Safeguarding Homeland Security

Simon Hakim · Erwin A. Blackstone
Editors

Safeguarding Homeland Security

Governors and Mayors Speak Out

Foreword by Edward G. Rendell

Springer

Editors
Simon Hakim
Department of Economics
Temple University
1301 N. Cecil B. Moore Avenue
Philadelphia PA 19122-6091
USA
simon.hakim@temple.edu

Erwin A. Blackstone
Department of Economics
Temple University
1301 N. Cecil B. Moore Avenue
Philadelphia PA 19122-6091
USA
erwin.blackstone@temple.edu

ISBN 978-1-4419-0370-9   e-ISBN 978-1-4419-0371-6
DOI 10.1007/978-1-4419-0371-6
Springer New York Dordrecht Heidelberg London

Library of Congress Control Number: 2009930368

Printed on acid-free paper

Springer is part of Springer Science+Business Media (www.springer.com)

This book is dedicated to the memory of Paul J. Andrisani, a scholar and a pioneer in the field of economics and management of privatization, a wonderful person, and a dear friend. We also dedicate this book to our wives, Marijane Blackstone and Galia Hakim, and our children and grandchildren.

Foreword

The terrorist attack of September 11, 2001, and the natural disasters of Hurricanes Katrina and Rita demonstrated the challenges that governments face in initial response and recovery efforts.

This book details the important steps that governors and mayors have initiated to address the serious problems illustrated by these recent disasters. The innovative solutions include developing more reliable communications, creating public–private partnerships to supplement public emergency services, establishing fusion centers that interpret information, and creating joint operations centers to manage the response to the event.

There are important lessons to be learned from the managerial and technological innovations that the governors and mayors describe in this book. As the Mayor of Philadelphia and now as the Governor of Pennsylvania, I have contributed to three books on best practices of state and local governments. I am pleased to participate in the efforts of the Center for Competitive Government of the Fox School at Temple University to address the important issues faced by governments. This book makes an important contribution to the public discussion on the public and private sectors' role in homeland security.

Commonwealth of Pennsylvania   Governor Edward G. Rendell

Acknowledgement

The editors would like to acknowledge Dr. M. Moshe Porat, Dean of the Fox School at Temple where the Center for Competitive Government is located. His strong contribution and support for the Mayors' Summits is most appreciated. Many chapters for our books including this one emanated from these Summits.

Contents

1   **The Role of the Private Sector in Homeland Security**   1
Simon Hakim and Erwin A. Blackstone

2   **Creating the Boston Medical Reserve Corps**   23
Thomas M. Menino

3   **The Hierarchy of Emergency Preparedness**   31
Rob Drake

4   **Border Security and State Safety and Security:**
Addressing Common Agendas   41
James Jay Carafano

5   **Lessons Learned from the 2004 Atlantic Hurricane**
Season: How This Highly Active Year Helped Jacksonville,
Florida, Build a Better Emergency Response System   53
John Peyton

6   **Disaster Management: Privatization as a Viable Alternative©** . .   61
Alan Kirschenbaum

7   **Caring for the Evacuees from Hurricane Katrina and Rita**   73
Bill White

8   **Sheltering and Evacuating from Hurricanes Katrina and Rita** . .   81
Henry Garrett

9   **Local Government Contingency Planning for Public**
Security and Public Safety – Innovative and Remedial Efforts . .   87
David G. Wallace

10   **Technological and Regional Cooperation Strategies:**
Securing the City and Port of Oakland, California   99
Ronald V. Dellums, Yolanda Burrell, and Michael O'Brien

11   **Innovative Anti-terror Information Sharing: Maryland's**
Federal, State, and Local Partnership Model   117
Robert L. Ehrlich

**12 Public Safety and Homeland Security Solutions:
An Evolution of Technology and Policy**   131
Edward G. Rendell

**13 Utilizing Technology Within the Delaware Information
and Analysis Center**   149
Ruth Ann Minner

**14 From Curiosity to Collaboration: Leveraging Technology
to Improve Situational Awareness**   159
Curt Pringle

15 How a Midwestern "Digital City" Serves and Protects the Public .   177
Frank A. Pasquale

16 Hurricanes and Modern Communications Infrastructure   185
Barry H. Axelrod and James V. Mudd

**17 The First Line of Defense: Cities Using Technology in
Homeland Defense**   191
David N. Cicilline

18 Full Interoperability for All South Dakota Public Safety   197
M. Michael Rounds and Otto Doll

19 Evolutionary Planning for the Technology Revolution   207
Bill Baarsma

**20 History of Regional Unified and Integrated Public Safety
and Public Service Communication and Transportation Systems** .   217
Will Wynn

**21 Interoperability in the City of Tampa: A Partnership
with the Department of Homeland Security**   233
Pam Iorio

**22 Capital Connections: Washington's Public Safety
Communications Suite**   241
Anthony A. Williams

**23 Information, Leadership and Decisiveness,
All in One Room**   253
Richard M. Daley

**24 Beyond an Information Technology Approach to
Continuity of Operations: The Commonwealth of Virginia Story** .   261
Timothy Kaine

25 The Soft Stuff is Still the Hard Stuff   269
Albert Morales and Todd S. Ramsey

Index   287

Contributors

Ruth Ann Minner Governor, The State of Delaware, (2001–2009), gminner@state.de.us

Barry H. Axelrod Information Technology Director, Collier County, FL, barryaxelrod@colliergov.net

Bill Baarsma Mayor, Tacoma, WA, (2002–present), bill.baarsma@cityoftacoma.org

Erwin A. Blackstone Faculty of Temple University, Philadelphia, PA, erwin.blackstone@temple.edu

Yolanda Burrell Technical Communications Specialist, City Oakland, CA, yburrell@oaklandnet.com

James Jay Carafano Assistant Director, Kathryn and Shelby Cullom Davis Institute for International Studies and Senior Research Fellow, Douglas and Sarah Allison Center for Foreign Policy Studies, Heritage Foundation, jamescarafano@heritage.org

David N. Cicilline Mayor, Providence, RI, (2003–present), mayor@providenceri.com; http://www.providenceri.com/government/mayor.php

Richard M. Daley Mayor, Chicago, IL, (1989–present), erika.zovka@ex.citychicago.org; http://egov.cityofchicago.org/city/webportal/home.do

Ronald V. Dellums Mayor, Oakland, CA, (2007–present), officeofthemayor@oaklandnet.com

Rob Drake Mayor, Beaverton, OR, (1992–2008), drarej@comcast.net

Otto Doll Commissioner of the South Dakota Bureau of Information and Telecommunications, otto.doll@state.sd.us

Robert L. Ehrlich Governor, The State of Maryland, (2003–2007), mdmanual@mdarchives.state.md.us

Henry Garrett Mayor, Corpus Christi, TX, (2005–present), lindale@cctexas.com

Simon Hakim Faculty of Temple University, Philadelphia, PA,
hakim@temple.edu

Pam Iorio Mayor, Tampa, FL, (2007–present), pam.iorio@tampagov.net;
http://www.tampagov.net/dept_mayor/

Timothy Kaine Governor, The Commonwealth of Virginia, (2006–present),
ima@governor.virginia.gov; http://www.governor.virginia.gov/index.cfm

Alan Kirschenbaum Associate Professor, Faculty of Industrial Management,
Technion, Israel Institute of Technology, Haifa, Israel,
avik@techunix.technion.ac.il

Thomas M. Menino Mayor, Boston, MA, (1993–present),
mayor@cityofboston.gov

Albert Morales IBM Global Business Services, General Manager Public Sector
Federal Industry Leader, albert.morales@us.ibm.com

James V. Mudd County Manager, Collier County, FL, (2002–present),
jamesmudd@colliergov.net

Michael O'Brien Port Facilities Security Officer, Port of Oakland, Oakland, CA,
mobrien@portoakland.com

Frank A. Pasquale Mayor, Bellwood, IL, (2001–present),
fpasquale@vil.bellwood.il.us;
http://www.villageofbellwood.com/html/mayor_s_page.html

John Peyton Mayor, Jacksonville, FL, (2003–present), jpeyton@coj.net

Curt Pringle Mayor, Anaheim, CA, (2002–present), sray@anaheim.net;
http://www.anaheim.net/article.asp?id=206

Todd S. Ramsey Managing Director, U.S. Federal, IBM Corporation

Edward G. Rendell Governor, The Commonwealth of Pennsylvania,
(2003–present), ra-govnews@state.pa.us; http://www.governor.state.pa.us;
governor@state.pa.us

M. Michael Rounds Governor, The State of South Dakota, (2003–present),
sdgov@gov.state.sd.us; http://www.state.sd.us/governor/

David G. Wallace Mayor, Sugar Land, TX, (2002–2008), dgwal007@aol.com

Bill White Mayor, Houston, TX, (2004–present), mayor.b.w@cityofhouston.net

Anthony A. Williams Mayor, Washington, DC, (1999–2007), awilliams@fbr.com

Will Wynn Mayor, Austin, TX, (2006–2009), william.wynn@lpbenergy.com;
http://www.ci.austin.tx.us/council/wynn.htm

About the Editors

Simon Hakim is a professor of economics and the director of the Center for Competitive Government at Temple University. He earned M.A. and Ph.D. degrees in Regional Science from the University of Pennsylvania. He also earned an M.Sc. degree in City and Regional Planning from the Technion, Israel Institute of Technology and a B.A. degree in Economics at Hebrew University in Jerusalem. His special areas of research and teaching are privatization, public policy, private/public police and homeland security. Dr. Hakim published fifty-eight scientific articles in leading economic, criminal justice, security and public policy journals. He wrote over forty professional articles and edited fourteen books. He wrote with Professor Blackstone a major book on the security industry.

Dr. Hakim conducted several funded research and consulting projects for the U.S. Departments of Justice and Labor, the Commonwealth Foundation, the Independent Institute, the Alarm Industry Research and Education Foundation, the City of Philadelphia, the Philadelphia International Airport, and leading security companies. For the complete CV see http://astro.temple.edu/~shakim; for the Center for Competitive Government see http://www.fox.temple.edu/ccg.

Professor Blackstone received his AB from Syracuse University where he was elected to Phi Beta Kappa. He received his PhD from the University of Michigan. He has taught economics for over 35 years. Prior to coming to Temple in 1976, Dr. Blackstone taught at Dartmouth College and Cornell University. His research areas and publications include the Economics of Industrial Organization, Health Economics, and Privatization. He has published on a variety of antitrust topics including mergers, dominance, reciprocal buying, collusion, and damages. His publications include over 40 articles in major economics and public policy journals, chapters in books, an edited book, a monograph on private policing, and a book on the electronic security industry. Dr. Blackstone has taught courses from the introductory to the PhD level. He was given in 1976 the Clark Award for distinguished teaching at Cornell and at Temple, the Andrisani-Frank Award for Excellence in teaching in 2001, and the Musser Excellence in Leadership Award for teaching in 2006.

Chapter 1
The Role of the Private Sector in Homeland Security

Simon Hakim and Erwin A. Blackstone

Abstract Chapter 1 reviews the budgetary requirements of state and local governments for homeland security and suggests how restructuring both security and emergency services and greater use of public–private partnerships could address a significant portion of such needs. Specifically, governments could shed services that are private in nature, contract out public services that could be more efficiently provided under market conditions, charge cost-based prices for services that are provided free or at nominal prices by governments like ambulance services, require businesses and other organizations to have security insurance, and provide incentives for private sector involvement. Private managerial talent and security officers as well as capital could be enlisted to provide effectively the excess demand for manpower and capital when homeland security events occur.

Introduction

In 2002, the total homeland security budget was $20.6 billion with a supplemental as a result of 9/11 of $12.36 billion. The proposed federal budget for 2008 is $61.16 billion, an almost 100% increase in 5 years. In 2008, one-third is spent on border and transportation security, almost another one-third on protecting critical infrastructures and key assets, and about 8% on emergency preparedness and response (OMB, 2008).

In spite of the substantial increase in federal spending, only one quarter of state emergency operations plans and 10% of municipal plans are sufficient to cope with a natural disaster or terrorist attack (Flynn, 2007, 5). In addition, a well-regarded non-governmental commission argued that additional funding of $98.4 billion over 5 years was required to cover potential emergency response needs. This figure does not include overtime, training, and police force needs across the United States (Council of Foreign Relations, Rudman Report, 2003, 31). There is an obvious lack of financial resources, and all expect the federal government to carry the burden.

S. Hakim (✉)
Faculty of Temple University, Philadelphia, PA, USA
e-mail: hakim@temple.edu

S. Hakim, E.A. Blackstone (eds.), *Safeguarding Homeland Security*,
DOI 10.1007/978-1-4419-0371-6_1, © Springer Science+Business Media, LLC 2009

   The financial burden is huge since the amount of critical infrastructures includes 15,000 chemical facilities, 489,862 miles of pipelines for hazardous liquids and natural gas, 5,389 public use airports, 16,024 publicly owned wastewater treatment facilities, 700,000 miles of drinking water system, and 64 nuclear power reactors (Critical Infrastructures, 2008).

   After 9/11, billions of tax dollars have been spent creating a new capability to deal with crises in the United States. The US Department to Homeland Security was established and increased funding was made available to emergency responders. Exercises to prepare for mass casualty events were held across the United States. Nevertheless, Hurricanes Katrina and Rita proved that we were no more capable of responding to a major catastrophe than we were on 9/11 (Clarke et al., 2006, 1).

   The attack of 9/11 and the natural disasters of Rita and Katrina showed that the United States lacked appropriate communications, supplies, and possibly suffered from inappropriate management during emergency events.

   The objective of this chapter is to provide guidance for the following:

1. Improving the public sector's structure and responsibilities to better meet demands in major homeland security events.
2. Engaging the private sector in fulfilling homeland security obligations, providing incentives and challenges, and appropriate regulations.
3. Establishing regulated insurance programs to achieve business survival following a major uncertain homeland security event. The insurance program will also motivate businesses and individuals to take appropriate precautions to minimize adverse effects.
4. Introducing technological products that could supplement or substitute for regular labor efforts. Since 9/11 many IT companies have been developing products to avoid the problems faced in New York City during and following the attack. The chapter will review the problems associated with response and recovery from homeland security incidents and present technological solutions employed by state and local governments.

Background

As a result of the 10th amendment to the US Constitution, the states have all the powers not expressly delegated to the Federal Government. This has been interpreted as the "police power" where the states have the ultimate control of most emergency services. In practice, the states allow local governments to be the principal responders and managers in case of disasters. When a terrorist or natural disaster occurs, the local jurisdiction responds while the State may aid with the state police, the National Guard, and other resources. However, the ultimate control is with the governor who may choose to exercise control under unusual circumstances. The Governor may declare a State of Emergency in order to mobilize and send in the National Guard.

The federal government basically provides assistance to states and localities when an emergency occurs beyond the capability of the state. The Federal Emergency Management Agency (FEMA) often supplies medical equipment, temporary housing, food, and other essentials. The President may make a Disaster Declaration in order to provide greater federal assistance. This includes loans or grants to homeowners, businesses, and local governments to recover from the disasters.

The management of disasters is done by the mayor under the authority of the state and is usually handled by the chiefs of the police and fire departments. The mayor can clearly choose personally to manage the response and recovery efforts.

Small natural and manmade disasters occur often and thus sufficient response and recovery experience exists. There are, after all, the lessons learned from the multitude of small terrorist attacks in Israel and from "regular" natural events here in the United States. However, such catastrophes as 9/11 and Hurricanes Katrina or Ike show that the usual practices and material support are insufficient for major disasters. Government at all three levels has responded by developing either new departments for homeland security or created positions to deal specifically with homeland security.

Homeland security (HLS) is viewed as a pure public good. If adequate HLS services are provided, then most residents will enjoy the benefits. Further, private marginal costs of homeland security are higher than private marginal benefits, and the latter are significantly lower than social marginal benefits. Thus, there is little incentive for individuals to expend resources on HLS services. Given these facts, it is not surprising that HLS services are considered by all as a primary responsibility of government at all three levels. The federal government is expected to cover the cost since it has the greatest ability to pay and the negative externalities associated with disasters are normally far more widespread than within any individual state.

Market failure also exists in the private sector and especially with respect to corporate resource allocation. Long-run profit maximization may suggest greater corporate spending on security. However, the interest of top corporate executives is to earn short-term profits even at the expense of the long term. Executives' personal interest is high immediate profit since that is what determines their compensation and tenure on the job. Also, short-term profits keep the stock price high and prevent hostile takeovers. Executives do not maintain their positions for too long, and thus the consequences of lack allocation for security will inure to others. Supporting the notion of the short-term horizon of corporate executives is the fact that since 2002 Sarbanes-Oxley Act, corporate turnover has increased. Specifically, there was a 91.3% increase in the departures of the top 100 Fortune CEOs compared with the previous 5-year period. The global business environment adds to the competitive pressures for short-term profits and to reduced incentives for security spending. Almost 20% of Fortune 500 companies do not even have a corporate security officer to manage threats and security risks (Blades, 2008).

The next question is how to allocate limited resources among the three categories in homeland security: preparation-prevention, response, and recovery in a manner that maximizes security. It is commonly believed that most resources should be spent on target hardening which is the form of prevention. Others argue that static or inflexible measures are inefficient. The number of critical infrastructures is huge; the terrorist has complete choice of target, timing, and attack method. Effective prevention measures are very costly and ineffective; a well-prepared team of terrorists could easily overcome a static, unprepared group of guards. Instead, efforts should be placed on effective response and recovery. For example, it is possible to place a guard at the entrance of each school and build a high fence to prevent an attack on students. Clearly, such measures could not deter or prevent a team of terrorists who plan an attack on a specific school. Instead, digital data could be maintained on the buildings, hidden cameras installed at the school, and a well-trained and mobile SWAT team could be available for each metropolitan area to deal with any attack on critical infrastructures.

The government could encourage deployment of technology to improve homeland security. Technological innovations that could improve homeland security relate to a computerized automatic protocol response system, managing the event over the Internet, sufficient and durable communication channels among the key people during the event, data mining to anticipate and perhaps prevent an event, reverse 911-emergency notification systems, and use of digital monitoring devices.

Technological products could serve both as a substitute for and as a complement to labor. Unlike the private market, signals of need or incentives of profit are less present in the public sector. Even though officials at the IT departments of government may know their needs, there are no markets to encourage appropriate or prevent excessive adoption of new technology products. Unlike the private sector, financial incentives are weaker for government decision makers, the bureaucracy is greater, and therefore adoption of new products is less likely to occur. The more rapid diffusion of e-commerce versus that of e-government supports our argument (Blackstone et al., 2005, 4).

Managerial innovations include establishing a separate command and response structure once an emergency event occurs, creating emergency forces for such an event, creating emergency positions and responsibilities for public employees, and sharing relevant security information among public and private agencies.

Restructuring Public Emergency Services

State and local governments provide emergency response services, some of which lack public goods attributes. In this section, we shall identify services that should not be provided by public police, fire, and ambulance entities; estimate their magnitudes; and analyze whether social welfare will be affected by their elimination from the public sector. Other emergency services are public in nature but could be contracted out and provided under competitive conditions. In both cases, government could provide such services within a competitive market context. We shall then outline how the saved resources could be shifted and used for homeland security purposes.

Police services that do not involve public good attributes include attending and investigating minor traffic accidents, escorting funerals and oversized vehicles, animal control, unlocking vehicles, recording citizen complaints, checking on people's welfare, and traffic control during road construction. The largest single item on police budgets is response to burglar alarms of which 94–99% are false. Elsewhere we showed that police response is a public good only when a real burglary occurs, and there is a chance of apprehending a burglar. When alarm owners accidentally activate their systems or when a system malfunctions, there are no social benefits when police respond. If police eliminate provision of the above non-public services, private entities will enter under competitive market conditions. Further, non-users of these services in the community will then not be required to subsidize those who use them, the service will be provided to its users by private entities, and social welfare will not diminish. Alternatively, police should charge their long-run average total cost and allow competitors to also respond to alarms. Our calculations show that if police indeed eliminate the delivery of non-public goods, 13% or 55,000 patrol officers could effectively be used for other services with no social loss. In dollar terms, the total annual savings will be $2.8 billion (Blackstone et al., 2007).

Police are a public monopoly in providing most of their services. Some public services could be produced under market conditions where many potential suppliers exist. This will most likely improve efficiency in their provision. Police could contract out such public good services as handling abandoned vehicles, providing criminal information databases, enforcing traffic and parking regulations, providing lost and found services, guarding prisoners, protecting court rooms and public infrastructures, processing reports, and fulfilling office administrative duties. Government should employ Activity-Based Accounting (ABC) where expenses are attributed to particular functions or activities that are considered for contracting out. Only then can government assure that the lowest bidder actually saves resources.

Basically, wherever civilian workers replace expensive sworn officers, savings on the order of 30% will be realized. Contracting out will lead to an additional annual savings of $1.15 billion or the equivalent of 23,000 officers (Hakim et al., 2007). In small communities, the police may have to provide services since the market is too small to accommodate competitive entry. In any event, the police should charge for non-public services and competitive entry should always be allowed.

Extinguishing fires is a public good since fires spread and cause harm and injury to others. However, responding to a false alarm is not a public good. If a resident overheats his stove causing a false alarm and a fire engine responds, other community residents gain no benefits while bearing a long-run marginal cost between $365 and $1,050. Fifty-eight percent of fire responses are to false calls. By charging for false activations, the number of false alarms will be significantly reduced and they will not burden public budgets. Also private companies or other response entities should be allowed to compete with the public fire department. We estimated that if false alarms are eliminated, between 18,600 and 48,900 firefighters or equivalently between $0.93 and $2.44 billion could be saved or reallocated to other uses. By pricing false alarms and enabling competitors to enter, cost of production will diminish, service level would remain the same, and social welfare will rise.

Ambulance services are not a public good, since individuals are served with no external effects and service could be denied to those unwilling to pay. However, government involvement is justified on the basis of the high value of life. In any event, government provision is not necessary since private ambulance services do exist.

A maor problem facing ambulance services is the 25% or $8.5 million calls a year are false. Local governments bear most of the $0.92 billion cost for the false service responses, or equivalently, they could shift 18,300 first responders to more productive uses. Indeed, some use ambulances to reach the hospital for minor illnesses. This adds an additional burden on hospitals and governments (Blackstone et al., 2007).

Evidence exits that private providers are more efficient and may provide higher quality care than public ambulances. Thus, exposing government ambulance companies to competition or contracting out through competitive bidding is desirable. Successful managed competition requires that the public provider price at long-run marginal cost and entry by other public or private providers is allowed.

Under the assumption of perfect information, the solution of managed competition would be preferred to contracting out where temporary monopoly is awarded after competitive bidding. Ambulance service companies, however, must be able to provide timely, high-quality service anywhere in the community. Users of emergency services are usually unaware of quality differences among providers. Thus, in this imperfect information environment, contracting out where government assures quality service at a certain price may well be the preferred solution over managed competition.

Annual savings from elimination and contracting out of services

First responders	Annual savings (billion)	Number of responders that could be reallocated
Police		
Elimination of false alarm response	$1.8	35,000
Elimination of other non-public goods activities	$1.0	20,200
Contracting out services	$1.15	23,000
Fire		
Elimination of false alarm response	$0.93–2.44	18,600–48,900
Ambulance		
Elimination of false alarm response	$0.92	18,300
Total	$5.80–7.31	115,100–145,400

Source: An earlier version appeared in Blackstone et al. (2007), 319.

Some suggest that in times of emergency, all emergency resources will be devoted in any case to homeland security. Homeland security activities, however, are not restricted to the time of the occurrence. On-going homeland security efforts include training of first responders who will operate during such events; developing plans, procedures, and protocols to manage emergency situations; conducting desktop exercises; and acquiring equipment and facilities. Other activities include acquiring special supplies like medicines, canned food, rescue equipment; purchasing, installing, and training with interoperable communication systems; developing and training with robotic technology to dismantle bombs; and building and equipping an emergency center. The resources expended on non-public goods or the resources saved by encouraging greater efficiency could be used to accomplish the above activities.

Previously we reported that the Council on Foreign Relations (The Rudman Report) concluded that there was a $98.4 billion shortfall in homeland security spending over a 5-year period. Specifically, by eliminating non-public goods and exposing other public goods to competition through contracting out, between 30 and 37% of the required funding could be obtained entirely from within the emergency services sector.

Engaging the Private Sector in Homeland Security

Demand for emergency personnel and equipment is higher when an emergency occurs than in normal circumstances. This is similar to the case of electricity where the capacity of power stations must be sufficient to meet peak-time demand. Since electricity cannot be stored, capacity and production need to accommodate fluctuating demands. In order to save on infrastructure investment, prices could be established such that peak demand is smoothed out; the success of course depends upon price elasticity of demand.

Instead of a summer peak for air conditioning, HLS involves a natural disaster or a terrorist incident. However, most personnel and equipment are designed for off-peak demand and there is no a priori knowledge about the probability of an event's occurrence, the nature of the event, the extent of the damage expected, and the types and extent of necessary resources to cope with the event. Since a homeland security event involves unknowable information, most, if not all, communities are unprepared for a major event and indeed may have little incentive to be prepared for the peak-time demand. Unlike electricity where considerable experience exists about capacity utilization, no such information is available for terrorist events.

A consequence of the above peak time unknowable information situation is that most communities do not expend sufficient resources for homeland security and instead expect the federal government to undertake the responsibility. However, the amount needed to provide for a nationwide preparedness for major events is huge and cannot easily be accommodated by the federal budget. The experience of Rita and Katrina in Louisiana 5 years after 9/11 proved that the United States is still unprepared. Given this lack of appropriate incentives by the players, it is apparent that government at all three levels is still not prepared for another major event.

In view of the above, we suggest forming a public–private partnership that could fulfill any conceivable excess demand resulting from a major event when public resources are insufficient. The objective is to provide financial incentives that will encourage private participation in homeland security efforts. Emergency legal homeland security jurisdictions should be formed to incorporate an entire affected area. In case of a catastrophic event, the emergency jurisdiction will likely encompass an entire metropolitan area and will not necessarily correspond with political boundaries.

In terms of personnel, private security forces are three times as large as the sum of federal, state, and local law enforcement officers (Blackstone et al., 2007, 315). The majority of them are low paid hourly workers with limited or no fringe benefits. It is possible to form civilian reserve units that can be mobilized in case of a catastrophic event. Also, retired police officers, firefighters, and ambulance paramedics, as well as emergency managers could serve in these units. Training including emergency exercises could be performed during the year and the assignment of emergency personnel could be arranged for emergency situations. These people would be paid for their reserve duties. These earnings would probably be an adequate inducement to participate in such reserve force. In case of a real event, these reserve officers report to their pre-assigned responsibilities to perform the services for which they were trained.

Mayor Menino of Boston in Chapter 2 discusses the creation of reserve medical units that can be mobilized in case of an emergency. In case of a major event like a biological attack, the existing medical personnel may not suffice. Pre-arranged and trained medical units composed of various medical and administrative volunteers handle the peak-time demand. Mayor Drake of Beaverton, OR, evaluates (Chapter 3) the establishment of a regional emergency response organization, which included public, private, non-profits, and volunteer groups. Volunteer groups play an important role in emergency response and recovery plans and efforts. During a major flood in 1996, a church staffed a flood information and referral line. Volunteers in an organization termed the Minutemen already operate on the southern US border to locate and identify illegal aliens who can then be apprehended by the US border patrol. This group's presence presumably deters some illegal entry. However, their activities raise such liability issues as illegal arrests and improper use of weapons. James Carafano suggests in Chapter 4 that volunteers could be integrated within a State's defense forces to function under the Governor's control. This could alleviate some of the control and liability problems posed by vigilantes. Mayor Peyton of Jacksonville, FL, indicates in Chapter 5 that his city has also been training volunteers to supplement first responders during an emergency. Further, Jacksonville firefighters, sheriff deputies, and many civilian city employees have been trained in disaster response. In particular, some city employees have been trained as call takers to serve during disasters or other peak-time situations. Kirschenbaum shows in Chapter 6 how Israel overcomes suicide bombing and other terrorist attacks against civilians; volunteers play an important role when an attack occurs. Included are civilian watch, reserve medical officers, and religious organizations that gather body parts. Since so many Israelis have military experience, even unorganized volunteers assist in emergencies.

An issue in integrating private security guards and retired emergency services' officers in homeland security efforts is whether such integration is likely to succeed. Indeed, there are many examples of successful cooperation between police officers and private guards. In New York City, more than 1,000 private security organizations are linked with the police to prevent, prepare for, and respond to homeland security incidents. They work together on building evacuation plans, security screening of vehicles entering facilities and adjacent parking, checking suspicious individuals and packages, and sharing terrorism alerts (BJA, 2005, 11). In Las Vegas, private security forces guide police in casino-related criminal events, and the police train private security in proper procedures for handling the usual criminal incidents (BJA, 2005, 15).

An interesting issue is obtaining recruits for the top and mid-level reserve emergency management positions. Current practice in the United States is that the local political leader is in charge of all emergency services in both regular and emergency situations. However, since the areas impacted during a catastrophic event are often larger than political jurisdictions, there could be a management cadre different from existing political structures. Successful local business and corporate leaders may be challenged by the opportunity to manage significantly large public security obligations. Already, local private executives occupy top local public positions like weak mayors in such major cities as Phoenix, AZ, and Charlotte, NC, or chair county executive boards like Orange County, CA. The incentives for top and middle level homeland security management personnel clearly differ from the financial incentives already suggested for the lower level personnel. The public sector could not offer financial rewards that could attract suitable leaders.

Emergency situations require adapting to varying conditions, developing innovative solutions, and being able to move beyond simple and traditional solutions. In the vernacular of today this is termed "thinking out of the box." Combined with the political jurisdictional issues, the appropriate leadership for emergency situation may not necessarily be the same as the political leadership. Private sector leaders who advanced in the competitive environment, were successful entrepreneurs, and showed strong survival attributes could be challenged to get involved. Mayor White of Houston, TX, states in Chapter 7 that his city did exactly that in the response to the challenges of sheltering thousands of refugees from Hurricane Katrina. The city used successful business and civic leaders to manage provision of certain services. The mayor created "Virtual organizations." Specifically, the city set up field hospitals managed by hospitals and pharmacies, enrolled 20,000 evacuated children in schools and raised funds to help students who are behind their grade level, and used hotel and apartment managers to arrange housing for the refugees. A similar effort by Mayor Garrett of the City of Corpus Christi (Chapter 8) involved absorption of several thousand of evacuees from Hurricane Katrina, and later the city itself evacuated its own residents and the previous evacuees north to safety. The city government even arranged transportation and food for the sick and the infirm.

We often witness successful business and corporate leaders turning to politics. Mayor Bloomberg of New York City, Governor Corzine of New Jersey, Governor Shapp of Pennsylvania, Senator Lautenberg of New Jersey, and Governor Romney of Massachusetts are just a few examples. They changed careers and brought private solutions to public problems. Their involvement in government may be motivated by the desire for new challenges in the public sector after having been successful in the private sector. They may also desire the esteem garnered from high-level government service and the possibility of further advancement in the political sphere. It has proved to be a win–win situation. The public sector may even enjoy additional financial support from the new political leaders, in addition to their talent and introduction of private management practices into the public sector. Mayor Bloomberg works for $1 a year. He contributed a new computer system to city government, and his companies provided financial support to community and social groups. Further, high-level executives' involvement with the public sector often attracts other private sector younger leaders who wish to be associated with the senior executives.

The private sector executive might well direct all regional homeland security responsibilities, including preparation for and the response and recovery efforts from an event. Preparatory activities are on-going and include the establishment of a personnel structure and their periodic training, acquisition or emergency drafting of equipment, and development and construction of databases. When a homeland security event occurs, all political jurisdictions and their staffs, including police, fire, and ambulance services, come under the control of the director.

A major event requires far more equipment than government normally maintains. This equipment includes fire engines, rescue vehicles, heavy construction type vehicles, medical, and other equipment that is event dependent and is difficult to anticipate. Since the private sector owns most of such equipment, we need to develop a process by which equipment could be transferred to the management of the event. The state legislature could grant the homeland security directors the power to requisition with appropriate compensation necessary personnel and equipment from the private sector. Kirschenbaum (Chapter 6) reviews the existing Israeli practice where the government requisitions and pays private companies and individuals for using their equipment and buses during emergency situations.

Numerous legal, administrative, and payment issues arise whenever private resources are shifted to the public sector to respond to natural or terrorist events. Responders have to be assured that they will enjoy protection against liability for their interjurisdictional activities performed with usual care and diligence. Prior agreements for private sector resources including personnel and equipment have to be arranged to include their authority, duties, protection against liability, and payments for damages or injuries incurred in the course of their public deployment.

Interstate transfer of resources is more complicated. Public interstate involvement requires the US Congress to approve any interstate compact between states. In the absence of prior agreements, deputizing has to occur before personnel enjoy sovereign immunity. In the aftermath of Hurricane Katrina in 2005, Louisiana officials deputized Blackwater security guards who helped patrol New Orleans. The guards were even authorized to use deadly force (Scahill, 2005). Incidentally, similar issues arise when police officers assist from outside the state. Police officers generally have the authority to enforce the state law everywhere within the state.

When the Rita and Katrina natural disasters occurred, the government at all levels encountered difficulties in the prompt delivery of food, water, and other emergency supplies to the affected region. At the same time, chain stores had sufficient supplies through use of their normal distribution systems; they transferred supplies from unaffected stores to the stores in the affected region. Also, emergency supplies were even delivered to the New Orleans Dome but could not be distributed because they were unable to gain access. Inventory management including delivery of goods is a normal business function. In preparation for emergencies, the private sector should be contracted to fulfill these functions. Local communities often experience a shortage of supplies after 2 days of responding to an emergency. Mayor Wallace of Sugar Land, TX (Chapter 9), was instrumental in creating the Regional Logistics Center that was managed by a private company. The regional authority in effect established a public–private partnership (PPP) to handle more effectively the management of supplies. The city's leadership was also instrumental in helping to develop a prototype agreement for distant cities to provide aid in emergency situations. The agreement is an attempt to resolve state sovereignty issues that delayed responses to Hurricane Katrina. Baltimore, MD, and Trenton, NJ, have such a mutual aid agreement.

Mayor Dellums describes in Chapter 10 an interesting PPP that was established to protect the Port of Oakland, CA, and its environs. The agreement involves many government and private entities and makes coordinated response and recovery efforts easier. Oakland was instrumental in forming committees along functional and geographical lines and in employing technology like video surveillance around the Port. The unified regional command structure worked well when a ship crashed into a bridge and caused an oil spill.

A form of public–private partnership incorporating volunteers occurred in response to evacuation from Hurricane Katrina. Corpus Christi (Chapter 8), a city of 285,000, received several thousand refugees from Hurricane Katrina. City personnel and volunteers converted the Coliseum for the evacuees, some of whom were sheltered in neighboring communities. Volunteer restaurants provided food. Medical services, Internet access and other communications, and travel assistance to reunite families were also provided. An emergency operations center and a mobile command post were used. Then, Hurricane Rita forced the city to evacuate the refugees and its residents, including, 350 special needs citizens who were transported to a Senior Center and then evacuated to San Antonio. Corpus Christi employees are considered essential and are not allowed to evacuate. The city operated a "refuge of last resort." Jacksonville, Florida has developed a special needs database so that this group can receive necessary services in a timely fashion (Chapter 5). The Special Needs group includes those who are homebound, dependent upon electricity to power oxygen dispensers and other life-saving equipment, or dialysis patients. The city has developed a plan for evacuating special needs individuals to special shelters.

Establishing Regulated Insurance Programs

The problem that society faces is that businesses under-invest in protecting themselves against homeland security events. Businesses also under-invest in protecting society against the adverse effects that their actions cause others. We shall outline the reasons for such under-investment and suggest how regulated insurance could encourage firms to take more appropriate precautionary measures.

Homeland security incidents, whether natural or terrorist disasters, could be significant in scope and even lead to business bankruptcy with no fault attributable to the individual firm. HLS incidents are uncertain with unknowable probability of occurrence, magnitude, and duration of damage, which could all lead to the destruction of the firm. There are insurance programs to protect businesses from such events; however, because of the uncertainties involved, insurers that often deter businesses from subscribing to them set premiums at high levels. Thus, businesses choose to under-invest in protecting themselves against the direct effects on themselves of HLS events.

Firms may also take insufficient HLS precautions that cause adverse effects on other firms. These adverse indirect HLS effects require government intervention to encourage firms to act in a manner that minimizes such effects. Private markets will under-invest in indirect security precautions for the following reasons. First, the adverse effects of an incident are wider ranging than the direct harm to the individual business. Thus, businesses may insure and/or act in order to protect against their own expected suffering without taking account of the indirect adverse effect that the disruption of the business may cause other businesses. Second, a chemical plant may insure and/or take precautions protecting the facility up to its full value. However, a terrorist may steal and use chemicals from the plant to contaminate the entire water supply of the city. We would have liked the plant to take security precautions that significantly reduce the chance of such a theft. Unfortunately, the effort is not worthwhile for the plant itself but is desirable for society, considering the expected social costs. Third, the public is not aware whether buildings they visit contain the necessary security in case of an incident. There is asymmetric information because the owner of the building knows the insufficient level of security he/she provides while the "customers" are unaware of the potential danger of working in or visiting the building. Fourth, a company will take precautions to protect its assets up to the value of bankruptcy. The company will not take precautionary actions beyond that level even at a very low cost. However, the social cost of inaction beyond the bankruptcy level may be great and could be avoided at low cost. Fifth, if a company knows that the government will compensate businesses in case of a disaster, it will take no or a low level of necessary security precautions. For example, buildings may be designed and built to sustain an earthquake but since the company expects the government to compensate victims in case of such disaster, the company will not spend the additional money to improve the sustainability of the building. All these points suggest government intervention to achieve socially desired level of precautions (above discussion is based on Orszag, 2003). There are also the market failure issues emanating from the short-term interest of corporate managers.

The problem of negative externalities caused by under-investment in security is similar to the environmental issue of controlling pollution (Auerswald, 2005). The solution suggested by economists and implemented by governments involved introducing direct regulation and then market-based auctioning to regulate the amount of allowed pollution. Government regulation was necessary because the adverse effects often occur after many years and their causes cannot be attributed to individual firms. In the case of under-investment in security that causes social costs to other agents, the effect is immediate and the link to the responsible firm can be more easily identified. Thus, reliance on markets and individual HLS insurance is appropriate.

It is obvious that markets are inefficient with regard to uncertain substantial homeland security events. In order to correct the under-investment, government intervention could take the form of regulation, required insurance, or subsidization of security precautions. Government intervention in this case is aimed at correcting for both the inadequate amount firms spend for a HLS event and the amount needed to correct or avoid the external or spillover negative effects.

An important criterion in evaluating the above three alternatives is to select the one that requires minimum government intervention in this marketplace. Insurance is the least intrusive and allows the most opportunities for market forces. But, some regulation is often necessary to take account of asymmetric information or to assure minimum standards of security. For example, regulation may appropriately specify armed guards for nuclear facilities. Subsidization of businesses for undertaking appropriate security precautions has all the usual shortcomings of encouraging unnecessarily expensive investments, sparking lobbying to obtain the subsidy, providing funds for activities that might be taken in any event, and causing undesirable distributional consequences (Orszag, 2003, 9).

Through requiring insurance market forces are unleashed to encourage a more efficient investment in precautionary efforts. There are numerous insurers, and all businesses will be required to obtain HLS insurance. Thus, a competitive market will develop, and insurers should earn close to normal profits. Depending upon the specifications of the regulation, a monopolistically competitive market is expected where insurers will offer various policy packages to businesses. Businesses will have the option of paying lower premiums and spending more and/or undertaking greater precautionary efforts. Or, alternatively businesses can pay greater premiums and take fewer precautions. Businesses will select the least cost option, a situation that is socially desired.

Before 9/11, there were few companies that insured against acts of terrorism and the premiums were quite modest. For example, before 9/11 O'Hare airport in Chicago had $750 million in terrorism protection for an annual premium of $125,000. After 9/11, O'Hare could only obtain $150 million of coverage for $6.9 million per year. In fact, prior to 9/11 terrorism protection was usually included within normal commercial insurance. However, soon after 9/11, most policies, including worker's compensation, excluded terrorism protection so that by September 11, 2002, very few companies had terrorism insurance (Kunreuther and Michel-Kerjan, 2004, 203).

Since 1996 catastrophe bonds have been used in the United States to defray part of the risk of insurance losses from natural disasters. They yield higher than normal interest. However, if a natural disaster occurs, either the principle or the interest payments cease depending on the specifics of the bond. To date, they have not been used in the terrorism realm.

The magnitude of potential losses is another issue. Hurricane Andrew, which occurred in 1992, had insured losses of $19.6 billion dollars in 2001. The insured losses in the 9/11 attack, the largest catastrophe in US history, amounted to $30–70 billion (Joint Economic Committee, 2002, 1). As of May, 2007, the Insurance Information Institute (May, 2007) reported that total insurance claim payments were

$35.9 billion. The total surplus of the insurance industry in 2001 was somewhere between $300 and $427 billion. But the surplus associated with or available to pay high-risk commercial targets in 2001 was only $100 billion. Thus, 9/11 consumed about one-third of the relevant insurance industry surplus. All other attacks were much smaller in magnitude; the first World Trade bombing and the Oklahoma City bombing had insured losses of $725 million and only $145 million, respectively. The Joint Economic Committee of the US Congress concluded that the insurance industry could pay the 9/11 claims but the payments will significantly impair the industry ability to withstand another catastrophe (Joint Economic Committee, 2002, 3).

Following 9/11, $22 billion of the $33 billion were paid by reinsurance companies (Auerswald, 2005). The high cost and the uncertainty then led these companies to cease offering terrorism coverage. Accordingly, since 2002, the federal government has had a program to cover insurance companies' losses in case of a terrorist attack. The provisions of the program have increased the portion that insurance companies must bear before the federal program comes into play.

In 2007, the US Government would underwrite 85% of insurance companies' losses emanating from a terrorist act in excess of 20% of insurance companies' premiums. The federal government underwrites up to $100 billion above the $27.5 billion that insurers will spend. The insurance companies must then pay a surcharge not to exceed 3% for premiums covered by the Terrorism Risk Insurance Act and its extension (TRIEA) to reflect government exposure. The provisions are similar to those of Great Britain whose program has been in effect since 1993. Insurance companies must now bear a larger portion of the damages before the federal program coverage begin. Clearly, if a company does not carry terrorism insurance, it does not receive any government support. In spite of reserves that seem adequate, we witness here a market failure that seemingly requires government underwriting of catastrophic HLS events. The impact on the overall economy of a catastrophic event helps justify such government involvement.

It is noteworthy that indirect business losses to non-direct victims are not covered unless specifically included in the terms of the insurance policy. A federal district court in Chicago has held that O'Hare Airport was not entitled to compensation under its terrorism insurance policy as a result of 9/11 when all flights were grounded by order of the FAA and therefore the airport incurred substantial losses (City of Chicago v. the Factory Mutual Insurance Co., 2004). This is the standard legal interpretation of insurance policies where direct victims are fully covered but indirect victims are not covered for their business losses. A business would seem to be better off being a direct victim than being an indirect victim.

If a HLS event occurs then some suggest that government should step in and help businesses survive. Relief from an event and recovery efforts appear to be "public goods" because of the spillover effects on society. However, some may claim that it is not the role of government to rescue businesses. Also, if government is expected to help in the aftermath of major HLS events, there is little incentive for businesses to take precautions in advance to prevent such major harms. Businesses should know for certain that either government will not aid them or know the extent of aid in the aftermath of devastating events. In any case, the objective is to avoid a collapse of the economy emanating from a major terrorist event. Federal compensation is designed to prevent devastating negative social externalities caused by the attack. For example, the Federal Reserve provided billions to rescue Bear Sterns whose failure would have threatened to collapse the financial system in the wake of the subprime fiasco.

Employing Technology

Technology improvement is crucial for the four categories of gathering intelligence, preventing attacks and natural disasters, responding to events, and recovering from them. Correspondingly, technology is used for data mining in order to detect irregularities; digital cameras with face recognition can observe known terrorists. Computer-assisted systems can help to manage an event and the recovery efforts. Mainly the federal government does intelligence gathering through data mining with some intelligence work done by state governments. State and local governments are establishing emergency centers where all relevant services are located during disaster situations and where communication channels are provided to the field forces.

The question in the area of investment in technology is whether the allocation of spending for the four categories is efficient Economists claim that efficient use of resources requires that the last dollar spent on each category yields the same benefit. Even if we spend the right amount on each category, it is still uncertain whether resources are spent on the right type of technology and at the appropriate time.

These allocation problems always exist. However, where governments are the primary decision makers, the appropriateness question is exacerbated. Government lacks the profit motive which guides business in the decisions about which technology to adopt and when. In private markets, prices and inherent demands provide signals to producers about the appropriate rate and direction of innovative activities. These signals are lacking in the homeland security field. Government often is unaware of products that might improve security and lacks channels to communicate needs to technology companies. When developing or even contemplating developing security products, technology companies have limited knowledge of government needs because of perceived conflict of interest issues. It is important to maintain forums at which government and private technology personnel interact. Under existing conflict of interest regulations, such forums could be convened by neutral entities like universities.

Information gathering using technology includes data mining, digital cameras, fusion centers, improved telecommunications, and the use of the Internet to transmit the information. Governor Ehrlich of Maryland outlines in Chapter 11 the creation of a fusion center that collects information from all sources and mines the data in order to detect irregularities that suggest terrorist activities. The public is encouraged to provide information through a "tip line." The Center has federal, state, local, and private sector participation representing 250 agencies or organizations. A principle objective of a fusion center is to develop a pattern of cooperation and information sharing. Governor Rendell of Pennsylvania (Chapter 12) created a unified database for criminal, judicial, and corrections, which is being expanded to include HLS usage and information from federal, state, local, and adjacent states. First responders will have access to the information. In Chapter 13, we learn from Governor Minner of Delaware about the fusion center that started operation in 2005. It is unusual because law enforcement members are joined by agricultural, transportation, and health experts, the National Guard and other governmental agencies. The fusion center has a "tip line" and is helped by the uniform reporting system employed by all the law enforcement agencies in the State. The Center was instrumental in de-escalating the action plan by fusion Center stakeholders after a 2004 crash of a US Air force C-5 transport plane.

Mayor Pringle of Anaheim, CA (Chapter 14), created a virtual operations center to manage emergency situations. Authorized users could now manage events from any computer. It has a landing page where users can access information ranging from building blueprints to traffic flow around the incident. Regional communities also participate in the virtual center. The system has worked well in the case of fires and in a simulation of a major disaster.

Cameras deployed throughout a jurisdiction could help gather information. The data are mainly used for operations but they could be used for data mining. Bellwood, Illinois in 2005 (Chapter 15) created an integrated wireless surveillance network focused on 2.5 miles of public streets, sidewalks, and alleys. The system has both audio and video and can focus on sounds of breaking glass or gunshots. Cameras were also installed at intersections to catch red light runners, illegal right on red turns, violators of railroad crossing signals, and even overweight trucks. The system has reduced 911 calls for service and such property crimes as auto theft. Bellwood also instituted a wireless communications system that allows data, pictures, and other information to be provided to officers on patrol and firefighters in transit to an emergency. The sophisticated system allows personnel to view traffic cameras so they can often determine the situation before arriving on the scene. Intelligent cameras are already being used elsewhere for surveillance with facial recognition, and some can identify suspicious objects through quasi x-ray ability. When the cameras detect any such elements, an alert is generated.

Adequate communications are necessary for effective rescue operations. Rescue efforts on 9/11 were impeded when the cellular antennas at the top of the Twin Towers collapsed. Access calls are usually diverted to other antennas but the magnitude of the calls caused a collapse of the entire cellular system. Thus, rescue efforts relied more on personal contacts and with the leaders "on the scene" than on communication systems. Collier County, FL, experienced similar communication problems during Hurricanes Charlie and Wilma. Disruptions occurred in the public-switched network, the cellular systems, and the Internet. In response to that experience, Chapter 16 by Collier County officials James Mudd and Barry Axelrod reports on its improved public safety system. The County added more automotive radios, which are less reliant on antennas, developed a private optic data network, improved the connectivity between the private data network and the Internet, and improved the telephone system through reduced reliance on one central office. It also enlisted volunteers who are "ham" radio users to provide communication during an emergency. The latter are least dependent on any infrastructure and therefore their communications are robust. Mayor Cicilline of Providence, RI, states in Chapter 17 that his city was one of the first cities to make data in a digestible form available to field officers. The officer in the field has information equivalent to that at the station and can complete reports that enter the database. The Internet is making such practice commonplace.

The lack of interoperable communications between the police and the fire forces contributed to the loss of lives of responders. Interoperable radio communication is the solution promoted and funded by the federal government. The failure of the communications and the lack of interoperability have also been dominant themes raised by governors and mayors. To achieve interoperability the federal government supports state and local governments by grants of around $2.7 billion. Governor Round and Otto Doll of South Dakota (Chapter 18) report on how a statewide radio system was developed that allows its more than 14,000 public safety officials (local, state, federal, and tribal) to communicate with each other. The digital, trunked system permits voice and data transmission in a cost-effective manner. The trunked feature ensures efficiency because the computer searches to find the first available channel rather than dedicating a particular channel to a particular user. Tacoma, WA (Chapter 19), established a region-wide cooperative effort to promote, evaluate, implement, and manage technology applications for law enforcement. The technology incorporates police, HLS, and the courts under one organization where relevant data are maintained, evaluated, and distributed to the appropriate law enforcement agencies. Mayor Will Wynn of Austin, TX, describes in detail in Chapter 20 the history and process of integrating the communication systems in the region. In Chapter 21, Mayor Iorio of Tampa outlined the development of a regional cooperative, interoperable police, fire, and emergency management systems and a joint operations center where each maintains its own system to satisfy special requirements.

The communications policy has not been free of controversy. In a testimony before US Congress, one expert stated that not every firefighter or police officer needs an interoperable radio. Only those actually at the scene should be so equipped. A simple mobile interoperable communication system at the scene valued at merely a million dollars will suffice. Only a few such systems need to be purchased by each major city (O'Hanlon, 2007). This suggests possible over spending on technology. Further, political issues enter into the allocation of government funds. For example, rural states like Wyoming or Montana have received larger per capita homeland security funds, including presumably communications grants, than major cities like New York and Washington that are prime targets for terrorist attacks.

Emergency operations centers have an interesting history. Former New York Mayor Rudolph Giuliani completed in 2000 his innovative emergency center at the Twin Towers in the financial district of the city. The Center also had a conference room for all the commissioners and the mayor. The Center was used a few times for specific emergency situations like water breaks and electricity shutdowns. The Center became the emergency operational facility where critical city and public utilities migrated during a crisis. In a disaster, all phone lines are diverted to it. The Center's location at the Twin Towers was decided after a thorough analysis of various locations in the city. It was determined that only a direct atomic bombing of the building could endanger the center. Unfortunately, no one could have predicted the vicious attack on the Twin Towers that prevented its use at the most critical time of that attack. Incidentally, an emergency center does not normally perform data mining and the opposite is also true.

Many other cities followed NYC's project while employing new technologies that became available. Washington, DC, under Mayor Williams (Chapter 22) has developed innovative technologies for homeland security. The improvements included the establishment of a command center that is in operation at all times. It has the capability for voice, video, wideband, and wireless communications. Remote backup capability was created. Interestingly, the Center was located in an economically deprived section of the city in part to stimulate the area's development. The technology allows viewing activities throughout the city, adjusting traffic patterns, and the deployment of forces. The Center was used to control major events like July 4th celebrations and the 2005 Presidential Inauguration.

Chicago under the leadership of Mayor Daley (Chapter 23) developed a Joint Operations Center, which brings together in one room federal, state, municipal, and utility emergency personnel to monitor and react to events like storms, utility interruptions, and terrorist attacks. Digital cameras are monitored at the Center. Detailed digital floor plans of all tall building and major infrastructure are available on the Center's computers. Chicago also has a mobile unit that can perform all the functions of the Joint Operations Center. This unit, which could serve as a backup Center, can be dispatched to the place of an incident and would prevent the situation of 9/11 in New York City where the Center was destroyed. Chicago employed the mobile unit to handle successfully the 2007 New Year's celebration, which occurred at the same time as a major playoff football game.

Virginia (Chapter 24) developed and implemented a continuity of operations plan for all disasters including a possible flu pandemic. Continuity plans include provision for use of alternative facilities in case a disaster disables the primary department or agency facility. Virginia also created a new Emergency Operations Center with sufficient space to accommodate individual departments and agencies that have had their facilities made inoperable. The Emergency Operations Center has sophisticated computer and communications technology, which permits operational management of a disaster. Especially important is the redundancy aspect so that the Center is resilient to failure of any individual system.

The human element and the specific culture of the targeted population are most important for successful implementation of technology in homeland security. Morales and Ramsey argue in Chapter 25 that the IT people are important in educating other members of the organization.

Conclusions

Since 2001, government at all three levels face increased demand for homeland security services that could be partially met through restructuring of existing emergency services, shedding non-public services, and contracting out public good

services. Homeland security services include preparation and training for anticipated events and assisting in satisfying the unknowable peak load demand. We suggested ways to engage the private sector in preparing and providing homeland security services before and during such events. We also suggested requiring insurance
against catastrophic events that will encourage businesses to take appropriate security precautions. Technology is often an efficient substitute for labor. However, since
government is not motivated by profit and the social net benefits are unknowable,
the appropriate technology may not be developed or deployed. Governments could
either over or under spend on technology for homeland security.

Specific recommendations include verified response to false alarms for police
and charging prices that cover the long-run avoidable cost for fire and ambulance response to false calls, and shedding non-public police services like animal
control, escorting funerals, and unlocking cars. We suggest establishing reserve
units for homeland security. Private security guards and directors will be trained
and deployed to pre-assigned obligations in case of an event. Retired emergency
services' officers could also be invited to join such a force. Personnel should be
paid for the time they serve on the force. We also suggest that the commanding officers could be police chiefs or private executives who volunteer. Private executives
are often interested in public service and obviously have the requisite managerial
and entrepreneurial skills. Finally, our suggestions for public–private partnerships
are consistent with the current emphasis of expanding the role of the private sector
in providing public services.

Improving homeland security in the public sector will probably encounter a
few problems. Several years have passed since 9/11 and no other terrorist attacks
occurred within the United States. It may become difficult for elected public official
to justify local and state spending on homeland security. This excludes activities
related to natural disasters. It is more popular to exhibit achievements in services
that contribute directly to the constituents. Besides, the public expects the federal
government to cover all defense and homeland security expenses.

In the background section, we discussed the asymmetric information problem
where the terrorist has the freedom of choosing the target, the timing, the nature,
and extent of an attack. Public budget constraints make target hardening in the form
of prevention activities thin and ineffective across the many critical infrastructures.
One solution is to maintain limited personnel at most facilities and employ technological advanced sensors to alert and provide necessary information about attacks.
Obviously, high-risk targets like nuclear plants require strong security measures.
Most of the financial resources should be spent on effective response and recovery
efforts. Another possible preventive measure is to respond by randomly securing
most critical infrastructures. Thus, the policy might be to respond in a random fashion to the terrorist, creating uncertainty on their part.

The other problem relates to the lack of incentives to promote managerial and
technological innovations in the public sector. Unions of public employees often
object to merit or incentive payments, preferring across the board increases in compensation. Encouraging innovations including obtaining patents, however, requires
significant financial incentives. State and local governments have technology experts

working at the IT and the homeland security departments and in other security-related departments. State and local governments could establish incentive systems.

Ordinary disasters have been and are successfully managed by state and local governments. National homeland security efforts should mainly address major catastrophic events that could occur in various locations in the United States. For example, a terrorist attack that might simultaneously destroy sewer facilities in many metropolitan areas or a major natural disaster might affect many states. Society has to prepare for a low probability event that could have significantly large adverse effects. The United States has enough emergency resources to handle almost any event; it is basically an issue of peak-time demand where the existing resources must be mobilized to confront the calamity with minimum disruption. We suggest establishing public–private partnerships that will prepare and train for such an event and where private resources could be added to the existing public emergency resources. Thus, an appropriate role for the US DHS or the National Governors Association would be to induce states to establish regional compacts to share governmental resources while incorporating private resources and private sector ideas. The objective is to mobilize emergency resources from non-affected areas and from the private sector to assist the impacted area. We are optimistic that unleashing the private sector will help minimize the disruption from any natural or terrorist attacks.

References

Auerswald, P., et al. (2005). The challenge of protecting critical infrastructure. *Issues in Science and Technology*, Fall. Obtained from http://www.issues.org/22.1/auerswald.html. Last accessed September 19, 2008.

Blackstone, E.A., A.J. Buck, and S. Hakim (2005). Evaluation of alternative policies to combat false emergency calls. *Evaluation and Program Planning* 28(2): 233–242.

Blackstone, E.A., A.J. Buck, and S. Hakim (2007). The economic of emergency response. *Policy Sciences* 40(4): 313–334.

Blades, M. (2008). Helping hands: the FBI is working with the private sector to enhance corporate security and to promote national security. *Security Technology and Design* May: 36–38.

Bureau of Justice Assistance (BJA) (2005). Engaging the Private Sector to Promote Homeland Security: Law Enforcement-Private Security Partnerships, US Department of Justice, Office of Justice Programs, NCJ 210678, September.

City of Chicago v. Factory Mutual Insurance Co., 2004 U.S. District Lexis 4266.

Clarke, R.A. and R. Beers, et al. (2006). *The Forgotten Homeland: A Century Foundation Task Force Report*. The Century Foundation, New York.

Council of Foreign Relations (2003). *Emergency Responders: Drastically Underfunded, Dangerously Unprepared*. The Rudman Report, NY.

Critical Infrastructures, 2008. Chemical plants-go well beyond well prepared. *Newsweek*, November 5, 2001. Obtained from www.newsweek.com/id/76228/page/1 Last visited 9/16/2008.

Flynn, S. (2007). *The Edge of Disaster: Rebuilding a Resilient Nation*. Random House, New York.

Hakim, S., A.J. Buck, and E.A. Blackstone (2007). Funding the local war on terror. *Milken Institute Review* 9(1), First Quarter: 46–56.

Insurance Information Institute (2007). *9/11 and Insurance: The Five Year Anniversary*. New York, NY. Available from www.iii.org. Last accessed May 19, 2008.

Joint Economic Committee of the US Congress (May, 2002). *Economic Perspectives on Terrorism Insurance*.

Kunreuther, H. and E. Michel-Kerjan (2004). Challenges for terrorism risk insurance in the United States. *Journal of Economic Perspectives* 18(4), Fall: 201–214.

Office of Management and Budget (2008). *Analytical Perspective on the Budget of the US, Fiscal Year 2008.* Obtained from www.whitehouse.gov/omb/budget/fy2008

O'Hanlon, M., 2007. *A Broad Take on America's Current Homeland Security,* Testimony before the House Committee on Homeland Security's Subcommittee on Boarder, Maritime and Global Counterterrorism, March 8.

Orszag, P.E. (2003). *Homeland Security and the Private Sector,* Testimony before the National Commission on Terrorist Attacks Upon the Unite States, November 19.

Scahill, J. (2005). *Blackwater Down.* The Nation, October 10. Visit http://www.thenation.com/doc/20051010/scahill. Visited May 6, 2008.

www.apwa.net/Advocacy/Infrustructure Last visited 9/16/2008.

www.fpl.com/environment/nuclear_power_serves_you.shtml Last visited 9/16/2008.

Chapter 2
Creating the Boston Medical Reserve Corps

Thomas M. Menino

Abstract Boston learned from the 9/11 disaster and the devastation following Katrina and Rita that volunteers are willing to help the people in need even by taking personal risks. The Boston Medical Reserve Corps trains public health emergency response volunteers to assist in case of need. Within 48 h, the volunteers can distribute medication to the entire population of the city. Basic training, exercises, and refresher courses are provided to prepare volunteers for biological, nuclear, or communicable disease events.

Introduction

There have been many lessons learned in the area of public health preparedness since the 9/11 disasters and the devastation that followed Hurricanes Katrina and Rita. The lessons about security, communication, and preparation are well documented. One of the more inspiring lessons learned is that in the event of a disaster, whether natural or manmade, Americans are willing to help those in need. Often with little regard for the danger to themselves, thousands of Americans from near and far did not wait to be asked before deciding to head to the affected areas and volunteer.

The City of Boston has taken these lessons to heart. We have developed our public health emergency response volunteer program, the Boston Medical Reserve Corps, to help ensure that we have a cadre of skilled, trained volunteers ready to support our city's public health response efforts. The Boston Medical Reserve Corps serves as an example of how a city government and its constituents can partner effectively to serve a community.

T.M. Menino (✉)
Mayor, Boston, MA, (1993–present)
e-mail: mayor@cityofboston.gov

S. Hakim, E.A. Blackstone (eds.), *Safeguarding Homeland Security*,
DOI 10.1007/978-1-4419-0371-6_2, © Springer Science+Business Media, LLC 2009

The Boston Medical Reserve Corps

The Medical Reserve Corps (MRC) was created in response to President Bush's 2002 State of the Union address, where he called for increased volunteerism in support of our nation's security. The MRC is run out of the Office of the Surgeon General and is designed to be operated locally to meet the specific public health needs of the communities they serve. Currently, there are nearly 700 recognized MRCs around the country, with nearly 125,000 volunteers. The Boston MRC was created in 2003 and operates out of the Boston Public Health Commission's (BPHC) Emergency Preparedness Division.

The City of Boston and the Boston Public Health Commission's Emergency Preparedness Division designed the Boston Medical Reserve Corps to meet the Cities Readiness Initiative (CRI) objectives. The CRI is a federal effort to prepare major cities in the United States to distribute oral medications to their entire residential population within 48 h of the decision to do so. The federal government provides assistance to cities to help them increase their abilities to receive and dispense medicine and medical supplies from the Strategic National Stockpile. Large-scale public health emergencies could include bioterrorism attacks, accidents at nuclear facilities, or major disease outbreaks such as pandemic influenza.

The main model used to dispense medication in a CRI event is Points of Dispensing (PODs). These PODs allow for the distribution of medicine and/or other health-protecting supplies to people in the affected area during a large-scale public health emergency.

Operating the number of PODs necessary to provide mass prophylaxis to all Boston residents is a huge task. Thousands of volunteers working around the clock providing medical and logistical services will need to be activated in a very short-time period. This creates a serious human resource challenge. Each POD is really a small clinic. Patients requiring care will rely on medically trained volunteers to screen and treat them. Yet many more non-medical volunteers will be needed to handle supplies, to make sure the lines run smoothly, to maintain the needs of the facilities, to provide language translation, to distribute information, and a variety of other tasks essential to the smooth operation of a POD.

The Boston MRC provides volunteers to staff these PODs. "Response level" volunteers make up the majority of the Boston MRC. These volunteers go through a basic orientation and will be called upon in the event of an emergency. "Leadership level" volunteers, who complete nearly 10 h of additional training, will be responsible for managing volunteers as they run part of a clinic. In a large CRI event, Leadership level volunteers will be needed to perform key managerial roles.

Volunteer Recruitment

As our CRI planning ramped up, we began to ramp up our volunteer recruitment efforts. In the summer of 2006, we had about 400 volunteers, many of whom had signed up following the disasters of Hurricanes Katrina and Rita. With those disasters moving off the front pages, and the newness and lack of notoriety of the MRC program, volunteer recruitment had dropped off considerably.

In response, the city developed a comprehensive advertising campaign designed to reach both medical and non-medical volunteers. The campaign was designed to call upon the best of Boston residents. Using the tagline *Be One of Boston's Everyday Heroes*, the campaign showed a variety of people – medical and non-medical, young and old, students and parents – in heroic poses. The ads described key concepts of the program: ease of joining, free training provided, minimal time commitment, providing a valuable service to the City of Boston.

The campaign ran on the web sites of Boston's two major newspapers, *The Boston Globe* and *The Boston Herald*, as well as the free daily, *The Boston Metro*. The city placed advertisements on subway cars and at public transportation stations, with a particular focus on subway lines and stations that served hospitals. Placements were made in Boston's community newspapers and advertising kiosks around the city. We launched the campaign with a press conference at city hall where I spoke alongside then BPHC Executive Director John Auerbach and a Boston MRC volunteer. This campaign, launched in September 2006, has encouraged more than 1,200 new volunteers to join the Boston MRC, quadrupling the size of this critical volunteer group. Because of its success, this campaign was re-launched in June 2007 to continue to expand our volunteer numbers.

Basic Training

Having such a large group of volunteers would be useless without providing them with the quality training needed to allow them to succeed in the event of activation. In order to serve effectively during emergencies, volunteers need to know about the management structure during a response, potential roles they might hold, how they would be contacted in the event of an emergency, how to prepare themselves and their family before an emergency ever happens, and much more. Prior to the launch of the recruitment campaign, this basic training required of all volunteers was provided in person. Due to staffing limitations, training was only provided monthly, in the evening, at the BPHC offices, which are not so easily accessible by public transportation.

With ambitious growth goals, we had to identify a new way to train the expected sizable influx of new volunteers. The answer came in the form of new technology: online distance learning. In partnership with the Harvard School of Public Health's Center for Public Health Preparedness, an online version of our response level training was developed. The training is an interactive experience, with the volunteer going through a series of narrated power point slides, with checkpoint quizzes at the end of each section. Volunteers learn the purpose of the Boston MRC, and their roles and responsibilities, in addition to how to prepare themselves and their families before an emergency happens. The volunteers have the opportunity to hear a sample activation call and must also successfully complete a quiz at the end of the training in order to stay active.

Leadership Training

We have additional trainings that we require of our leadership volunteers. In the event of a CRI, we will rely on Boston MRC leadership level volunteers to perform managerial roles at PODs. Four additional trainings were created to give volunteers the skill they will need in order to perform these critical tasks.

The first of these additional trainings is our Managing Mass Dispensing Clinics training. In this 2-h training, volunteers get a refresher on the reasons for the activation of a POD. The roles and responsibilities of POD managers are explained in detail. The leadership staff that first arrives at the POD will be responsible for setting up the stations, organizing supplies, and doing all of the work necessary to prepare the POD before the rest of the volunteer staff arrives. In order to do this, the leadership volunteers must have an in-depth knowledge of the POD layout, the supplies they will have at their disposal and how they are to be used, and a sense of how the patients coming to the clinic will flow through the dispensing process.

In a large-scale operation such as this, there are bound to be many issues that will affect the way the clinic will operate. Weather, staffing limitations, distribution bottlenecks, and safety issues are just some of the factors that could create havoc during clinic operations. This training helps our leadership volunteers to identify and address a variety of issues affecting the opening and operation of a POD. A scenario-based discussion also allows Boston MRC volunteers to talk about how they might handle various situations.

The second leadership training is on Incident Command System (ICS), the management tool used by all response agencies to run emergencies response efforts. In a potential activation, Boston MRC leadership volunteers will need to understand how public health incidents are managed within a clinic as well as the overall incident response structure.

In the ICS training, Boston MRC volunteers learn about the key concepts of the structure, and how that structure is specifically implemented for POD operations in Boston. They are taught how to maintain specific channels of communication with supervisors and supervisees in order to ensure that information gets to the people who need it. The use of ICS forms is discussed, with particular attention paid to the job action sheet (JAS).

JASs are a list of immediate, ongoing, and demobilization tasks that are required of each job at a POD. Boston MRC leadership volunteers learn how to read and utilize a JAS to perform their job function correctly and to facilitate the transfer of their position to another volunteer when their shift is over.

We train our leadership volunteers in key concepts of disaster behavioral health and psychological first aid as the third component of leadership training. In any emergency situation, coping with stress must be an important consideration. Imagine a public health scenario where a potentially fatal disease affects large portions of our city, as people are told to wait in lines to receive life-saving medication. Even with a strong public messaging campaign, volunteers at a POD are likely to encounter some level of confusion, fear, and panic among the patients and staff.

This 3-h training gives Boston MRC volunteers an understanding of how to provide the most basic support to those experiencing stress at a POD. They are taught how to recognize the signs of extreme stress in themselves and others. In situations involving their own stress, they are taught ways to practice self-care. In situations involving patients or other staff, the volunteers are taught methods for de-escalating a situation and for directing someone to mental health resources that are part of the POD staff structure. Finally, volunteers are given the chance to practice self-care as they are led through scenarios that role-play situations requiring psychological first aid that they might encounter as volunteers.

The last leadership level course is on volunteer management and leadership skills. In CRI events, Boston MRC leadership volunteers will likely have the responsibility of supervising other volunteers. This course helps the volunteers learn how to motivate volunteers and how to work effectively with other professional cultures that will be involved with the response, such as the Police Department, Fire Department, Emergency Medical Services, and the media. Volunteers are also taught to identify their own leadership skills, and how to utilize those skills to make the POD more effective.

Lectures to Maintain Interest of Volunteers

Once our volunteers are trained, they are available to be called upon at any time. However, even small-scale public health emergencies are rare, and it is likely that volunteers could go years without being asked to respond to an emergency. This makes the retention of volunteers very difficult. To aid in this effort, there is a quarterly Boston MRC lecture series to keep volunteers involved in the program. We present special topics of interest to Boston MRC members that help them stay current with public health issues. We have offered a session on Pandemic Flu, in which volunteers learned what influenza is and how it develops into a pandemic, how to prevent contracting influenza through use of respiratory precautions, and ways BMRC volunteers might be involved in a response to pandemic influenza.

We also offered a session on the Strategic National Stockpile, which is a federal program that assures the availability of essential medical materials to any community in the United States in a time of disaster. We explain how federal and local supplies get to our PODs, and how this supply chain relates the work Boston MRC volunteers do.

We held a lecture series event to describe how mass care has been used in the past and lessons learned from those events. Mass care is a means of providing shelter and other assistance to victims following a major disaster. While not a main volunteer role of Boston MRC volunteers, we may rely on them to assist with mass care operations in different types of emergencies. We discussed ways in which volunteers might be utilized in these instances. Upcoming lecture series events will be held on safety issues at a POD and an update on pandemic influenza. Other topics are in development.

Exercises

One of the best tools we have at our disposal for retaining volunteers, as well as preparing them to be effective POD staff and managers, is the use of exercises. As the Emergency Preparedness Division works to test its activation plans, Boston MRC volunteers are utilized to give them experience in the POD setting and to ensure that they are being taught the skills necessary to do their job safely, accurately, and efficiently.

In the summer of 2006, the EPD tested its capabilities to open a POD. It was important to learn how long it would take to open a POD, the resources needed to support a throughput of 1,000 doses per hour, and the staffing requirements needed to open the clinic in a relatively short amount of time. As part of that exercise, we invited some MRC leadership volunteers to participate. The volunteers were given their work assignments on the day of the event. Using their leadership training, the volunteers were effectively able to perform a variety of roles. They unloaded and sorted medical and non-medical supplies. Most importantly, they were able to work collaboratively, respond to problems, and come up with ideas to improve plans on the spot.

We rely on exercises to help us inform our planning efforts. The feedback from Boston MRC volunteers proved to be invaluable. One of the main lessons learned from this exercise was about our clinic setup. The staff initially envisioned a clinic with three lanes of traffic for dispensing the medication. One lane would be a standard dosing lane, or "express lane," for those receiving the most common medication. A second lane would be for those requiring suspension dosing, meaning those who would need their medication broken down and mixed with water to make it easier to swallow. The third would be for complex treatment, which would apply to families in which some members required standard dosing and others required suspension dosing. Our volunteers noted that such a system could cause a long wait time for clinic patients, which could mean that bottlenecks may form at the entrance of the clinic, within the clinic, and at the clinic exit.

We took these suggestions and used them to update our CRI plans. Instead of three different lines, all medication lanes were made "express lanes." In this plan, anyone can go to any line. Each station will have all the medications necessary for the particular response. If suspension dosing is required, every station will have an information sheet with directions for suspension dosing. This allows for shorter processing time per patient, reduces any confusion that could arise by having lines with different functions, and helps ensure that each patient receives the same information.

This information was added to our trainings, and we used this new streamlined model in our exercise in the summer of 2007. The 2007 exercise picked up where we left off in 2006. This time we were testing our ability to dispense medication, both in terms of time and in terms of accuracy. To meet our CRI goal, we determined that we needed to have a throughput of at least 1,000 doses per hour. For this exercise, we used Boston MRC volunteers to serve as clinic staff: nurses who were dispensing medication; triage staff who greeted and screened incoming patients; queue management staff, who managed the flow of patients into and out of the clinic; and medical evaluation staff, who handled patients with special medical conditions. In addition, we used other MRC volunteers as patient simulators, who played different "characters" with different ages, medical histories, children, etc.

The first part of this exercise was an activation call to our clinic staff volunteers using the Mayors Emergency Alert Notification System, or MEANS. This system performs a callout to selected people registered in the MEANS to alert them to a specific condition. In this case, the condition was that MRC volunteers were needed to run a POD in response to a simulated Anthrax release. Virtually all of the volunteers were able to listen and respond to this activation call successfully.

The second part of the exercise was a just-in-time training of our POD staff. This is the type of training that volunteers would receive prior to being sent to a POD site. Here volunteers receive incident-specific information, as well as a refresher on POD layout, staffing, and management. The volunteers were registered and trained at the DelValle Institute for Emergency Preparedness just as they would be in the event of a real emergency.

The final part of the exercise was the running of the POD. Patient simulators went through the clinic in virtually the same way they would in a real CRI event. They were screened, led through the clinic, and treated by Boston MRC volunteers. Our goal was to dispense at a rate of 1,000 doses per hour. Largely due to the efforts of the Boston MRC volunteers, we were able to dispense at a rate of more than 1,800 per hour and no one was given the wrong medication.

Support for Non-CRI Events

CRI events, thankfully, do not occur very often. But many other types of public health emergencies occur more regularly, and often these emergencies will exceed the resources of the Boston Public Health Commission's staffing resources. Boston MRC volunteers are utilized in these situations. Since the Boston MRC was created in late 2003, there have been a number of activations of support clinics to curb outbreaks of Hepatitis A, Meningitis, and most recently, measles.

In the summer of 2006, there was a measles case at the John Hancock building, the largest building in Boston, located in the heart of the city. The exposed person had contact with employees on multiple floors of the building, where 80% of the air is recycled. There were many potential exposures within the building and elsewhere, and the BPHC's Communicable Disease Center made the decision to open a clinic in the building to treat those potentially exposed who did not have proof of vaccination. Boston MRC volunteers played critical roles that ensured the success of our clinic operations: Volunteer nurses helped dispense medication and a volunteer pharmacist and two of his students helped to prepare vaccines. Having this cadre of volunteers available made the job of seeing thousands of patients a very manageable task.

Future

In the coming months and years, the Boston MRC will continue to grow to help reach our goal of more than 4,000 active volunteers. As new exercises are conducted, and as the threats that affect the public health change, trainings will be updated in order to keep our volunteers as prepared as possible for potential activations. In addition, a yearly refresher course is being developed which will keep our volunteers up-to-date with the most current information and allow us to update our database as contact information changes.

The Boston Medical Reserve Corps is a key element of our emergency preparedness strategy and a great example of a partnership between constituents and government.

Chapter 3
The Hierarchy of Emergency Preparedness

Rob Drake

Abstract The mayor of Beaverton promoted cooperation between organizations and through use of technology to prepare for disasters. Local police and fire personnel participate on each other's calls to develop a cooperative relationship. Regional emergency response organizations, including public, private, non-profits, and volunteer groups, have been developed. Volunteer groups play an important role in emergency response and recovery efforts and plans. During a major flood in 1996, a church staffed a flood information and referral line. The region has developed region-wide plans and procedures for disaster response. Interoperable communications now enable emergency responders from the region to communicate during a disaster.

As the mayor of the City of Beaverton, OR (population 87,000), the western neighbor of Portland, there are relatively few things that wake me up in middle of the night. However, there is a recurrent question that can play havoc with my sleep: How would my community react to a major disaster? Are city personnel appropriately trained and ready to respond? How would residents cope if emergency assistance were delayed by 24–72 h?

I am not alone in these concerns. It is hard not to feel more vulnerable post-911 or after seeing the incomprehensible damage of Hurricane Katrina. I toured New Orleans in November 2007 and was stunned by the pervasive devastation and human displacement 2 full years after the hurricane. New Orleans is comparable in size to Portland, and it is hard to fathom how the "Rose City" could survive the dislocation of half its residents and the devastating loss of its many businesses.

R. Drake (✉)
Mayor, Beaverton, OR, (1992–2008)
e-mail: drarej@comcast.net

S. Hakim, E.A. Blackstone (eds.), *Safeguarding Homeland Security*,
DOI 10.1007/978-1-4419-0371-6_3, © Springer Science+Business Media, LLC 2009

Local Threats

It is important to be realistic about the threats that our local communities do and do not face. There is little reason to believe that my city would be the target of terrorist act, and our weather, while wet, is typically pretty benign. However, there are always exceptions. I was 13 years old and had already developed an avid interest in the weather when the Columbus Day Storm hit in 1962. It was late afternoon and the storm arrived with little warning. Peak wind gusts of 129 mph were recorded in Portland and left a path of death, injury, and severe property damage the length of the Willamette Valley and the entire upper northern California and Oregon coastlines. My newly purchased weather station was bolted to the fence along side the house, and after the high winds hit neither was ever seen again! With the electricity out for 3 weeks, the fireplace in our living room became the focal point of family life. Today, the possibility of wind speeds half as strong prompt local television to break-in with special "weather alerts," but we veterans know better.

Much more recently, just 25 miles west of Beaverton, a severe storm in December 2007 dropped over 13 in. of rain in Oregon's coast range in less than 24 h. The town of Vernonia sustained dramatic flooding that was televised throughout the world. It was the second time in 11 years that this community was nearly washed away.

And then there is the "big one." Less than 60 miles due west of Beaverton, the floor of the Pacific Ocean is sliding slowly under the North American continental shelf. While the enormous forces involved are largely hidden, every now and then they make themselves known. This happened in dramatic fashion in 1980 when Mt. St. Helens erupted. More common are the low-to-moderate intensity earthquakes. Geologists tell us that every 300 years or so the pent-up forces require a major adjustment and a severe earthquake occurs. There is strong scientific evidence that the last severe quake occurred in 1700, so the chances of a major event are steadily increasing.

While not a worrier by nature, I think it is understandable and appropriate that I experience that periodic sleepless night and nagging question: Are we ready? Because of my involvement with the National Leagues of Cities, I know the same question is asked in communities across the nation. The natural threats vary based on location, as does the likelihood of and type of possible human-caused emergencies. Yet, there is also a random quality at work, as evidenced by incidents such as the Amish school shooting in Pennsylvania in 2006 and the wintertime tornado that tore through Vancouver, WA, in January 2008. Whether predictable or an aberration, it does not matter; when an emergency confronts your community, you get one chance to respond correctly.

The Hierarchy of Emergency Preparation

The American psychologist Abraham Maslow is famous for his theory on the hierarchy of human needs. The basics of physiological survival – food, water, air, rest, etc. – form a foundation that all humans require. Once met, individuals are able to

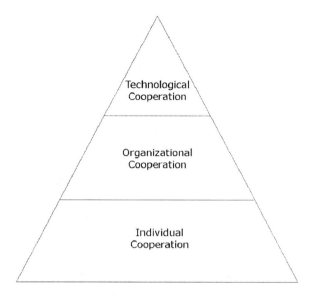

move, one step at a time, to subsequent levels in the hierarchy (safety, love and belonging, and self-esteem). The content of Maslow's steps does not apply here, but I have definitely experienced a hierarchy of need for successful emergency preparation. The foundation is individual cooperation, followed by organizational cooperation, and then technological cooperation.

Individual Cooperation

The larger the emergency, the greater the likelihood that people from multiple agencies will be working together. If they know one another and something about respective roles and responsibilities, the chance of quickly moving to purposeful and coordinated action increases. Encouraging these relationships and awareness is the first step in the emergency preparation hierarchy.

Officers from the Beaverton Police Department (BPD) regularly ride-along with crews from Tualatin Valley Fire & Rescue (TVFR), the regional service provider that serves our city and eight others. The opposite is also true with a TVFR officer tagging along for a shift with a BPD officer. Ask anyone with a law enforcement or fire fighting background and you will discover quite a rivalry exists between these two professions. Sometimes it is counterproductive to working together at an emergency incident. The ride-along program has become a simple but effective way to begin to break down some of the "silo" thinking that can be incredibly destructive when responding to a major emergency.

Tualatin Valley Fire & Rescue has taken this relationship building a huge step forward with its Incident Management Teams (IMT). Conceived to provide a supporting command and logistics presence during a significant event, each IMT is on call a week at a time. Rather than rely solely on TVFR personnel to staff the various positions, representatives are included from local law enforcement, public works, ambulance providers, large employers, and other public safety responders from the cities, county, and other special districts. The teams train together several times a year and relationships are established. At the request of the State of Oregon, a TVFR IMT assisted with the recent winter floods in Vernonia in the neighboring county. They were deployed for a week and provided timely support to the county staff in the Emergency Operations Center. A key member of the responding IMT team is the Public Works Director from another city served by TVFR. His contribution during the flood deployment was irreplaceable because his community had been inundated in 1996 and he led that recovery effort.

This kind of interdisciplinary relationship building is common in Washington County, where Beaverton is located. This tone of working together has been set for the past two decades as elected and appointed officials work across jurisdictions and boundaries. Particularly useful for me has been the County Managers group, which brings together the top managers of the county, cities, and special districts on a monthly basis to navigate difficult public policy issues. Certainly there are points of departure where we agree to disagree, but the foundation of respect and cooperation is always retained.

And it is not only government that is trying to steer a common direction in Washington County. Formalized linkages and relationships are in place with individual leaders in business, non-profits, education, citizen organizations, and the faith community. These connections are regularly tapped to work on issues that challenge our livability, such as homelessness and affordable housing – but they take on a more pressing importance when a crisis occurs. The 100-year flood of 1996 was such an event. With its emergency response infrastructure still young at the time, Washington County accepted the offer of the local LDS Church to staff the phones at the Flood Information and Referral center and the church members performed admirably for a full week.

Organizational Cooperation

Progressive emergency response organizations use of the Incident Command System (ICS) and the more recent federal adaptation, the National Incident Management System (NIMS), provides a rational organizational structure with clear reporting channels during times of emergency. While very supportive of this move to a common command structure, I am personally far more concerned about how we organize ourselves and advance emergency preparedness when the crisis is not upon us. Like a world-class athlete, we must use our "off season" to collaborate across organizations to build, test, and train systems and personnel that will be stressed to dramatic levels when a major emergency actually occurs. It is far too late when the disaster is knocking on our door or happens without notice to worry about what to do if we have not prepared for the worst. Again, we get only one chance with our citizens to get it right.

A Regional Model

I have served as Chair of the Portland-area Regional Emergency Management Group (REMG) since 1993. REMG is the vehicle by which the public and private sectors in the Portland, Oregon/Vancouver, Washington region work together to organize, plan, and define regional needs and develop common policies and procedures to follow in the event of a disaster. The group is dedicated to providing a long-term model for regional coordination and planning, driven by operational necessity, not by financial incentives.

This is a voluntary group formed through intergovernmental agreement between special districts, city, county, and regional agencies in the five-county, bi-state Portland/Vancouver Metropolitan area. It includes the American Red Cross and steady participation from utility providers and local and global businesses.

Some key initiatives for REMG include the following:

- Identification and publication of regional emergency transportation routes;
- Development of the Great Portland/Vancouver Area Emergency Alert System (EAS) Operation Plan in coordination with broadcasters across the region;
- Development of a regional disaster debris management plan in cooperation with "Metro," Portland's regional government and local solid waste program managers;
- Voluntary agreement between local governments to address emergency management issues for the benefit of the entire region, regardless of resources or participation in the group;
- Staff deployment from participating agencies, without compensation, to work with the regional partners; and,
- Involvement of policy level representatives from each signatory agency who provide structure to the group and assist in developing sound policies and procedures for use in disaster situations.

REMG works effectively because its signatory agencies believe in the value of a regional plan, which ensures the integration of all individual plans under the umbrella of one common plan. Local agencies and entities retain their own identities, but we work together leveraging our resources into a stronger whole. The regional focus yields many advantages including proactive partnerships between likely co-responders, collective knowledge for the benefit of the entire region, and a reduction in duplicate efforts, which helps identify and allocate finite resources, maximize resource utilization, and ensure communication of a consistent message to the public.

Local Government Cooperation

In response to the early success of REMG, the leadership of the larger emergency responders in Washington County concluded that there was tremendous room for improvement in coordinating our own emergency planning and preparation efforts. Rather than assign the "emergency manager" function to individual staff positions in disparate locations and jurisdictions, the decision was made to form and jointly fund a cooperative organization that brings the expertise and resources under a common roof. Established in 1995, the Office of Consolidated Emergency Management (OCEM) is staffed by individuals with direct connections to key law enforcement, fire, and public works agencies in the county and cities. In turn, the OCEM staff actively coordinates with area hospitals, medical emergency transporters, schools, major employers, Red Cross, non-profits, social service providers, local CERT groups, and many other groups and institutions that must actively coordinate to ensure an effective response during a real emergency.

Key responsibilities of the OCEM team include the following:

- Develop, maintain, and test functional primary and alternate Emergency Operations Centers (EOC, DOC, FOC) in each OCEM jurisdiction.
- Prepare and maintain comprehensive emergency management plans and procedures addressing preparedness, response, recovery, mitigation, and continuity of operations.
- Identify and assign staff to major emergency/disaster duties and train and exercise them in their assigned responsibilities.
- Develop and deliver a public education program that provides information and/or programs on emergency preparedness for individuals, families, businesses, and industries.
- Guide and facilitate agency-level implementation of homeland security program requirements (e.g., NIMS implementation) and participation in homeland security grant program processes.

The creation of REMG and OCEM are two of many examples of organizational cooperation in our community that is taking advantage of the present to prepare for the potential emergencies of tomorrow. Sadly, the sound logic of cooperating to share ideas, personnel, services, training, and equipment to stretch taxpayer dollars and promote efficiencies is sometimes lost on policy makers and those who implement those policies on a daily basis. Examples abound where elected officials, public agencies, and local non-elected folks miss opportunities to perform better, more effectively, and efficiently. Several years ago, I was a speaker on a panel at a National League of Cities (NLC) meeting. During the question and answer portion of the panel, I was asked how local people could promote better cooperation between the public agencies and the local businesses. The audience participant identified himself as the owner of the local hardware store on Main Street, an elected City Councilor, and served on the local Chamber of Commerce Board of Directors. He was in an outstanding position to facilitate discussion between the public and the private interests – yet apparently it was not happening. I suggested that he peer into the mirror and take an honest look at why his community could not solve its problems. Working together begins with each one of us at the lowest levels and is facilitated by those in decision-making positions at the top.

Technological Cooperation

Much is made of the need for government to work smarter and to make better use of technology, which is a frequent prescription for what ails the public sector. I do not disagree, but the promise of technology is easily over-sold if it is applied in situations where individual and organizational cooperations do not already exist. This is certainly true when we talk about it as a tool for better emergency response. By contrast, when organizations and individuals are accustomed to working together, enhancement of the technological systems that link them together can have a dramatic impact on their ability to respond effectively in times of crisis.

For many communities and regions across the country, the challenge of interoperable voice and data communications represents an immediate threat to the viability of their public safety operations. If these communities and regions do not knock down the barriers and "silo" mentalities, they will not maximize their opportunities to leverage cooperation and hard-earned taxpayer dollars. Though the federal government is requiring cooperative efforts and the ability to have interoperable voice and data communications, it is happening very slowly due to parochial thinking, technological challenges, and the never-ending shortage of public dollars.

In my hometown of Beaverton, OR, that is part of the greater Portland metropolitan area, we approach interoperable communications from a regional perspective because public safety is an issue that does not respect political or geographic boundaries. For example, we are already at level-4 interoperability communications that gives us the ability to interact during a crisis or disaster to fully implement our mutual-aid agreements and cooperative problem-solving efforts. We have more to do, but the region has been cooperating and moving in the right direction for quite some time.

Congress should support mechanisms that encourage, facilitate, and fund-coordinated planning on a regional level. The challenge of integrating levels of service provision is daunting. I have helped guide regional cooperation among local officials for the last 15 years. It has taken hard work and commitment to keep us on task.

Local governments have always resisted state and federal mandates that require certain performance levels without a funding mechanism to implement those requirements. In Oregon, several years ago our independent-minded voters adopted a statewide ballot measure that prohibits the state government from mandating anything without providing the necessary funding to implement that requirement. The federal government can and should mandate programs that encourage and require voice and data interoperability – but should also help provide the funds to make it happen! Included in the idea that funds should accompany the mandates would also be a federal policy that recognizes not everyone is at the same technological sophistication levels or has the same long-term funding capabilities for training, purchasing, and maintaining the systems. Nationally, local police, sheriff, fire, and medical emergency transportation agencies have a broad range of technology and funding capabilities. That range of technology and funding capabilities prohibits a single cure all for full voice and data interoperability.

Nationwide, the age and types of communications equipment vary immensely. Some local agencies have, in recent years, purchased new communications equipment and are not about to abandon these expensive acquisitions. These systems can still be in an analog format and pose hurdles in being capable of communicating with the newer digital format communication systems. To overcome those gaps in capabilities to be able to communicate, some software technologies have been created to "patch" the two analog and digital systems together. Until recently, no national standards had been adopted to guarantee that the equipment "patches" would actually work between the analog and the digital systems. Some manufacturers had alleged that the two systems would "patch" together, but this was not always the case. Along came the P25 standards working group to test and verify that systems will actually be capable of working together when certain types of "patches" are utilized or new equipment additions were purchased. This will allow the taxpayer investment to be maximized until the older system can be abandoned or has served its useful working life.

I would recommend the following to strengthen the federal role on interoperable communications:

1. Elevate the visibility of project SAFECOM.

Project SAFECOM at the Department of Homeland Security is a great example of a federal agency incorporating the input of local governments to improve interoperable communications plans and guidelines. Both the SAFECOM Executive Committee (EC) and the Emergency Responder Community (ERC) are comprised of mainly local government elected officials and everyday practitioners. Elevate the visibility of Project SAFECOM and its mission because interoperable voice and data communications influences hometown security directly.

2. Build on the "spine" of existing communications networks.

The federal government should design programs that benefit first responders at the local level, but within a national scheme. Build on the "spine" of communications networks that promote enhanced public safety and all-hazards disaster response capabilities across multiple jurisdictions. In Oregon, the Portland region is willing to share towers and communication capabilities with the State to leverage existing infrastructure and public dollars already invested in communications capabilities.

This approach not only leverages costly infrastructure appropriately but also creates an environment that fosters solid working relationships to the benefit of the public that we all serve.

3. Funding flexibility.

The NLC has urged Congress to allow more flexibility in the use of federal public safety funds for upgraded technology communication systems and training. The federal government should provide funding directly to local governments for homeland security, emergency preparedness, and response because we are the initial focal point of all disaster mitigation and recovery activities.

4. Federal commitment to "Date Certain" for return of analog spectrum.

While NLC acknowledges the political challenges that led to a "date certain" return of analog spectrum by February 2009, the NLC and others have reminded Congress that more lives than necessary may be lost between now and then because of a lack of spectrum. NLC urges Congress to lead the efforts to accelerate, if possible, efforts to resolve interoperability problems that affect emergency communications and data systems throughout the nation.

Congress has moved in a positive direction with the creation of the Public Safety Broadband Trust (PSBT) legislation in 2007. Unfortunately, there is no "silver bullet" or quick results. Yet to be fully implemented, this legislation finally establishes the "spine" of a national network for communications capabilities. The PSBT allocates certain spectrum for a national interoperable communications network. The initial plans call for a 75% implementation in 4 years and 95% implementation in 7 years. This is the foundation and first step for the creation of such a national policy. This will facilitate significant cost savings on a national basis and be the foundation for a national network plan. Though the news is significant and positive, much detail is yet to be resolved and will be the determiner of success or failure. Common standards have yet to be established and will significantly determine whether the program meets the initial high expectations.

Conclusion

Interoperable communications technology will be a huge step forward in our nation's efforts to prepare for and respond to natural and human-caused disasters. Certainly the federal government must take the lead in this area, ideally in a manner that builds cooperatively on existing state and regional investment, emphasizes common standards, and is mindful of the needs of local emergency responders. But enhanced communications alone will not prepare a single US community for even the smallest emergency incident. Equivalent or greater attention must be paid at the local and state government levels to ensure that response systems are developed and then regularly tested. Most importantly, at both the individual professional and the organizational levels, there must be a clear understanding that effective disaster response demands teamwork and discipline. The only time to successfully build the cooperation that a crisis will demand of us is before it occurs.

Chapter 4
Border Security and State Safety and Security: Addressing Common Agendas

James Jay Carafano

Abstract This chapter shows how state and local government can reduce illegal border crossing and entry of criminals. On the southern border, community policing can combat trans-border crime and deter illegal border crossing. On the northern border, states can help make cross-border traffic both more rapid and secure. Borderland states ought to promote public–private partnerships to build more resilient and higher capacity infrastructure that will enhance efficient border crossing, trade, and security.

Introduction

The United States shares about 2,000 miles of border with Mexico. That border is an economic engine that generates hundreds of billions a year in benefits for both countries. It is, however, a border out of control. The most serious threat is transnational criminals; specifically the cartels are fighting over control of a corridor that ferries a multibillion-dollar-a-year business of drugs, people, and weapons. According to the 2008 National Drug Intelligence Center threat assessment:

> Violence is often associated with drug trafficking along the border; however, law enforcement officials have noted a significant escalation in the level of violence in recent years. Much of the violence occurring along the Southwest Border is a result of conflict between the Gulf Cartel and the cartels composing The Alliance for control of key drug smuggling routes into the United States, particularly through Nuevo Laredo, Tamaulipas, Mexico.[1]

The cartel wars and violence and lawlessness they breed are making the southern border a dangerous place, destroying property and putting lives at risk. The cartels work in conjunction with international gangs who often provide the foot soldiers for criminal activities on the border that range from stealing cars to attacking border patrol agents.[2]

J.J. Carafano (✉)
Assistant Director, Kathryn and Shelby Cullom Davis Institute for International Studies and Senior Research Fellow, Douglas and Sarah Allison Center for Foreign Policy Studies, Heritage Foundation
e-mail: jamescarafano@heritage.org

S. Hakim, E.A. Blackstone (eds.), *Safeguarding Homeland Security*,   41
DOI 10.1007/978-1-4419-0371-6_4, © Springer Science+Business Media, LLC 2009

In addressing border violence, dealing with illegal immigration is part of the mix. Serious criminals hide among the 500,000 individuals who illegally cross the border each year. A significant drop in illegal crossings would allow law enforcement to focus resources on criminals victimizing people on both sides of the border.

By even the most conservative estimates, the United States has an unlawful population of at least 12 million. This population serves as a magnet for further illegal migration. According to a Pew Hispanic Center study in 2003, individuals working in the United States sent almost $30 billion to their families in Latin America and the Caribbean. As the single largest form of direct foreign investment in the region, these remittances have become the economic engine of Latin America. As long as the unprecedented economic importance of remittances remains, individuals will seek access to the US labor market by legal or illegal means. That pressure has overwhelmed America's ability to secure its own border.

The challenges of illegal border crossing reach well beyond the border. Unlawfully present persons are largely the source of undocumented workers. The costs of low-wage, undocumented labor are foisted on state and local communities, from providing various entitlements to the law-enforcement expenses involved in incarcerating criminal aliens. As a result, while immigration overall has a net-positive effect on the US economy, the fiscal costs of illegal migration often fall disproportionately on small communities. Up to 3 million people who illegally crossed the border, for example, live in Texas. The public benefits they receive– like education and emergency-room care – are a crippling burden.[3]

Illegal border crossings introduce other problems as well, like public health concerns. Recently, the case of Andrew Speaker, the globetrotting honeymooning lawyer infected with tuberculosis, gained the attention of thousands of newspaper articles and hours of TV coverage because of his ability to slip past border officials. What the media largely missed is that the United States already has a major communicable disease problem. And the individuals entering the United States legally through legitimate points of entry are the least part of it. Tuberculosis (TB), including strains that are increasingly drug resistant, is one of the fastest-spreading diseases in the world. In part, this is because of the spread of HIV/AIDS, which reduces the human immune system and leaves individuals more susceptible to TB. According to the World Health Organization, more than 8 million people get TB each year, and about 98% live in the developing world. Most illegal migration comes from the developing world to Europe and the United States. Many of these individuals never pass through a point of entry, a key node in preventing the introduction of infectious diseases into the United States.

Finally, the US-Canadian border is not devoid of problems. Cross-border drug trafficking is an issue, as is the transit of individuals on the US terrorist watch list. Additionally, as with the US-Mexican border protecting cross-border trade from acts of terrorism or other malicious activity is also a concern. Indeed, Canada is the most important trading partner of the United States. The US-Canadian border is an economic engine that generates over $1 billion dollars a day. Making that engine run as smooth and efficiently as possible is equally important as thwarting terrorist travel, combating criminal activity, and enforcing immigration laws. Adopting strategic solutions that ensure prosperity, security, and sovereignty requires a strategic approach that starts to address problems long before they get to the border – and then add security at the border that makes sense.

Safeguarding the Borders

There are four activities where state and local governments can play an important role in enhancing border.

(1) Securing the southern border requires combating organized border crime and enhancing security at the border to prevent illegal crossings and smuggling along the border and at points of entry. States on the southern border can best contribute to safeguarding the US-Mexico border by increasing "community policing operations" in border communities and participating in federal task forces that combat organized border crime, transnational terrorism, and gang activities.
(2) Securing the US-Canadian border requires a different strategy. A sound US-Canadian strategy must give equal weight to safeguarding the North American perimeter; policing the homeland and diminishing the radicalization threat; and sensible border security enhancements. States can contribute to this effort by participating in federal task forces that combat organized border crime, gang activities, and transnational crime. States should also ensure that their state drivers' licensing is compliant with the standards of the Real ID Act and participate in pilot programs to employ licenses as authorized border-crossing documents under the Western Hemisphere Travel Initiative.
(3) States on both the northern and the southern borders can support border security by promoting public–private partnerships that enhance transportation and other critical infrastructure facilitating cross-border trade.
(4) All states can contribute to promoting border security by combating unlawful presence in the United States. This can be done through a variety of programs with federal, state, and local law-enforcement cooperation.

State and Local Cooperation on the Southern Border

While there has been much emphasis on building walls and having guards to patrol the border that alone is not the answer. A "static" defense cannot keep up with a "dynamic" enemy that is always thinking of new ways to cross the border. Active interdiction and investigative operations that target smugglers and smuggling routes show a lot more promise. The United States needs to take these to the next level with operations that provide a persistent law enforcement presence up and down the border.

Enhanced law enforcement in border communities in the form of more robust community policing should be a key component in rapidly enhancing security on the US-Mexico border. Local law-enforcement officers are ideal because they often have the best intelligence on threats in their areas, are most familiar with the local people and geography, and are trained experts in community policing techniques.

The value of community policing is primarily to deter the types of crime that are associated with illegal human trafficking along the border (e.g., trespassing, theft, and document forgery), not to enforce federal immigration laws. Deterring this criminal activity will in turn make the federal government's challenge of policing the border more manageable.

State and local governments should support these programs because they have a vested interest in making their communities more safe and secure. In addition, since the focus of their efforts is deterring crime – not arrest, prosecution, and incarceration – these programs should not substantially increase the burden on state and local judicial and penal systems. The federal government should support their efforts because they contribute directly to a federal mission. This recommendation is an important policy shift away from the federal government's tendency to subsidize routine local law enforcement through wasteful and ineffective programs such as the Office of Community Oriented Policing Services (COPS) toward enlisting local law enforcement to help secure the nation's borders.

The efficacy of local support for border security is already proven. In Texas, federal, state, and local law enforcement have run a series of interdiction operations along the border and in the interior, using community policing and investigations to identify, target, and disrupt human and drug smuggling operations. What is most important about these efforts is that they show what needs to be done to really ramp up border security and what can be achieved. Operation Rio Grande, launched February 2006, for example, reduced all crime by an average of 60% in sheriff-patrolled areas of border counties.

Equally important is state participation in task forces that combat organized crime. The Department of Homeland Security has developed Border Enforcement Security Task Forces (BESTs), which operate on the southern border with Mexico. There are currently five such teams. They are located in Laredo, El Paso, and Harlingen, TX, as well as in Tucson, AZ, and San Diego, CA. The BESTs provide information sharing, operational coordination, and collaboration among the federal, state, and local agencies combating criminal activity and violence on both sides of the border.

In addition to the BESTs, the federal government operates other task forces that deal with a range of criminal issues including human trafficking, arms trafficking, gang violence, and money laundering. The FBI also runs Joint Terrorism Task Forces (JTTFs). Currently, JTTF operations include every state in the country. Fully supporting and participating in these activities with qualified personnel contributes significantly to combating organized illicit border activity.

Operations and intelligence centers also play an important role in supporting law enforcement on the border. Texas operates a centralized state border security center to coordinate the activities of state and local law enforcement both in border communities and in the interior of the state along smuggling routes and at the terminus of smuggling operations. Texas, and many other states as well, also operate centralized intelligence and information-sharing "fusion centers" that distribute information to state and federal task forces as well as various state and local law-enforcement agencies.[4]

States should look to a variety of federal grants that can enhance the capabilities of local law enforcement in conducting community policing and participating in federal task forces. For example, the Public Safety Interoperable Communications (PSIC) Grant Program provides matching grants. The PSIC Grant Program also assists public safety agencies in the planning and coordinating acquisition, deployment, and training for the use of interoperable communications equipment and software. Other homeland security and law-enforcement grants may also be applicable to border law-enforcement activities.

Volunteer Groups and State Defense Forces

Volunteer groups could perform functions to augment law enforcement. One cost-effective option might be to encourage border security volunteer groups as part of state defense forces. These groups might also have utility in other homeland security tasks including disaster response.

The willingness of Americans to volunteer reflects a healthy civil society. Volunteer groups could perform many tasks that would enhance the nation's capacity to control its borders. As with all volunteer associations that interface with government agencies, there are three minimum requirements to making operations safe and effective: accreditation, standards, and practical employment concepts that are consistent with volunteer service.

The Minuteman Project demonstrated both the propensity for volunteers to serve and a range of useful activities that they could perform, from conducting surveillance to undertaking search and rescue operations. However, the project also demonstrated the limitations of volunteers. The Minutemen deployed an average of almost two dozen volunteers per mile, 24 h a day to monitor border activity. Manpower requirements for sustained operations would require tens of thousands of personnel every day, which is unrealistic. In addition, Minuteman activities raised a number of safety and liability issues. An alternative would be to integrate volunteers into an established organization and develop employment concepts that are safe, sustainable, and organized to complement government border control activities.

States should consider promoting their defense forces (SDFs), which are authorized under federal law (32 USC § 309) as the principal volunteer organizations for assisting in border control. An SDF is under the command of the governor and reports to the state's adjutant general. The state's constitution and laws prescribe the SDF's duties and responsibilities. These forces are state troops and are not funded by the federal government. To use armories, train on military installations, and receive in-kind support, states must comply with federal standards for the National Guard in matters of accession, training, uniforms, and discipline. SDF personnel receive no pay for training but may be paid for active duty under state control.

The Department of Homeland Security (DHS) and the Department of Defense should encourage border states to organize in support of the border control mission.

Within the DHS, the Customs and Border Protection and the Coast Guard should manage programs cooperatively. Regional DHS offices should help states to coordinate SDF programs. Funds should be authorized for establishing a system of accreditation and standards for volunteer border operations and for developingemployment concepts, plans, and exercises.

On the Northern Border

Sharing intelligence and law-enforcement information within and along the border with Canada is equally important. This can best be accomplished through state and local cooperations with the Integrated Border Enforcement Team (IBET) program, a joint US-Canada initiative that combines the intelligence and law-enforcement capabilities of five agencies to identify and stop the movement of high-risk people and goods between the two countries.

While law-enforcement cooperation is important, state and local governments have an even more important role to play in relieving the pressure at the border. Traffic volume at the US-Canadian border has decreased since 9/11, but average wait times for vehicles have increased. This is both a by-product of uncoordinated screening processes and a catalyst for further trade and travel delays at our ports of entry. Today, people crossing land and seaports are only required to orally declare their citizenship.[5] Customs and Border Protection officers may request a travel document for further inspection, at which point any one of 8,000 documents may be presented. At best, the officer may be familiar with the document and be able to quickly verify its authenticity. For a car with 4–5 people, this verification process takes approximately 10 min. The greater threat arises when an officer, under pressure from the mounting traffic behind the vehicle, fails to discern between a valid document and a phony.

Agencies on both sides of the border have recognized this inefficiency, but steps to address it have been arduously slow. Widespread implementation of the Western Hemisphere Travel Initiative (WHTI) has been hampered by delays and will not come into effect until January 31, 2008, when travelers crossing the border into the United States will be required to submit a WHTI-compliant document or at least two government issued identification documents.[6] But this alone is not enough to assuage the growing border traffic and security concerns.

The most effective way to rapidly implement WHTI is to use state-issued drivers' licenses and identification cards based on common standards. Enhanced driver's licenses would transition the screening process from a car-based system to a person-based system, thereby decreasing the wait time per vehicle. For the United States, this will require full implementation of the Real ID program, which provides for creating common standards. The administration should work with the states to implement Real ID regulations and agree on sensible contribution of federal dollars to move the program forward. Border states such as Washington, Vermont, and Arizona have already moved forward on this issue. Other states should follow suit and collaborate with their neighbors to ensure that their programs are compatible.

Infrastructure Improvement

Effective security at the points of entry and exit is essential not only to keep bad things and bad people out of the United States but also to protect the border-crossing cites, key nodes in the networks that connect America to the world of global commerce. This security has to be provided while facilitating the free of flow goods, people, services, and ideas that are the lifeblood of the American economy and a key competitive advantage for the United States in the worldwide marketplace.

The United States and Canada have underinvested in the most important components of an effective border control system: infrastructure. Investments in adequate bridges and roads leading to ports and land border crossings are vital to network-centric security. However, the primary object should not be to harden infrastructure against terrorist attacks. Trying to turn every port and crossing site into a little Maginot Line is a losing strategy. Like the French defenses for World War II, this approach would be both very expensive and likely to fail because an innovative enemy will find a way around the defenses. Points of entry and exit must have the physical assets to support screening, inspection, and gathering, evaluating, and sharing critical information.

Today, most bridges are designed for tax and duty collections. This is not realistic in the post-9/11 world. Infrastructure such as road networks that connect to rail terminals, seaports, and airports is essential to providing the capacity, redundancy, and flexibility required to ensure that the free flow of trade and travel is not disrupted. The best way to accomplish this goal is to encourage public–private partnerships (PPP) that invest in border infrastructure. The United States has utilized the PPP model for its public highways and other infrastructure projects. For example, the General Services Administration (GSA) owns, builds, and leases border and port entries. It develops and maintains standard processes and procedures to ensure that land ports of entry are developed consistently and to an acceptable standard.[7] Creating opportunities for GSA, CBP, and private firms to work together on improving the infrastructure at points of entry would be the most cost-effective and sustaining strategy for a safe and secure border.

Infrastructure investments should be focused on constructing an effective system of systems. Points of entry and exit must have the physical assets to support screening, inspection, and gathering, evaluating, and sharing critical information.[8] In addition, adequate infrastructure – including bridges and roads, especially road networks that connect to rail terminals, seaports, and airports – is essential to providing the capacity, redundancy, and flexibility required to ensure that the free flow of trade and travel is not disrupted. This is particularly vital at the small number of transit nodes that handle most of the cross-border traffic.[9]

Border-crossing infrastructure should be given high priority. The roads, bridges, inspection points that span the border are the most congested and the most vulnerable to delays and disruption.[10] Joint assessments by American, Canadian, and Mexican officials estimate that infrastructure shortfalls total about $24 billion.[11]

Establishing priorities and providing revenue for these investments is not solely or, in many cases, even primarily a federal responsibility. For example, local governments own most of the 26 motor vehicle crossings on the Texas–Mexico border.[12] Likewise, airports and seaports are owned and operated by a mix of public and private entities. An investment strategy will require better public–private partnerships, including targeting national transportation trust funds so that they are spent on national priorities rather than pork-barrel projects.

One possible solution could be to turn back the trust funds, such as the federal Highway Trust Fund, to the states or to allow states to opt out of the program in return for agreeing to meet a series of quantitative performance criteria.[13] Additionally, rather than relying heavily on subsidized public funding of infrastructure, investments should focus on "project-based" financing that shifts the risks and rewards to the private sector.[14]

Interior Enforcement

Interior enforcement is an essential component of border security because it can effectively deter further illegal border crossings. In addition, about half of the unlawfully present population in the United States entered the country through legitimate ports of entry, either by using fraudulent documents or with legitimate visas that they then overstayed. Thus, border security alone will not address the undocumented population already in the country. Indeed, a review of the social science literature on the effect of border enforcement on illegal immigration shows mixed results. Some studies find no effect, while others indicate a positive or negative relationship between border enforcement and illegal immigration. Additionally, the literature indicates that increased border enforcement appears to slow the flow of illegal immigrants leaving the United States. Thus, immigration law enforcement that is overly reliant on border enforcement may actually make the unlawful population in the United States bigger, not smaller.

On the other hand, state and local cooperation in combating unlawful presence could not only serve to help deter further illegal entry to but lessen the burden of undocumented workers on local communities as well address the public safety threat of criminal aliens (convicted of conducting violent crimes and other felonies).

Section 287(g) of the Immigration and Nationality Act (INA) could serve as a basis for state and local law enforcement to cooperate effectively with federal authorities in rapidly building up capacity to gain operational control of US borders. This section gives local and state governments the authority to investigate, detain, arrest, and deport illegal immigrants on civil and criminal grounds under federal immigration law. Section 287(g) was added to the INA in 1996 to enhance Immigration and Customs Enforcement. In many cases, local authorities along the border are often the first to witness immigration violations and in the best position to stop illegal immigrants who are trying to enter the United States. Under Section 287(g), states could secure adequate training for state and local law-enforcement officers, who would then be authorized to deal with immigration offenders and enforce the INA. The month-long training focuses on immigration law, civil rights, racial profiling issues, and identifying immigration violators.

Using Section 287(g) would strengthen cooperation among federal, state, and local law-enforcement agencies while still adhering to constitutional principles of federalism, protecting the rights of US citizens, and combating threats to the nation. Currently, only Alabama, Florida, Arizona, North Carolina, and California have established Section 287(g) programs, but none of them are used for border control.

The best way to integrate Section 287(g) programs into border control is to expand the BESTs, which act as fusion centers for federal, state, tribal, local law enforcement, and intelligence entities in identifying and combating emerging and existing threats. Other effective models of this approach include Project Seahawk at the port of Charleston, the Joint Interagency Task Force in Key West, the FBI's JTTFs, and Canada's IBETs.

In addition to the BESTs, the Department of Homeland Security has organized Document and Benefit Fraud Task Forces (DBFTFs). Immigration and Customs Enforcement administers these task forces. They target criminal organizations that exploit the immigration process through fraud. As of 2007, task forces are operating in Atlanta, Boston, Dallas, Denver, Detroit, Los Angeles, New York, Newark, Philadelphia, St. Paul, Washington, DC, Baltimore, Chicago, Miami, Phoenix, San Francisco, and Tampa.

ICE also operates Fugitive Operative Teams (FOTs) for apprehending and removing criminal fugitive aliens. FOTs rely on the assistance of state and local law-enforcement agencies. These agencies can assist the FOTs by participating in local Joint Fugitive Task Forces.

States can also avail themselves of other DHS programs and resources. According to the department these include the following:

(1) Asset forfeiture and sharing. Criminal organizations that conduct cross-border crimes earn illicit proceeds that sustain their criminal activity and fund other criminal endeavors. Asset forfeiture laws allow ICE agents to seize and forfeit these illicit proceeds and other criminally derived assets. ICE uses asset forfeiture to disrupt and dismantle these organizations across all ICE investigative areas, such as money laundering, bulk cash smuggling, worksite enforcement, and alien and drug smuggling investigations. The proceeds of these forfeitures are deposited into the Treasury Forfeiture Fund and are returned to member agencies to pay for a variety of important law-enforcement operations.

(2) State, local, and foreign law-enforcement support of federal investigative and prosecutorial initiatives is essential; and the sharing program has proved invaluable in fostering enhanced cooperation among the law-enforcement agencies. In fiscal year 2006, ICE coordinated payments of $5.65 million in overtime costs for state and local police officers working alongside ICE agents throughout the United States and provided $43.46 million in direct payments of equitable sharing of forfeited assets to 362 state and local agencies, four federal agencies, and one foreign government. These payments allow agencies to cooperatively combat crimes in their jurisdictions through joint operations with ICE and have increased goodwill and partnership with these agencies.

(3) The Criminal Alien Program (CAP). CAP focuses on identifying criminal aliens who are incarcerated within federal, state, and local facilities, thereby ensuring that they are not released into the community by securing a final order of removal prior to the termination of their sentence.

(4) Customs cross designation. Title 19 United States Code 1401 (I) allows for federal, state, local, and foreign law-enforcement officers who participate primarily on US Immigration and Customs Enforcement task force operations to be cross designated as "Customs Officers" and be granted the authority to enforce US customs law. These cross-designated task force officers supplement ICE's investigative mission of combating narcotics smuggling, money laundering, human smuggling, and trafficking and fraud-related activities.

(5) Law Enforcement Support Center (LESC). LESC provides immigration status and identity information to local, state, and federal law-enforcement agencies on aliens suspected, arrested, or convicted of criminal activity. The LESC operates 24 h a day, 7 days a week assisting law-enforcement agencies with information gathered from eight DHS databases, the National Crime Information Center (NCIC), the Interstate Identification Index (III), and other state criminal history indices.

Participation in these federal programs is an appropriate means for state and local governments to support immigration enforcement. Programs can be tailored to address state and local public safety and law-enforcement concerns.

Conclusion

America's borders are broken, but sensible policies can meet the challenge of fixing them. State and local governments have an important role to play. On the southern border community policing can make an important contribution to combating trans-border crime and deterring illegal border-crossing activities. On the northern border, states should invest in efforts that will make legitimate cross-border traffic both more rapid and secure. Equally important on both borders, borderland states ought to increase their efforts to promote public–private partnerships to build more resilient and higher capacity infrastructure. Finally, all states can make important contributions in supporting enforcement of US immigration laws.

Notes

1. The Alliance, also known as The Federation, is a cooperating group of Mexican drug trafficking organizations (DTOs) that share resources such as transportation routes and money launderers. See, National Drug Intelligence Center (October, 2008). Southwest border region – drug transportation and homeland security issues. *National Drug Threat Assessment*, available at www.usdoj.gov/ndic/pubs25/25921/border.htm#foot2.
2. In 2002, the National Youth Gang Survey estimated that there were 21,500 gangs and 731,500 active gang members in the United States, 85% of whom reside in large cities. The National

Youth Gang Survey is a nationally representative sample drawn from law-enforcement agencies. See Egley, A., J.C. Howell, and A.K. Major (2004). Recent patterns of gang problems in the United States: results from the 1996–2002 national youth gang survey. In Esbensen, F.-A., S.G. Tibbetts, and L. Gaines (eds). *American Youth Gangs at the Millennium.* Long Groves Press, Long Groves, IL , pp. 103–104.

3. The fiscal burden of unlawfully present persons remains a controversial subject. See, for example, Edmonston, B. and R. Lee (eds.) (1996). *Local Fiscal Effects of Illegal Migration: Report of a Workshop.* The National Academies Press, Washington, DC.

4. National Governors Association Center for Best Practices (July 7, 2005). *State Intelligence Fusion Centers: Recent State Actions,* available at www.nga.org/Files/pdf/0509FUSION. PDF.

5. Press Release, Department of Homeland Security Office of the Press Secretary (June 20, 2007). *WHTI Land Sea Notice of Proposed Rulemaking Published,* available at www.dhs. gov/xnews/releases/pr_1182350422171.shtm.

6. The Department of Homeland Security (June 20, 2007). *Remarks by Homeland Security Secretary Michael Chertoff at a Press Conference on the Western Hemisphere Travel Initiative Land and Sea Notice of Proposed Rule Making,* available at www.dhs.gov/xnews/speeches/ sp_1182430462235.shtm.

7. US General Services Administration, at www.gsa.gov/Portal/gsa/ep/home.do?tabId=0.

8. For example, even before 9/11, the General Accounting Office found that inspection space and inadequate roads connecting ports of entry were among the most significant factors contributing to northbound congestion at the border. US General Accounting Office (March, 2000). *U.S.–Mexico Border: Better Planning, Coordination Needed to Handle Growing Commercial Traffic,* GAO/NSIAD–00–25, p. 14, available at www.gao.gov/archive/2000/ns00025.pdf.

9. For example, about 70% of Canada–US cross-border truck traffic goes through just six crossing points. On the southern border, Laredo, TX, is the gateway for 43% of the total tonnage moving across the US–Mexico border. Likewise, nearly 95% of all non-North American foreign trade arrives by ship, but 50 of the over 350 US ports account for 96% of all cargo tonnage, and 25 ports account for 95% of all container shipments. U.S. House of Representatives, *Maritime Transportation Act of 2002,* H. Rpt. 107–777, p. 4; National Chamber Foundation, US Chamber of Commerce (March 2003). *Trade and Transportation: A Study of North American Port and Intermodal Systems.* In 2000, the top 20 US gateway airports accounted for 90% of non-stop international air travel to and from the United States. See US Department of Transportation, Bureau of Transportation Statistics. *Overseas Travel Trends,* available at www.bts.gov/publications/us_international_travel_and_transportation_trends/ overtrends.html.

10. For example, in the wake of the 9/11 attacks, border security was tightened significantly. As a result, many truckers were delayed at border crossings for several hours. Because truckers are permitted to drive only 10 h per day, significant delays at the border can add an extra day to delivery time. For example, after 9/11, Dairy Queen experienced huge delays in getting key ingredients for its ice cream cakes from Canada, and Ford Motor Company idled five US manufacturing plants because of slow delivery from parts suppliers in Canada. Martha, J. (January, 2002). Just-in-case operations. *Warehouse Forum* 17(2), available at www.warehousing-forum.com/news/2002_01.pdf.

11. Shane, J.N. (August 16, 2005). "Innovative Finance and Border Infrastructure," speech at FHWA/SCT Border Finance Conference, San Antonio, TX, p. 3, at ostpxweb.dot.gov/S-3/ Data/Border%20Finance%20Conf-San%20Antonio%20(8-16-05).pdf.

12. The state and federal governments own several, and several are privately owned. Phillips, K.R. and C. Manzanares (June, 2001). Transportation infrastructure and the border economy. *The Border Economy,* Federal Reserve Bank of Dallas, available at www.dallasfed.org/research/ border/tbe_phillips.html.

13. Utt, R.D., Ph.D. (March 7, 2005). "Congress Gets Another Chance to Improve America's Transportation: Should It Be Its Last? (Draft)," Heritage Foundation *WebMemo* available at www.heritage.org/Research/SmartGrowth/highway-reauth2005.cfm.

14. Project-based financing focuses on obtaining stand-alone investment from private investors and could include multiple investors, each with a different level of investment, varying rate of return, and different timeline for realizing those returns. Such strategies not only shift risk to the private sector but also should lead to improved decision making about needed infrastructure investments. Luberoff, D. and J. Walder (March 28, 2000). *U.S. Ports and Funding of Intermodal Facilities: An Overview of Key Issues*, unpublished paper.

Chapter 5
Lessons Learned from the 2004 Atlantic Hurricane Season: How This Highly Active Year Helped Jacksonville, Florida, Build a Better Emergency Response System

John Peyton

Abstract In Jacksonville, FL, firefighters, sheriff deputies, and many civilian city employees have been trained in disaster response. In particular, some city employees have been trained as call takers to serve during disasters or other peak-time situations. The city has developed a special needs database so that this group can receive necessary services in a timely fashion. The Special Needs group includes those who are homebound, dependent upon electricity to power oxygen dispensers or other life-saving equipment, or dialysis patients. The city has developed a plan for evacuating special needs individuals to special shelters. Jacksonville has contracted with private contractors to assist in debris removal operations. The city has trained volunteers to supplement first responders during an emergency.

The 2004 Atlantic Hurricane season particularly impacted Florida from mid-August through late September. Four storms made landfall in the state, and a fifth hit east Alabama close to the Florida border. Approximately 6 million homes statewide were without power at one point or another, some for several weeks. The persistence and magnitude of these and other storms prompted the National Hurricane Center to characterize 2004 as the most intense hurricane season in more than a century. In fact, there was tropical activity involving at least one named storm every day from August 5 to October 11 of that year.

It had been 40 years since Hurricane Dora struck just south of the Jacksonville area, and 5 years since Hurricane Floyd posed a serious threat to the region. Back then; Jacksonville's population was about 455,000. Today, it is nearly 850,000, so dealing with a major incident is more complicated because it demands more resources and more responders. The City of Jacksonville employs about 7,000. All 1,200 uniformed firefighters are trained in various levels of emergency response. The Jacksonville Sheriff's Office has 1,600 sworn officers who have key roles during incidents. Another 204 civilian employees have received at least an introductory level of disaster management training.

J. Peyton (✉)
Mayor, Jacksonville, FL, (2003–present)
e-mail: jpeyton@coj.net

S. Hakim, E.A. Blackstone (eds.), *Safeguarding Homeland Security*,
DOI 10.1007/978-1-4419-0371-6_5, © Springer Science+Business Media, LLC 2009

Although no hurricanes directly struck Jacksonville in 2004, the city's emergency responders were heavily tasked, due to close calls with Tropical Storm Bonnie and Hurricanes Charley, Frances, and Jeanne. During this period, the city's Emergency Operations Center (EOC) was activated for an unprecedented number of days in such a short time span.

The active season and the short recovery time between storms affecting Northeast Florida placed significant pressure on government and non-profit services to address myriad problems: prolonged power outages for thousands of the city's residents and businesses, windstorm damage throughout the county, and numerous incidents of localized flooding. Downed trees and other debris also presented an enormous challenge for the city (which encompasses the entire 840 square miles of Duval County, since Jacksonville has a consolidated government). Communicating details to the public was also a challenge because of the volume of calls to the EOC's information center. The center was staffed by a mixture of city employees, some of who had received no training in emergency response.

More than ever before, the storms' effects tested Duval County's preparedness, response, and recovery efforts. But the season also helped identify several strengths and weaknesses in the implementation of emergency plans, delivery of services, and coordination of agency activities.

Mayor John Peyton, along with other city leaders and executive decision makers, identified Jacksonville's key strengths as the following:

- Participants of all responding agencies at the local levels demonstrated excellent collaboration.
- The participating local agencies successfully demonstrated an initial capability to manage a citywide incident, including the supply and operation of temporary shelters.
- Participants recognized shortfalls in the city's Comprehensive Emergency Management Plan as they were uncovered and reacted appropriately to adjust operations.
- Areas for improvement included these following recommendations:
- Development of Standard Operating Guidelines for internal and external communication procedures.
- Improvement of the management procedures of the Special Needs database.
- Development of policy and guidelines outlining expectations of FEMA and mutual aid reimbursements.
- Development of a Duval County Debris Management Plan.
- Development of Standard Operating Guidelines for meeting human needs.
- Mandatory Emergency Operations Center training for all key employees.

The value of these recommendations and their subsequent implementation are detailed in this chapter. So is the city's migration from an Emergency Services Function response methodology to the National Incident Management System (NIMS), which includes all hazard incidents that threaten public safety, not just hurricanes. Jacksonville officials implemented this system when the city hosted Super Bowl

XXXIX in February 2005. NIMS also played a part in Jacksonville's relief effort for victims of Hurricane Katrina in 2005.

Development of Standard Operating Guidelines for Internal and External Communication Procedures

The large-scale demands of the 2004 hurricane season prompted Duval County's Emergency Operations Center (EOC) to review and enhance its internal and external communications plans. During the four tropical storm-related EOC activations in 2004, there were roughly 1,500 calls per day from the public to the EOC and the city's call center. At some points, there were more than 300 calls in the queue.

This activity level overwhelmed the EOC's experienced staff, which had to scramble to recruit and organize additional human resources to answer the call volume. To meet the demand, the EOC was forced to rely upon untrained manpower. Suddenly, employees with no EOC experience were fielding calls. In some cases, their lack of experience compromised the integrity and timely delivery of public information. Experienced operators had to handle their own calls while also assisting inexperienced operators.

Using this lesson from 2004, an executive team of city personnel has since developed EOC training for all civilian employees who will function as operators during EOC activations. The executive team, which included staff from the city's Emergency Preparedness Division (EPD), has since built a database of trained employees, each of whom is called up during an emergency event to staff one of three shifts in the Citizen Information Center, the EOC's call center, also known as the CIC. There also are now standard operating guidelines for information gathering and dissemination, but more on that later. Designated city staff update the EOC-trained employee database twice annually and maintain a centralized "communication tree" containing contact information for key city officials, including the mayor's office, city council, and department leaders.

The executive team also addressed the integrity of the information relayed to the public. Even with CIC training, no two emergencies are the same; there were still protocols and other contingencies that had to be addressed. The team's solution involved a web-based "white board" within the EOC that is activated and continuously updated during an event. Public Information Officers work with EOC staff to update the board. Prior to 2004, these data were released less frequently during the EOC's situation report, which summarizes the status of various responder units whose missions are providing specific disaster service and support. How often a situation report is issued depends upon the severity of an event or any sudden change in status. What's more, the report is quite detailed and not easily discerned by untrained operators, so the "white board's" utility is high because it offers operators prepared scripts that address calls requesting similar information during a specific event. So under the new guidelines, CIC operators now have a dynamic resource to help them relay the information that the public demands during a storm or catastrophic event.

After 2004, Jacksonville's EOC modified its management, transitioning from an Emergency Support Function (ESF) paradigm to the National Incident Management System (NIMS). The NIMS framework facilitates collaboration between government and private entities during an incident. There is a unified command (in Jacksonville's case, it's the mayor) over four reporting sections: operations, planning, logistics, and finance/administration.

In terms of communications, NIMS also provides a more streamlined information flow with specific responsibility reporting up and down the chain-of-command within each section. ESF does not possess this chain-of-command reporting concept and tends to isolate information with respective areas versus sharing it across the system. ESFs are traditionally organized around agency-specific responsibility for completion of the assigned tasks. NIMS is an entire management system grouped around dynamically organized units designed to provide specific disaster services/support. This structure also enhances communications when the EOC is nearing initial activation or upgrading the current level.

NIMS also coordinates media relations through one Public Information Officer (PIO) who arranges for interviews and reviews and distributes all press releases. Under ESF, each responding agency tended to have its own PIO that would provide information from his or her agency perspective versus the City of Jacksonville's. Now, all agency and department PIOs funnel information through the Mayor's Office PIO during an emergency. This way, there is consistent messaging and everyone is on the same page.

Improving the Management Procedures of the Special Needs Database

The Emergency Preparedness Division's Special Needs database was heavily taxed during the 2004 hurricane season. Even though Jacksonville was spared a direct hit from the hurricanes, there were numerous, prolonged power outages, which are a serious problem for some homebound, electrically dependent patients, such as those on dialysis. The most common special needs residents are geriatrics (75 or older), oxygen dependent, and wheelchair bound. The most critical, such as those on ventilators, are sheltered in designated hospitals outside of an evacuation zone.

When the season started, there were 10,000 registrants in the Special Needs database. But this did not present a realistic picture because of outdated information. Allocating resources to anticipate the needs of these individuals became a problem. Recognizing this weakness, the EPD now requires annual registration and promotes this through public service announcements. But EPD also makes it convenient. Residents who are already registered receive a new form by mail in January. They may also register online or pick up a form at one of several customer service centers operated by the local utility. They may also call the city's call center or EPD directly.

Another point of contact with special needs patients is the numerous home health-care agencies. To enhance registration, the Duval County Health Department (DCHD) and EPD held a training and education session about special needs registration and emergency shelters with the home health-care agencies. EPD also designated the DCHD nurse as the lead shelter manager who coordinates admitting the clients to the shelter during an event. That way, there is a command structure in place, expediting the staging of shelters.

Shelters start opening once evacuations are ordered. Prior to an evacuation order, tourists and visitors are asked to leave if they are able. When an evacuation order is given, it will always identify the zones that are being evacuated. Before the general population is given this order, the Health and Medical Group contacts every individual registered in the special medical needs database within those evacuation zones to determine if they need assistance evacuating. The group arranges with the Jacksonville Transportation Authority (JTA) for evacuation of special needs residents. They pick up the residents and transport them to a special needs shelter (the location is not publicized). This operation starts at least 8 hours prior to a general evacuation order being given.

Duval County has a hospital evacuation plan that would be carried out if an evacuation were required where hospitals are located. The beaches hospital would be the first to evacuate. In this plan, each hospital identifies the facility where they will be relocated. County resources are used to assist the hospitals in accomplishing this feat.

Dialysis patients were another concern in 2004 because they require the right equipment no matter where they are displaced. The DCHD has since strengthened relationships with dialysis centers and educated them about the necessity of registering with special needs. Dialysis patients register with EPD and are assigned to one of two shelters so they can have the right equipment at those shelters or for transportation purposes to open dialysis centers following a disaster.

Finally, although this came out of the 2005 season, another refinement to the Special Needs Database is registering transportation-dependent residents. This is critical for people who use public transportation and have no other means to get to a shelter during an evacuation.

Development of Policy and Guidelines Outlining Expectations of FEMA and Mutual Aid Reimbursements

Duval County received $13.1 million in FEMA reimbursement resulting from 2004 hurricane response costs. Locally incurred costs of disaster response and recovery efforts for Federally Declared Disaster events – such as Hurricanes Frances and Jeanne in 2004 – are eligible for reimbursement under published Federal Disaster Assistance Programs like the Stafford Act. Local governments should have plans and procedures in place that follow these program guidelines to expedite reimbursement to the local agencies for the cost of providing these services to impacted communities.

As of this writing, the City of Jacksonville is facing shortfalls of approximately $50 million stemming from the Florida Legislature's property tax reform. A reduction in property taxes will reduce revenue for the city's general fund. This is devastating on its own, but it would be more severe if the city and other responding agencies had not received the disaster recovery reimbursement.

So now it is particularly critical to educate those who are responsible for filing reimbursement claims following a disaster. Since the 2004 hurricane season, EPD has conducted workshops wherein FEMA and Florida's Division of Emergency Management explained the process of seeking reimbursement to local governments and non-profit agencies.

Development of a Duval County Debris Management Plan

Although Jacksonville did not suffer a direct hit in 2004, the proximity of four hurricanes over 40 days produced enough collateral damage and debris to overwhelm the City of Jacksonville's solid waste collection resources beyond capacity. Hundreds of city employees' normal routines were disrupted for weeks as the city and its contractors gathered, cut, loaded, hauled, dumped, and mulched more than 150,000 tons of yard waste. That equates to 619,000 cubic yards, an amount that would have overflowed Jacksonville's 80,000-seat municipal stadium several times. That debris was transported to four temporary dump sites over several months. In fact, debris collection during September and October 2004 was the equivalent of what would normally have been collected over 12 years.

As late as mid-November 2004, city crews still roamed the city, picking up the vestiges of the summer's storm damage. Six weeks after Hurricane Jeanne brushed the city, officials closed three of four temporary dump sites created in the storm's aftermath and contractors hauled the mulch piled there to a site at Cecil Commerce Center – a former naval base – for ultimate disposal.

Using this lesson from 2004, the city developed a debris grid management plan, dividing Duval County into hundreds of areas – 10,000 × 5,000 feet grids – and mapping them on the city's Geographic Information System (GIS). Each grid can be remotely monitored for status and prioritized for debris removal.

In the future, the City of Jacksonville will deploy a Public Works Group (PWG) – part of the NIMS model – for debris management operations. Whereas 2004's cleanup was highly reactive, a proactive team is now clearly defined. It includes city engineers; debris planning consultants; a streets and drainage superintendent; maintenance personnel; a traffic engineering representative; designated support agencies; utility companies (more than one serves Duval County); specialized debris collection contractors; waste management firms; and trucking companies to facilitate the debris clearance, collection, reduction, and disposal needs of the city.

The team also resolves drainage problems following a disaster. PWG will be responsible for removing debris from the public right-of-way and from other city-owned property. PWG will further stage equipment in strategic locations around the city, as well as regionally if necessary, to protect the equipment from damage and allow clearing crews to employ the apparatus and begin work immediately after the disaster.

Because of the limited quantity of city resources (e.g., vehicles and apparatus) following the disaster, PWG will rely heavily upon private contractors to remove, collect, and manage debris for reuse, resource recovery, reduction; and disposal. The city will bid contingency contracts, pre-storm; and per FEMA contracting guidelines, for most if not all contractor services. In the initial "cut and toss" phase, contractors will be pre-positioned at select fire stations with a bucket loader and cleanup crews to support search and rescue operations. As required, other contractor crews may be put on notice to support streets and drainage crews, which are responsible for initiating the "cut and toss" phase in clearing priority roads. Crews also can request an exterior electrical utility linesman to accompany them to deal with downed electrical lines and expedite clearance operations. As the search and rescue operations wind down, those contractor crews may be asked to shift over to clearing public roads to relieve the city's streets and drainage crews who will be shifting over to priority drainage work. As this work is ongoing, PWG will formulate a debris management strategy for each affected territory as damage assessments become available.

Development of Standard Operating Guidelines
for Meeting Human Needs

Following the 2004 hurricane season, the EPD created a human needs assessment procedure, organizing all city and outside agencies that specialize in meeting disaster victims' needs. EPD also has conducted training for all agencies that are part of the plan. This was essential so everyone would have buy-in of the plan and a clear understanding of the human needs assessment role.

To properly allocate the agencies' resources, EPD created a post-disaster assessment plan. Post-event assessment teams will identify target-affected areas and then determine the community's immediate needs, environmental hazards, animal issues, and labor issues. These teams will consist of Duval County Health Department members and volunteers from the city's Community Services Department. Following their assessment, they will send their data to the Planning Section – part of the NIMS structure – to create an action plan which meets needs. A recovery task force will carry out this plan, be it short- or long-term or both.

With all of our emergency plans – known as interagency coordinating procedures and hazard-specific plans – we involve every agency whether government, volunteer, private, or non-profit that may play a part in response and recovery. Their roles include mitigation, preparedness, and public education. The Community Emergency Response Teams, or JaxCERT, play a big role. JaxCERT training provides Duval County residents with basic disaster-response skills necessary to address the urgent needs of their community when professional first responders and emergency personnel are not immediately available. Another aspect is the Volunteer Reception Center. It falls within the structure of the EOC in charge of coordinating all unaffiliated volunteers after a disaster.

Mandatory Emergency Operations Center Training

The EOC's prolonged activation in 2004 season required additional employees to answer calls and staff other functions. Many employees were filling a variety of roles for the first time. They adapted, but it made the need for training apparent.

Since then, the Emergency Management Training Series has been offered to all city employees as well as any agency staff working in or with the EOC. Offered by the EPD, the series covers the fundamentals of emergency management, emergency preparedness, fundamentals of Duval's EOC operations, and E Team Emergency Management Software introduction. E Team Software is not unique to Jacksonville, but it allows responders to collaborate and manage their efforts and assets across multiple organizations using a real-time interface. The interface is graphical and can quickly display detailed countywide status. To date, more than 1,000 employees have received all or part of this training series. The EPD also offers media relations training to the city's numerous PIOs. Also, hundreds of employees from the City and other local agencies have completed a 40-h course in the MINS Incident Command Structure.

Conclusion

Having evaluated its strengths and weaknesses in terms of emergency response and having implemented new structures and strategies, Jacksonville is better prepared to effectively respond to future disasters. This recent evolution of the City of Jacksonville's Emergency Preparedness Division yielded a program sophisticated enough to make Jacksonville the first local jurisdiction in the country to earn full accreditation from the Emergency Management Accreditation Program (EMAP) in 2005. The EMAP process fosters benchmarking against consistent standards and continuous improvement in local and state government emergency management.

While Jacksonville has analyzed its own capabilities and improved its capacities, the scope of a response is not limited to the city's limits. No one can predict when or where a catastrophe will occur, but there is reassurance in knowing that neighbors are not only willing to help but also more equipped to do so.

Chapter 6
Disaster Management: Privatization as a Viable Alternative©

Alan Kirschenbaum

Abstract This chapter details the use of the private market to prepare for and respond to disasters. A survey of Israeli citizens was conducted to determine their "readiness to pay" for services provided free by the Home Front Command. About one-quarter to a third said they were ready to pay for additional quality services such as assuring their safe room could handle a chemical or biological attack. Age and ethnic-religious status affected the readiness to purchase. Also, private companies were paid to provide equipment including buses for emergencies. Volunteers such as a civilian watch group and reserve medical workers play an important role in homeland security. Since so many Israelis have military training volunteers, even unorganized, play important roles in emergencies.

The Ideal Disaster Organization

Let us just imagine for a moment that we have all the resources in the world, no political restrictions, the best advisors and the support of the populace to devise a scheme that will assure us, as individuals and a community, the ability to survive disasters. What do we do? As a start, it is likely that someone would advise us to look at what has already been done. Doing this would lead to the conclusion that disaster management is organized, controlled, and financed primarily as a public sector enterprise. There are no other serious forms of alternative formal organizing that neither seem apparent nor sought after.

We also begin to discover from a number of specific case studies that these organizations are not very successful. Researchers seem to point out all kinds of organizational problems. The usual turf wars, inter-agency discord and problems in coordination, overlapping and redundant services, and of course political power

A. Kirschenbaum (✉)
Associate Professor, Faculty of Industrial Management, Technion, Israel
Institute of Technology, Haifa, Israel
e-mail: avik@techunix.technion.ac.il

S. Hakim, E.A. Blackstone (eds.), *Safeguarding Homeland Security*,
DOI 10.1007/978-1-4419-0371-6_6, © Springer Science+Business Media, LLC 2009

struggles. What seems to be the rule is that as the number of agencies involved in a disaster or emergency increases, the effectiveness of these agencies decreases. In some cases, the consequences of the disaster multiply in terms of damage and deaths. And, even more instructive is that despite the investment and growth of public sector disaster agencies, the number of both natural and human-made disasters is increasing rather than decreasing (Coppola, 2007).

A Critical Introspection

Of the literally, thousands of studies and opinion articles that have been written about disasters and their management – however rigorous or anecdotal – there has been practically no critical empirically based analysis of the disaster management system as it exists (Kirschenbaum, 2002). There are the usual complaints about bureaucratic bungling, the need for more and better equipment, technological gadgets, and the quest for more power in the halls of government. More significantly, research available points to specific critical trouble spots. Let me briefly state some of the hard evidence.

First, disaster management organizations tend to be characterized by centralized bureaucratic structures that focus their resources on internal issues, retarding them from fulfilling their mission of preventing, mitigating, or preparing the population for disasters.

Second, disaster managers' understandings of their organizational goals do not match the potential victim's perceptions of what those goals should be.

Third, disaster organizations make the erroneous assumption that people will automatically listen and respond to their directives.

A Complementary Path: Privatization

Putting these corrosive issues on the table should act as a catalyst for public sector policy makers to reevaluate what disaster management is all about. To start this ball rolling, I would like to explore a complementary path of thinking, namely privatization. The ideological basis for this perspective is a running assumption that the private market, at less cost and greater efficiency and effectiveness, can replace public monopoly services (Rondinelli, 1989; Pack, 1987). This approach has been tried all over the world with various degrees of success (Farazmand, 2001; Cowan, 1990). Governments, for a combination of ideological, political, and economic reasons, have used all types of mechanisms in an attempt to divest public service agencies (Armstrong et al., 1997; Samson, 1994; Massey, 1993). Not only have they tried to divest budget draining and highly subsidized government monopolies in such industries as gas, oil, coal, communications, and transportation but other services in the area of education (Bennett, 2000), mental health (Upshur et al., 1997), art, and culture (Campbell, 1999).

Privatized Disaster Market

The few studies that have focused on the public–private link in the area of disaster management have emphasized the clear-cut economic benefits of having the private for-profit sector replace the responsible government agencies (Horwich, 1993). This, general trend, as I have already pointed out, has been going on for some time. It is now being bolstered by an economic justification that favors the development of the private market in a broad range of disasters services. But, disaster service companies can make money only if they provide equitable services. "The simple fact, from an economic perspective, is that in the absence of a functioning price system (*sic competition*), neither central authorities nor well intentioned altruistic outsiders are likely to come close to knowing and responding effectively to the circumstances and preferences of afflicted populations" (Horwich, 1993). One of the major reasons why this is so is that disasters affect, on the whole, private property and how individuals use the market to prepare for, mitigate, or recover from a disaster. From the individual's point of view, this means buying goods in the open market that will increase chances for survival. The bottom line is that disasters are potentially big business.

Private Market Attractions

Given the enormous flow of public money involved in the area of disasters, it would seem only natural for private market firms to be attracted into this market niche. To some extent insurance companies have triggered this growth with the largest part of the private market being taken up by specialized firms that deal in crisis reduction and risk aversion. The major buyers have included firms dealing with information technology, transportation, and energy resources. For the most part, such private consultant companies deal with disaster issues at an organizational level, focusing on specific types of industrial plants, a particular company, or corporate organization. Few, if any, focus on individuals, families, or communities. Only in the area of non-profit or NGO organizations like the Red Cross, do we see an effort to deal with the victims. Even here, public sector disaster management agencies continue to act as the public oversight and manager, controlling guidelines and policy. Such management is done at the macro-organizational level that focuses on internal organizational concerns. But where do the "victims" fit into this scheme of privatization?

People Power

For the most part, the generous funding from governments usually ends up in other public disaster-related organizations. An example illustrates this: FEMA providing funds ($21 million) through the national citizen's corps to local governments and sub-contractors eventually flowing into another FEMA project related to communities (CERT). But if disasters are big business, and involve private property, should not the consumer be part of the privatization formula? The consumer in this case is the (potential) victim of a disaster and at the end of the day is the reason and justification for disaster management organizations. As consumers, the potential victims should, according to basic economic theory, affect the supply and demand of goods and their prices. As consumers, they also have a choice of what and where to purchase disaster survival goods and services! This perspective flies in the face of regulated non-competitive public sector disaster management agencies that decide and price what services they supply. It is probably why the private market providing disaster items and services to individuals and households stays clear of the types of services the government supplies; they simply cannot compete. But "what if" a competitive market was available?

A Case Study in Israel

A unique study in Israel[1] may clear up the place of the consumer in this privatization process. It should be recalled that the only legal public disaster agency in Israel, the Home Front Command (HFC), is required to protect the public in cases of emergencies and disasters. Its services are given without extracting a direct cost to the individual. This includes a series of specific missions, some of which are the distribution of gas masks, their maintenance of protective equipment, shelters, and provision of guidelines in case of conventional and non-conventional attacks by terrorists or general war. As part of a national representative survey, Israeli heads of household were asked about their readiness to pay for a series of disaster-related services. Most of these services could be obtained free of charge either through the Home Front Command or through other public agencies. In some cases, they were simply items related to being prepared for an emergency or disaster. But the overall concept was to judge the degree to which consumers would be ready to enter the private market to purchase these critical disaster services.

Ready to Pay

The readiness to purchase disaster-related services in the private market meant that individual respondents would act upon their conviction that the private market could provide them with better disaster-related service than that already in the public realm. People were simply ready to put their money down to pay for and have these services. The use of the term "ready to purchase" was not chosen by accident as it is as close as you can get to the actual behavioral act of purchasing. This is a far cry from the problematic use of such terms that are employed in opinion polls as a 'willingness' or "intent" to do something. In this sense, the question reflects potential purchasing power. It is also, in its reverse form, an evaluation of public services that they feel should be provided.

A glance at Table 6.1, which lists disaster-related services open for purchase, shows that between one-quarter and one-third of the respondents indicated a

Table 6.1 List and proportion of households who are "Ready to Pay for Disaster-Related Services Provided by Private Organizations"*

Disaster service	Ready to pay
Supply food and water	31.4
Provide quality gas mask	28.3
Prepare children in schools in emergency	28.3
Have electric supply if stoppage	32.9
Evacuate to safe place if necessary	32.7
Check readiness of shelter/sealed room	28.3
Guard home in case need to evacuate	27.5
Provide radio, batteries, and flashlight	22.6
Psychological advise or therapy	26.7
Provide detailed instructions on what to do	27.8
Materials and information on biochemical war	24.6
Materials on atomic warfare	24.4
Provide medical services	34.8

*Based on a random national sample of households in Israel. See Kirschenbaum (2004b).

readiness to make purchases of disaster-related services in the private market. This proportion sheds considerable light about the potential market for private disaster services as well as about the services already being received. Looking at the alternative services in more detail is also important as it provides a window into what families are interested in purchasing. What seems most obvious is that the demand for private market services does not replace what is already provided by public sector disaster agencies but expands the breadth of services that are related to being prepared and/or coping with disasters.

Quality Services

What appears is that the "*quality*" ingredient of the services is most sought after. For example, there is a readiness to pay a private vendor to make sure that a quality gas mask and basic supplies of food or emergency equipment are available. These are recommendations made by the Home Front Command but are not part of the disaster service package. Nor is there a way of knowing the quality of the equipment or item; are they the best, the most reliable and most likely to help me and my family to survive? Perhaps for these reasons, there is a demand for services provided by private vendors to assure the respondents of the quality of the items that are critical for their survival.

Family Safety Net

In addition, another set of private sector services was in demand by the respondents. Specifically, these services have to do with making sure that their and their *family's physical protection* is maximized. In this case, private vendors are sought after to prepare and confirm the readiness of a sealed room and shelter. As most of the national sample had experienced the Gulf War, they were keenly aware of the threat of a biological or chemical ballistic missile attack – and of its potential consequences. Seeking out this service from a private vendor provided an alternative means of making sure they were optimally protected. Along these same lines, a third of the respondents also sought out private firms who would make sure that an alternative source of electricity was available if disrupted, place a guard in their home if the need ever came to leave or evacuate, and have both the means and the place to go in case their own home was damaged or destroyed.

Seeking Information

Another set of safety net services, which drew attention to the private market, had to do with information. It can be speculated that this was related to their lack of trust in information made available by official authorities. In any case, there was a demand for material about non-conventional biochemical warfare as well as the possibility of an atomic attack. Along with this came a similar readiness to pay a private vendor to provide expert detailed instructions about how to behave and what to do as the threat of a disaster (war) progressed into an actual disaster. This category of services encompassed not only providing instructions about the proper care and use of gas masks but when and how to get themselves and family fully prepared for the worst.

The last set of services, which family heads felt they would be ready to pay for, was for medical assistance and psychological therapy. Both these services are provided through highly subsidized HMO's but it appears that despite being able to receive them at minimum direct cost, there seems to be a question as to their quality and availability. Perhaps the rationale that drives the demand for both services may be due to the fear of an overloaded and perhaps collapsed medical system during a disaster. The readiness to purchase psychological advice or therapy before, during, and after a crisis reflects a deep understanding among the respondents that both body and mind can be seriously affected in times of great stress especially if accompanied by potential death or injury.

Who Wants to Pay?

The fact that between one-quarter and one-third of the Israel national sample indicated a readiness to purchase private sector disaster services also means that two-thirds did not. How can we explain why someone is ready to purchase disaster services from the private market while others are not? We asked ourselves what is it that attracts people to be ready to pay for services that most can obtain free of charge? A number of possible explanations come to mind. I examined four possible explanations and found the following.

Wealth, or income, by itself, has little impact on whether or not an individual will purchase disaster survival services from the private market. Likewise, *knowledge* (education) was discredited as a prime suspect in why people choose private over public disaster service vendors. *Age* was also examined with the analysis clearly showing that for each of the alternative disaster services, age makes a large and significant difference in the readiness to pay for private market vendors. The older one is, the less ready he or she is to make use of the private market for disaster services. Finally, *marital status*, being married, led to significantly greater potential use of private market services than single-headed families.

Are the Rich Safer?

The analysis has so far shown that certain characteristics of consumers significantly affect whether or not they will be ready to pay for private market disaster services. Younger people, Jews rather than Muslim Arabs,[2] and traditional cohabiting families were found to favor private market purchases. What is still a mystery is which one of these characteristics can best predict being ready to purchase such private sector services?[3]

The results of the analysis found that the *age* of the consumer and his or her *ethnic-religious status* are the prime significant predictors, who will seek out private market disaster service vendors. *Family status*, being a traditional cohabiting family unit or single-head household, also appeared but only in the case where a decision had to be made concerning a quality gas mask. Overall, it appears that among the numerous possible characteristics of the consumer that would affect her or his readiness to purchase private market disaster services, age and ethnic-religious affiliation is the most critical. This is extremely telling as it provides both public and private vendors not only what the specific market niche is available but to whom to pitch their marketing strategies.

A Social Decision

Being ready to pay private market vendors, as the analysis has shown, has little to do with being rich or poor, educated or not. It was found to be linked to the age, ethnic-religious affiliation, and family status of the respondent, variables that reflect inherent behaviors associated with cultural imperatives, social norms, and values. *This can be interpreted to mean that the decision by individuals to purchase private market disaster services is not so much an economic decision but really **a social decision**.* It is a decision that a fairly sizeable proportion of people are ready to make. Apparently, perceptions of risk that may be linked to the safety of one's family seem to have a powerful impact on whether or not services that increase survival and minimize harm are purchased. This basic assumption about disaster behavior has significant consequences for the configuration that private–public interactions are likely to develop in disaster scenarios.

Organizational Adaptation

In Israel, natural disasters (earthquakes, floods) along with human-made technolog-ical/industrial accidents and terrorist attacks are not a theoretical issue; they are very real and painful phenomenon. For this reason, disaster managers, first responders, and the general population have adapted their community's and organizations to deal with these occurrences. Many of these adaptations reflect private–public organiza-tional cooperation that has been successful in dealing with emergency incidents. I will enumerate a number of these as examples for potential best practices elsewhere.

Sharing Resources

In the case of Israel, over 60 years of plain hard experience has led to a variety of organizational adaptations that has taken various forms. The legally mandated *Home Front Command* (HFC) is a case in point. Like the Department of Homeland Security, it is authorized to protect the civilian population in case of national emer-gencies. This disaster management agency has evolved as the prime mover in coor-dinating all the relevant agencies – both private and public – in dealing with national disasters.[4] To some extent, the HFC has resources available based on a reserve of basic equipment and manpower for local emergencies but with the ability to tap into other private and public sources.[5] In addition, there has evolved a well-coordinated, private–public sharing system. In the area of transportation, for example, private bus companies can be held on "retainer" in case of need to evacuate populations or bring emergency workers to critical areas.[6] The companies would be responsible for the logistics, maintenance, and supply of buses and would be compensated if utilized. Another arrangement has been made with private companies specializing in heavy equipment for use in infrastructure recovery, airline companies for transportation, as well as medical services and facilities.

Manpower Reserves

The development of a national reserve of manpower specifically for the Home Front Command is part of the general military reserve system that calls up personnel for training exercises and in case of an emergency for active duty. This means that among the general population is a large number of trained "disaster managers" who can act as truly first responders in terms of organizing responses and aiding victims until official rescue units can arrive. This has been in fact the case, for example, where homicide bombers have wrecked havoc in public places, buses, or shopping centers. In addition, a grass roots response initiated among private sector businesses due to the ongoing Palestinian terror led to creating specialized security person-nel to protect all public and private establishments. Private manpower companies responded to the demand for such security needs and put on the streets an additional large number of trained potential first responders.

NGO Volunteers

Other adaptive organizational forms evolved that filled gaps not provided effectively by public agencies. The HFC, rather than see these groups as obstacles, welcomes them. One such group is composed of voluntary community organized civilian "watch groups" members. Under the auspices of police supervision and supported by local private businesses, these volunteers are trained in basic medical and police skills. During emergencies they form a community-based leadership cadre as well as community first responders and "on the ground" source of information for the HFC operational decisions. In another case, a voluntary group emerged that developed highly mobile quick response teams to provide medical assistance at the scene of an attack as well as the care and collecting of bodies (and body pieces) after a terror event. This was in response to the sometimes frustrating efforts of ambulances and "official" personnel to get to the scene quickly. Other volunteer groups emerged that provided financial help, social services, counseling, and even legal help to terror victims. In most cases, this type of assistance is supported by contributions made by the general public and private corporations. These groups encompass already existing volunteering organizations that realign their goals as well as emergent groups that arise in response to the situation.

Flexibility and Change

After the recent rocket 2006 bombardment by Hezbollah on the Israel civilian population in Northern Israel, a building manufacturing company began marketing mobile and modular "safe rooms" to the public by stressing it had the approval of the Israel Standards Institute and the Israel Home Front Command. This organizational transition to generate incentives for greater private sector involvement in providing end-user disaster-related services was initiated by the HFC. It follows a growing recognition that the private sector can better provide specific *preparedness* services to the public at greater efficiency and less cost.[7] The implication of this structural change from a formalistic bureaucratic organization that is intent on controlling disaster management to a *knowledge generating organization* providing the guidelines, priorities, and format to allow private sector vendors to give the customer the best protection available has slowly evolved. Another step in this direction has been the recent establishment of *the Israel National Research Center for Disasters* to provide vital input – including evaluation of private–public cooperation – to disaster management policy makers.

Pro's and Con's

Why seek ways to mesh private and public sector disaster management agencies? And what is the best way to do so? One argument for keeping disaster management solely in the public sector is in being able to control, direct, and determine disaster management activities for the public good. This argument fails in light of the reality of increasing numbers of disasters, their intensity and economic damage, and numbers killed or injured. It also fails the mark as witnessed by the descriptions in numerous case studies of disasters when public sector organizations are at cross-purposes with each other. A technological fix or a colorful organization chart cannot solve turf wars and non-interoperability in communications.

The argument for cooperative links between the private and the public sectors in disaster management, along with economic benefits, is that such a perspective offers an attractive alternative means of managing disasters. For one, it allows experienced non-political experts in the private market to do what they know best. For another, it encourages the marketing of products and services that are crucial for being pre-pared. As we have seen in the Israeli case, such cooperative linkages do work when the organizational "bottom line" goals are intended for the people who are at risk and threatened. In addition, such mutual goal attainment has created large reserves of skilled "first responder" manpower and community volunteer groups who fill in important gaps that private and public sector organizations are not equipped to handle. In summary, it is an economically viable and socially preferable alternative means of providing disaster-related services to future satisfied customers than to victims.

Notes

1. This study was funded by the Israel Home Front Command (Kirschenbaum, 2000) and sought to provide evidence-based policy recommendations on and operational guidelines to prepare the Israeli general public for the possibility of a major non-conventional and conventional attack on the civilian population.
2. A separate analysis was performed by religious identity, namely, being a Jew or Muslim Arab. Significant differences were found with the Arab population choosing the public sector services. A more detailed explanation for this pattern can be found in Kirschenbaum, A. Chaos Organization and Disaster Management (Marcel & Dekker, 2004).
3. To answer this question requires a more sophisticated type of analysis as the dependent variable, purchasing services in or not the private market is a dichotomous variable. This means that unlike ordinal or interval type scales which measure various degrees of more or less, our focus will be on a "zero"–"one" scale. For this reason, a special type of regression will be used called a logistic regression statistic, which is based on the log probability of an event occurring. It asks what will be the probability of a person wanting to purchase disaster services on the private market against what is provided by public sector agencies. If the answer could have been given on the basis of simply random chance, it would not be considered significant. But, if the odds are not random, then there is something special about that person or in our case his or her characteristics that can explain a choice of a private service vendor.
4. The Home Front Command is a military-structured organization that has embedded within its structure a core unit that provides expert advice on population behavior to commanders at all levels in the field. These experts have taken a specialized officers training courses in disaster behavior and are on call in emergencies as career or reserve officers. The balance between the Home Front Command organizational preparedness and that of the potential victims needs – the two major stakeholders – is therefore represented.
5. One major source is a parallel organization that provides vital national reserves during emergencies.

6. This is the case in Israel that has proven to be extremely successful. Originally, the private bus companies were called in to provide transportation for moving reserve military personnel to critical locations.

7. This process began in preparation for the first Gulf War bombardment of Scud ballistic missiles on the civilian population when a private company was designated to develop and distribute gas masks. It has been recently followed by similar private–public collaboration for the recall of gas masks for renewal.

Acknowledgment   The theoretical and empirical basis for this manuscript was derived from previous work and field surveys conducted in Israel and particularly my book *Chaos Organization and Disaster Management*. Marcel & Dekker, 2004.

References

Armstrong, H., P. Armstrong, and M.P. Connelly (1997). Introduction: the many forms of privatization. *Studies in Political Economy* 53: 3–9.

Bennett, E. (2000). Time for a change in public education, but what change? *Nature, Society and Thought* 13: 181–214.

Campbell, M.S. (1999). New trends in culture policy for the twenty-first century. *Social Text* 17: 5–15.

Coppola, D.P. 2007, *Introduction to International Disaster Management.*Butterworth-Heinemann (Elsevier), Burlingtom, MA.

Cowan, L.G. (1990). Privatization in the developing world. *Contributions in Economics and Economic History*, No. 112. Greenwood Praeger Press, Westport, CT.

Farazmand, A. (ed.) (2001). Privatization or public enterprise reform? International case studies with implications for public management. *Contributions in Economics and Economic History*, No. 112. Greenwood Praeger, Westport, CT.

Horwich, G. (1993). The role of the for-profit sector in disaster mitigation and response. *International Journal of Mass Emergencies and Disasters* 11: 189–205.

Kirschenbaum, A. (2000). Preparing the Population of Israel for Conventional and Non-Conventional Attacks. Israel Home Front Command, Jerusalem.

Kirschenbaum, A. (2004a). Measuring the effectiveness of disaster management Organizations. *International Journal of Mass Emergencies and Disasters* 22: 5–28.

Kirschenbaum, A. (2004b). *Chaos Organization and Disaster Management*. Marcel & Dekker, New York.

Massey, A. (1993). *Managing the Public Sector: A Comparative Analysis of the United Kingdom and the United States*. Aldershot Press, London.

Pack, J.R. (1987). Privatization of public-sector services in theory and practice. *Journal of Policy Analysis and Management* 6: 523–540.

Rondinelli, D.A. (1989). Decentralizing public services in developing countries: issues and opportunities. *Journal of Social, Political and Economic Studies* 14: 77–98.

Samson, C. (1994). The three faces of privatization. *Sociology* 28: 79–97.

Upshur, C.C., P.R. Benson, E. Clemens, W.H. Fisher, , H.S. Leff, and R. Schutt (1997). Closing state mental hospitals in Massachusetts: policy, process and impact. *International Journal of Law and Psychiatry* 20: 199–217.

Chapter 7
Caring for the Evacuees from Hurricane Katrina and Rita

Bill White

Abstract lllllIn September 2005, Houston delivered essential services to well over 200,000 Americans displaced by Hurricanes Katrina and Rita. It used business and civic leaders to provide services and established volunteer virtual organizations of experts to handle such specific needs as field hospitals managed by medical professionals. The city enrolled 20,000 evacuated children at schools, raised funds to help poorly performing students, and used hotel and apartment managers to arrange housing for the evacuees.

Introduction

In September 2005, Houston, TX, efficiently and compassionately provided essential services to well over 200,000 Americans displaced by Hurricanes Katrina and Rita. By the end of 2005 approximately 160,000 evacuees remained in the Houston area, most living in approximately 37,000 apartments and houses provided under a locally designed emergency housing program. As of mid-2007, an estimated 90,000–100,000 remained in Houston, with the majority intending to reside in their new hometown for the longer run.

According to the numerous surveys undertaken from hurricane landfall to the date of this writing almost 2 years later, the overwhelming majority of evacuees from these enormous tragedies believe that Houston dealt with their tragic circumstances effectively. Anecdotally, as mayor of Houston I encounter new residents once or twice a week who express appreciation and awe at the scale and effectiveness of Houston's response. The most typical words are "Houston saved me" and "I still can't believe what Houston did." In at least 18 months only a handful of evacuees have approached me with a criticism of the local response, though hundreds have criticized the response from public entities outside our region.

B. White (✉)
Mayor, Houston, TX, (2004–present)
e-mail: mayor.b.w@cityofhouston.net

S. Hakim, E.A. Blackstone (eds.), *Safeguarding Homeland Security*,
DOI 10.1007/978-1-4419-0371-6_7, © Springer Science+Business Media, LLC 2009

Houston responded effectively by creating a virtual organization, consisting of the most capable individuals and organizations – typically outside of government – to accomplish each clearly defined task.

Our goals, which we believe should have been America's goals, were articulated by me and Harris County Judge Robert Eckels immediately after the New Orleans levees broke: (1) we should move as quickly as possible to allow evacuees to get on with their lives with security and dignity, so they could live where they chose; (2) we should treat evacuees as we would wish to be treated in similar circumstances; and (3) evacuees themselves had to immediately accept responsibility for getting on with their lives, students in school, and able-bodied adults at work.

Though Harris County's Judge and I have received numerous public recognitions for this remarkable effort, the credit belongs to numerous individuals and organizations in our community who responded magnificently when called on. Finally, although some media reports emphasized the destitution and complaints of evacuees, or some lawless conduct by a small minority, I can assure all Americans that the overwhelming majority of evacuees themselves were strong, resourceful, and resilient, looking with hope to their future and not with despair toward their loss.

This chapter will briefly sketch out Houston's response to the evacuations from Hurricanes Katrina and Rita and will then identify in more detail lessons learned from our experiences. These lessons also apply in many cases to making government more efficient and consumer oriented in providing a wide range of services.

What Happened

Most of the population of southern Louisiana evacuated during the weekend of August 26–28, before Hurricane Katrina hit, late Sunday and early Monday. Most heeded the weather forecast and mandatory evacuation order. They headed in all directions, but somewhere between one-third and one-half headed to Texas on Interstate Highway 10. They filled the houses of friends, hotel rooms, Red Cross shelters, and ad hoc emergency shelters throughout Northern Louisiana and East Texas. Because Houston is the largest city close to Southern Louisiana, most of those who headed west filled our city.

Those who evacuated over the weekend planned to return in 72 h or less after the storm or storm threat passed.

On Monday morning I learned that the levees had broken. At lunch the CEO of Shell USA, the largest private employer in the region, gave me a damage assessment. From my knowledge of the levee system and experience with electricity and water/sewer infrastructure, I understood that New Orleans as we knew it had become uninhabitable. That afternoon we began preparing to deal with a "city within a city." Within 24 h the post-hurricane evacuation began, including thousands of airborne medical evacuations and 40,000–50,000 who arrived in buses, vans, and anything that could move.

We prepared our two largest public facilities–the Reliant complex (the Astrodome and a convention center) and the George R. Brown Convention Center. We called on our major hospitals and pharmacies to open large field hospitals to process these evacuees, many of whom came exhausted, dehydrated, and hungry.

At each of the two large emergency centers we established virtual organizations headed by individuals. The Judge and I observed them to have judgment and command presence. From the outset, we superseded the local emergency response plan because those organizations simply lacked the operating experience to run small cities.

The emergency evacuation from New Orleans took almost a week, for tragic reasons, which can be described elsewhere. During that week I initiated daily, 1-h meetings with the business, spiritual, and non-profit leadership of our city to ensure that needs were met in a matter of hours. This encompassed everything from laundry, airplane tickets, databases that reunite families, clothing, food, and small amounts of cash to allow people to leave shelters.

Our paramount goal was to place people in modest but habitable, furnished apartments, with electricity. I had ordered vouchers to be printed up, and we enlisted over 500 local apartment owners. Within a week, a volunteer organization was moving evacuees into apartments. Many hundreds were moved from shelters, hotel rooms, and houses of Houstonians every day from the first week of September until the end of December, when we announced Houston was "full."

All Red Cross shelters were vacated by the third week in September, when Hurricane Rita hit. Perhaps the most remarkable, unreported aspect of the entire relief effort occurred during Rita when those in hospitals along the Texas Gulf Coast joined those from Southern Louisiana in a variety of ad hoc field hospitals staffed by medical professionals in the Houston region.

Hundreds of thousands of Houstonians took part in relief efforts, largely through their employers and faith-based organizations.

Sixty thousand evacuees lived in hotels and motels in September and October, with that number steadily diminishing during November and December.

On one day, I recall learning of two motels and one small church, each of which was housing more than a hundred families. The evacuees and hosts ran out of cash. I called a corporation to adopt the families at one motel, and the group, the Ismaili Muslims, to adopt another. I asked a large local private business headed by a lay Christian leader to adopt the church and its evacuees. My request was simple: handle any needs and set folks back on their feet. They figured out how.

The local FEMA representative, Tom Olson, did three enormous things of great benefit to us. (1) He gave to me a letter assuring us that reasonable public expenditures could be reimbursed. (2) He expedited a cash advance for the housing program, and "blessed" it. (3) He did not try to "take charge" and worked as a team member, even when that meant disregarding ludicrous directives from DC such as FEMA's "order" to head the evacuees into cruise ships, to live in isolated dependency.

We opened our schools to evacuees and let people know that parents must get students into the classroom. Over 20,000 had enrolled by mid-September. We raised millions of dollars of private funds to assist these young people, many of whom were not performing at a Houston-area grade level. For some, it took tutoring and summer school, but now most are doing well.

Our housing program provided housing for an average, 12–24 months. For many able-bodied people who found jobs, it was 12 months more or less. A number of seniors and disabled individuals are still in the program. We housed a substantial percentage of those displaced in Southern Louisiana who had no savings or home-owners insurance. Total cost to FEMA? About $350 million. Total cost of FEMA's trailer program? Over $7 billion. I would wager that it is harder for people to become self-sufficient in trailers than in cities.

By 2 years after the disaster, I estimate that about 90,000–100,000 of the Houston-area's new residents lived in Southern Louisiana before the storms. Of this number, perhaps 20,000–30,000 people were higher income with savings and insurance and jobs and businesses, which could move. Another 20,000 or so are seniors or disabled people, with FEMA paying for housing but our local United Way agencies providing for casework and special needs. Most of the balance has found gainful employment, often after re-training.

With jobs in Houston and uncertainty concerning the more than $10 billion in federal grants to Louisiana for housing, most intend to stay in our region.

We do not care where law-abiding evacuees live. We do care and care passion-ately that we respect their decision as free Americans about where they want to live.

Lessons Learned

The most important lesson to be learned is to have sound management by an experi-enced executive. None of the five basic management principles critical for Houston's effective response would work unless there is good executive leadership. Sometimes a senior elected official may have that experience, and on other occasions he or she may not. Where they do not, that kind of expertise should be brought in.

We successfully applied six basic principles, dealing with: goals, tasks, person-nel, accountability, identification of the "consumer," and flexibility. For each, I will describe an example of how we applied it, and how that contrasts with "business as usual," or "good enough for government work."

Carefully Defining Goals

At the beginning of this chapter, I defined the three goals, which governed our program. These goals were simple and clear and allowed various alternatives to be quickly sorted. For example, because we wanted to allow people to live with independence, looking to the future, we rejected strong pressure from FEMA to herd evacuees into cruise ships. We acted with speed because we knew that stu-dents would fall behind for every day they missed in the classroom. As a result, we moved the 60,000 people who had been processed through the organized shelters, and closed those shelters, in less than 4 weeks after the evacuation. A "business as usual" response would have been to settle evacuees in trailer villages, which has been done in other areas. This would have been "easier," though far more expensive, because FEMA's rules and standard operating procedures had employed trailers rather than apartments. However, trailer cities would not have offered as much opportunity for independence and flexibility in seeking employment and getting kids back to school.

Break Big Jobs Down into Manageable Tasks and Empower Those Assigned the Task to Make Decisions

In emergency situations, one must create virtual organizations, particularly if you are to plug in the "best available people," and not simply rely on emergency professionals. One good rule we employed every single day was to assign one organization to one clear task. So, for example, we requested that a large corporation "take care" of all the needs of over 100 families jammed into an apartment complex, when the families had arrived by bus and none had transportation. One strong faith-based organization was assigned to another complex and marshaled medical and other resources, including employment, to meet all of those evacuees' needs. A national pharmaceutical retailer was asked to set up a pharmacy at a shelter and dispense medication without regard as to who would pay. A coalition of major churches was assigned responsibility for organizing about 10 warehouses with over a million square feet, which was packed with food, clothing, household supplies, furnishings, and the like. They organized their lay leadership for everything from a trucking operation, to a forklift operation, to indexing the various pallets of supplies.

The "business as usual" response would have been to ignore the incredible capability of large corporations and non-profit organizations and try to meet all of these needs either with public sector employees or organizations such as Red Cross who have defined emergency responsibilities.

Enlist the Most Competent People in Organizations for each Task

The keys to any successful organization are experienced people. For emergency short-term housing, we enlisted hundreds of hotel owners and managers. For housing after the first 2 weeks, we enlisted over 600 apartment owners and their management. We created virtual organizations staffed by people who provide temporary shelter (hotels and motels) and affordable shelter for a longer term (apartments) to help us design and implement these programs. By using the entire resources in the hotel and apartment industry, and adapting the forms and inspection procedures that are utilized for HUD programs, we did not have to deal with the "learning curve" of teaching government emergency professionals or contractors the housing business. "Business as usual" would have been to buy trailers or to have a "cost plus" contractor working for FEMA to develop a "housing plan." The extensive use of consultants is one of the reasons why the apartment reconstruction program within Louisiana got off to a slow start.

Strict Accountability

In a crisis, some excel, some perform beyond all expectations, some stumble, and some fall. It is critical that performers replace non-performers in mission critical tasks. Sometimes this is a challenge in governmental organizations or virtual organizations where the leadership does not have the power to hire or fire individual employees. Nonetheless, one can re-assign responsibilities using some simple rules. First, take advantage of multiple organizations performing similar tasks so that their relative performance can be evaluated, and stronger organizations can assume some of the responsibilities of weaker ones. Second, have discussions concerning the expansion or contraction of responsibilities in an open, public manner, which reduces the ability of people or organizations to fight for "turf." Third, make clear that there is a task for *everyone*, which should be suited to his or her capacity. One classic example of choosing "the best person for the task, regardless of job title" was the assignment of a Coast Guard officer as the site commander of relief efforts at the Reliant complex (including the Astrodome) during the Katrina evacuation. The facility was owned by Harris County and the Red Cross provided some of the organizational infrastructure, designed for 72-h emergencies. Of course, this was more than a 72-h emergency and required the skills of someone with a command presence that cared nothing about ego and could innovate to obtain results. We spotted these skills in a Coast Guard commander and made him the site commander, dealing with the operation that became a small city for several weeks.

The "good enough for government work" solution would be to simply use organizational charts prepared for a much more modest emergency, and ignore whether the person in a particular box had the stamina and charismatic leadership capacity to both improvise and command the respect of thousands of people filling out a virtual organization.

Improvise and Use What Works

President Eisenhower said on a number of occasions that plans are useless, but planning is indispensable. Great sports coaches understand that well, as do mangers that are able to manage fluid situations involving a great deal of uncertainty. However, journeyman managers or people who believe that management consists of memos, budgets, and procedures, as do many in the public sector, do not appreciate the critical importance of freedom to deviate from the plan. This tendency toward inflexible management is reinforced by the tendency of some auditors and professional critics to review emergency response, with the benefit of hindsight, and test it against established plans or procedures, which may or may not be applicable to the situation. Countless millions of dollars were wasted in Houston by the insistence of some within FEMA that all records concerning housing expenses be organized by evacuee household in hard copy, rather than having records organized by vendor and related occupancy units as you would normally do to track purchases and payables in an orderly basis. (Eventually, after many millions of dollars of expense, this requirement of FEMA was dropped.) What may make sense in a small emergency may not make sense in a large emergency. What may make sense for a devastated community may not make sense for a community hosting a new evacuee population. Emergency response requires the type of skills that you see in tactical military operations, or trading and investment banking operations, or successful serial entrepreneurs, where people need to make decisions quickly and innovate.

Finally, the pressures of such a response coupled with uncompromising insistence on accountability can add to the stress of a situation, which is inherently stressful – a natural disaster. Many of us believe in the healing power of prayer. We began and ended our daily meetings with prayer, which reminded all participants of the common values, which make us strong rather than our inadequacies.

Chapter 8
Sheltering and Evacuating from Hurricanes Katrina and Rita

Henry Garrett

Abstract Corpus Christi, a city of 285,000, received several thousand refugees from Hurricane Katrina. City personnel and volunteers converted the Coliseum for the evacuees, some of whom were sheltered in neighboring communities. Food provided by volunteer restaurants, medical services, Internet access to other communities, and travel assistance to reunite families were provided. An emergency operations center and a mobile command post were used. Then Hurricane Rita forced the city to evacuate the refugees and its residents, including, 350 special needs citizens who were transported to a Senior Center and then evacuated to San Antonio. Corpus Christi employees are considered essential and are not allowed to evacuate. The city operated a "refuge of last resort."

Corpus Christi is a city of 285,000 located on the Texas Gulf Coast. As a result of Hurricanes Katrina and Rita, our city faced back-to-back challenges in September 2005. In a continuous operation that lasted over 3 weeks, our city was tasked with providing shelter for several thousand evacuees from New Orleans, only to transition into a mandatory evacuation of our own city as record-breaking Hurricane Rita approached the Texas Coast.

Like most Americans, our community had been following the events unfolding as a result of Hurricane Katrina. On Friday, September 2, the morning news continued to carry stories of the dire situation at the New Orleans Superdome. At 10 o'clock that morning, I had received a call from the Governors Office of Emergency Management inquiring as to whether Corpus Christi could provide shelter for several thousand evacuees. Our immediate response was that although our city itself is in a potential evacuation zone, we understood the seriousness of the situation and would offer any assistance that we could provide. We learn later that many of the people arriving in our city had been at the Superdome.

On Friday, September 2, we were advised that the evacuees would be arriving on Monday morning allowing 2 days to prepare. Planning sessions were held

H. Garrett (✉)
Mayor, Corpus Christi, TX, (2005–present)
e-mail: lindale@cctexas.com

S. Hakim, E.A. Blackstone (eds.), *Safeguarding Homeland Security*,
DOI 10.1007/978-1-4419-0371-6_8, © Springer Science+Business Media, LLC 2009

throughout the day at the Emergency Operations Center. By the end of the day, a rough plan had been developed to convert the Memorial Coliseum into a shelter. The conversion of the coliseum into a shelter was a massive undertaking. The Coliseum was being used as a practice skating arena for the hockey team and had not been open to the public for some time. Believing they had approximately 72 h to prepare, staff believed it would be difficult but not impossible to remove the ice rink and equipment and get the building in shape by Monday. Those plans were shattered when on Saturday morning at 7:00 a.m., we received a call that planes "were in the air" and would be arriving in a few hours.

By early Saturday morning, the Emergency Operations Center was in full activation, a mobile command post had been placed at the coliseum, shelter teams were activated, and schedules were set. Employees had worked throughout the night on the coliseum, and by that afternoon, as planes began to land, the coliseum was ready to accept the evacuees.

Initially, concerns were raised regarding media reports of rampant crime that had occurred in the New Orleans Superdome. We decided early on that the evacuees had suffered terribly and that they were to be treated as guests of the city from the moment they arrived. During the next several weeks, only one or two minor issues of criminal conduct occurred. This is an amazing fact considering the events these folks had just suffered, the close quarters they were now living in, and the unknown future ahead of them.

As the planes continued to land that first day, we faced the fact that the Coliseum would soon reach capacity. The situation was relayed to the State EOC. However, due to the chaos on the ground in New Orleans and the lack of coordination between federal and state agencies, the planes kept coming and no one could say for sure when they would stop.

Emergency Management staff began coordinating with neighboring communities and local churches for help. Eventually, the neighboring communities of Port Aransas, Kingsville, and Portland were also caring for evacuees in their communities, and local churches in Corpus Christi were providing assistance as well. Daily counts, information, and needs were coordinated through the Corpus Christi EOC.

By implementing portions of our own hurricane emergency plans, and with the assistance of city employees and volunteers, we were able to rapidly provide essential services including food, medical, financial, travel, clothing, housing, sanitary facilities, and even a Wi-Fi café.

The Parks and Recreation Department manages the Meals and Wheels program on a daily basis and was the logical choice to manage the evacuee food program. The strategy was to utilize existing contracts as much as possible for this event, including food preparation. The city has a contract with a local vendor to provide food services for the newly opened Convention Center, and this contract was expanded to provide food to the Katrina evacuees. During the next few weeks, local restaurants provided free meals, and a former resident who now owns a chain of restaurants donated a mobile kitchen, complete with food staff to conduct meal operations for several days.

The Public Health Department, working with our Emergency Medical Division, quickly set up a clinic at the Memorial Coliseum. Evacuees were provided with medical evaluations and provided medications if necessary. A pharmacy system was instituted with the cooperation of local pharmacies, and medications were delivered to the Coliseum site as needed.

Sanitary and shower facilities were inadequate or non-existent at the Coliseum. Contracts were made for additional sanitary facilities, but a provider for portable showers could not be located. As part of our Homeland Security strategy, we ensure that equipment purchased with grant funds can also be utilized in the event of natural or man-made disasters. This strategy was especially useful as the Fire Department converted decontamination tents into showers, command tents into donation centers, and outdoor eating areas. Portable generators that had been purchased for terrorism response purposes supplied power. The mobile command post was especially useful as command coordinated with the EOC.

The City of Corpus Christi has been at the forefront of Wi-Fi technology, and this technology was put to use at the Coliseum. The Fire Department Command Post utilized Wi-Fi and WebEOC (electronic emergency management program) to coordinate with the EOC. Two issues, locating relatives and travel planning, were the impetus to creating a Wi-Fi café in the coliseum. A Wi-Fi system was installed, and a bank of computers was set up to allow the evacuees access to e-mail and to search web sites dedicated to locating relatives. One of the State established priorities was to unite families, and travel vouchers were offered for relocation. Municipal Information Services (MIS) stepped up to the plate and created a virtual travel agency. As relatives located each other, the MIS staff created necessary databases and coordinated travel plans for the evacuees. A voucher system was instituted with cab companies to provide transportation to the airport.

For a small city such as ours, the task of supporting an operation to care for several thousand displaced evacuees in need of the most basic necessities, while continuing to conduct normal day-to-day business placed a major strain on our employees and our abilities.

In mid-September things had slowed down somewhat as many evacuees had found permanent housing or had relocated to other cities to be near friends and families. Several refuge sites had closed, and the Emergency Operations Center, although still in operation, had scaled back to a reduced level. There were several hundred evacuees remaining in local shelters.

On September 18, our eyes were on a small tropical storm off, the coast of Florida. Her name was Rita. The situation grew more ominous the following day as Rita was now a hurricane and was projected to strengthen to a major storm. Corpus Christi now sat in the long-range projected path of a catastrophic storm, and it was time to consider evacuating the evacuees, as well as our own citizens.

Two days later, on September 20, the EOC operation was escalated to work two operations: the evacuation of Hurricane Katrina evacuees and preparations to evacuate the City of Corpus Christi. Although it was not quite time to call for a general evacuation, it was necessary to implement the special needs and transportation-dependent operations due to the length of time these operations require.

Several years ago a draft plan for evacuating citizens with special needs was created, but never completed. With our minds fresh with the images of Katrina, it was time to dust off the proposed plan and make it happen. Within a few hours, with cooperation from the Regional Transit Authority, and local community groups, a working plan was developed for a special needs and transit-dependent evacuation.

The implementation of the special needs operation began with notification utilizing media and our emergency telephone call-out system. Citizens were provided with a telephone number to contact for instructions. The plan called for a para-transit bus to transport citizens from their homes to a central "depot." A senior community center served as the depot for outbound special needs citizens. The center was an ideal site as the staff had considerable experience working with seniors and the disabled. Once at the site, they were provided with water and a small snack, and then boarded charter buses (provided by the State Operation Center) to depart for shelters in San Antonio. Approximately 350 citizens made use of this service.

The concept for the transit-dependent operations was very simple; citizens that were without transportation could board a Regional Transportation Authority (RTA) bus on its normal route to reach the "depot" (City Hall in this case). Once at the site, necessary information was obtained and a snack and water for the trip were provided. Corpus Christi has a large diabetic population and a small snack would ensure the 2-h drive could be completed without complications. Once registered, the citizens boarded Corpus Christi Independent School District buses for the trip to San Antonio. Approximately 300 citizens utilized this service, although we transported slightly more on the return trip to Corpus Christi several days later.

The next morning was September 21. Hurricane Rita was a Category 4 hurricane and was projected to strengthen during the day. Corpus Christi remained in the projected path. In cooperation with the State EOC, the remaining Katrina evacuees (those that had not found housing) were evacuated by air to Tennessee, and our two bus operations were underway.

Previously, no authority existed to call for "mandatory" evacuations, and earlier evacuations had been termed "recommended." Changes in the statute had recently occurred, and on the evening of the 21st· as we faced a record setting hurricane, I called for the first ever "mandatory" evacuation of the city. To their credit, the citizens took the mandatory order seriously, and the evacuation of the city began.

We quickly realized that the term "mandatory" created its own set of problems as essential employees such as pharmacists, bank employees, gasoline sales clerks, baggage clerks, and others quickly evacuated as well, leaving citizens with little ability to obtain cash, medicines, or fuel.

To compound the situation, Rita was a record-breaking hurricane, with its path still uncertain. Not only were our residents evacuating, but almost every city on the Texas coast was calling for evacuation as well. Although nursing homes had pre-existing contracts with bus companies, these buses quickly became scarce as nursing homes all along the coast initiated their contracts. Most nursing homes were able to obtain necessary resources, and the EOC was able to obtain transportation for the few that could not.

The city appeared to be a ghost town on the 22nd. Parking lots were empty, stores and restaurants were closed, and little to no traffic existed. Although no official count is available, it appeared that a many citizens had obeyed the mandatory evacuation order.

Fortunately for Corpus Christi, the storm began to make its turn away from our shores, and by the 23rd, all storm warnings had been lifted and we were able to begin the process of returning our citizens home.

Contributing Factors

In most states, evacuation zones are established along storm surge zones near the immediate coastline; however, the State of Texas includes a "wind zone" in addition to the storm surge zone when designating evacuation zones. The addition of the wind factor greatly increases the size of the evacuation zone and places the entire city in the zone (including portions of the city well inland). The National Red Cross will understandably not place a shelter in a hurricane evacuation zone.

Having learned from past experience, we understand that not all of our citizens can evacuate for various reasons; some lack transportation and some simply refuse to leave. Additionally, we understand that a total evacuation policy is not without risk. In light of these issues, the city is forced to operate its own "refuge of last resort" program. In addition to the shelter program, employees are assigned to functional teams such as food and water operations, debris management, and damage assessment. All city employees are considered essential and cannot evacuate during a storm (special case waivers are available).

Managerial Strategies

- Today's municipal employees face an ever-increasing workload, and EOC's are seldom activated. This naturally results in a situation in which employees may not take these duties as seriously as they should (does not happen often and it takes away from daily activities). We have worked to create more "ownership" of EOC duties by assigning sections to high-profile managers. Although the Office of Emergency Management operates within the Fire Department, Assistant City Managers now have year round functional responsibilities within the EOC such as Operations, Logistics, and Administration. Each of the functional teams, i.e., refuge (shelter) management, food and water distribution, damage assessment, etc., is assigned a Team Leader that reports to an Assistant City Manager (ACM) in the appropriate NIMS section. Once a plan is created, teams are established and trained; there is little impact to the ACM's workload.
- City employees (3,000+) are considered "essential" and cannot evacuate (waivers are available for special circumstances). Employees are assigned to functional teams, i.e., staff for "refuge of last resort", food/water/ice distribution, internal

food supplies, transportation, evacuation, special needs, etc. Teams conduct full scale or functional exercises annually if necessary.
- A shelter site is dedicated to employees, families, and their pets and is opened early on in the process.
- As much as possible, a multi-purpose use strategy is employed when deciding on expenditure of Homeland Security funds. At the Katrina Shelter, HAZMAT decontamination tents became evacuee showers. Fire Department mobile command vehicle became the onsite command post. Portable generators supplied power, and tents were converted to various uses.
- Providing outside agencies and community groups to be included in developing and implementing the plans is essential. The city had recently partnered with the "Assisted Living" agency to begin implementing a special needs registry, and this operation could not have been accomplished without their help.

Technological Strategies

- Corpus Christi is at the forefront in developing a citywide Wi-Fi umbrella project. Wi-Fi was utilized to create the "Internet café" at the coliseum allowing evacuees to e-mail, track relatives, and for city employees to create a "travel agency" to relocate evacuees. This proved to be a major benefit in assisting the evacuees to locate relatives and reunite families.
- The city uses the WebEOC electronic emergency management program. The program is Internet based and allows us to create a "virtual EOC" very quickly and simply.
- Wi-Fi was also utilized at the Fire Department command post to allow incident command access to WebEOC.
- The special needs registry was created and placed into WebEOC, creating an Internet-based portal in which all participants (RTA, EOC, "depot" sites) could maintain situational awareness of the process at all times. Additionally, the emergency call system was activated to contact the special needs citizens and inform them of the evacuation operation.

In Conclusion

The ability to bring this project together in such a short time frame was a result of the culmination of separate but integrated strategies including hurricane preparedness, homeland security, and technology. Relationships between area governments, the emergency management community, and local volunteers were critical as well.

Chapter 9
Local Government Contingency Planning for Public Security and Public Safety – Innovative and Remedial Efforts

David G. Wallace

Abstract Local communities often experience a shortage of supplies after 2 days of responding to an emergency. Sugar Land, TX, was instrumental in creating along with neighboring communities a Regional Logistics Center that was to be managed by a private company. The area in effect established a public–private partnership to handle more effectively the management of supplies. The city's leadership was also instrumental in helping to develop a prototype agreement for distant cities to provide aid in emergency situations. The agreement is an attempt to resolve state sovereignty issues that delayed responses to Hurricane Katrina. Baltimore, MD, and Trenton, NJ, have a mutual aid agreement.

Introduction

The terrorist incidents and natural disasters of the last decade have significantly influenced local government priorities and the role of the chief elected official – the Mayor. The need to ensure homeland security and public safety in each city has required local government to reallocate resources and administrative attention. As mayor of Sugar Land (TX), and as Co-Chairman of The US Conference of Mayors (USCM) Homeland Security Task Force (HSTF), I have had to learn about and adapt to security and safety issues and the needs that are new and challenging.

As an active participant in the HSTF, I have had the benefit of discussing security and safety issues with mayors across the nation. The Task Force provides a forum for mayors to discuss these challenges and forge plans and innovative approaches to deal with them effectively. Two of these innovative approaches (establishing regional logistics centers and promoting inter-metropolitan mutual aid agreements between cities) are described below.

D.G. Wallace (✉)
Mayor, Sugar Land, TX, (2002–2008)
e-mail: dgwal007@aol.com

S. Hakim, E.A. Blackstone (eds.), *Safeguarding Homeland Security*,
DOI 10.1007/978-1-4419-0371-6_9, © Springer Science+Business Media, LLC 2009

As mayor of Sugar Land I was involved in one of the most far-reaching public disaster incidents to strike our area in decades. This experience and a post-mortem review of the public safety effort launched by the area governments indicates that many, if not all, cities would be well served to review their emergency management plans to ensure they are modernized. Some of these remedial actions are also described below.

The City of Sugar Land is geographically situated in the heart of the Houston-Galveston Area Council (H-GAC). The H-GAC is the region-wide voluntary association of 133 local governments in the 13-county Gulf Coast planning region of Texas. Its service area is 12,500 square miles and contains almost 5.4 million people.

The H-GAC mission is to serve as the instrument of local government cooperation, promoting the region's orderly development, and the safety and welfare of its citizens. The H-GAC is governed by a Board of Directors composed of local elected officials who serve on the governing bodies of member local governments. There are 35 members on the H-GAC Board.

The H-GAC provides many tools: information, region-wide plans, and services to support the region's local governments. Key H-GAC governmental services include transportation planning, cooperative purchasing, homeland security, air and water quality planning, forecasting, and mapping. H-GAC also serves the region through workforce development, criminal justice, 9-1-1, trauma care planning, small business finance, and other programs contributing to the region's quality of life and economic competitiveness.

Innovative Security and Safety Approaches – Regional Logistics Center

Emergency Response and Recovery Gap

Recent local government's experience with the 2005 hurricane season and previous hurricanes have prompted local elected officials to critique the state of emergency preparedness and emergency responses to disaster incidents and local capacity to effectively deal with them and the post-disaster recovery period. Additionally, mayors have concerns in relation to past terrorist disasters such as the Oklahoma City Federal Building bombing and the multiple 9/11 airline hijackings and subsequent targeted crashes. Some lessons learned from examining these disaster incidents provide local decision makers with information to guide future homeland security and public safety efforts.

First, historical and 2005 hurricanes impacting the Gulf Coast region (e.g., Texas, Louisiana, Alabama, Florida, Mississippi) indicate that local emergency preparedness and response capacity are ordinarily exhausted in a short period of time (24–48 h) and are usually adequate to address disaster events of limited physical geography and limited impacts.Local supplies, equipment, and manpower are, for all intents and purposes, exhausted after this short-term period. Communities can and do rely on state and federal emergency response aid, but when major disasters occur it takes from 72 to 120 h for such aid to begin to ramp-up and longer for it to reach adequate levels of aid to effectively address the need to protect public safety, private property and public infrastructure, and natural resources. Thus, there is a "response gap" between exhaustion of local emergency aid and ramp-up of outside aid. This "response gap" period should and can be addressed via planning and capacity building.

A second lesson learned from the Oklahoma City and 9/11 incidents is that in addition to the short-term local emergency response gap, there is also a mid-term and long-term gap in the ability of local government to provide adequate post-incident disaster recovery aid (a "recovery gap"). Officials involved with the Oklahoma City incident emergency recovery period called on the public to bring shovels to the disaster scene to dig for survivors once the local emergency response resources were exhausted. The 9/11 disaster sites in New York City and at the Pentagon also experienced some equipment exhaustion, although information on those disaster sites is more complicated and not easily assessed. These post-incident recovery events have in common a general lack of emergency response/recovery logistical support. The information suggests that the readiness and deployment of equipment, supplies, and manpower may not be managed to their maximum capabilities. Local government has recently learned what military planners have practiced for decades – if not centuries – and have determined that you cannot address major disasters without the appropriate logistical support to provide needed equipment, supplies, and manpower in the right place at the right time.

Sugar Land and the H-GAC communities have worked for the last 2 years on developing a mechanism to enhance local first-responder capabilities for natural and terrorist disaster events. The mechanism is referred to as a Regional Logistics Center (RLC). The H-GAC communities adopted a resolution in 2004 to support the establishment of an "all-hazards" logistics center that would service the region in a disaster event. Sugar Land and H-GAC convened a local/regional government Summit in October 2004 to further develop the concept, and it garnered considerable political support.

The idea behind the concept was to establish a mechanism that would pool the resources of cities in a region to deal more effectively with first-responder activities during a major catastrophe. While individual communities are adding to their disaster supplies and equipment inventories with homeland security federal financial assistance granted from Washington through the states, the scattered state of supplies and equipment, as well as the lack of military-like logistics support enhances the opportunities for a lack of coordination in the event of a major disaster. The RLC approach remedies that shortcoming by pooling some of those emergency response resources (thereby being more fiscally conservative for *all* participating cities) coupled with professional grade logistics management to a pre-positioned cache of equipment that is maintained and managed for a response-ready deployment.

Enhance Logistics Capabilities

Integrating logistics capabilities into local government provision of public security and safety services is desirable, but local government normally lacks a sophisticated capability in this area. The military and the private sector, on the other hand, have an abundance of demonstrated logistics capability. One firm in particular that has been researched, LION Apparel, has a long history of providing municipal government with public safety services and suggests that their TotalCare® concept and their work for the US military in supplies logistics is well suited for cities. The TotalCare® concept, in short, provides city fire departments with a cradle-to-grave acquisition, maintenance, and replacement program for firefighter's personal protective equipment. The basic idea is that a private party be tasked with ensuring that the personal protective equipment always be available and "response-ready." Thus, firefighters are free to fight fires and provide emergency management services, and the lower order, yet very important, job of providing protective gear is performed by a private service provider. LION has demonstrated cost savings in this area and the opportunity to establish a public–private partnership is appealing to cities because of the support for public safety and the additional cost savings over traditional protective gear maintenance and replacement practices.

Second, LION has provided similar services to the United States Marines for some time. The services to the military demonstrate that the concept is useful and proven. The same benefits apply to the military as they do to the cities where LION provides the TotalCare® services.

The concept was adapted to apply to the H-GAC, a group of Gulf Coast Texas cities, to modernize inter-city cooperation to provide a greater level of public security and safety. H-GAC is pursuing a program to establish logistical capabilities to address many of the problems associated with the disaster emergency "response gap" and the post-incident recovery activities. The H-GAC Board has endorsed the establishment of a Regional Logistics Center (RLC) whose purpose is to provide logistical support to communities in the H-GAC region in the event of a natural or a terrorist disaster event.

The RLC program envisioned by H-GAC is intended to support local emergency response and post-incident recovery efforts and will be fully integrated into the current plans. The program takes local mutual aid agreements to a higher level of effectiveness by pooling emergency response resources and coordinating the supply chain to address needs. It is obvious that no single community can gather and maintain the resources necessary to adequately address a regional disaster. That is why the RLC approach is a superior planning approach. Participating communities can transfer and pool "excess assets" from their emergency resources inventory and the regional community can mutually benefit from sharing these "excess inventories." The participating communities can work together to identify additional emergency response equipment and supplies that can be procured for the RLC inventory that would not otherwise be "affordable" to individual communities. Simply put, apart from an "insurance premium-style inventory management and availability fee," the municipalities do not acquire the equipment until the need presents itself.

Furthermore, the municipality can redeploy the capital it receives as it is conveying its "excess inventory" to the private sector operator of the RLC. This is a significant benefit of using the public–private partnership.

The H-GAC Regional Logistics Center (RLC) is designed to warehouse a response-ready centralized cache of supplies and equipment and, in some instances additional "life support" supplies to local residents that can be deployed on demand, to first-responder field needs in time of need. It will also be responsible for establishing the necessary supply chains to replenish emergency response equipment and supplies that would otherwise be exhausted during the first 5 days of a major disaster. In short, it serves as the 5-day bridge of response, relief, and recovery supplies and equipment until state and federal authorities can mount effective relief efforts.

The centralized logistical cache system is a successful time proven method of sustaining an intense campaign used by both the military and the industry. Logistical management and deployment concepts can be applied to address meso (one that triggers mutual aid agreement activities) to major-scale disaster emergency events. Planning for a pre-determined level of response and ensuring field delivery of supplies shifts one burden from the first-responder team to a support team. This frees up the first responder to pursue the operational objectives of the incident relief and recovery efforts.

Defining the Role of an RLC

The RLC will be assigned a number of responsibilities related to servicing H-GAC communities in emergency response and disaster relief efforts. These responsibilities may change over time, but are initially as follows:

- Logistical planning efforts involving RLC managers with the H-GAC community emergency management personnel to develop local emergency resources needs assessments and the combination of equipment and supplies which will be pooled at the RLC facility.
- RLC managers will be responsible for operations and maintenance (O&M) of the RLC warehouse facilities.
- RLC managers will be responsible for maintaining the pooled equipment (equipment that has been conveyed from the warehouses of the subscribing municipal partners plus additional new equipment) and supplies in response-ready mode. This includes inventory management, replacement, and rotation; equipment calibration; and, certifying that all equipment is operational when needed.
- RLC managers will be responsible for ensuring that equipment and supplies are properly bundled and transport ready. Community emergency managers will be responsible for communicating with incidence response leaders and transporting equipment and supplies from the RLC to specified staging areas.
- RLC managers will be responsible for tracking and accounting for the use of supplies and equipment and will provide deployment and usage records to H-GAC.
- RLC managers will be responsible for reporting inventory replacement needs on a regular basis to the H-GAC.

- RLC managers will coordinate with the various response agencies and will be responsible for identifying and activating pre-existing arrangements to procure designated equipment and supplies to support post-incident recovery efforts
- RLC managers will create an after action report for the H-GAC emergency management oversight committee. The report will detail all of the specific activities that the RLC was engaged in during the incident and provide documentation for the appropriate reimbursement of material utilized during the incident. Some of the specific items or activities included in this report are as follows:
- Any item utilized during the incident, items that were where damaged, destroyed, or lost.
- Items that were consumed.
- Specific special activities not predetermined in the original service agreement.
- Labor overtime or additional labor or other resources.

A Public–Private Partnership Approach

The H-GAC plans to secure a service provider in a public–private partnership to procure these services in conjunction with a service agreement. Cities already hire, train, and certify personnel to perform emergency response duties, but for the RLC model the H-GAC will choose a service provider that has demonstrated previous experience in military-like logistics operations. Generally speaking, the service provider will have sophisticated training and skills. Logistics skills rather than administrative skills will be the most important skill level in choosing an appropriate service provider. H-GAC has determined that the preferred service provider will have the right balance of training and experience in logistical skills and a full understanding of disaster relief and emergency response protocols.

The H-GAC anticipates that member cities and/or counties will accumulate and warehouse fixed and mobile emergency equipment and supply asset inventory, which will be maintained in operational stature by the service provider. The service provider will be required to rapidly replenish equipment and supplies from outside an impacted disaster event area under adverse conditions. The service provider must also be able to ensure additional contingency resource capability in the event of infrastructure damage. It is anticipated that the partnership approach will yield cost savings and can be designed at an H-GAC designated level of funding and financing that meets the changing needs for security and safety over time.

Innovative Security and Safety Approaches – Inter-metropolitan Municipal Mutual Aid Agreements

The US Conference of Mayors (USCM) Homeland Security Task Force (HSTF) hosted Mayoral discussions describing what went right and wrong in the public response to the 2005 hurricane season. Many cities were affected by Hurricanes

Katrina, Rita, and Wilma; and both the recovery and the emergency public safety response efforts were widely varied. One of the topics discussed was how cities prepare for and respond to disaster events and the role of municipal mutual aid agreements.

Mutual aid agreements likely date back to the original colonies in America. They establish protocols for one or more cities to bring fire, police, or other public safety and emergency aid to a city experiencing a natural or other disaster. The Gulf Coast cities have a long-established history of hurricane disasters as well as mutual aid agreements in place. The pre-existing agreements often provide the requisite help that impacted cities need. Hurricane Katrina, however, while not unique, was certainly a wake-up call to local government that the traditional mutual aid agreements are not adequate to address disasters of such magnitude and that encompass such a broad geographical area.

The HSTF discussions included many of the impacted cities, such as Gulfport, MS, the landfall site of Hurricane Katrina. Gulfport, like many of the surrounding cities, was overwhelmed by the sheer magnitude of wind and water destructions. The public infrastructure was severely damaged. Roads were washed out, which impeded the deployment of emergency equipment and personnel. Electricity was lost, as well as most communications capabilities, drinking water, and wastewater services. Cities surrounding Gulfport were similarly impacted. Thus, each city could neither provide nor receive aid from their neighboring cities. They were more or less on their own.

Mayors participating in the HSTF discussion remarked that the national media was broadcasting live feed of the destruction in the aftermath. Helicopter crews were filming the flooded areas, the people stranded on rooftops, and the heroic yet slow pace of emergency response. The nation looked on with a feeling of helplessness. State and federal emergency aids in the multi-state Gulf Coast area (Florida, Alabama, Mississippi, Louisiana, and Texas) were beginning to ramp-up but appeared to be too slow.

One of the problems identified by the mayors was that calling on mutual aid from outside the impacted cities and states was impeded. One impediment was the temporary loss of communications with the impacted cities' local government leaders. Coordination of efforts was near impossible until the communications channels were re-established.

"State sovereignty" protocols, however, proved to be another unintended factor. While many cities outside of the disaster impact zone geared up emergency aid, they could not cross state borders without permission from the impacted state's Governor. It would be misleading to suggest that the Governors were not prepared to grant permission for the emergency aid from other jurisdictions to enter their states. Yet, there was a combination of temporarily delayed communications between the states and the impacted cities, and therefore the needs of the impacted cities were not fully understood. Also, state decision makers were cautious about allowing even more people into the hazard areas and becoming exposed to life-threatening danger. The breakdown in communications led to confusion; and the confusion prolonged the disaster's impact. This emergency response "confusion conundrum" can be better addressed.

The HSTF has called for modernization of interoperable communications since shortly after the 9/11 disasters. Interoperable communications could effectively reduce the confusion encountered in the Hurricane Katrina disaster relief effort. Modernizing interoperable communications requires major federal actions that are beyond the ability of local government to achieve on a national scale. The "state sovereignty" issue can be managed to some extent by local government, and the USCM adopted a resolution to promote the interregional "Mutual Aid Agreement" (attached at the end of the chapter).

An innovative aspect of the resolution adopted by the USCM is to create a link to mutual aid from outside a large, regional disaster impacted area with a preconceived arrangement that could avoid the emergency response "confusion conundrum." The model approach (hopefully a Best Practice) has three key elements.

First, the aiding city agrees to send "...public safety (fire and police), public works, transportation, and other personnel, equipment, and resources as may be of assistance to the city confronting an emergency." The two cities entering a mutual aid agreement have specified the broad categories of aid in advance of an incident; and the cities can notify their respective state leaders with such information. The aid-sending city can reserve resources necessary to protect their people and property. The cities of Baltimore (MD) and Trenton (NJ) have established the first known interregional mutual aid agreement as outlined by the USCM resolution. It has not yet been tested, and it is not yet known whether the "state sovereignty" concerns will be satisfactorily dealt with.

The second element is ambitious. It stipulates that the aid-sending city will agree to bear the cost of sending resources (subject to reimbursement efforts by the city receiving the assistance) to the city confronting the emergency. This is a "help-first/cost-later" approach. Yet the resolution states that the two cities will jointly seek reimbursement through normal channels such as the Federal Emergency Management Agency (FEMA).

The third element of the resolution recognizes the need for organizational order. The aid-sending city agrees that emergency resources will "...operate under the command, control, and supervision of the appropriate responsible officials in the city confronting the emergency." This provision recognizes that coordination and cooperation is critical and that local officials on the emergency disaster scene are most knowledgeable about the current disaster incident.

The public benefits of the interregional mutual aid agreement can be significant. Normally no one single city has the resources to address a disaster emergency of the magnitude of Hurricane Katrina. It takes a lot of resources, most of which can be attracted from elsewhere (but not similarly impacted neighboring cities). The goal is to protect the public, property (both private and public), and natural resources. The model also recognizes that most of the emergency response resources are at the local government level. The new mayoral awareness is that local government needs to build disaster relief capability and not rely solely on the federal or state governments to save the day.

Contingency Planning

The scale of terrorist and natural disaster incidents has vast implications for emergency planning and implementation. Emergency preparedness, response, and recovery require that efforts match the scale of the incident, and therefore, contingency planning is required to ensure the proper level of community action. Cities have proven that they are capable of managing local emergencies of limited scale or short duration. The adequacy of such emergency efforts was tested in the 2005 hurricane season when large-scale incidents (Katrina and Rita) occurred in the Texas Gulf Coast area. Local leaders learned where remedial planning was required to address certain inadequacies, and some of the lessons learned by local government are described below.

Reverse 911

Reverse nine-one-one (9-1-1) is, simply stated, the local government sending out emergency calls to the citizens, instead of citizens calling in to report an emergency. In the case of Hurricane Rita, Sugar Land, Texas arranged to have its contract 9-1-1 auto-dialer service send a taped message to its residents to encourage evacuation for those having medical or physical disabilities/impairments. Due to the unanticipated large geographic scale of the potentially impacted area, the planned arrangement with the service provider was found, in retrospect, inadequate.

It was determined after review that the contract "reverse 9-1-1" service provider was also used by numerous cities, counties, etc., in the H-GAC area; and it was inundated by a myriad of city and county agencies sending similar evacuation messages. The queue of calls was so long that when Sugar Land placed its "Noon" order for the call, it fell behind over 750,000 other "reverse 9-1-1" calls, and the "emergency message" was not received by our residents until 8:00–9:00 p.m., a full 8–9 h later. The weather patterns adjusted materially during that period, and the auto-dialer message continued to be sent after the decision was made to halt the evacuation encouragement and to suggest residents to shelter-in-place.

Now Sugar Land contracts with alternative auto-dialer services to increase the rate of calls per minute and to ensure a remedy for the cueing situation. Also, local officials are asking service providers to disclose their other client demands in a large-scale disaster event to avoid the problem encountered during Hurricane Rita.

Evacuation Transportation Capacity

Many sensitive populations in public and private institutions such as hospitals, nursing homes, hospices, and other health-care facilities housing or treating disabled patients have established contracts with emergency evacuation transportation service providers. Yet, many of these institutions found themselves waiting for services that came late or did not come at all during the Hurricane Rita evacuation.

The post-incident review revealed that the list of available emergency transportation service providers was relatively limited in the immediate region. It was found that the service providers had sufficient vehicles and personnel for limited evacuations, but were "oversubscribed" in the case of a major disaster event where several institutions would be affected.

Institutional consumers of emergency evacuation services are urged by Sugar Land officials to contract for redundant local evacuation need situations and ensure sufficient capacity to meet large-scale evacuation needs. Institutions responsible for evacuating clients or patients should ask service providers to disclose their other client demands in a large-scale disaster event.

Coordinated Regional Evacuation Planning

Local governments are responsible for warning citizens of impending natural disasters. When Hurricane Rita hit land in the Texas Gulf Coast area, the evacuation effort was led by Houston/Harris County. Although the evacuation was successful and the citizens of one of the nation's largest urban areas were moved to safety, there were some clear challenges.

The regional evacuation plan had not been fully adopted by all affected local jurisdictions. Police in small towns along the evacuation route were not fully coordinated to move traffic through their jurisdictions (i.e., a red light in Giddings, TX, literally backed-up traffic to Brenham, TX). Construction on major highway routes caused immediate traffic problems. There were shortages of food, water, and fuel supply on major evacuation routes.

These evacuation factors can be dealt with through contingency planning and coordinated regional evacuation efforts. It will, however, require integration of state and regional emergency planning efforts to move large populations.

Role of the Mass Media

Local government often relies on the media to help in emergency situations, but in the case of Hurricanes Katrina and Rita, the massive media coverage in the Houston/Sugar Land area resulted in a considerable amount of public confusion. The post-incident review pointed out a number of things that can be discussed with the media community to improve the emergency response efforts of the future.

The video and print media did a good job of providing images of devastation along the Gulf Coast, but this undoubtedly fueled the public's perception of danger and resulted in an urge to flee the region ahead of the storm in areas in the region that are not normally required to evacuate during a hurricane. The tendency for the media to predict the most devastating outcomes of a Category 5 hurricane resulting in widespread devastation reinforced the public's urge to flee. This type of warning provides a good public service if it accurately reflects danger, but it should be tempered with information that better defines the likely impact areas. The aftermath of

Hurricane Rita suggested that the actual destruction was far less than the potential destruction, and there is a fear among public officials that the future calls for evacuation are likely to be met with skepticism and reluctance on the part of the public. Future emergency planning (and especially evacuation planning) will benefit from briefing the local/regional media in advance on sensitivity to reporting information to the public with greater accuracy and balance.

Hosting Emergency Evacuees

The state of Texas, in its efforts to provide care and compassion to its Gulf Coast neighbors, offered to accept Hurricane Katrina evacuees. State and local officials were forced to make many procurement decisions based on out-dated or incomplete information from federal partners, including FEMA, as well as the Red Cross because of real-time emergency and "life-threatening" requirements. There was a general lack of contingency planning and a dearth of accurate information that could have helped local decision makers to more adequately assess the impact that a sudden influx of people would have on local governments.

Inaccurate or insufficient information leads to adjustments in the normal local government procurement process, which hinders the ability of municipalities to obtain reimbursement for response, care, and recovery expenditures. This has had an impact on local government budgets and liquidity. It also could adversely affect the business economics of vendors who came to the aid of the evacuees. If situations such as this are not dealt with fairly, and if new policies and procedures are not adopted to reflect such situations, then it may have a chilling affect on municipal mutual aid and disaster response efforts in the future.

Emergency Planning Scale

Soon after Hurricane Katrina hit land it became clear to many observers that government response efforts at the local, state, and federal levels were overwhelmed by the impacts and the sudden demand on resources. FEMA appeared to be underprepared for an incident of this magnitude. The Red Cross was overwhelmed with requests for shelters and could not staff or operate the number of shelters required in outlying areas. The efforts of good Samaritans (faith communities, service organizations, and other groups) were critical to supporting evacuee needs. However, at times the effort was fragmented and lacked coordination.

The unfortunate lesson learned from the post-incident review was that in the case of disasters of great magnitude that overwhelm affected local governments, states and federal response agencies were not adequately accounted for in existing emergency response and recovery plans. No longer can local government rely on emergency response and recovery plans that anticipated disaster events of limited geographic scale and scope of impact. Emergency plans and various assumptions contained in those plans must be examined for accuracy, adequacy, and be modified to address disasters of great magnitude. The mass evacuation and sheltering process that resulted from Hurricanes Katrina and Rita will provide a template for revision of plans needed to address bioterrorism, radiological dispersal devices, nuclear, and other events that may result in mass population relocation. Both events required seamless federal, state, and local coordination. Regional coordination proved invaluable in these incident experiences. Working with the state, the region should move forward with the development and adoption of a broader, full-scale regional-based emergency response plans. In fact, the state of Texas has performed such research and has previously developed a regional proposed plan for deployment of personnel and equipment in 12 pre-selected regions of the state. It is this sort of pre-planning that each state in the nation should be researching, considering, and adopting.

APPENDIX: MUTUAL AID AGREEMENT

WHEREAS, the cities of _____ and _____ (collectively the "parties") recognize the value and the potential need of assisting each other in the event of some emergency, and each city has personnel, equipment, and resources that could assist the other in an emergency,

NOW, THEREFORE, the parties agree as follows this ____ day of _____, ____:

1. In the event of an emergency as declared by the mayor of one of the cities that is a party to this agreement, and upon the request of the mayor of that city, the mayor of the other city commits to send forthwith and without delay such public safety (fire and police), public works, transportation, and other personnel, equipment, and resources as may be of assistance to the city confronting an emergency. This obligation to provide assistance shall be subject to the right of any city sending resources to withhold resources to the extent necessary to provide reasonable protection for the safety and protection of its citizens.

2. The city sending personnel, equipment, and resources to respond to an emergency in the other city agrees to bear the cost of its action pending the execution of any necessary contracts or other documents to seek reimbursement from any agency of the federal or state governments, including, without limitation, the Federal Emergency Management Administration, or any similar or counterpart state emergency management agency. The parties shall work together closely and cooperatively to obtain any federal or state reimbursement that may be available. In the event that reimbursement for some or all provided services is unavailable, the city sending personnel, equipment, and resources shall be entitled to request reimbursement from the other city and that city shall make a good faith effort to provide in a timely fashion reimbursement for all unreimbursed expenses.

3. All personnel, equipment, and resources made available to a city confronting an emergency shall, while in the city confronting an emergency, operate under the command, control, and supervision of the appropriate responsible officials in the city confronting the emergency.

4. Within 45 days of the parties' execution of this mutual aid agreement, each city shall, to the extent necessary, modify or amend its respective emergency management plans to reflect the obligations set forth in this agreement.

Chapter 10
Technological and Regional Cooperation Strategies: Securing the City and Port of Oakland, California

Ronald V. Dellums, Yolanda Burrell, and Michael O'Brien

Abstract The City of Oakland, CA, with the nation's the fifth busiest maritime shipping port, has persevered through several major disasters in recent years. The region's geography and its designation as a high value terrorist target present an unquestionable public safety challenge. This chapter discusses the characteristic strategies the city and Port employ to protect its people and resources against potential threats and hazards in an environment of limited multi-jurisdictional resources. Through the collaboration of a broad coalition of stakeholders, active information sharing, and the use of various enabling technologies, the city and the Port are able to prepare, prevent, respond, and recover from potential risks both natural and man-made.

When I became the 48th mayor of Oakland, I challenged the citizens of Oakland to see ourselves in larger terms, to have the audacity to come together to create Oakland as the model city. What is a model city? Succinctly stated, it is a cohesive, coherent city, anchored in a vibrant economy, where its citizenry is healthy, well educated, well trained, well informed, and capable of effective interactions with the civic, economic, social, and cultural institutions of our community. For a model city to truly realize its potential it must be a city that works, it must have logic, and it must have a rationale. A model city should work for everyone; it must be open, aboveboard, accessible, and transparent.

There is no quick fix to confronting the struggles facing urban America in the twenty-first century. These concerns have evolved over a long period of time and will require innovative and strategic action. We can create a model city by taking a holistic approach to addressing our concerns in the context of one another; nothing happens in a vacuum and all things are interrelated. I have challenged the community and our partners to engage in a level of collaboration unprecedented, in the hopes that we begin to feel the strength of our collective power to change the status

R.V. Dellums (✉)
Mayor, Oakland, CA, (2007–present)
e-mail: officeofthemayor@oaklandnet.com

S. Hakim, E.A. Blackstone (eds.), *Safeguarding Homeland Security*,
DOI 10.1007/978-1-4419-0371-6_10, © Springer Science+Business Media, LLC 2009

quo. By tapping the brilliance that resides in our community and with the assistance of a broad coalition of community partners, there is nothing that we cannot achieve.

A prime example of unprecedented collaboration is our collective effort to protect the people and resources of the Port of Oakland (Fig. 10.1). We have brought together many public, private, and community partners to address the issues of regional preparedness and security. The city and Port of Oakland, together with local and regional public safety agencies and a broad coalition of stakeholders have joined forces to ensure that we can withstand inevitable disasters, manmade or natural, and assure the continuity of operations of vital economic engines and public safety services. Oakland has faced several devastating events in recent memory; and we will strive to make continuous improvements to our level of readiness by honing our procedures, processes, and strategic relationships.

Fig. 10.1 The Port of Oakland, CA

The Port of Oakland

The Port of Oakland (Port) is an autonomous department of the City of Oakland. The Port area is situated along approximately 20 miles of Oakland's waterfront. Oakland has operated a public harbor to serve waterborne commerce since its incorporation in 1852 and is one of the pioneers of large-scale containerization in the United States. The Port has also operated an airport since 1927. The seven-member Oakland Board of Port Commissioners (Board) has exclusive control and management of the harbor and the airport under the City Charter. The Port Commissioners are nominated by the mayor of the City of Oakland and appointed by the Oakland City Council. The Port Commissioners are residents of the City of Oakland and serve staggered 4-year terms without compensation.

The Port has three major business lines. The Port's *Aviation Division* operates Oakland International Airport, a passenger, cargo, and general aviation airport, which offers more than 188 commercial passenger non-stop flights daily to 33 domestic and international destinations and 46 all-cargo flights. The Port's *Maritime Division* manages the fifth busiest cargo container port in North America by twenty-foot equivalent unit (TEU) volume with 2,388,182 TEUs having moved through the Port in CY 2007.[1] Approximately 86% of the Port's trade is with international trading partners/regions and 14% is domestic. Asia is the most significant trading partner of the Port of Oakland. In CY 2007, 80% of the TEUs that moved through the Port was either originated from or destined for Asia.

In addition, the Port's *Commercial Real Estate (CRE) Division* oversees a total of 876 acres of land along the Oakland Estuary, which includes warehouses, parking lots, hotels, offices, shops, and restaurants. The Port of Oakland also acts as a trustee for waterfront property serving commercial, recreational, and other public access purposes as well as for all its other Tidelands Trust properties. The Port of Oakland supports approximately 55,000 direct and indirect jobs in the region and approximately 668,000 related jobs in California and the United States, and impacts the generation of approximately $7 billion in economic impact.

This chapter discusses the challenges and practices of coordinating local public safety agencies to maintain the security of the Port's maritime infrastructure and operations.

Protecting the Port Infrastructure

The goal of the security system at the Port of Oakland is to prepare, prevent, respond, and recover from potential incidents through the following:

- trained and motivated people;
- current policy and procedures;
- effective security equipment and systems; and
- regular exercises.

Through these actions the security system will reduce the risk from incidents that may impact the Port's key assets and critical infrastructure, disrupt regional business activity, or negatively affect the citizens and environment of the City of Oakland.

Even though the primary focus of the security system is the prevention and response to Chemical, Biological, Radiological Nuclear and Explosive (CBRNE) incidents in the San Francisco Bay Area, the extensive planning, interagency cooperation, public–private collaboration, and continuous drills and exercises all contribute toward our region's readiness for all hazards, both natural and manmade.

Interagency Cooperation and Collaboration

The security system for the Port of Oakland has evolved and significantly improved over the past 7 years. While the initial focus of the Maritime Transportation Security Act of 2002 was on security program implementation for regulated vessels and marine facilities, the Port and associated response and regulatory agencies have taken these security mandates several steps forward toward an integrated and holistic approach to improve awareness, prevention, response, and recovery from all hazards.

Several maritime-related coalitions, councils, and committees have been formed around functional and geographical lines. These groups have established forums to address port-wide systemic issues, improve interagency cooperation, develop greater public/private collaboration, and promote best security practices (see Fig. 10.2).

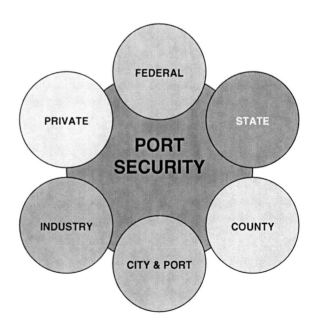

Fig. 10.2 Port security partnerships[2]

In the San Francisco Bay and Delta Region, port security partnerships include the following:

- Federal – Coast Guard, Federal Bureau of Investigation, Transportation Security Administration, Customs and Border Protection, and Immigration and Customs Enforcement.
- State – Governor's Office of Homeland Security, Governor's Office of Emergency Services (State Operations Center), California Highway Patrol, California National Guard Bureau, Department of Fish and Game, and California State Lands Commission.
- County – Sheriff Department, Office of Emergency Services (Coastal Region Operations Center), County Fire Department Resources, and County Medical Resources. There are 12 counties in this area to be considered.
- City – Police Department, Fire Department, Emergency Services (Emergency Operations Center & Departmental Operations Centers), Seaport District and Emergency Medical Services.
- Industry – Marine Exchange, Pilot Association, Maritime Labor, Ferryboat Operators, Tugboat Operators, Barge Operators, Fishermen, Water-Taxi Operators, Vendors, Truck Drivers, Waterside Facility Operators, and Vessel Operators.
- Private – Yachtsmen, Waterside Homeowners, Fishermen, General Boaters, and Beachcombers.

The Area Maritime Security Committee (AMSC) has a regional focus and is chaired by the Coast Guard Sector Commander. This group is generally focused at the security policy level and oversees the development and implementation of the Area Maritime Security Plan. This plan covers the Port of Oakland and all associated federal, state, and local agencies and regulated maritime entities from the California/Oregon border south to Monterey Bay. The 33 members of the AMSC are representatives of their maritime industry or agency. The benefit of area-wide interaction is derived from the concept that the Coast Guard will be the lead federal agency for all hazards incident response on all waterways in the San Francisco Bay. An incident of national significance at one port in the San Francisco Bay region will likely affect all ports and private entities associated with the bay.

Real Life Scenario: The M/V COSCO BUSAN

On November 7, 2007, at approximately 8:30 a.m., the M/V COSCO BUSAN struck a support tower of the San Francisco–Oakland Bay Bridge in very heavy fog. Initially, damage to the bridge and ship was thought to be negligible with a spill estimate of only 100–400 gallons of fuel oil. When weather conditions improved and local and federal officials made more accurate assessments, the actual magnitude of the spill jumped to approximately 58,000 gallons of fuel oil. The oil spread north and south of the Golden Gate, affecting fish, birds, and marine mammals along the sensitive coastline, tidal areas, lagoons, and wetlands.

The economic short-term and long-term costs to the region are yet to be determined. The San Francisco Bay Area has an extremely rich and sensitive diversity of ecological life that many commercial industries are dependent upon including fishing, shipping, and tourism. A spill of this magnitude severely distressed the ecological diversity in the Bay Area and was of paramount concern to municipalities and agencies around the Bay.

Even though the prevailing tides and currents initially pushed the brunt of this ecological disaster toward the entrance to San Francisco Bay and the beach areas outside the Bay, there was significant impact on areas in the East Bay and Oakland as well. Shortly after the magnitude of the spill was made apparent to the public, the Port of Oakland activated the Port Emergency Operations Center and immediately coordinated with the East Bay Regional Park District to conduct an assessment of the Middle Harbor Shoreline Park – a recently restored sensitive habitat closest to the spill site. Measures to prevent additional beach impact and to protect the public were put into place. Additionally, the Port coordinated with the City of Oakland Fire Department to ensure the Lake Merritt Estuary was boomed off to prevent any contamination in anticipation of tidal shifts. Both the Port and the city positioned representatives at the Coast Guard led Unified Command to ensure our cleanup priorities were integrated into the Planning Section along with 19 other federal, state, and local agencies in the region-wide mitigation effort. This interagency communication and response coordination minimized the consequences of the spill and facilitated a rapid recovery from the incident.

The M/V COSCO BUSAN incident response was coordinated by a Unified Command composed of representatives of several federal, state, and local response agencies, cleanup contractors, and many other stakeholders. The Ports of Oakland and San Francisco were part of the incident command, ensuring the coordination and collaboration between their individual port efforts and those entities involved in the overall response and cleanup operations. The Port of Oakland efforts were further integrated with those of the City of Oakland via partial standup of their respective Emergency Operations Centers to ensure the protection of sensitive habitats and advocate cleanup priorities to the Unified Commander.

The Neptune Coalition is composed of 15 participating Bay Area Law Enforcement Agencies and is a cooperative effort to enhance the safety and security of the ports within the Bay Area and Delta. The Coalition accomplishes this primary objective through monthly meetings, joint training and law enforcement operations, and participation in annual marine events such as Navy Fleet Week. Coalition partners agree to support and participate in local Port Security drills and exercises to coordinate response activities during a real maritime emergency/incident. The Coast Guard notifies partners of any upcoming High-Valued Assets entering the San Francisco Bay Area and coordinates maritime security measures with Neptune Coalition partners. These multi-agency, training, and event opportunities have facilitated a common agreement on very high frequency (VHF) communications protocol during events, led to understanding of different marine patrol capabilities, and established a basis for mutual aid and support across jurisdictions in the event of future incidents.

The Port of Oakland hosts Quarterly Security Meetings between the marine tenants, Oakland Police, Fire and Emergency response agencies, Coast Guard, Customs and Border Protection (CBP), and other local security and operations stakeholders. The purpose of these meetings is to identify local maritime area issues of concern including increased incidents of metal theft, access control and credentialing procedures, and to report on new initiatives that require revised procedures or agreements.

One example of positive outcome from these meetings was the determination of how to respond to reports of unaccounted for persons on the marine terminals. Cooperation between CBP, Oakland Police, and the marine terminals resulted in documented procedures to detain suspicious persons, compare identity against known terrorist watch lists, and proceed with a citation or an arrest for trespassing.

In addition to regular meetings of Port response stakeholders, it is important to document response requirements and expectations to ensure consistency of operations going forward. Toward that end, a Memorandum of Understanding (MOU) was established between the Oakland Police Department (OPD) and the Port of Oakland that establishes resource and operational requirements for both landside and waterside presence by OPD officers that is dependent upon the Maritime Security (MARSEC) level set by the local Coast Guard Captain of the Port. The MOU also details and documents the financial support from the Port to the police department for operational fuel costs.

The Port of Oakland and City of Oakland have also made efforts to leverage security system technology to enhance the patrol effectiveness of the Oakland Police Department. Through Port Security Grant funding, the Port of Oakland established a Port roadway video surveillance system. This system is used to monitor intermodal access points and provides the ability to remotely view vehicle activity in a particular area. It could be expanded to aid in the enforcement of designated routes to keep trucks out of the nearby West Oakland neighborhood. This capability will also be essential to any response involving a hazardous material spill or event, which precludes access to response resources. The system has been particularly helpful to OPD staff when used to monitor illegal street racing in the Port area at night, directing their patrol vehicles to specific locations to control the situation. Future security projects are being designed with the concept of interagency information sharing such as the surveillance system just described.

Regional Collaboration Efforts

The regional collaboration efforts of Bay Area mayors and local government officials began modestly in 2000 with agreement to draft a regional emergency plan using Urban Area Security Initiative funding (UASI). The process was a multi-year effort involving hundreds of stakeholders including local government, special districts, state agencies, non-profits, and private sector representatives to develop a comprehensive emergency coordination plan for the nine Bay Area counties.

The critical elements of the plan have the potential to be incorporated throughout the state with the cooperation of the California Governor's Office of Emergency Services.

Regional efforts intensified when the Bay Area Super Urban Area Security Initiative (SUASI) was created in January 2006 by federal government consolidation of the separate urban areas of San Francisco, Oakland, and San Jose, along with ten counties. The Bay Area SUASI also includes representatives from the Governor's Office of Emergency Services. Within its jurisdiction are 7 million people and over 100 incorporated cities. The Bay Area region attracts millions of visitors each year. In addition to the Port of Oakland, some of the nation's most notable landmarks are located in the Bay Area, as well as three international airports and six professional sports teams. In early January 2008, Mayor Dellums together with Mayor Gavin Newsom of San Francisco and Mayor Chuck Reed of San Jose held a press conference to roll out the UASI-funded Regional Emergency Coordination Plan (RECP).

The Bay Area SUASI is widely viewed as having an important, groundbreaking regional approach that is widely recognized and may be replicated throughout the state and across the country. The governance structure of the Bay Area SUASI recognizes the leadership and collaboration of the three UASI cities (Oakland, San Francisco, and San Jose) as well at the surrounding counties and the Governor's Office of Emergency Services – Coastal Region by the formation of an Approval Authority, which balances and coordinates local and regional planning efforts. Through strategic, well-defined, multi-year program plans, the Approval Authority builds on work that started with the Regional Emergency Coordination Plan and directs funding to projects that have regional impact.

The benefits of participation in the work of the Bay Area SUASI are tangible for the City of Oakland. Oakland's staff and management have provided leadership and local expertise to the planning efforts. Oakland has benefited from the opportunity to build solid working relationships with the network of resource organizations with whom we will respond during a catastrophic event. Participation in the on-going SUASI workgroups provides continuing opportunity to broaden and deepen relationships that are called upon on in everyday work and during an emergency. As national disasters such as Hurricane Katrina and 9/11 have demonstrated, regional collaboration in the event of a disaster is central to an effective response. Enhancing regional capability through regional collaboration is the fundamental goal of the SUASI program.

Regional Exercises and Skill Building

The City of Oakland and the Bay Area SUASI are committed to supporting homeland security exercises throughout the ten-county SUASI region. The exercise and evaluation program is an important component of emergency preparedness. Oakland's preparedness has been improved by successful participation in Urban Shield, Golden Guardian, and BayEx 2008 exercises. Exercising capabilities to prevent, respond to, mitigate, and recover from a terrorist or another kind of disaster is an essential part of the mission for public safety, health, and emergency management agencies. It is during these exercises that strengths are identified and shared as best practices. Gaps, needs, and weaknesses are identified and addressed to strengthen capabilities. Oakland is an active participant in a functional exercise coinciding with the 140th anniversary of the last catastrophic earthquake on the Hayward Fault in October 2008. The *Silver Sentinel* exercise recognizes that the damage from the next catastrophic earthquake will be extensive in the region and will require a regional response. SUASI funding has supported adding city-specific data building on existing data from the Hazards US (HAZUS), a nationally applicable standardized methodology Geographic Information System (GIS) software program that estimates potential losses from earthquakes, hurricane winds, and floods. The Federal Emergency Management Agency (FEMA), under contract with the National Institute of Building Sciences (NIBS), developed this software. Updated HAZUS information includes soil and building data for a more realistic determination of shake intensity in various sections of the city, damage to infrastructure and utilities, and estimated sheltering needs. On a regional level, updated information includes damages to hospitals, highways, and debris. Analysis of the data by first responders and emergency management staff will increase the realism of the situation as well as the likelihood of various response options. Oakland has reached out to local utilities, a major medical hospital employer, and the American Red Cross to participate in the City Emergency Operations Center. In addition, the city will participate in a regional Joint Information Center for coordination of public information with local, state, and possibly federal representatives.

The City of Oakland Medical Reserve Corps (MRC) is yet another example of regional leadership. Recently established to provide volunteer medical professionals and resources, Oakland's MRC will assist the City of Oakland and Alameda County Public Health with the distribution of mass prophylaxis in the event of bioterrorism or epidemic.

Maritime Interdiction Training

The Port of Oakland has been designated as the number two terrorist target in the state according to the SUASI project manager for the Infrastructure Protection working group. Recognizing the potential threat, six law enforcement teams from throughout the Bay Area SUASI Region received 2 weeks of intensive training in maritime interdiction. This marked the first time that the region has had formal maritime interdiction capability. The courses were designed to provide law enforcement personnel with the tools and techniques necessary to identify, intercept, and safely board non-compliant vessels at sea. The training was provided by veteran Navy Seals and was funded through the Bay Area SUASI. Having maritime interdiction capability greatly enhances our ability to protect against and respond to terrorism-related and other incidents in San Francisco Bay.

Real-Life Scenario: I-80 at I-580/I-880 Freeway Deck Collapse

On Sunday, April 29, 2007, at 3:44 a.m., a fuel tanker truck carrying over 8,000 gallons of fuel and traveling at excessive speeds on a major East Bay transportation corridor attempted to change lanes and overturned in a burst of flames. The fire sent heavy black smoke over the entire area. The heat of the fire melted the steel beams and bolts of the freeway structure, causing the roadbed to slip off its supports. Minutes later, the upper connector ramp buckled and collapsed on to the road below.

The two routes, bordering downtown Oakland and the city of Emeryville, make up a major transportation artery for 280,000 commuters a day and funnels traffic onto the Bay Bridge. Temporary road closures and rerouting of traffic resulted in a significant financial impact to the region. Regional transit planners estimated the economic loss from bridge fare tolls and round-the-clock efforts to clear the twisted wreckage and restore the structure cost the state of California an estimated $5.9 M.

Oakland and Emeryville Fire Departments responded immediately. Despite obstacles to accessing the incident site, including extreme heat, the actual area of the collapse, and unknown integrity of the surrounding structure, the incident was declared under control by 6:00 a.m. An Emergency Operations Center (EOC) was activated to coordinate efforts of the California Department of Transportation (Caltrans), Bay Area transit agencies, and other response teams to deal with immediate issues related to traffic engineering and detour design, cross agency transit coordination, and Oakland's Public Works Agency response (enhanced signage, lane restriping, barricade replacement, traffic signal retiming, etc.). Real-time, technology-enhanced impact identification and the ability to track and monitor conditions and changes resulted in maintained mobility for Bay Area residents and businesses for the duration of the emergency.

Caltrans made repairing the interchange a top-level priority and a contract for the construction work was fast-tracked. The structure was repaired and reopened in a record 25 days.

Real-Life Scenarios: Loma Prieta Earthquake and Oakland Hills Fire

In October 1989, a magnitude 7.1 earthquake struck the Oakland/San Francisco Bay Area at the start of the evening rush hour and just before the third game of the World Series at Candlestick Park. The worst since the infamous 1906 quake, this tremor collapsed a section of the San Francisco–Oakland Bay Bridge and stranded thousands of commuters. Damage was estimated at almost 3 billion dollars in San Francisco alone, which was approximately one-half of the total damage figure for the entire earthquake zone (Fig. 10.3).

On October 20, 1991, a devastating fire occurred in the scenic hills above the cities of Oakland and Berkeley, California. Burning embers carried by high winds from the perimeter of a small but growing brush fire ignited overgrown vegetation

Fig. 10.3 Freeway collapse after 1989 Loma Prieta earthquake

Fig. 10.4 Oakland Hills fire, 1991

and led to the further ignition of trees and combustible construction materials of adjacent homes. The result was a major wildland/urban interface fire that killed 25 people, including a police officer and a firefighter; injured 150, destroyed nearly 2,449 single-family homes and 437 apartment and condominium units; burned over 1,600 acres, and caused an estimated $1.5 billion in damage (Fig. 10.4).

Response by public safety agencies to the Oakland Hills fire and communities devastated by the Loma Prieta earthquake was massive and swift. In both instances, however, the efforts of responding public safety agencies were hampered by the inability of the initial on-scene responders to establish effective perimeters around the catastrophe areas. Additionally, and more importantly, coordination by incident command staff was significantly hampered by the inability to directly communicate with mutual aid public safety agencies arriving from around the state.

Enabling Technologies

Technology plays a critical role in disaster preparedness and effective response. As we learned from the Oakland Hills fire and the response breakdowns of 9/11, coordinating technology resources between public safety agencies and other partners is vital in bringing coordinated, cohesive, and timely response in critical situations.

The City of Oakland has long recognized the significance and importance of enabling technologies and effective use of various tools and techniques in public safety. In addition to the local technology projects, Oakland has also played an important and active role in local, state, and national technology initiatives, from developing the regional crime data sharing applications to building interoperable communication systems. There are numerous active technology projects in Oakland, where we are sharing our skills, human capital, infrastructure resources, and knowledge with the other Bay Area regional partners. Our goal is to use the proven technology to bring efficiency in government, improve public safety, reduce crime, and enhance quality of life for Oakland residents. As part of Oakland's model city initiative, we are implementing a number of "public safety districts," a unique service delivery model to bring all city agencies together in the effort to improve community safety and enhance quality of life.

Interoperable Communications

Voice interoperability and data sharing is a primary concern and identified gap with first responders in the Bay Area who are challenged with protecting the region's 7 million residents. As with urban areas across the nation, the fragmented assignment of radio frequencies and the lack of public safety communications standards during the population growth of the 1970s and 1980s have resulted in a patchwork of disparate voice and data communications networks on both sides of the Bay. Prior experiences with incompatible radio frequencies during emergency operations have highlighted the need for interoperability for both the Oakland and San Francisco Metropolitan Statistical Areas (MSA). Public safety agencies throughout both jurisdictions have experienced situations where tactical officers were unable to communicate with one another during high-risk encounters, placing personnel in unnecessary danger. Further, incompatible communication systems negate the ability of public safety agencies to work in a cooperative atmosphere or respond to calls for mutual aid. Coupled with disparate frequencies, the respective agencies are unable to share information, data, or intelligence in "real-time" during exigent circumstances.

Since 1989, when the Project 25 interoperable digital two-way wireless communications standard was still a concept, Oakland has been working collaboratively with the Bay Area Rapid Transit (BART) and many neighboring cities. We have been advocating for interoperability standards, developing partnerships, and seeking technological solutions to achieve it. Today, Oakland is an active partner of Bay Area Regional Interoperable Communication System (BayRICS), working with the leadership of the City of San Francisco and many neighboring counties and cities to achieve the goal of a seamless P25 network build-out in the urban areas that will be expanded to include all ten Bay Area counties in the SUASI area. The vision of the SUASI is to provide seamless roaming and connecting various public safety networks throughout the Bay Area, up through the I-80 Corridor and into the Sacramento Valley. This initiative provides our first responders with the ability to communicate with other cities and counties across the Bay Area, further improving the way our emergency teams can respond.

Data Sharing, Reporting, and Analysis Strategies

Today, public safety agencies rely heavily upon the availability of real-time, reliable, and accurate digital and voice information. Newly deployed field-based data collection and reporting systems are becoming essential tools in crime fighting and mission critical in protecting communities. Public safety agencies are recognizing the need to share information, not only in day-to-day activities among their departments but also with their neighbors and other outside agencies for those situations requiring a multi-agency and multi-jurisdictional response. Data sharing will ensure that all cooperating agencies are aware of any threats, persons, trends, or conditions that may exist. However, there are very few standards-based, user-friendly systems in place today that can easily enable information sharing among jurisdictions in an effective manner. Data sharing systems will assist with efficient deployment of resources by more accurately pinpointing anomalies upon which law enforcement can focus its response.

Currently the Oakland Police Department is confronting an inability to sift through the massive amounts of information maintained in several, unconnected databases to discover the critical facts that could make a difference in crime prevention and effective enforcement. A potential solution to this problem is use of the ComStat (COMputer analysis of crime STATistics), a sophisticated data integration and reporting system, which has been used in several major cities resulting in a dramatic downturn in crime once it was implemented. ComStat allows for geographic responsibility to be applied with weekly meetings using mapping information to address crime trends in particular areas. ComStat can provide a single platform that instantaneously sifts through large amounts of information producing data driven law enforcement strategies.

Acoustic Sensor and Image-Processing Technologies

In last few decades, sensor technologies have made significant improvements in accuracy and reliability, and perfectly fulfill many public safety requirements. Applications such as video surveillance, airborne video, gunshot locator systems Radio Frequency Identification (RFID), Infra Red imaging, biometric sensors, license plate recognition, and mesh-based wireless networks are available to commercial markets for mass deployment. These various sensor and transport technologies are emerging as helpful tools for public safety personnel.

Oakland adopted Gun Detection and Location System (ShotSpotter) technology at a very early stage and has it currently deployed in a targeted 6 square mile area. Implemented throughout the city's highest crime areas, these acoustic sensors detect and locate gunshots in seconds, sending critical data, and enabling police to arrive on the scene of a gunshot event far more quickly.

Similarly, using image-processing technology, we have deployed a fleet of police vehicles equipped with an automatic License Plate Recognition (LPR) system to identify vehicles by their license plates. The system has been well received by the Police Department and has assisted in the retrieval of stolen vehicles and apprehending criminals. Although the mobile LPR units have proven to be successful, implementation of fixed units in high crime areas to augment these mobile units will increase the overall visibility. LPR technology can also be used by the Port to track and monitor vehicles as they enter and exit the terminals.

Surveillance Camera Technologies

In an effort to reduce crime, the City of Oakland, in partnership with private entities, has a limited deployment of security cameras throughout the city. Leveraging the deployment of a broadband wireless network, the city intends to expand the use of this technology to provide a cohesive electronic video surveillance system.

In a disaster scenario, surveillance cameras allow public safety personnel to survey damage and plan an appropriate response to the incident via the utilization of live video. In the event of a toxic chemical or gas disaster, the cameras and live video allow responders to determine the inner and outer perimeters of the hazard area. Live video also enables responders to plan access and evacuation routes, reduces risk to personnel and equipment, and can be shared by collaborating emergency response agencies in the event of critical incidents.

Oakland's Citywide Broadband Wireless Initiative

Broadband wireless access is becoming an essential part of today's mobile society. The new wave of wireless handheld devices and mobile phones necessitate a broadband wireless infrastructure. Many municipalities are also coming to rely on wireless infrastructure to improve a host of services to their citizens.

The My Citywide Broadband Wireless Initiative in Oakland will provide access to the Internet, assisting the community, businesses, and schools as well as government. The broadband wireless network provides mobility and secures high-speed access to critical information resources to police and fire personnel. The potential for increasing the use of wireless applications by Public Safety personnel that heavily depend upon the Wi-Fi technology infrastructure is enormous:

- Police and Fire field-based reporting, replacing handwritten reports, and paper tracking
- Traffic citations in the field, directly transmitted to the Court
- Video surveillance and monitoring of critical infrastructure, crime areas, and incident sites
- Mobile command and control center for effective field response
- Gunshot locator with video
- Crime mapping/GIS reports for tactical planning and field response
- Field-based personnel systems reporting for resource management and field deployment
- Mugshots
- In-car video streaming to the command center
- Real-time crime alerts
- Messaging/e-mails
- Scheduling and time reporting

Vision for the Future – Resources and Funding

Port and City of Oakland Integrated Monitoring and Coordination System

There are several federal, state, and local drivers, combined with various grant funding programs, that are encouraging the city and Port of Oakland to expand and integrate landside domain awareness with what has been established in the waterside domain. This increased domain awareness, when combined with situation analytics and reporting, environmental monitoring, actionable intelligence, and state of the art dispatching, communications, and coordinating technology, will result in vastly improved readiness to prevent, respond, and recover from major events in the Oakland region and ensure better multi-agency coordination across the larger

San Francisco Bay area. The requirements of the Maritime Transportation Security Act of 2002 are to establish a security focus on regulated marine terminals and vessels that call on those terminals. The only regional collaboration that was mandated in that Act was the establishment of the Area Maritime Security Committee, which is essentially a policy-focused group that is a forum for public/private interaction on maritime security issues.

The SAFE Port Act expands that initial, single point port security focus and requires ten Coast Guard Captains of the Port zones to establish Interagency Operations Centers (IOC). The IOC's will have the capability to facilitate routine operational planning between agencies, the ability to monitor current Port activities comparing them with the planned and normal events, and the authority to initiate a coordinated initial response to an incident. To accomplish this involvement and awareness requires sharing information and intelligence, creating a common risk picture/common operating picture, and transparently integrating the day-to-day maritime security business practices and operational activities across echelons of government and industry.

What will be needed in the future is a true integration and coordination of private industry operations with public prevention and response resources and command and control capability that will significantly reduce the risk of incidents in the Marine Transportation System. To address this concern, a Port Coordination Center will bring together the various perimeter intrusion detection systems, smart surveillance systems, asset tracking systems and environmental monitoring systems, and will enhance situational awareness for the entire Port area. This increased awareness will improve threat analysis and enhance response coordination. The Port Coordination Center would also be the focal point for increased tempo of operations in response to an incident, facilitating a common operating picture, and actionable information for responsible agencies and decision makers. This concept, once established in the Port of Oakland, could be expanded to the rest of the San Francisco Bay Area to include the Ports of San Francisco, Richmond, and Stockton in addition to the vital private industry infrastructure along the waterways. This Bay Area wide security system would provide redundancy and alternatives for operations coordination, and greatly facilitate recovery operations in the event that an incident impacts an entire Port area.

In addition to the on-going efforts at the Port of Oakland, the Bay Area SUASI, City of Oakland, and the Oakland Police Department (OPD), these entities are increasingly being tasked with finding ways to improve efficiency and risk management through the use of technology. As the city and region build capability to meet these demands, additional specialized space will be required. The combination of a maritime monitoring and coordination center with the City of Oakland's interagency, landside monitoring, and coordination center could have great potential and benefits in protecting the people and the critical infrastructure in both the city and the Port area.

The build-out of an Urban Integrated Systems Monitoring Center in existing and currently underutilized OPD space will satisfy many of the surveillance and response needs in a centralized secure facility. The monitoring facility will be used to manage the following projects:

- Monitoring of existing and proposed public CCTV systems in city and Port areas
- Monitoring of vulnerable infrastructure, existing semi-private and other-governmental systems related to the management of special events and public safety that include
- The Coliseum
- Port of Oakland
- BART
- City-funded cameras on problem liquor establishments
- Potential for monitoring key locations during a pandemic influenza such as the exterior of hospitals in case of medical surge
- Potential for monitoring CBRNE Detection devices
- Traffic management
- Emergency operations and the City's Emergency Operations Center (EOC) backup
- Disaster response
- Criminal investigations
- OPD in-car video
- Red light electronic enforcement and monitoring
- Basic police response to emergency calls for service
- Covert police response and investigation into emerging crime
- Electronic monitoring of high-risk parolees and probationers
- LPR monitoring
- Management and monitoring of the "ShotSpotter" system

Oakland's Police Department, Fire Department, Department of Information Technology, the Office of Emergency Services, the Port of Oakland, and Transportation Services have all expressed interest in participating in this collaborative project. The increased awareness and coordination resulting from this collaboration will improve threat analysis and enhance response coordination for our region. The project will further the Bay Area SUASI's position as a front-runner in the use of technology to improve government efficiency, the environment, and public safety for it citizens.

There are many challenges for the city and Port of Oakland, but the benefits of establishing a capability to monitor and coordinate information sharing and threat detection information between industry and response agencies, across the entire Port area, are well worth the effort and expense. The on-going costs to maintain and operate this system should be borne by the participating and affected stakeholders. These efforts will enhance awareness of threats, more accurately pinpoint suspicious behavior and activity, and enable the rapid deployment of appropriate resources to prevent, respond, or recover from large-scale incidents.

Contributors

The following individuals also contributed to this chapter:

- Daphne Markham
- Ahsan Baig
- Paul Martin
- Kathleen Crawford
- Marilyn Sandifur
- Roberto Bernardo
- Ron Yelder
- Renee Domingo
- Chris Peterson
- Trina Barton

Notes

1. AAPA North America Port Container Traffic 2007 (represents total loaded and empty containers and includes those moving in domestic and foreign trade).
2. Paul R. Martin, USCG Sector San Francisco.

Chapter 11
Innovative Anti-terror Information Sharing: Maryland's Federal, State, and Local Partnership Model

Robert L. Ehrlich

Abstract Maryland created the first fusion center which collects and analyzes disparate data or information to try to "connect the dots" to prevent acts of terrorism. The public is encouraged to provide information through a "tip line." The Center has federal, state, local, and private sector participation representing 250 agencies or organizations. The Maryland Center is led by members of all three levels of government. A principal objective of such a fusion center is to develop a pattern of cooperation and information sharing.

Introduction

I was in my office on Capitol Hill when terrorists struck the World Trade Center and the Pentagon. As a four-term member of the United States House of Representatives, I stood with my staff and watched the tragedy unfold on live television. But I also viewed the horrific events of that day through the eyes of an American citizen whose Nation was under attack. For many Americans, the shock seemed like it would never fade. However, over the weeks and months that followed, something changed. The grief of the Nation gradually transformed itself into resolve. United we stood. Citizens across the Nation rediscovered their passion for the freedoms that America represents. Patriotism was rekindled. Federal, state, and local leaders pledged to take whatever steps were necessary to prevent such an attack from ever happening again.

Fourteen months later in 2002, I was elected Governor of the State of Maryland.

Partnerships Produce Results

The protection of Maryland citizens has been a top priority for my administration from day 1. Public safety stands as one of the five pillars of my administration — the roadmap, which guides our efforts to make Maryland a cleaner, safer, more

R.L. Ehrlich (✉)
Governor, The State of Maryland, (2003–2007)
e-mail: mdmanual@mdarchives.state.md.us

S. Hakim, E.A. Blackstone (eds.), *Safeguarding Homeland Security*,
DOI 10.1007/978-1-4419-0371-6_11, © Springer Science+Business Media, LLC 2009

prosperous place to live. Protecting people and property from the threat of terrorism is a significant part of these efforts. In 2003, I created the Governor's Office of Homeland Security (GOHS) to develop a continuous, cost-effective, and sustainable approach to homeland security. By leveraging federal, state, and local security assets, as well as coordinating with private sector initiatives, GOHS has played a key role in making Maryland safer today.

We must, however, share the credit for our successes. Maryland's significant achievements in homeland security, in addition to our day-to-day operations in this area, would not be possible without the coordinated efforts of our federal, local, and private sector partners. In January 2003, during my first State of the State Address to the Maryland General Assembly, I spoke of the importance of principled cooperation in the legislative process. My message that day was that great achievements could be made in critical policy areas if we embrace the spirit of cooperation. The theory has applications beyond lawmaking. For example, in combating terrorism, cooperation across jurisdictional, institutional and disciplinary lines leads to otherwise unobtainable gains. One clear example of how principled cooperation works in practice to protect Maryland citizens from the threat of terrorism is the Maryland Coordination and Analysis Center (the "MCAC" or the "Center").

Fusion Centers: A New Approach to Information Sharing

The MCAC is indicative of the innovative approaches the State of Maryland has taken to homeland security operations since I took office. When the MCAC opened in November 2003, it was the first fusion center established in the United States. According to the federal Department of Homeland Security (DHS), 38 fusion centers are currently in operation across the Nation, and more are in the planning stages.[1]

What is a Fusion Center?

One post-9/11 focus of the law enforcement and intelligence communities has been on developing new approaches that improve information sharing between organizations – specifically, the sharing of information relating to threats of terrorism. The advent of fusion centers (so named for their core function to integrate or *fuse* threat information from multiple sources) is one example of this new approach that has proved extremely effective in these efforts.

One of the innovative features of fusion centers is that they bring together representatives from separate federal, state, and local entities, often under one roof, to engage and assist one another in achieving a shared purpose: to combat terrorism. Another term used for this bringing together of different entities is called integration.

We have learned since 9/11 that providing a setting where federal, state, and local law enforcement can share information with each other is critical to defending against terrorist threats. However, it is important to note that this process should not be limited to only law enforcement agencies. The bringing together of entities from across many different disciplines (e.g., health and medical or environmental agencies) for the purpose of information sharing is also valuable. This so-called horizontal integration is another significant advantage in establishing a fusion center because the early indications or initial clues of a terror plot may lie in the hands of non-law enforcement entities. Fusion centers provide a forum for non-law enforcement partners to openly, effectively, and securely communicate with law enforcement about matters relating to potential terror threats.

The notion that this approach would bring improved results stemmed from the painful lessons learned 5 years ago. Before 9/11, the terrorism intelligence community was close-knit and largely focused at the federal level. Over the past several years, intelligence activity aimed at preventing acts of terrorism has been evolving into more of a joint effort and common mission among interdisciplinary federal, state, and local partners. This new approach makes sense. These partners share common interests and therefore have a shared responsibility to protect those interests. It logically follows that the most effective way to maximize the protection of these shared assets is through the sharing of resources.

What Do Fusions Centers Do?

As I mentioned above, fusion centers are named for what they do. But why is it necessary or beneficial to fuse information relating to terror threats? The benefit lies in the comparative value of the fused information. Fused intelligence is more actionable (i.e., valuable) than the separate data used to create it. Simply stated, the fused outflow is more useful for thwarting potential attacks than the separate informational inflow. A metaphor will help to illustrate how the fusion process adds value by transforming a collection of separate items into one single more useable product.

In science, fusion is the act of liquefying or melting by the application of heat.[2] Picture a saucepan resting upon a source of heat. Now add a cup of sugar and a tablespoon of water to the pan. At first, there is little change to the contents of the pan – it is now simply thousands of damp sugar crystals. But over time, with heat and a little stirring, the water and crystals lose their individual and separate characteristics to take a new combined form as a single puddle of liquid sugar. If you know your confections, you know that with more heat and more time, the transformation continues to eventually produce delicious caramel – a much more appetizing (i.e., useful) product than its separate components of sugar, water, and heat.

Returning to the topic of terrorism, the ingredients with which fusion centers work everyday are individual and sometimes seemingly unrelated bits of information. These data can come from numerous different sources such as partner agencies, law enforcement, citizen tips and even public sources of information such as the Internet. The data are then integrated or fused by professional analysts into products that are more useful than their individual components. In simplified terms, the process of fusion transforms disjointed and otherwise unhelpful information into a more valuable and more actionable intelligence product.

Case Study: Part 1

The MCAC is Maryland's fusion center. To understand how the MCAC protects citizens by preventing terrorist attacks, consider this fictional but not unlikely scenario.

London, England – August 2006

British law enforcement agents arrest and charge a man with plotting to carry out a terrorist attack against the Chunnel – the 31-mile tunnel beneath the English Channel, which connects Great Britain and France. In the course of the investigation, authorities learn from the suspect that similar attacks are being planned against unnamed US targets. During the search of the suspect's London flat, hundreds of items are seized. One of these items is a small piece of paper on which is written a man's name and a United States phone number, but no other information. Following protocols, which have become routine for local law enforcement since 9/11, the information on the piece of paper is immediately relayed to British intelligence officials.

According to the findings of the 9/11 Commission, law enforcement and intelligence agencies failed to "connect the dots" which could potentially have allowed authorities to uncover the specifics of the hijackers' plot before the attacks were carried out. In Part 2, we will revisit this scenario to detail what happens next and how the MCAC facilitates the connecting of dots today to thwart potential terrorist attacks in Maryland and elsewhere.

An Overview of the MCAC

Bolstered by the support of my administration, the founding of the MCAC in 2003 was made possible by the coordinated and cooperative efforts of an unprecedented federal, state, and local partnership. To this day, cooperation continues to provide the operational backbone of the Center. The MCAC is staffed around the clock by personnel from the Center's diverse group of partners such as law enforcement, the US Military, first responders, Maryland National Guard, state transportation agencies, and state public health agencies, to name a few. These dedicated men and women sit side by side, putting their significant combined experience to work to further the mission of the Center.

Brief History

In the immediate wake of 9/11, US Attorney General John Ashcroft declared the fight against terrorism to be the "first and overriding priority" of the Department of

Justice.[3] Each of the 93 US Attorney Offices[4] was directed to establish an umbrella organization of local, state, and federal agencies responsible for coordinating activities, developing policies, and implementing strategic plans which combat terrorism within its district. The directive further required these organizations, known today as Anti-Terrorism Advisory Councils (ATACs),[5] to be established by and placed under the leadership of an experienced career federal prosecutor.

The ATAC[6] has four organizational objectives, which are served and advanced by a corresponding functional component. The four objectives of the ATAC are the following:

1. To facilitate intelligence and information sharing among federal, state, and local authorities, as well as with relevant private sector participants. (Intelligence and Information-Sharing component);
2. To prevent and disrupt terrorism activity within the State through aggressive investigation and prosecution. (Investigation and Prosecution component);
3. To assure that the organizational structure and plans exist to effectively plan for, and respond to, any future terrorist incidents in the State (Emergency Preparedness and Response component);
4. To provide relevant training to its members in order to better equip them to perform their anti-terrorism responsibilities more effectively (Training component).

The ATAC is comprised of an equally large and diverse number of participating agencies. ATAC membership includes federal, state, and local agencies working in law enforcement, fire/rescue, public health and emergency planning/management organizations, as well as representatives from the military, intelligence, and private sectors. As of this writing, over 250 agencies or entities have joined the ATAC – clear and convincing evidence of the truly collaborative efforts involved in combating terrorism in the State of Maryland.

Mission

The MCAC is the intelligence and information-sharing component of the ATAC. The MCAC is a 24/7 operation, which collects, analyzes, and integrates myriad pieces of information collected from a variety of public and private sources. These data are then reformatted into products, which are more usable and intelligible than they were when the data existed separately. The MCAC then distributes these products to any number of the appropriate governmental and non-governmental partners of the Center.

The MCAC is principally, but not solely, dedicated to combating terrorism within the State of Maryland. The MCAC has a well-developed network of contacts with other fusion centers throughout the United States. Occasions arise where threat information relating to another state or region is obtained by or flowed through MCAC. In these situations, the MCAC will immediately contact the out-of-state jurisdiction and the appropriate national entity (e.g., the National Operations Center, the National Counterterrorism Center, the Transportation Security Administration Operations Center, FBI CT Watch, or the Terrorist Screening Center) to share the threat information and offer any requested assistance. The information sharing flows both ways. The MCAC provides other states and federal entities with a single point of contact to receive threat information, which relates to Maryland. The MCAC is then able to immediately disseminate the information to the appropriate local jurisdiction for investigation and offer any requested assistance.

In addition to producing and disseminating intelligence products to its public and private partners across the State and Region, the Center is constantly re-analyzing existing intelligence and products for changes or emerging trends. Although the MCAC is closely tied to the FBI's Joint Terrorism Task Force (JTTF) and its Field Intelligence Group (FIG), the Center is not an investigative body. The MCAC's focus is on filling the analytical gaps such as those which the 9/11 Commission brought to light in its report. In the terms used by the 9/11 Commission, the MCAC connects dots.

The MCAC's mission is primarily related to preventing potential acts of terrorism. However, persons or organizations whose aim is to carry out acts of terror are often involved in other non-terrorism-related crimes and the lines between the two are not always clear. Therefore, the MCAC has the capability and is often called upon to analyze information relating to general crimes such as violent or drug-related felonies. Often, these circumstances arise when a partner agency has requested the assistance of the MCAC in one of their ongoing investigations. Regardless of the subject matter involved, the MCAC operates to support, not supplant, the efforts of statewide law enforcement, public health, and homeland security organizations.

Organizational Structure

The MCAC has two main sections, which contribute to its efforts: the Watch Section and the Strategic Analysis Section (SAS). The two sections have distinct, but complementary functions which serve to further the overall mission of the MCAC.

The Watch Section

The MCAC Watch Section operates 24 h a day, 7 days a week, and is currently staffed by representatives from numerous different federal, state, and local agencies.[7] The Watch Section's core functions are as follows:

a. To receive and process tips regarding suspicious persons or activity;
b. To receive and process agency or organization requests for information (RFIs);
c. To monitor all available intelligence resources for significant or high profile events in order to determine the impact the event may have upon the State;
d. To coordinate Maryland law enforcement resources;
e. To disseminate and communicate intelligence information to federal, state, and local entities.

Information can flow into the Watch Section from any one of several sources outside the MCAC or can be collected on their own initiative by analysts within the Center. These inputs can originate from public heath agencies, first responders, emergency management agencies, law enforcement, the military, or even the general public. Informational data can come by fax, by e-mail, or by telephone.

The Strategic Analysis Section

The MCAC Strategic Analysis Section (SAS) is overseen by a Supervisory Special Agent (SSA), who is also the supervisor of the FBI's Field Intelligence Group. The SAS Commander leads a group of trained intelligence analysts representing the broad array of federal, state, and local partners as are utilized throughout the MCAC.[8]

The mission of the SAS is to harmonize or "fuse" information and intelligence products from numerous public and private sources. This process also allows for duplicate or contradictory information to be identified for clarification. The priorities of the SAS reflect the general priorities of the MCAC – to engage in activities that enhance homeland security and, wherever possible, disrupt the activities of those engaged in planning or carrying out acts of terrorism within the State and the Nation. The SAS may also become involved in analyzing criminal activity that may not appear, at first blush, to be terrorism related (e.g., violent or drug crimes) because these crimes sometimes have a nexus to the individuals or organizations engaged in terrorist activity.

The professional analysts in the SAS are trained to identify trends or patterns in often seemingly unrelated events or criminal activity occurring in the State of Maryland. These patterns can either be trends of activity occurring within the State that are specific only to Maryland, or they can be evidence of national trends manifesting themselves in Maryland for the first time. The MCAC's comprehensive network of contacts is well equipped to handle either situation. In the former instance, the SAS can draft an intelligence bulletin for distribution to the MCAC's statewide partners alerting them to the pattern of activity. In the latter instance, the MCAC is able to immediately share the intelligence with the appropriate national homeland security or law enforcement partners, as well as fusion centers in other states.

The Role of the Public

The public also plays a key role in homeland security in Maryland. Citizens carrying out their daily routines are often the most capable eyes and ears for noticing suspicious activity. To facilitate the communication between citizens and the MCAC, a toll-free telephone number (the "TIPS line") has been established for use by anyone wishing to report suspicious activity directly to the Watch Section. The general public has been educated about the TIPS line through various means such as by prominent placement on certain state web sites and display of the number upon electronic sign boards mounted above Maryland's major highways. Also, anyone can e-mail a tip to the Center through links, which have been prominently placed on certain state web sites (e.g., http://www.gov.state.md.us/homelandsecurity.html).

Products

Information about potential threats is of limited utility if it is not disseminated to the appropriate partners who are in a position to investigate or take further action on the item. The Watch Section and SAS produce and distribute numerous products to their partners, which allow the recipient (e.g., local law enforcement agencies) to be informed about potential threats that may affect their jurisdiction.

The Center's comprehensive distribution channels are also utilized by its partners to quickly disseminate information about a time-sensitive threat or emergency situation. For example, a local jurisdiction may report a suspect vehicle it has lost visual contact with in hopes that the vehicle may be sighted traveling through a neighboring jurisdiction.

A non-exhaustive list of MCAC products includes the following items:

a. *Daily Watch Reports* – A daily summary of calls received through the TIPS line over the previous 24-h period is distributed to all of the MCAC's law enforcement partners. This enables all partner agencies to remain up-to-date on all security-related issues within the State. In addition, when circumstances warrant, these reports are distributed to any non-law enforcement entities that could be affected by an item in the report (e.g., a state health or transportation agency, or even a certain shopping mall).

b. *Suspect Reports* – Law enforcement agencies will occasionally contact the Watch Section requesting information about a suspect or a person the agency wishes to locate. The person often has connection to an ongoing investigation. The Watch Section has developed working relationships with federal, state, and local agencies that allow analysts in the Center to quickly obtain information from these partners that may be either unobtainable by the requestor or significantly delayed without the assistance of the MCAC. This product is a written report, which is hand delivered to the requestors seeking information about the person of interest.

c. *Bulletins and Alerts* – The MCAC Watch Section serves as an efficient and effective disseminator of public safety/homeland security products such as BOLOs ("be on the lookouts"), missing person reports (e.g., Amber Alerts), and alerts relating to officer safety issues. The MCAC's established and open lines of communication with its nationwide network of public and private partners make for an extremely powerful communications tool that can be used to instantly reach out across the state, region, and the Nation.

d. *Event Threat Assessments* – The MCAC continually monitors the calendar for public events, which could be targets of terrorist attacks. International or domestic terror groups may choose a particular event for its political significance, degree of press coverage, or simply because of the number of people expected to attend. The SAS will monitor intelligence sources for indications that a particular event may be subject to increased risk for any reason. A report is generated and distributed to all the jurisdictions or partners who may be connected to the event.

Governance and Leadership

Any organization whose responsibility includes protection of citizens should be led by a group of dedicated and principled individuals whose commitment to their mission never wavers. The group providing this leadership for the MCAC is the Executive Committee of the ATAC of Maryland. The members of the Executive Committee, which serves as the Center's governing body, are chief executives from 16 different federal, state, and local law enforcement and non-law enforcement organizations. The Committee is chaired by a senior Assistant United States Attorney (AUSA) appointed by the US Attorney to serve as the ATAC Coordinator.

Beyond the policy decisions made by the Executive Committee, there are day-to-day operations of the Center, which also require strong and dedicated leadership. To carry out these operational duties, the Executive Committee appoints a Director and two Assistant Directors who serve 18-month terms. It is the policy of the Executive Committee to fill the three leadership positions with representatives from one federal, one state, and one local jurisdiction.

The MCAC also has a dedicated Chief of Information Technology under contract to handle the technology, network, and equipment aspects of the operation. Operating largely behind the scenes, the IT Section has two primary functions critical to the continued operations of the Center. First, it is responsible for protecting the integrity of the digital information held by the MCAC. Protection of data is not only critical for preventing outsiders from gaining unauthorized access to MCAC data. The IT Section is also responsible for performing frequent backups to prevent catastrophic data loss due to fire or flood in the Center. Research and development is the second primary function of the IT Section. The Section is constantly exploring new hardware and software products in the marketplace, which could enhance the efficiency or effectiveness of the MCAC.

One clear value of having numerous agencies represented at the MCAC is the pool of experienced and qualified individuals that are available to fill the operational leadership positions. For example, the current Director overseeing the Center is a Captain in the Baltimore County Police Department, one of Maryland's major local law enforcement agencies. The Assistant Director in command of the Watch Section is a Lieutenant in the Maryland State Police. The Assistant Director serving as the SAS Commander is a Supervisory Special Agent (SSA) of the FBI. These individuals bring a wealth of professional experience and skill to the Center, which provide valuable guidance and learning opportunities for other staff members, thus enhancing the overall efficiency and effectiveness of the MCAC.

Case Study: Part 2

Now that we have examined the working components of the MCAC, let us take a look at how they function by returning to the hypothetical terrorist plot introduced earlier in this chapter. Recall that the investigation by British authorities revealed that the plot possibly extends to unknown US targets and that the search of the suspect's London apartment uncovered a piece of paper with a US telephone number written on it.

Baltimore, Maryland – October 2006

A Maryland woman is driving on her daily commute home from work. She passes a car parked in the breakdown lane near the opening of the Fort McHenry Tunnel – an eight-lane portion of I-95 where the highly traveled interstate crosses Baltimore Harbor.

As she is driving, the woman sees a man crouching next to his vehicle holding a camcorder. He appears to be videotaping the tunnel. When the man realizes that she is looking at him, he quickly tucks the camera into his coat and pretends to be inspecting his tire. For a moment, the woman ponders what she just saw, and then remembers the overhead electronic sign board she passes on the same stretch of road ten times every week. She has never given much thought to the sign before now, but its image is clear in her mind. The sign reads: "To Report Suspicious Activity, Call 1-800-492-TIPS."

She dials the number on her cell phone and immediately is connected to the MCAC Watch Section.

Following protocol, Watch Section personnel contact the law enforcement agency with primary jurisdiction over the Fort McHenry Tunnel – the Maryland Transportation Authority Police (MdTAP). The Watch Section relays the information reported by the woman such as the plate number and description of the vehicle and the individual she saw. Officers on patrol of Interstate 95 immediately begin attempting to locate the vehicle. Meanwhile, the Watch Section has also contacted the on-call investigator at the Threat Squad of the Joint Terrorism Task Force (JTTF).[9] This results in the assignment of a JTTF investigator who will follow up with MdTAP about the incident.

As it turns out, an MdTAP patrol officer locates the vehicle and conducts a brief field investigation. During the roadside interview, the man states that he is an architectural student interested in the construction of the tunnel. The officer records the subject's name, address, and local contact information. The officer also notes that the man reports that he is studying architecture at Towson University. The man is sent on his way. When the JTTF investigator contacts the MdTAP officer, the officer reports all of the information she collected from the subject.

The Value of the MCAC's Information-Sharing Function

I stated earlier that information not shared is of minimal value. Parts 1 and 2 of the case study demonstrate two important benefits of the MCAC, which illustrate this point.

First, the MCAC facilitates valuable connections between state or local law enforcement officers and the federal entities, which are charged with disrupting terrorist activities. For example, by simultaneously contacting the JTTF and the MdTAP about the taping of the tunnel, the MCAC prompted action by both agencies, which directly led to the exchange of information between them about the incident.

A second and equally important benefit of the MCAC is that it promotes and facilitates better citizen involvement in combating terrorism. The establishment of a 24-h a day TIPS line enables citizens to immediately report suspicious activity to professionals who are trained to interpret it. It is important to note that the TIPS Line is not intended to prevent citizens from utilizing the local 911 system to report an emergency situation. The Watch Section's protocols call for immediate contact of local law enforcement partners whenever the circumstances surrounding the tip warrant. The value of the MCAC is the additional support and terrorism-related expertise it can provide to local law enforcement agencies. Had the woman motorist simply called 911 instead of 1-800-492-TIPS, the MdTAP may still have been dispatched to the scene, but the connection between the MdTAP and the JTTF might not have been timely made, if at all, and information about the incident would not have been shared between them.

Part 3 of the case study will provide another, and perhaps the most dramatic, example of how information sharing facilitated by the MCAC leads directly to the prevention of terrorism in Maryland.

Case Study: Part 3

So far, we have examined two separate incidents, which occurred 2 months and 3,600 miles apart – a thwarted terror attack in London and an architectural student studying a tunnel in Maryland. Investigators in both cases have collected numerous pieces of physical and informational evidence. Beyond the fact that both incidents involve tunnels, there is no clear connection between the two investigations. The dots do not make sense.

After speaking with the MdTAP officer, the JTTF requests assistance from the MCAC in confirming the information the man taping the tunnel gave to MdTAP officers. Utilizing its statewide contacts and resources, the MCAC learns from Towson University officials that the man is not listed as a current or former student.

The architectural student's contact information is also flowed through the analysts working in the SAS. Following protocols, MCAC shares the information from the roadside stop with its partners within the state, federal, and even international intelligence community. It is determined that the subject's telephone number is identical to the one British Intelligence has passed to the US Government from the search of the London apartment. This student's information is immediately relayed to the JTTF investigator who reports her findings to her supervisor at the FBI.

Effective sharing of information includes coordination among federal agencies as well. Pursuant to the US Attorney General Guidelines, the FBI contacts the US

Attorney's Office to discuss the facts of the investigation and what next steps are appropriate. At this point, two of the options for proceeding are to conduct further investigation or to initiate a federal prosecution. The file is assigned to an Assistant US Attorney who immediately begins to provide legal assistance to the investigative team as they explore whatever legal options are available.

A potential plot to attack the Fort McHenry Tunnel in Baltimore has been uncovered as a direct result of information sharing facilitated through the MCAC. Principled cooperation in this case led to otherwise unobtainable results. Before the MCAC was established, the motorist might never have alerted authorities of the suspicious behavior she witnessed. In addition, the information collected by the officer would likely never have been cross-checked against the information obtained from British officials in London. The MCAC has helped to connect the dots.

Conclusion

I am pleased to have had this opportunity to write about the MCAC and I am proud of what the Center has accomplished during its first 3 years in operation. As home to one of the busiest ports in the country, and the closest neighbor of our Nation's Capital, Maryland must remain at the forefront on homeland security operations. The MCAC is clear and convincing evidence of Maryland's continuing success in this area.

Cooperation has been the pervasive theme throughout this chapter. The theme is appropriate because it is the foundation upon which the MCAC was built. Indeed, cooperation continues to drive the work of the MCAC. With confidence acquired through experience, I believe that principled cooperation is the key to the success of all other fusion centers throughout the Nation. Partnerships produce results.

Finally, I would like to close with sincere words of appreciation for the dedicated individuals and organizations that have contributed to making the MCAC a model example of how fusion centers can contribute to state and national homeland security. There are too many deserving of merit to list on these pages. The success of the MCAC is only made possible by the hard work and dedication of countless extraordinary individuals over the past 3 years. Each one of these individuals can be proud that their personal commitment to the mission of the MCAC has made Maryland a safer place to live.

Notes

1. *DHS Strengthens Intel Sharing At State and Local Fusion Centers.* Department of Homeland Security Press Release, July 27, 2006.
2. For a comprehensive definition of fusion as it applies to physics, music, and cooking, see http://www.answers.com/topic/fusion (last visited on October 4, 2006).
3. *United States Department of Justice Strategic Plan for Fiscal Years 2001-2006. A Message from the Attorney General,*available at http://www.usdoj.gov/archive/mps/strategic2001-2006/index.htm (last visited September 19, 2006).

4. There are actually 94 federal judicial districts. However, Guam and the Northern Mariana Islands share one single US Attorney, hence there are only 93 US Attorney districts. The entire State of Maryland resides within a single district, called the District of Maryland.
5. Prior to September 24, 2003, Anti-Terrorist Advisory Councils (ATACs) were known as Anti-Terrorism Task Forces (ATTFs).
6. Although there are up to 93 separate Councils in the United States and Territories, from this point forward the term "ATAC" will refer solely to the Anti-Terrorism Advisory Council of Maryland, unless otherwise noted.
7. There are currently 23 different agencies or entities represented throughout the Watch Section and SAS. Although many agencies have representation in both sections of the Center, their memberships are not identical. There is some overlap, but some agencies may only have representation in one section or the other.
8. For more information about how many entities are represented in the MCAC, see footnote 7 above.
9. The JTTF Threat Squad is under the command of a Maryland State Police lieutenant. The JTTF is a collaborative federal, state, and local law enforcement entity housed at and staffed by the FBI. The primary function of the JTTF is to investigate terrorism activity and individuals who may be engaged in such activity. The goal of the JTTF is to prevent and/or aggressively act to disrupt terrorist activity and, where it advances the interests of national security, referring certain matters to the US Attorney to initiate federal prosecutions.

Chapter 12
Public Safety and Homeland Security Solutions: An Evolution of Technology and Policy

Edward G. Rendell

Abstract Before 1990 Pennsylvania's four justice systems each had its own information system and encountered difficulties in sharing information. Homeland security requires addressing the laws, policies, and business cultures that resist information sharing across communities while at the same time satisfying data security requirements.

Pennsylvania's Public Safety Continuum

Public safety technology has a long history in Pennsylvania – ever since 1929 when the Pennsylvania State Police implemented the nation's first statewide law enforcement teletype system. In 1929, though the challenge was not mass destruction and terrorists, it was bootlegging and organized crime. To the average citizen, public safety was a law enforcement problem and remained so for many years.

Since that first statewide teletype system, public safety has evolved along a continuum from that single-agency issue into a multi-disciplinary challenge. In more recent years, this continuum can be divided into three distinct phases, each characterized by specific policies and trends in the underlying technology. The phases are Justice Silos, Integrated Justice, and Homeland Security. Early in the evolution, the underlying technologies presented the biggest barriers to solutions, but as public safety evolved, policy constraints have become much more significant (Fig. 12.1).

In Pennsylvania's public safety evolution, there are also a few pivotal events that mark the transitions between phases, and we will discuss these as we look at each phase.

E.G. Rendell (✉)
Governor, The Commonwealth of Pennsylvania, (2003–present)
e-mail: ra-govnews@state.pa.us

S. Hakim, E.A. Blackstone (eds.), *Safeguarding Homeland Security*,
DOI 10.1007/978-1-4419-0371-6_12, © Springer Science+Business Media, LLC 2009

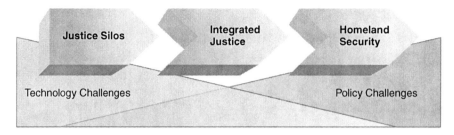

Fig. 12.1 Pennsylvania's public safety continuum

The Starting Point – Justice Silos

The first phase of this evolution is characterized by siloed justice systems. Prior to 1990, Pennsylvania's justice "Big Four" (the Courts, Corrections, Probation and Parole, and the State Police) each had their own information systems that supported their own business processes. The Courts and Corrections both had custom-developed IBM mainframe solutions. Probation and Parole utilized a client-server data solution running in Windows NT, and the State Police utilized a Unisys messaging switch and a custom Unisys Computerized Criminal History database, both mainframe based. There was no common data standard between the four, no recognized common business architecture, and each agency handled governance internally without collaboration with the others.

These independent systems resulted in a fragmented justice environment in which information sometimes took days or weeks to get to the appropriate agencies. In many cases, databases that should have contained consistent information were highly divergent; yet, from a business perspective, each of these agencies managed the same offenders as one or more of the others.

Technology and Policy Factors – Justice Silos

Though individuals in each of the agencies recognized that they needed to share information more directly, at the time their systems were developed, they were limited primarily by the technology environment:

- Processing power was expensive. The market was dominated by mainframe and mini-computer implementations, and client–server systems were new and underpowered.
- Storage was expensive, too. In the early 1980s, a megabyte of storage cost anywhere from $100 to $500.
- Connectivity was primarily point-to-point; the Internet, when it was available, was new and struggling, and bandwidth was expensive.

- Standards for both hardware and data were still in their infant stages. Almost every implementation was a custom build designed to improve an agency's access to its own internal data, not share that data with another agency.

From the policy perspective, there was no public mandate that agencies share information. Because computers really had not become household appliances in the early 1980s, the public really was not even aware of the potential for agencies to move information electronically, so there was little or no perceived benefit to expensive integrations.

Significant Event – 1994 Pennsylvania Gubernatorial Race

The 1994 gubernatorial race pitted Democratic Lieutenant Governor Mark Singel against Republican challenger, Tom Ridge, and the race was a close one. During the race, though, the Pennsylvania Board of Pardons, chaired by Singel, recommended to release Reginald McFadden from state prison where he had been sentenced 25 years before at the age of 16 for the murder of a Philadelphia woman. Upon his release, McFadden made his way to New York where he was again arrested in October for multiple murders, kidnapping, and rape. His case became a widely publicized campaign issue and likely decided the race for Ridge.

McFadden's case highlighted information-sharing problems in Pennsylvania's justice system and provided the public mandate for better integration. There was a public outcry for initiatives that would eliminate "preventable" crime by ensuring the correct facts were available. When Governor Ridge took office, he called a special session of the legislature to address the problem of crime, and Pennsylvania's most significant integrated justice initiative, the Pennsylvania Justice Network (JNET), was born from that session.

Pennsylvania's Integrated Justice

Background

To address the problems highlighted by the McFadden case and to address recommendations of the Governor's special session on crime, the Governor's Office of Administration established the "Integrated Criminal Justice Project" to develop a strategic vision for information sharing between justice and justice-affiliated agencies. This project produced documents including a strategic vision, requirements analyses, and an action plan. These documents stressed business practices, which promoted:

- Cost effectiveness;
- Information sharing;

- Timely and appropriate access to information while recognizing the independence of each agency.

The following year saw the creation of the JNET and the development of the JNET blueprint. While JNET has grown into a *secure virtual single system* that allows authorized users from municipal, county, state, bordering state, and federal justice agencies to share justice and public safety information, it began as a solution to allow Pennsylvania's Courts, Corrections, Probation, and Parole, and State Police to bridge their respective silos of information in the context of the technology and policy of the mid 1990s.

Technology and Policy Factors – Integrated Justice

Pennsylvania's Integrated Justice environment benefited from significant improvements in technology that reduced the barriers to justice solutions:

- Processing power became significantly less expensive. The market was dominated by a trend away from mainframes and mini-computers, and client–server systems developed to the point that they could challenge those larger systems for all but the most high-volume, mission-critical applications.
- Storage had become very affordable. In the mid to late 1990s, a megabyte of storage cost anywhere from 3¢ to 10¢.
- Networking had matured and was much faster and more reliable. Internet use had exploded, with nearly half of US households having access by the year 2000. The dot-com industry was booming.
- Hardware standards were the rule except for emerging technologies, and justice data standards like GJXDM gained acceptance. Commercial hardware and software products began to tout built-in adapters and interoperability.
- Messaging became an accepted method for exchanging data in real or near real time.
- Finally, object-oriented programming set the stage for much simpler integration projects.
- These same improvements, however, opened the door to much more substantial business and policy challenges.
- Pennsylvanians expected their government to share information so "preventable" errors like those in the McFadden case never occurred again. This expectation was fueled by the information sharing they were beginning to see in their homes on the Internet and through the media coverage of the dot-coms.
- In developing governance for the JNET initiative, we faced several hurdles for turf and ownership. Even though our "big four" justice agencies shared clients and many business requirements (not to mention a public mandate), there were significant legal and cultural barriers to sharing information. In these cases, JNET's executive sponsorship was critical to its success.

- There was a drive toward accurate, coordinated record-keeping within this newly recognized (at least from the citizens' perspectives) "justice community." This still represented, however, a records-based approach to law enforcement and justice.

Pennsylvania's Integrated Justice Initiative – JNET

JNET was developed to simplify and standardize information sharing between multiple justice agencies and reduce the costs of point-to-point integration. To meet these goals while still allowing agencies to keep their existing systems and maintain independent control of their data, JNET uses a hub and spoke configuration over which information is exchanged in event-driven messages. JNET serves as the message broker, and performs data translation, user authentication, and transaction logging. It also supports a web interface that provides users with a "virtual single system" for searching data from participating agencies.

JNET's first integration took place within the Commonwealth Metropolitan Area Network (MAN) (Fig. 12.2 – center). Because most justice data originates at the

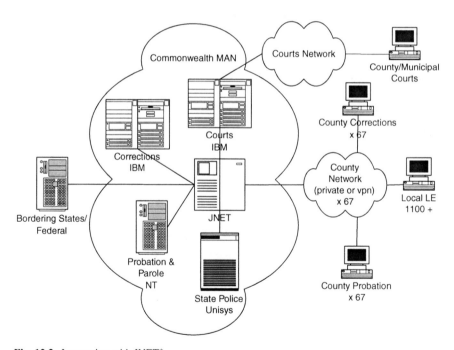

Fig. 12.2 Integration with JNET*
*This is a very high-level representation of JNET's integration strategy. It does not include all data sources/contributors. It is also worth noting that JNET maintains connections only to the county networks; counties must connect county and local agencies.

county and local levels, though, JNET quickly moved to add county and local trans-actions to its portfolio. Federal agencies and surrounding states were added later.

JNET Technology Advances

When JNET started, commercial software was either prohibitively expensive, or did not meet the justice community's needs. After evaluating options, JNET chose to build a custom messaging infrastructure (MI) with its own data adapters to access agency data. It also developed its own web interface to provide users with access to that data. JNET spent several years building and tuning this application. The formats were proprietary, and it required substantial vendor support to maintain the system as a whole.

Within the last 2 years, though, commercial software has improved to the point that it now meets many of JNET's requirements without exceeding its budget. JNET transitioned, therefore, from a proprietary message switch and web site to a COTS switch and portal. The switch now includes many standard data adapters that reduce JNET's need for custom integration. Both of these transitions are key to JNET's pending move to enterprise service bus technology and better web services.

On the hardware side, JNET began with very limited production equipment. Some of the components were running on laptops instead of servers. Much of the software JNET runs now would not have run on its original equipment. Today, JNET maintains formal development, test, and production environments with pro-duction servers housed in co-location at the state's Commonwealth Technology Center (client/server/web data center). JNET has formal service level agreements with data providers and because of its robust infrastructure consistently meets or exceeds its levels.

JNET Service Expansion

JNET's initial service offering included a "virtual single system" query of Courts, Corrections, and Probation/Parole databases. It also included event messages for arrests, wants, and dispositions. As these transactions became (recognized as) suc-cessful, JNET was able to implement other queries and messages. They also began serving as a host agency for criminal justice applications like the PA Commission on Sentencing's Sentencing Guidelines Software. Eventually, JNET was able to pro-vide additional services to agencies or reduce agencies' workloads by providing citizens a service normally handled by those agencies (certified driver history and certified vehicle registration information for PennDOT) (Fig. 12.3). Together with a growing user base (see Fig. 4), these added services sometimes drove changes to JNET's technical architecture.

JNET Data Standards – Proprietary, GJXDM, and NIEM

JNET's data standards followed a similar evolution, initially driven primarily by technology, and later driven more by policy.

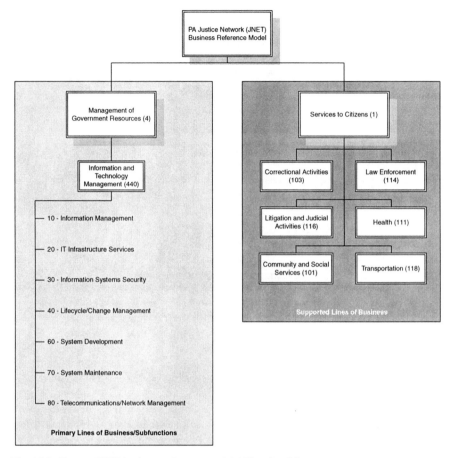

Fig. 12.3 Current JNET business reference model (abbreviated)*
*This is based upon Pennsylvania's draft business reference model for the Commonwealth. It is abbreviated to omit many standard financial and human resources functions and focuses only on lines of business central to JNET's mission.

When JNET started, there were no national justice data standards. Pennsylvania participated in pilot activities for the Justice XML Data Dictionary (JXDD), the Global Justice XML Data Model (GJXDM), and the National Information Exchange Model (NIEM) (as it applies to justice integration) specifically because of our recognition of the need for data standards.

Because these standards did not exist, JNET originally developed its own messaging standards: JNET Message Volumes I & II. The standards were largely controlled by the agencies owning the messages implemented under each volume, and while they facilitated information exchange within state agencies, they made exchange outside those agencies problematic because of the need for greater coordination with applications outside state control. When the JXDD/GJXDM standards came out, Pennsylvania participated because of our recognition of the need

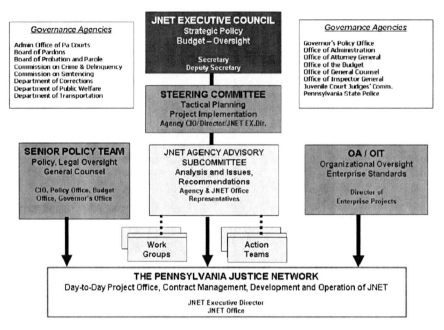

Fig. 12.4 JNET governance structure

to exchange data with counties, municipalities, other states' justice agencies, and federal agencies.

With the inclusion of GJXDM as a component of NIEM, JNET was faced with a decision to continue with its current data standard or move to the newer NIEM format. JNET has made a policy decision to investigate NIEM formats because they will enable Pennsylvania to work more efficiently outside justice in the homeland security environment.

JNET Business Reference Model

JNET's primary lines of business have remained substantially unchanged since its pilot phase (though the scope of some of its sub-functions has changed). Where JNET has really expanded, its model is in the number of lines of business it supports for other agencies. At the outset, its supported lines of business included law enforcement, correctional activities, litigation and judicial activities, and some parts of transportation. As it has added data sources and functionality, it has expanded further into all these lines and has added community and social services and health.

JNET Governance

JNET is a coalition of individual agencies, at different levels and in different branches of government, working together to share information and achieve common goals. Having the executive sponsorship necessary to build relationships and collaboration was critical to JNET's success. The Governor's office established a formal governance structure by Executive Order in 1999 and updated that structure with Management Directive 245.16 in 2003.

The JNET Steering Committee is at the heart of both daily and strategic directions for integrated justice in Pennsylvania. It is comprised of members from 17 Commonwealth agencies who are appointed by their respective agency heads. Each Steering Committee Member has a voice in JNET's strategic direction, how and what data are shared, and how JNET addresses policy and technical issues affecting their organizations and integrated justice. Steering Committee members chair and staff the JNET Agency Advisory subcommittee (JAAS) which directs workgroups and action teams that research and work on tasks from the Steering Committee as a whole.

In addition to the Steering Committee and JAAS, JNET's governance includes its Executive Council and Senior Policy Team, and oversight from the Governor's Office of Administration/Office for Information Technology. The JNET office supports this structure and conducts development, support, and communications/outreach activities.

Significant Events – September 11 and Katrina

As Pennsylvania was making strides with its JNET-integrated justice solution, events occurred in 2001 that radically changed the nation's view of public safety.

The terrorist attacks in New York, Washington DC, and Pennsylvania on September 11, 2001 (and events in London, Japan, and elsewhere), shifted the national perception of public safety to "homeland security." Though the terrorist threat had existed "remotely" for years, the nation was now acutely aware that it included not only traditional criminal activity but also weapons of mass destruction, and chemical, biological, and nuclear dangers.

On the heels of the "nine-eleven" attacks, Hurricane Katrina hit the United States in August 2005. While the nation did not expect the government to prevent hurricanes, it was appalled by its perceived inability to predict the level of damage and manage response and recovery.

Pennsylvania's Homeland Security

Background

Reports following the 9/11 attacks spotlighted the need for information sharing beyond the justice community into and between communities for defense, emergency management, transportation, health, agriculture, environmental protection, and finance – even into private industry. Additionally, these reports indicated that information sharing alone was insufficient. To be useful, information required trained analysis. Information sharing, therefore, evolved into "information fusion."

These attacks also caused another shift in the national perspective. Traditionally, crime prevention meant reducing the risk that a citizen would become a victim of crime, and citizens and businesses held the primary responsibility for prevention activities. Following the attacks, prevention and protection came to mean preventing something of that scale from happening again, and citizens looked to government to step up intelligence activities to protect citizens, critical infrastructure, and key assets.

Hurricane Katrina expanded the government's mandate even further to include protecting citizens, critical infrastructure, and key assets from all hazards. It also increased the emphasis on disaster recovery and continuity of government.

These shifts present a new set of challenges for public safety and homeland security, and while some of the challenges are technology based, they are secondary to ones based in legislation, governance, and culture (trust).

Technology and Policy Factors – Homeland Security

As Pennsylvania began to address the challenges Homeland Security, we found that policies and business practices were far more limiting than technologies – a significant difference from previous phases.

- Processing power and storage, though expenses within projects, are seldom limiting factors. In fact, server technology has become so inexpensive to procure and so powerful that agencies are looking at virtualization to reduce the number of servers in their inventories to realize savings in ancillary costs like personnel, software licenses, maintenance, power, and cooling. Studies of Commonwealth agencies have shown that most servers are underutilized.
- Despite the collapse of the dot-com industry, over half of US households have broadband Internet access. Cities are commissioning their own high-speed wireless networks, and major cellular carriers are rolling out third-generation (3G) networks for their subscribers. There is a movement toward device convergence (radio/phone/computer/internet/geospatial/television).
- Hardware standards are part of hardware life cycle, and justice data standards like GJXDM are expanding to national cross-business standards like NIEM.
- Enterprise service bus technology adds significant business intelligence and monitoring tools to existing messaging.
- The industry moves to service-oriented architectures and IT commoditization.
- As the information technology becomes easier to manage and more powerful, however, the business and policy challenges become increasingly difficult.
- Pennsylvanians expect their government to share sensitive information outside of traditional communities so all terrorist incidents are anticipated and prevented. In the case of natural disasters, they expect the government to eliminate risks, mitigate damage, and restore to normal operations with minimum interruption of their lives. These expectations are driven in part by media coverage of the

after-action reports from 9/11 and Katrina, and in part by fictional portrayals of government in movies and television.

- Post 9/11 legislation and planning also set business challenges. (Patriot Act, National Preparedness Goal, National Infrastructure Protection Plan, National Incident Management System, National Response Plan, etc.)
- The borders between traditional communities (justice, health, education, private sector, etc.) begin to blur as they begin to work toward "all hazards" planning. Governance becomes extremely challenging, and this blended approach leads to a need to classify levels of information in a manner similar to the military/federal model.
- There is a need to move from records-based justice to intelligence-led security. Having information becomes important only if that information is analyzed and acted upon regardless of its original source.
- All of these challenges take place in a culture designed to protect individual rights and civil liberties. Often, what appears to be operational necessity conflicts with long-standing civil liberties legislation.

Pennsylvania Homeland Security Initiatives

Pennsylvania's work on Homeland Security addresses initiatives across all phases of the incident management life cycle: prevention, protection, recovery, and response. This section will address four of Pennsylvania's initiatives:

1. Governance structure;
2. The move from integrated justice initiatives to a fusion environment for information sharing;
3. Identity protection and management;
4. Continuity of government.

Governance

Pennsylvania's Homeland Security governance structure (originally established in 2002) was updated by the Governor's office through an Executive Order in 2006. The order establishes three governing entities:

1. The Pennsylvania Office of Homeland Security;
2. The Governor's Homeland Security and Emergency Preparedness Executive Cabinet;
3. The Homeland Security and Emergency Preparedness Advisory Council.

In addition, Pennsylvania's Chief Information Officer established the Homeland Security Information Technology Governance Board to advise and assist these groups on technology issues.

The Fusion Environment

Because the Fusion Environment is the next phase in the evolution of integrated justice, and because it clearly demonstrates many of the challenges facing Homeland Security, we will address it in more detail than other Homeland Security initiatives.

Challenges

Integrated justice is based upon existing rules and agreements for sharing information among agencies that have established processes for managing offenders and cases. For the most part, agencies already had agreements about who was entitled to exchange information, and the real challenge was in effectively using developing technologies to facilitate that exchange.

As we look at information fusion and homeland security, however, we must acknowledge a need to exchange information that is often protected by law and always protected by business culture outside its normal community. There are two very clear examples in the law enforcement and health communities:

- Law enforcement intelligence and investigative information in Pennsylvania is severely restricted from electronic dissemination (even between law enforcement agencies) by the state's Criminal History Records Information Act (CHRIA) and is restricted to a lesser degree by federal statute (28 CFR, Part 23). Beyond the legislation, law enforcement agencies protect intelligence activities and active investigations from dissemination out of valid concern for the safety of their undercover officers and the success of their prosecutions.
- In the health community, the federal Health Insurance Portability and Accountability Act (HIPAA) governs information dissemination, but in addition to the legislation, health-care providers protect information out of valid concern for the privacy of their patients.
- This is by no means an exhaustive list; there are many similar examples in other communities. If we consider a bioterrorism incident, though, it is clear that health agencies will need information from law enforcement in order to prepare for and respond to an emergency, and law enforcement agencies will need information from health agencies in order to apprehend the criminals and prevent other incidents.

Pennsylvania's Fusion Starting Point – PaCIC

In 2003, Pennsylvania took its first step toward its fusion center by establishing the Pennsylvania Criminal Intelligence Center (PaCIC) within the Pennsylvania State Police. PaCIC serves as a focal point for both law enforcement and homeland security information gathering and analysis. PaCIC gathers information from many sources (with active support from other state agencies), but because of the issues discussed above about the sensitivity of law enforcement information and because other agencies do not employ trained intelligence analysts, it has handled the analysis tasks independent of other agencies.

In order to support different levels of access to information within and across communities, Pennsylvania will build its fusion center as a partial virtual extension of PaCIC, using software and telecommunications to link analysts with differing levels of access.

The development will take place in three phases:

- *Phase I* – Fusion Center Expansion/Criminal Justice Agency Implementation;
- *Phase II* – Non Criminal Justice/First Responder Implementation;
- *Phase III* – Private Industry Implementation.

As each phase rolls out, Pennsylvania will establish information-sharing policy and protocol. The phases above will allow us to build policies in similar areas first and use that foundation to expand into more difficult areas.

Anticipated Challenges

Pennsylvania anticipates several process and technology challenges in its development and roll-out of the virtual fusion center expansion to PaCIC:

- Establishing sensitivity levels for information and protocols for sharing that information (or some redacted version of that information) outside its normal community (process).
- Establishing a trust model for identity management across communities so sensitive information can be shared with authorized individuals (process and technology).
- Developing analyst skill sets in subject matter experts outside the law enforcement community (process).

Fusion Data Standards

Just as Pennsylvania's integrated justice solution (JNET) is preparing to move to NIEM data standards, Pennsylvania's fusion center will also standardize on NIEM. This cross-community data set is even more important for information fusion that crosses agency/community boundaries.

Fusion Business Reference Model

Unlike the JNET integrated justice model, the model for the fusion environment directly incorporates information analysis services normally associated with many agencies rather than just facilitating information sharing that is already taking place between those agencies. Though the difference seems subtle, it drives a need for a more involved executive governance structure. When coupled with the challenges

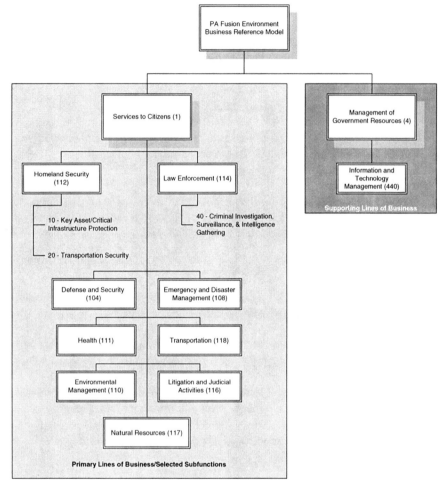

Fig. 12.5 Fusion environment business reference model*
*This is based upon Pennsylvania's draft business reference model for the Commonwealth. It is abbreviated to omit some lines of business indirectly supported by the fusion environment and some sub-functions in the services to citizens area.

listed above, it also drives the need for information classification similar to the military/federal model (Fig. 12.5).

Fusion Alignment

The fusion center is aligned primarily within the prevention and protection phases of emergency management as depicted below, though it also has roles in the other phases. Because of this alignment, its governance will be impacted by the agencies listed in lead and supporting roles in accordance with laws, agreements, policies, and protocols (Fig. 12.6).

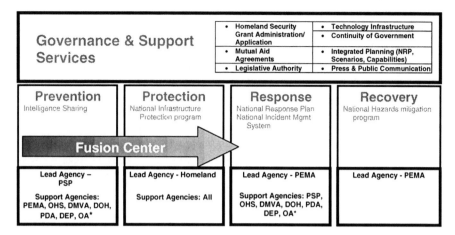

Fig. 12.6 Fusion center in emergency management
*This is not a comprehensive list of agencies.

Identity Protection and Management

Determining identity and associated certifications and authorizations is a core component of Homeland Security initiatives. Pennsylvania is approximately midway through a multi-year plan for addressing its enterprise technology solution for identity protection and management (IPAM).

This plan involves creation of a three-tiered enterprise personnel directory (employees, business partners, and citizens) through federated identity management and shared provisioning with Commonwealth agencies (and their existing directories). In parallel with this effort, Pennsylvania has participated with Department of Homeland Security in credentialing activities like the Winter Storm demonstration in February 2007, and we are also considering Real ID Act requirements in our solutions.

Because of industry support for standards like SAML 2.0 and FIPS-201, Pennsylvania has been able to select several commercial products that will allow us to create this directory, federate with existing agency directories, and credential our employees and first responders. Without minimizing the tasks associated with IPAM, this is significant because the technology is much less of a challenge in this initiative than the governance and management of a federated identity model across agencies and communities of practice.

Continuity of Government

Following 9/11 to some extent, and more so after Katrina, we recognized a clear need to plan for continuity of government following a disaster. When the possibility of a pandemic caused by a strain of avian flu became a concern in 2004–2005, continuity of government operations took on an additional dimension – not because facilities or infrastructure would be damaged or unavailable, but because we need to minimize the spread of disease.

In 2006 and 2007, Pennsylvania conducted tele-work evaluations that looked at several commercial solutions, both software based and thin-client device based, that would allow employees to work from home or another remote location. (We also evaluated thin-client devices as potential cost-saving desktop replacements.) Once again, it is important to note that we were able to evaluate commercially available solutions; technology was only a minor obstacle to the initiative. Most of the recommendations coming from the evaluations revolved around policy and training.

In looking at the user comments, though, there was one technology area that we did not adequately address in the evaluation scenarios – access to voice communications (office phone and remote meeting support). This is significant because it points to a user expectation that is being driven by advances in device convergence.

Planning for the Future

From a technology perspective, there are two trends that will substantially change how we address public safety and homeland security:

- Device Convergence;
- IT Commoditization.

Device Convergence

In the information silo phase, a phone was a phone, a radio was a radio, a television was a television, and a computer was a great big piece of equipment that took several people to maintain. In our homeland security phase, these devices are one item and can be carried in a user's pocket. We have a generation of IT users now who expect to be able to access audio, video, and data services wherever they are, and the implications to public safety and homeland security are considerable.

We already offer Amber Alert notifications via text message to cellular phones. In the wake of the Virginia Tech shootings, colleges and universities are working to establish policies and services for emergency notifications via similar media. Add to these devices GIS (which many models already support), and we will soon have to plan for location-based emergency notifications. Each of these requires substantial planning both from a technology perspective and from a policy perspective.

IT Commoditization

Pennsylvania has just begun an IT consolidation effort – moving the bulk of its IT services under a central agency for economy of scale and more efficient service delivery. Ten years ago, this would not have been possible in a government of our size. With advances in standards and technology, though, IT service delivery has become increasingly commoditized. Agencies do not need to buy servers, for example. They need to buy sufficient processing power to achieve their objectives. They do not really need to buy office computers and phones, they need to buy seat services from a provider that can get them up and running in short order. Now, consolidation is not only possible, it makes the best business sense.

Some of these "commoditized" services will be internally managed, and some will likely be contracted to commercial vendors with specific expertise. Again, there are significant implications for public safety and homeland security. As one example, how are these services prioritized? In the event of an emergency, will centrally managed or contracted services be able to support first responders and emergency workers despite increased demand from their other clients? Certainly communications problems in New York City after 9/11 suggest that this is a very real concern. In a commoditized environment, policies and service agreements become critically important. In some cases, some items may not be candidates for commoditization at all.

Conclusions – From Technology to Policy

The public safety/homeland security continuum – from justice silos through integrated justice to homeland security – has presented Pennsylvania with an evolution from technology challenges to policy challenges.

At the front end of the continuum, technology was clearly the limiting factor. There were certainly legal and policy issues with integrating justice information sharing, but the challenge to those issues was making developing technology support established policy.

This is no longer the case. For the most part, our integrated justice initiatives have identified the technologies we need to share information. Homeland security requires that we address laws, policies, and business cultures that resist information sharing across communities, but this is a far greater challenge than we faced in implementing the technology.

If we are to safeguard Pennsylvania's citizens, we must be able to combine data from different sources to produce valid intelligence assessments. We have to undertake this challenge, though, with recognition of each agency's requirements to protect that data and its sources, and with an eye toward protecting the civil liberties that are at the heart of Pennsylvania's constitution.

Early in Pennsylvania's history Ben Franklin warned: "Those who would give up essential liberty to purchase a little temporary safety, deserve neither liberty nor safety." (Attributed to Franklin in a letter dated November 11, 1755, from the Pennsylvania Assembly to the Governor of Pennsylvania.) With this sentiment rooted in our state's culture, we can expect the policy challenges to be far more significant than the technology ones.

Glossary

AOPC	Administrative Office of Pennsylvania Courts or "courts"
CHRIA	Pennsylvania Criminal History Records Information Act – legislation governing exchange of criminal history, investigative, intelligence, and other protected data
DEP	Pennsylvania Department of Environmental Protection
DMVA	Department of Military and Veterans Affairs (Pennsylvania National Guard)
DOC	Department of Corrections or "corrections"
DOH	Pennsylvania Department of Health
DSO	Domestic Security Office (Division of PSP)
DOS	Pennsylvania Department of State
EOC	Emergency Operations Center
FBI	Federal Bureau of Investigation
GATIR	Geospatial Analysis of Threats and Incident Reports – software that allows mapping of incidents
GFIPM	Global Federated Identity and Privilege Management
GIS	Geospatial Information Systems
GJXDM	Global Justice XML Data Model
HIPAA	Health Insurance Portability and Accountability Act
HSIN	Homeland Security Information Network (federal)
JAAS	JNET Agency Advisory Subcommittee
JCJC	Juvenile Court Judges' Commission
JNET	Pennsylvania Justice Network – integrated justice solution.
JXDD	Justice XML Data Dictionary
MAN	Metropolitan Area Network
MDJ	Magisterial District Judge (minor judiciary)
NIEM	National Information Exchange Model
NRP	National Response Plan
OA	Pennsylvania Office of Administration
OHS	Pennsylvania Office of Homeland Security or "homeland security"
OIT	Pennsylvania Office for Information Technology
PaCIC	Pennsylvania Criminal Intelligence Center (housed at PSP)
PBPP	Pennsylvania Board of Probation and Parole or "probation and parole"
PCS	Pennsylvania Commission on Sentencing
PDA	Pennsylvania Department of Agriculture
PEIRS	Pennsylvania Emergency Incident Reporting System – software that records and manages incident reports (housed at PEMA)
PEMA	Pennsylvania Emergency Management Agency
PennDOT	Pennsylvania Department of Transportation
PSP	Pennsylvania State Police or "state police"
RISS	Regional Information-Sharing System
SURE	Statewide Uniform Registry of Electors – system for voter registration (housed at DOS)

Chapter 13
Utilizing Technology Within the Delaware Information and Analysis Center

Ruth Ann Minner

Abstract The Delaware Information and Analysis Center, Delaware's fusion center, began in 2005 to analyze information and data to thwart terrorist and other criminal incidents. It is unusual because law enforcement members are joined by agricultural, transportation, and health experts among other participants. The National Guard also participates. The private sector, including the banking and finance industry, is heavily involved in the activities of the Center. The fusion center has a "tip line" and is helped by the uniform reporting system employed by all the law enforcement agencies in the state. The Center was instrumental in de-escalating the action plans by fusion Center stakeholders after a 2004 crash of a US Airforce C-5 transport plane.

Introduction

Following the terrorist attacks of September 11, 2001, the State of Delaware was confronted with the challenge of providing enhanced protection for its critical infrastructure and key resources realizing the potential with regard to both domestic and international hazards. Through the development of various strategies and systems, and the formation of assets that were not conceptualized prior to the September 11th attacks, Delaware successfully managed this challenge. Today, Delaware is recognized for the development of its fusion center, the Delaware Information and Analysis Center (DIAC) and a number of outreach programs that are now used as models for other states.

The analysis of the events leading up to the 9/11 terrorists attacks clearly emphasized the absence of linked intelligence between law enforcement agencies in Delaware and those around the nation. In today's environment, by utilizing the information sharing systems now in place, a simple traffic stop could lead to the

R.A. Minner (✉)
Governor, The State of Delaware, (2001–2009)
e-mail: gminner@state.de.us

detainment of a person who is known to, or suspected to, have terrorist or gang affiliation. Prior to September 11th, this was not possible. An example of this is on September 9, 2001, Ziad Jarrah, the hijacker pilot of United Airlines, Flight 93, was stopped by a Maryland State trooper on Interstate 95 for speeding. While it is still debated today whether Jarrah's name was on a terrorist watch-list, the fact is that the Maryland State trooper's only access to criminal information was through the National Crime Information Center (NCIC). NCIC is a computerized index of criminal justice information including criminal record history, fugitives, stolen property, and missing persons. NCIC is available to federal, state, and local law enforcement and other criminal justice agencies 24 hours a day, 365 days a year.

The NCIC system provides a database for quick access by a criminal justice agency making an inquiry and for prompt disclosure of information in the system from other criminal justice agencies about crimes and criminals. This resource also assists authorized criminal justice agencies in the protection of the law enforcement officers encountering the individuals described in the system (Pike, 2008).

Based on the information provided through NCIC, the Maryland State trooper found no reason to detain Jarrah. The trooper issued a traffic citation and allowed Jarrah to continuing driving. Jarrah traveled through Delaware and on to Newark, NJ, where he piloted United Airlines Flight 93, which crashed in Pennsylvania. It is important to keep in mind, this incident occurred prior to the tragic events of September 11th. Today, the Terrorist Screening Center would disseminate vital information to NCIC. This type of interagency information sharing would become the foundation for the Delaware Information and Analysis Center (DIAC), Delaware's fusion center.

Concept and Development of the Delaware Information and Analysis Center (DIAC)

In 2005, the Delaware Information and Analysis Center (DIAC) was created in direct response to an immediate need to gather, share, analyze, integrate, and disseminate information and intelligence among the many agencies protecting the citizens of Delaware against threats from numerous sources. The DIAC fuses together criminal intelligence and open source information to provide timely and actionable information and intelligence for law enforcement and our statewide partners including the private sector and key decision makers within the State.

The formation of the DIAC followed the US Department of Homeland Security's declaration of a high risk of terrorist attack against financial institutions along the East Coast in August 2004. Financial institutions in the New York City and Washington, DC areas were put on alert after the department received information that operatives of Al Qaeda had conducted detailed reconnaissance missions at the New York Stock Exchange, Citigroup headquarters in Manhattan, the Newark headquarters of Prudential Financial, and the Washington offices of the World Bank and IMF. As a result of the declared threat to the financial industry, the National Homeland Security Advisory System was raised from an elevated risk to a high risk.

With Delaware as one of the major money market and credit card centers in the United States, the threat to the financial industry was very concerning to Delaware officials. Many of the nation's largest banks, including Citibank, JP Morgan Chase, HSBC, and Bank of America, have a presence in Delaware. In conjunction with the heightened national security alert, Delaware officials took immediate measures to communicate with banking representatives throughout the State.

The Delaware State Police (DSP) Criminal Intelligence Section, without delay, assigned a detective from its Fraud Unit, to act as a liaison between the Unit and members of the State's financial sector. The DSP detective selected to serve as liaison was quite familiar with banking industry representatives and had numerous contacts within the financial sector. The action of designating a liaison was taken to establish an immediate two-way communication conduit with financial institutions throughout the state. At that time, communications had been limited to Situational Reports (SITREPS), generated by the DSP Criminal Intelligence Section via e-mail to primarily law enforcement and individuals in the private sector. This was one-way communication. A post-analysis of the agency's actions taken during the threat to the nation's financial sector resulted in the establishment of a permanent Critical Infrastructure Protection Unit. Today, the Critical Infrastructure Protection Unit complements DIAC personnel by sharing the current threat environment with Delaware's stakeholders and assists them with mitigation strategies.

The focus of the DIAC goes beyond the belief that law enforcement is the sole protector of the public. This proactive, multi-disciplined paradigm makes the DIAC a central conduit that builds partnerships between numerous agencies, both in the public and in the private sectors. The common goal remains the protection of our homeland and the prevention of criminal activity at all levels.

The DIAC incorporates the tenets of the State of Delaware's Homeland Security Strategy, the Office of Homeland Security's National Strategy for Homeland Security, Global's National Criminal Intelligence Sharing Plan (NCISP) and Fusion Center Guidelines, the White House's National Strategy for Information Sharing (NSIS), the Department of Homeland Security's National Infrastructure Protection Plan (NIPP), and the Office of the Director of National Intelligence's Information Sharing Environment Implementation Plan (ISE IP). The concepts within these strategies on fusion centers and their operations serve as guiding values and principles as the DIAC continues to evolve.

Technological Systems

Technology and analysis of data are at the heart of information sharing of every fusion center. Taking advantage of technology is a key element of an "All Crimes – All Hazards" concept, which the DIAC subscribes to. With the proper technology in data integration and quality data analysis, fusion centers are better poised to be successful. This must always be balanced with individual privacy and civil liberty rights to fulfill the mission of the fusion center. The DIAC has taken advantage of today's technology, building on existing systems while using the US Department of Justice's Global Justice Extendable Markup Language (XML) technology to integrate these systems.

The Delaware law enforcement community is unique from any other state, in which all law enforcement and criminal justice agencies within the state participate on the same electronic incident reporting or case management system. This system named LEISS (Law Enforcement Investigative Support System) is supported by the Delaware Justice Information System (DelJIS), a state agency with a multi-agency executive governing board. The LEISS system allows DIAC analysts to provide analysis of the LEISS data, looking for pre-incident indicators to a potential terrorist event. This analysis is done with integration of a graphical analysis tool used to discover patterns, trends, associations, and hidden networks in any number and type of data sources. This analysis is used in a number of ways to include crime and case analysis, and temporal analysis of pre-incident indicators and behaviors, located in and around Delaware's identified critical infrastructure.

In another way, Delaware Law Enforcement is unique in that every law enforcement agency within the state is trained in, shares, and utilizes the same highly advanced electronic operational intelligence system. This system, the Delaware State Intelligence System (DSIS) is housed and managed by the DIAC and enables secure data input from anywhere in the state, to include mobile data computers in police vehicles, of threat and criminal information. The ability for every law enforcement agency to share that same criminal information data enables the development of a much broader picture of an individual, group, or location, enabling agencies to more effectively identify threats and assign resources. This is an important step in the concept of "Intelligence Led Policing," which is predictive in nature rather than reactive, as is traditional law enforcement. This system also ensures that the DIAC complies with the *National Criminal Intelligence Sharing Plan* as adopted by the International Association of Chiefs of Police (IACP) in 2002.

One of the encrypted web-based systems used by the DIAC is the Regional Information Sharing System (RISS). RISS is a national program of regionally oriented services designed to enhance the ability of local, state, federal, and tribal criminal justice agencies to

- Identify, target, and remove criminal conspiracies and activities spanning multi-jurisdictional, multi-state, and sometimes international boundaries.
- Facilitate rapid exchange and sharing of information among the agencies pertaining to known suspected criminals or criminal activity.
- Enhance coordination and communication among agencies that are in pursuit of criminal conspiracies determined to be inter-jurisdictional in nature.

RISS supports a proactive, preventive approach, and offers services, tools, and resources to aid law enforcement and criminal justice entities to identify, disrupt, and prevent terrorist and criminal activities. Delaware is part of the Mid-Atlantic Great Lakes Organized Crime Law Enforcement Network (MAGLOCLEN), one of six regional RISS networks.

The nationwide encrypted electronic sharing network that RISS provides for law enforcement is called RISSnet. The fusion centers located in the northeast United States have formed a partnership called the Northeast Regional Intelligence Group (NRIG) and use RISSnet as one of their electronic communication tools within their fusion centers. RISS regional policy boards are made up of state and local police personnel, which give direction to the regional projects, such as MAGLOCLEN. This makes RISSnet a favorite tool of state and local law enforcement.

Another encrypted web-based resource utilized by the DIAC is the RISS Automated Trusted Information Exchange (ATIX), which is the private sector version of RISSnet. The RISS/ATIX web site is a secure encrypted network of information sharing between the law enforcement and the private sector, and the private sector within itself. This system is unique in that all disciplines share each other's information, so that information sharing across disciplines is achieved. RISS/ATIX was determined by DIAC personnel to provide an excellent source of information sharing with the private sector and is incorporated in the DIAC for daily use by the analysts. Due to outreach efforts and the system's capabilities and resources, Delaware has one of the largest ATIX user groups of any state and has become the model for ATIX outreach. Today, the DIAC has over 250 users of ATIX comprising 25 sectors, including state and local governments, state agencies, and corporate entities. In addition to the aforementioned, "private" sites within ATIX, have been developed at the request of the DIAC to facilitate secure information sharing between law enforcement and authorized users of the private sites for specific targeted crime initiatives in a confidential format.

In April 2006, the DIAC enhanced the ATIX system by incorporating the "Silent Partner Alert System." Recognizing the fact that information posted by the DIAC on RISS/ATIX can be critical and time sensitive in nature, the "Silent Partner" initiative was created to provide instant electronic notification of verified threats, as well as others need to know information. In the event that time sensitive information needs to be shared, the "Silent Partner" participants receive DIAC alerts via standard e-mail, text e-mail, text pager, cell phone e-mail, recorded telephone messaging, or palm device. This initiative has proven to be most helpful to DIAC stakeholders, who have the responsibility of putting action and mitigation plans into place, based on the threat information.

In 2004, the DIAC utilized the RISSnet/ATIX technology to provide information alerts to various users groups following an airplane crash at Dover Air Force Base. The Air Force's largest transport aircraft, a C-5, crashed on an approach to an emergency landing after experiencing engine problems. Upon impact the plane broke into several pieces. The 15-member crew exited the aircraft with minor injuries. With a DIAC forward deployed criminal intelligence analyst at the command post, the DIAC served a vital role in the minutes and hours after the crash, quickly disseminating critical details to northeast fusion centers via RISSnet and local RISS/ATIX users in the government, law enforcement, transportation, and private industry sectors. This immediate sharing of verified and validated information quickly led to the de-escalation of action plans put in place by the DIAC's stakeholders.

DIAC analysts also use a variety of other electronic information sharing platforms, such as the FBI's Law Enforcement Online network (LEO), and other non-classified federal government systems, such as the Department of Homeland Security's Federal Protective System (FPS), Homeland Security Information Network (HSIN), and the State and Local Intelligence Community (SLIC). All of these information sharing systems have specific uses and all are used within the DIAC to share information in a national network of fusion centers. DIAC analysts in the fusion center also have access to federal classified systems, all operated within strict federal guidelines.

During 2005, the DIAC conceptualized and installed a 24-hour anti-terrorism tipline. The anti-terrorism telephone tip-line provides the DIAC with information from the public regarding potential acts of terrorism. Citizens can report suspicious activity related to terrorism 24 hours a day, 7 days a week, by calling 1-800-FORCE-1-2. Information received via the tip-line is analyzed in the DIAC and then forwarded to the FBI's local Joint Terrorism Task Force (JTTF) or local law enforcement authorities for further investigation, if warranted. In Delaware, homeland security is hometown security. The citizens of this State are a valuable resource when it comes to recognizing oddities. They have been asked to help in the fight against terrorism by reporting suspicious activity related to terrorism with a public awareness program put together by the DIAC called "See Something, Say Something." This program is based on a 3-minute video educating the public on the seven signs of preoperational planning, used by terrorist organizations. In addition to educating the public on these suspicious activities, they are also educated on how and to whom to report the activity.

Current Status of the DIAC

Today, the DIAC, which occupies approximately 3000 square feet of office space, is run by a staff of more than 20 sworn law enforcement officers, civilians, and military personnel who are experts in various disciplines including counter-terrorism, illegal drug activity, chemical/biological/radiological/nuclear/explosives (CBRNE), and public health. The DIAC has partnered with the Delaware State Police and the Delaware National Guard in their "Counter-Drug Program" to provide full-time intelligence analysts to receive, review, and disseminate information. A strong partnership with the National Guard resulted in the appointment of full-time Intelligence Analysts to complement this staff. In addition, the staff has an Explosive Ordnance Disposal expert and a Public Health Epidemiologist who functions as a liaison for public health-related issues, and a Chemical, Biological, Radiological, Nuclear and Explosives (CBRNE) expert who procures equipment and provides training relating to these hazards for all law enforcement agencies throughout the state. Others represent the Joint Terrorism Task Force (JTTF) that investigates potential terrorism-related acts including tips generated by the public through the Anti-Terrorism Tip Line, 1-800-FORCE-1-2. The Critical Infrastructure Protection

Unit personnel are responsible for the outreach program to federal, state, and local governments, and private industry partners, through meetings, site visits, and promoting the RISS/ATIX and "Silent Partner" alert systems. Additionally, critical infrastructure vulnerability assessments are conducted by the unit and cataloged in a secure database. The National Guard personnel provide valuable input on illegal drug activity and assist with criminal drug investigations. The annual operating budget for the DIAC is approximately $500,000.

Delaware is leading the nation with its "all hazards" approach to information sharing and homeland security. Addressing all hazards that have the potential to negatively impact the state remains the goal of the Delaware Department of Safety and Homeland Security. Through the DIAC and with the assistance of many partners, the state continues to move forward with making the DIAC a true fusion center with the capacity and capability to network with numerous federal, state, private, and non-profit agencies. Since its inception, the number of DIAC partners continues to increase. In addition, members of Delaware's agricultural, transportation, and public health communities all have workstations in the DIAC. Bringing together these partners and others who have a vested interest in the welfare of Delaware citizens, makes the center's operation not only more efficient but farther reaching. Delaware is putting subject matter experts into its DIAC to assist intelligence analysts as they sift through an enormous amount of information looking for anomalies.

For example, with Delaware being one of the largest poultry producers on the east coast, having an agriculture expert in the DIAC who can identify concerns of the poultry industry, such as Avian Flu, is important. Delaware produced 245 million broilers in 2007. In 2006, approximately 76% of Delaware's cash farm income was from broilers and the broiler product was valued at $739 million (Delmarva Poultry Industry, Inc., May, 2008).

Another effort underway to expand the capabilities of the DIAC is securing a connection to the High Intensity Drug Trafficking Areas or HIDTAs. The mission of the HIDTAs is to improve interagency collaboration, promote the sharing of accurate and timely information and intelligence, and provide specialized training and other resources to HIDTA participating law enforcement and criminal justice agencies that will enhance their ability to provide superior services and meet their operational objectives (Office of National Drug Control Policy, 2008). Sharing of databases with the HIDTA's will provide Delaware with another link to valuable information. Just as a 9/11 terrorist traveled from Maryland through Delaware enroute to Newark, NJ, so do many others who are involved in criminal activity along the East Coast. With the US 95 interstate corridor providing a direct route through the eastern states and Washington, DC, the region is closely connected.

The DIAC is in its initial stage of releasing the first phase of the DIAC information sharing portal. This first phase will grant access to Delaware law enforcement personnel, where they can find "one stop shopping" for information and resources as it pertains to "All Crimes, All Hazards" in Delaware. Phase two of this project will include upgrades to the portal and access, by preset rights and permissions, to our private sector stakeholders, and other government agencies.

Information Resources

The DIAC receives its information from a variety of resources. Some of those resources are other state designated fusion centers, state and local law enforcement agencies, federal law enforcement agencies (including the FBI, the Department of Homeland Security, the private sector, the Delaware National Guard and Dover Air Force Base, other state agencies, maritime agencies and the US Coast Guard), the Information Sharing Analysis Centers (ISAC's), and open source information. All information goes through a validation and verification process before being disseminated and complies with all state and federal laws and guidelines.

Products

The DIAC provides a number of products to assist law enforcement and other homeland security stakeholders in the state. Products include tactical bulletins and assessments, strategic assessments, and case support including link analysis, association analysis, and temporal analysis.

In an effort to prevent overload to our private sector partners, the DIAC produces a Weekly Infrastructure Bulletin, designed to supply our stakeholders with the information that they need from a variety of resources, which is relevant to Delaware. This assists them with cutting through the large amount of information being bombarded upon them daily. This weekly bulletin is tailored to the DIAC's customers who are committed to infrastructure protection in government and the private sector. The purpose of the weekly report is to educate and inform. The details contained in the report are compiled from open source information to include the Department of Homeland Security. Various topics are covered including agriculture, banking and finance, chemical industry, emergency management, education, government, fire and emergency medical services, transportation, military, public health, telecommunications, and utility and water.

Privacy and Civil Liberties

The DIAC recognizes the balancing act between the ability to share information and the rights of US citizens pertaining to privacy and civil liberties. The DIAC strictly subscribes to all state and federal governmental laws pertaining to privacy and civil liberties. The DIAC has a published Privacy Policy in which the eight universal elements of the Fair Information Practices are subscribed. All employees and recipients of information are trained annually on the policy. This policy is a living document, in that it is reviewed for its comprehensiveness and validity annually.

Conclusion

Many of the fusions centers located across the country were designed with a focus on the law enforcement community. Delaware's fusion center is quite different as it brings together the many levels of law enforcement, government, private industry, and community. This unique collaboration makes the Delaware Information and Analysis Center a model in best practices for the development and operation of fusion centers Through the DIAC and the information sharing systems implemented, our State is diligently working to stay informed of potential risks. All Delawareans must remain vigilant in the fight on terrorism. The DIAC is providing our citizens and key stakeholders with the necessary information they need to protect the people and property of the great State of Delaware.

References

Christie, C.J. (May 2007). *Six Individuals charged with Plotting to Murder U.S. Soldiers at New Jersey Military Base*, United States Department of Justice. Retrieved August 20, 2008, from http://newark.fbi.gov/dojpressrel/2007/nk050807.htm.

Delmarva Poultry Industry, Inc. (2007). *Facts About Delaware's Broiler Chicken Industry.* Retrieved May 20, 2008, from http://www.dpichicken.org/index.cfm?content=facts.

Office of National Drug Control Policy (May, 2006). *High Intensity Drug Trafficking Areas.* Retrieved May 20, 2008, from http://www.whitehousedrug policy.gov/hidta/dc_baltimore.html.

Pike, J. (2008). *National Crime Information Center.* Retrieved March 20, 2008, from http://fas.org/irp/agency/doj/fbi/is/ncic/htm

Chapter 14
From Curiosity to Collaboration: Leveraging Technology to Improve Situational Awareness

Curt Pringle

Abstract The city created a virtual operations center as opposed to an operations center where many agencies and organizations congregate to manage an emergency. This approach enables management by authorized users from any computer. It has a landing page where users can then access information ranging from building blueprints to traffic flow around the incident. Regional communities also participate in the virtual center. The system has worked well in the case of fires and in a test simulating a major disaster.

Mayors and city councils around the nation share the same concern – ensuring that visitors and residents feel that their city is the best place to live and play. In today's world, where the threat of terrorism is more real than ever before, this responsibility raises questions that we think about a great deal. How can we best serve those who live in our city? How can we make sure our city remains a place where people are happy to visit? How can we safeguard the public welfare?

Most cities looked at questions like these with renewed vigor in the wake of September 11, 2001, and Anaheim was no different. Public safety is the first and most important responsibility of any municipality, and September 11 made us aware of whole new areas of vulnerability. Our stance on public safety had historically been very proactive, in part because there are economic drivers that make excellent public safety crucial to the city's economic well-being. The Disneyland Resort generates 54% of our city's general fund tax revenue, for example. Anaheim has always been seen as a safe and family-friendly place. But, to be sure the city sustained the perception and the reality, we could not stand still. We had to be prepared to respond to any emergency, even ones we had not imagined yet, anywhere in the city. We needed to continue to provide exceptional public safety support to a range of unique facilities with critical protection needs, including the Anaheim Convention Center, Honda Center, Angel Stadium of Anaheim, and the Disneyland Resort itself. In many respects, these were not new issues. While September 11 brought

C. Pringle (✉)
Mayor, Anaheim, CA, (2002–present)
e-mail: sray@anaheim.net

S. Hakim, E.A. Blackstone (eds.), *Safeguarding Homeland Security*,   159
DOI 10.1007/978-1-4419-0371-6_14, © Springer Science+Business Media, LLC 2009

anti-terrorism preparedness to the forefront, Anaheim had long dealt with the ongoing preparedness issues characteristic of our region, with readiness for wildfires and earthquakes being particularly vital.

Over the years, we had often turned to technology to help us serve public safety needs better. We had built up databases of information; we had a terrific Traffic Management Center; we strove to have state-of-the-art equipment. But in 2003, over the course of commissioning an information technology (IT) plan for the city, a few things became clear. First, we had a lot of strong IT systems in various city departments, but they did not talk well to each other. In addition, during an incident it took a lot of telephone calls and paging to obtain and share information. In short, we needed a better way of managing information during a crisis. By doing so, we hoped to increase collaboration in emergency situations and enhance overall team performance through better access to data.

To build the state-of-the-art emergency management tool we envisioned we knew that we wanted to build on the technology assets we already had but wanted to take a quantum leap forward. To help achieve this, we wanted to tap into the private sector's knowledge and talent base through a public–private partnership. We wanted to find a partner that had accomplished something similar for a private sector client (since this kind of solution did not exist in the public sector at the time) and could bring that expertise to address our needs. This emergency management tool could not be something that just made for an interesting demonstration; it needed to work, anytime and under the most challenging circumstances.

The private sector firm EDS immediately came to mind. At the time, the city and EDS were working on a full IT outsourcing partnership, an arrangement that is still in-place and continues to spark cross-team innovations. Because of this relationship, EDS had full knowledge of the city's IT assets and was aware of our communications needs. The team also brought a technical savvy that was crucial. Ultimately, I do not believe that the solution we collaboratively developed would have happened without EDS as a partner with the city.

The result of this dynamic partnership between the City of Anaheim and the EDS will be the development of a fully integrated crisis management system called the Enterprise Virtual Operations Center (EVOC). It is the first emergency management solution of its kind implemented at the local level that incorporates collaborative, real-time, secure, and virtual functionality. Never before has a system brought together critical information from a wide range of departments and jurisdictions on a single computer screen. EVOC allows all authorized users in the organization – not just top management – to view, through a web portal, what is happening in an emergency and provide the actionable information to best respond.

Business Issues and Background

Our goal was to provide a tool that not only enhanced collaboration but also thoroughly encouraged it. The genesis of EVOC arose from a basic desire to know what is happening and to share that information. Our hypothesis in pursuing EVOC as a broad-based tool was that our staff needed to know what was going on beyond their areas of responsibility. And that with a tool like EVOC in their hands, they would learn more about events occurring throughout the city – more shared information would then lead to collaboration. In turn, this would drive better, faster responses that could not happen without a tool like EVOC. As practical daily use of EVOC continues to extend into the field, we will have a better understanding of whether the hypothesis holds true. But the early results look promising.

In the interim, we have come a long way from where we started. A key challenge to taking a new approach was dealing with a problem commonly encountered in both the public and the private sectors: a tendency to keep information internal and not to share it. At first, the need to share information may not be obvious. The data serve a particular organization's purpose, but the data stay insular. And when the data stay insular, it defeats collaboration. Further complicating the problem, typically, are the legacy information technology systems themselves. Siloed or stove-piped communications systems, which allow little or no interoperability, have been identified as a problem on a national level. Our mission, then, was to demolish those silos, putting information in the hands of front-line responders and enabling incident managers and city officials to see the whole picture.

As part of that process, we needed to move forward with the idea of challenging a traditional understanding of jurisdictional boundaries as they relate to information sharing. During a major incident, there are many threads to weave together to create coherent situational awareness: fire and rescue operations, emergency medical response, evacuation procedures, law enforcement presence, and many more. And as incidents unfold across city, county and state lines (as they commonly will), gaining rapid, accurate situational awareness becomes even more complex. We imagined a tool that could give us instant access to information made available from multiple city departments, and even multiple cities. We also wanted to be able to share our own information with other regional governments, as well as state and federal agencies. How might that help us provide the best possible incident response for the public?

Appropriately, these ideas raised concerns among police, fire, and others about maintaining citizens' data privacy and security. We knew that this was the ultimate challenge to overcome – we simply could not pursue a solution that would compromise residents' sensitive information. But we felt confident that with the right technology approach, we could provide secure, authorized access to a wealth of information that could enhance our responsiveness and help us make better decisions during daily operations and major incidents.

In addition, existing physical and technological environments posed serious problems for situational awareness. Organizations in the public sector for many years have had emergency operations centers (EOCs), actual brick-and-mortar facilities or "situation rooms," where leaders and key staff members go during a crisis. It takes time to physically report to an EOC once it has been activated. And once the individuals are there, communications with field operations personnel usually take place via radio and telephone; much of the incident planning and management is done on a white board and conveyed by phone or e-mail to team members who are on the scene of the incident. In addition, the information provided for decision making is largely paper based. A couple of problems result from this setup. First, what if key members of the leadership team are out of town? Without a virtual command and control tool, they will have almost no visibility into events as they unfold, which may negatively affect decision making. Furthermore, what if the EOC location is compromised? In a worst-case situation, having most of a city's leadership in the same physical location is a potentially disastrous scenario. With all of this in mind, we began investigating whether we could conduct command and control operations virtually for major incidents, as well as everyday operations. For the leadership team in Anaheim, this was a critical distinction, as crises often begin as seemingly routine incidents.

We started the planning process during the summer 2003. Although we had been interested in finding ways to aggregate public safety and law enforcement information for some time, by 2003 there was increased emphasis nationwide on a cross-department and a cross-jurisdictional collaboration for incident management. One of our goals was to boost performance by providing decision makers and first responders with better access to data. Our vision was to break down organizational barriers through information-sharing technology that would leverage a common approach, framework, and solution set. We wanted it to be rapidly scalable, to readily integrate new technologies, and to easily extend to other agencies and regional governments. Ultimately, we wanted to transform how information is used. Applying approaches that were already available in the private sector, we wanted to enable our decision makers to visualize and connect with the situation in the field so they could make better decisions faster. To do this, we needed to facilitate complete synergy among our teams and the data they rely on – and create an entirely new way of using and applying intelligence.

We asked our technology partner, EDS, to help identify technology solutions that could address our business issues around collaboration. Previously, EDS had developed private sector knowledge management portals for critical information, aggregating data through a single program. Based on that experience and in response to our request, EDS created a basic framework called the Mission Support Platform. It was set up to allow us to monitor operations throughout the city, with a special emphasis on collaboration among emergency response organizations. At that point, we began to determine how the Mission Support Platform could be made more robust, with the idea of incorporating our computer-aided dispatch systems (CAD) for police and fire, traffic management cameras, and existing building security cameras. Several developments converged at this time, contributing to the system that eventually became EVOC. The Internet was becoming increasingly reliable and available for providing services, and it was increasingly possible to link in disparate systems. Wi-Fi was becoming available and hardware items such as cameras were going digital, and thus easier to link into the portal. So the timing and the partnership were critical elements, making Anaheim in 2003 the right place and at the right time to launch an innovative, proactive technology approach for emergency management.

The subsequent planning and design process was collaborative, with Anaheim's city manager's office, the fire and police departments, the City Council, and my own office providing key input. Throughout the process of refining the vision and designing the solution, a number of external agencies and experts were also consulted and given the opportunity to weigh in and provide input on early prototypes. These included the US Department of Homeland Security (DHS), the White House Department of Intergovernmental Affairs, Southern California congressional representatives and state legislators, Orange County law enforcement and fire associations, and EDS homeland security subject matter experts. The city also planned emergency management conference presentations to share the EVOC prototype and solicit feedback to enhance the overall concept.

As might be expected for any technology project of this scope and significance, funding presented a major challenge. In many respects, DHS played a formative role in developing EVOC and, very simply, Anaheim could not have accomplished its mission without the funding DHS provided to the region through Urban Area Security Initiative (UASI) grants. Anaheim has received these grants each year since their inception in 2004. Additional funding and other aid came from John Carnegis, then with the DHS Office for Domestic Preparedness; the State of California Office of Emergency Services, with specific support from Ron Iden; the Orange County police and fire chief's associations; and the regional UASI working committee. Key hardware and software providers were also involved in EVOC development, and in some cases invested their products to help the city develop a working prototype to share with others since funding was such a central issue.

EVOC and Its Supporting Technologies

So, on a basic level, what is EVOC? While its method and design have evolved over the years,[1] EVOC's core capability has remained the same. It is a virtual emergency management solution that centralizes existing information and live data feeds for decision makers. From a technical standpoint, EVOC is a secure, Web-based Microsoft (MS) SharePoint portal that uses MS Virtual Earth[TM] as a core means of displaying information, linking databases from all over the city.[2] While similarly robust portal technology had been used for corporate and retail project purposes, this marked its first use for managing emergency response. The portal presents a consolidated view of conditions and events for full situational awareness. EVOC provides access to data obtained across a wide range of platforms, allowing officials and emergency responders to review topographical maps, global positioning system (GPS) data, weather conditions, blueprints, utility plans, video camera feeds, radio transmissions, live news feeds, and more – all from a single application. EVOC makes it easy to share information almost instantaneously, both within and across departments; increased intra- and inter-agency collaboration has followed suit.

One of the system's real strengths is its ease of use. EVOC uses images from MS Virtual Earth to form the basis of its landing page, showing all incidents as

Fig. 14.1 EVOC – Anaheim incident map view

points-on-a-map (see Fig. 14.1). The viewer can toggle the image to show a standard map view, an aerial view, or a combination of the two. By rolling the mouse over an incident marker (labeled by municipality and color coded according to the department responding – for example, blue for police incidents, red for fire incidents), the user can obtain basic details. Clicking on the incident marker opens a window that provides more granular information, such as building blueprints, lists of any hazardous materials that may be located at the site, photos from the scene which may have been uploaded, and live streaming video if a city camera is positioned nearby. On the initial map screen, a box labeled "Layers Control" may be opened to allow the user to toggle additional information on or off on the map – such as the location of city vehicles, hospitals, schools, and traffic cameras (with live footage viewable by rolling the mouse over the camera marker). Major incidents, or threshold events, are highlighted in an alert box positioned to the side of the landing page, with supporting links available that lead the user to a detail page.

System monitoring, which designates threshold events and pushes them to a higher level of visibility, is another key element. This system monitoring is customizable and can be configured to indicate these events according to the evolving needs of the city. Currently, a threshold event for Anaheim is indicated, for example, by incidents for which seven or more fire units or eight or more police units respond. Power outages and street closures also appear in the alerts and notifications box, as they can have a significant impact on public safety. The system monitoring technology is also used on an ongoing basis to create a virtual perimeter around the Anaheim Convention Center; the system generates a call or e-mail to the convention center management if an incident occurs within 700 m of the facility. We created this perimeter at the request of the convention center management and can provide the same service for other locations as needed.

The robustness of the tool has proven extremely helpful. It currently merges information from seven fire departments and two police departments, with an unlimited degree of further expandability, opening great opportunities for collaboration regionally and beyond. The map function is also extremely flexible, allowing users to zoom, pan the map as far as they want, and go directly to a specific area. The tool, in combination with the GPS and Automatic Vehicle Location (AVL) technologies, enables us to locate our vehicles wherever they happen to be. We have been able to use this functionality to locate the position of public vehicles when they are in service within city limits, but also when working in other jurisdictions. For example, this tool was helpful when the Anaheim Fire Department provided support to firefighters in Malibu and when city participated in post-Katrina recovery efforts in Louisiana. This, in combination with all the other activities EVOC allows us to track, has already proven crucial during high-profile emergency incidents. When the 2007 wildfires struck Malibu, for instance, Anaheim Fire Chief Roger Smith happened to be out of town; yet he was able to locate every Anaheim unit that was providing support and track every development and communication, all on his laptop computer with secure remote access through EVOC. And using the aerial view of the map, he could assess the terrain his teams were facing – in some cases, before the teams on the ground were aware of that information themselves.

The portal setup and browser-based user interface speed the process of finding and retrieving information for most users, partly because of the familiarity of navigation and partly because of the portal's versatility. Vast amounts of information can be organized, categorized, and placed within a few clicks of the landing page (see Fig. 14.2). All of this is underpinned by the city's existing databases. That has been a key feature of EVOC: It leverages existing investments. "Enabling" software,

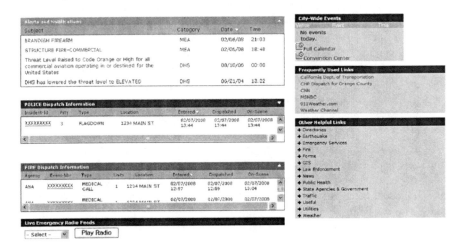

Fig. 14.2 EVOC – Anaheim textual incident data, radio systems, and custom links

or middleware, gives EVOC access to data from legacy applications, data repositories, and information systems without our having to re-engineer them. New functionality can be, and is, added on an ongoing basis. Now, all this information that once existed in silos (and which the public perhaps thought was already shared, but was difficult to share because of technology barriers) is available, collaboratively, across the city for any employee with authorized access. Key information from sources such as police and fire CAD systems, GPS on vehicles, databases of building plans, traffic cameras, and much more, once available only to one or maybe two agencies or departments, is now shared widely and securely. Other repositories, many of them linked through the Info and Links page or the Document Library tab, make an even richer set of information available: hazardous material data, parcel boundaries (shown as an overlay on the Virtual Earth map), tax roll information on properties, calendaring systems, phone lists, emergency evacuation plans, and more. Information from California's Electronic Data Information System (EDIS) has also been incorporated into the portal, making items such as fire advisories and fault-line maps directly accessible and enabling Amber alerts to be prominently displayed on the landing page.

We believe that broad information availability is resulting in a fundamental collaborative shift for the City of Anaheim. Traffic camera footage alone provides a great example. Before EVOC this footage could be viewed only in our Traffic Management Center, and thus, by default, only by members of our Office of Public Works staff. Today, the information is directly available to anyone with EVOC access and is routinely used by other departments to assess traffic congestion in various areas of the city. This has proven extremely useful for activities like managing major city events and mitigating and rerouting traffic following major accidents. The EVOC portal has been a cost-efficient, elegant solution to a complex problem: how to bring disparate data streams together and break down barriers to information sharing, making it possible for individuals to work better and faster. We hope that it will continue to shift the collaborative paradigm forward, allowing users to draw on their natural inquisitiveness and discover opportunities to contribute their expertise on an inter-departmental basis as they see events unfold on any given day. An example would be a fire department official that sees a wildfire become a threshold event in an adjacent city and immediately begins planning support efforts, before he is even contacted to do so. This is the kind of scenario we have already seen and strongly believe will become prevalent as EVOC continues to evolve and is brought out closer to the beat cop, the fire station, and the city worker out on his or her daily rounds.

Because of the volume, value, and distribution of the information available through EVOC, and of course its sensitive nature at times, security is an extremely high priority. We address security in several ways. Without going into depth about the technical aspects of our security measures, I think the guiding philosophy behind those choices is important to note. Primarily, we believe in taking an in-depth, layered approach to system security. First of all, data is encrypted and users are authenticated before they get on the network. In addition, permissions are assigned according to role on a need-to-know basis. In other words, a user is able (or unable) to view various kinds of information based on his or her identity and role. Currently, EVOC can be available to all 2,000 City of Anaheim employees, each of whom would have secure access. Users' access to features varies, with police officers generally having access to the broadest range of data; users outside the police group, for example, cannot access the police radio, among other features. Conversely, however, a police officer would not be able to access material stored on, say, the finance department drives. And on a broader, system-wide basis, each city can only access its own municipality's information, beyond a very superficial level, such as CAD information and vehicle locations. Beyond access authorization issues, naturally we take all the appropriate precautions considered essential to system security, such as maintaining firewalls, performing intrusion detection, and running virus scans. We perform due diligence on an ongoing basis to assure that we are constantly keeping a watchful eye on security issues.

To extend the benefits of EVOC further into the field and to provide additional communication services supporting Anaheim public safety, the city worked with EDS to develop an outdoor wireless network dedicated exclusively to city government use. This is a licensed, multi-frequency, multi-mode wireless 4.9 GHz and 802.11a/b/g public safety network – one of the first in the United States. We pursued this solution because we wanted employees to have access to their desktops while working in the field. In addition to improving overall situational awareness and collaboration through constant access to EVOC, we also wanted to address some practical concerns. For example, a police officer's job sometimes requires him or her to park visibly in a key position, and the officer's presence accomplishes the mission. But with the right technology support, officers can get other aspects of their job done while maintaining that presence. Rather than having to go back and forth to the station to complete and electronically file paperwork, we thought it would be extremely helpful if officers could do this work and upload it to the system while out on their beats. However, without a dedicated wireless system, this approach would have been cumbersome at best: the bandwidth was not available, ease of use was low, and security was a major concern.

The 4.9 GHz system solves a number of problems. It eliminates interference from telephones and other equipment in the public realm and it can be secured much more effectively. In addition, it prevents a problem we had encountered before: competition with the public for bandwidth during an emergency. Naturally during emergencies people tend to use their cell phones, tying up the lines, and this can become a major issue when emergency response teams are using public-available equipment and bandwidths. During the fall wildfires in 2007, for example, which affected neighboring communities and for which Anaheim was providing mutual aid support, a fire official from the affected area appeared on the local news asking residents to curtail nonessential cell phone use so that the fire department could communicate with their people. Now, with the dedicated public safety outdoor wireless system, we can make sure our first responders and incident managers have the bandwidth they need to get the job done. And in a major crisis that results in a drastic usage spike among network users, we can also prioritize bandwidth according to the individual and his or her role – something else that would not be possible if we were using a public entity for this service. Prioritizing the needs of incident managers and those on the front lines as they deal with a crisis will improve situational management and efficiency, enhancing overall mission support and improving outcomes.

Currently, there are about 100 wireless access points across the city. The defense strategy for the wireless network, similar to that of EVOC, is an in-depth, layered one; the network provides only authorized access and, even then, exclusively to the systems an individual user needs to access. Our goal is to provide a secure mobile experience comparable to hard-wired functionality for most applications – which includes providing uninterrupted service as a police officer, for example, drives from one neighborhood to the next. In addition, since the wireless network is our own system and we have the bandwidth available, we can control our future access needs and consider features like in-car access to video feeds. As EVOC and the systems supporting it continue to evolve, we hope that the wireless capability will be a useful tool for community interaction, as well. As more police cars are equipped to communicate as efficiently as possible with the wireless network (with in-car routers scheduled to be in-place fleet-wide for the police department during 2008), we believe we will see more occasions in which an officer brings his laptop into a resident's home or a community meeting to display and discuss patterns of crime in the community, using information that may be easily aggregated through EVOC. Thus the knowledge base that helps the officer on the job also extends to directly inform and involve the neighborhoods that officer serves.

Case Study: Windy Ridge Wildfire

EVOC proved instrumental for situational awareness during the Windy Ridge Fire (also called the 241 Fire at Windy Ridge) in 2007. On March 11, an abandoned stolen vehicle caught fire at a toll plaza on State Route 241, at the edge of the Weir Creek Regional Park. The toll plaza was upwind from an area with heavy growth that had not burned in 20 years. Fire swiftly swept through the park, stoked by high winds running parallel to the city, with flames moving at great speed toward homes in Anaheim Hills.

This kind of fire requires firefighters to move continuously and quickly to keep pushing the fire back. As the wind shifts and the fire advances or retreats, first responders are in constant motion. Under ordinary circumstances, without EVOC, it is very difficult to know where all your resources are – whether they are positioned correctly as the fire moves or if they are in a situation where it may rapidly become impossible to continue firefighting safely. With EVOC, incident managers and city officials could look at their screens and see exactly what was going on. They could locate every vehicle, to the point of even being able to track fire and public utility vehicles as they drove through Anaheim Hills. They could follow police and radio transmissions throughout the event. They could access ESI's WebEOC® application using EVOC, tracking significant events on a situational report screen where responders or incident managers enter key information, creating a real-time narrative of the event. They could check weather conditions, learn of power outages, review terrain maps, and evaluate other potential hazards. It represented an important opportunity to share information across jurisdictions. The Orange County Fire Authority was the lead response organization, with all communications coming through EVOC. Through EVOC, everyone involved in managing the incident could have a shared perspective – literally, since they could view the exact same data flow through their browser windows, whether they were logging in from Anaheim or from thousands of miles away.

This shared perspective was extremely helpful, particularly because Anaheim's Assistant City Manager Tom Wood, along with three City Council members, happened to be on the east coast that day. In fact, the fire had just started as their plane took off from Long Beach and headed for Washington, DC. As they flew over Anaheim and looked out the airplane windows, they could see plumes of smoke rising near the east end of the city; they could even see some first responders on the scene. As soon as they reached their destination, Tom and the council members booted up their laptops and logged into EVOC. As they listened to live radio traffic and checked the position of the units, they quickly learned the scope of the event and gained immediate situational awareness; then they continued to monitor the situation closely, contributing assistance as the situation evolved. In fact, they were able to notify the city's Public Information Officer (PIO), who was there on the scene, about an injured firefighter they had heard about over the radio transmissions. Because of EVOC, the team in Washington, DC, knew immediately that an injury had occurred to a firefighter on the front line and that medics were responding. Because the PIO was dealing with the immediacy of a chaotic situation, the news of the firefighter's injury simply had not reached him yet – but as soon as he received the information, he was able to deal immediately with the issues of communicating the information to family members and then the media.

Finally, the Windy Ridge Fire marked the first time we had used a new feature of EVOC to help us execute a major evacuation. Some of the problems encountered with evacuations in New Orleans motivated several Anaheim City departments to collaborate on ways to obtain evacuation information as quickly as possible in an emergency. They wanted to know everything they could possibly know about an area for evacuation – and they wanted the data to be available instantly. The city's information systems and public utilities offices worked closely with the fire and police departments to plan the functionality and assemble the information that now populates an application called Ready Anaheim, which is accessible through EVOC. It allows an incident manager to work either with a predetermined quadrant of the city or to draw a border around a perimeter of streets and immediately receive critical data for executing an evacuation. He or she can immediately retrieve information about the streets involved, the number of households, the addresses, census information (such as the names of property owners), and more. By using this information in their planning, emergency responders are better able to rapidly communicate with, evacuate, and support residents during a crisis. The system can even tell us how much food and water will be needed to support the people in that area for a given period of time. During the Windy Ridge Fire, more than a thousand residents were evacuated from the hill and canyon area in the path of the wildfire. We were able to be more exact about the information and addresses provided to law enforcement, so we knew that we were evacuating the right houses in the right areas. Pulling all that information together took seconds instead of hours. Ultimately, we plan to have the addresses in Ready Anaheim linked to a reverse 911 emergency notification system.

The Windy Ridge fire was brought under control with only one home damaged – no residents were injured or homes lost. Excellent communication and access to information helped. EVOC allowed us to access vital information quickly and be able to access it anywhere. Instead of managing this incident the old way – with maps spread out on the hoods of vehicles, with calls coming in from all over as officials try to determine what is going on, and with cumbersome methods for executing and tracking evacuations – we had a whole new way of managing a wildfire crisis: collaboratively and at unprecedented speed.

Case Study: Golden Guardian 2007

In November 2007, Golden Guardian, a California homeland security and disaster preparedness exercise, took place in Anaheim, along with two other cities. EVOC and the citywide Wi-Fi network were great assets to Anaheim emergency responders and to the other federal, state, and local agencies that participated in the drill. The full-scale exercise, based at Angel Stadium of Anaheim, was designed to test the region's ability to deter, prevent, respond, and recover from a potential terrorist attack or catastrophic natural disaster. An Amtrak station situated at the edge of the stadium's parking lot made the site well suited for simulating simultaneous attacks on mass transit and a sporting venue.

The exercise was extremely complex, with 12 hours of active drilling over 2 days. It drew upon safety personnel from the entire urban area and tested unified command – meaning that all police and fire personnel worked together under one command. In addition to testing the Incident Commander (or Unified Command), operations for the Joint Hazard Assessment Team, Urban Search and Rescue, Explosive Ordinance Disposal, and Emergency Management Services were also tested. The Orange County Transportation Authority, the Federal Bureau of Investigation, the Civil Support Team, and Amtrak/Metrolink all sent teams. More than 20 area hospitals participated, along with nearly 400 people playing the roles of incident victims. In all, roughly 20 jurisdictions took part in the exercise.

Following a massive blast that simulated a high explosive attack at the Amtrak station, first responders were dispatched from Anaheim and its neighboring cities. They arrived within minutes and encountered the realistically simulated chaos of a large-scale disaster. Car bombs had also been exploded and mock casualties were everywhere, needing immediate attention. The Orange Freeway was actually closed down in both directions alongside the stadium just before the exercise began to prevent traffic accidents that could have occurred in response to the explosions. (The freeway closure, of course, presented another aspect of planning and communications on the first day of the event.)

Given the scale and complexity of the exercise, EVOC and the wireless network helped in several key ways. One was by facilitating situational awareness and collaboration on a cross-jurisdictional basis. Because the system is web based and easy to use, every department can be on EVOC during a time of crisis. Departments that have never used EVOC before can be provided a password and connect with it right away. Typically, users get the hang of using the portal very quickly. During the Golden Guardian exercise, EVOC was pulled up and used by the various jurisdictions involved, and it was also set up at the mobile command post and in the Emergency Operations Center. It provided first field response and gave incident managers an eyes-on approach as the exercise unfolded. They had quick access to all the repositories of information and they could have confidence that the data were up to date. Without a system like EVOC, it is easy for emergency managers to find themselves using manuals, maps, or other materials that have become outdated and may no longer be accurate. Those items are now updated in EVOC; a single update can benefit scores of users, preventing them from having to rely on old material. The mapping and GPS functions were also extremely useful, showing the participating departments where each resource was deployed and enabling them to make better, faster decisions about where the resources should be. In addition to Orange County municipalities, the FBI, the California Department of Transportation, and other state officials could collaborate using EVOC to view live camera feeds, for example, or follow the development of significant events through the WebEOC application (see Fig. 14.3). EVOC was also useful for planning and reporting corrective actions as the event evolved.

The outdoor wireless network also helped facilitate constant readiness assessment during Golden Guardian. Prioritization software helped assure that wireless bandwidth was allocated based on individual need, ranking, or role as a participant. This allocation was modified as needed throughout the event. As roles were defined, or when they changed over the course of the 2-day exercise, and as various participants arrived on the scene, the roles for bandwidth priority were adjusted accordingly. Another wireless network innovation tested at Golden Guardian was video surveillance that was beamed from a helicopter to multiple locations. This enabled emergency managers and participating departments to have an immediate visual on developments so they could deploy resources right away. We see this capability as having several important emergency management applications – for example, helping with situational awareness during wildfires or earthquakes, as well as for terrorist incidents.

We found that live camera feeds accessible through EVOC during Golden Guardian significantly increased situational awareness and closed the downtime gap. More experts were able to receive and view information more rapidly – an important capability for public safety. Cameras at Golden Guardian allowed EVOC users, both on- and off-site, to see the size of the fire resulting from the exploded vehicle and the direction the smoke was going, as well as the location of the crowd, the direction of crowd movement, and area vehicle traffic patterns. Being able to view high-quality live data remotely can make a tremendous difference in decision quality and response accuracy.

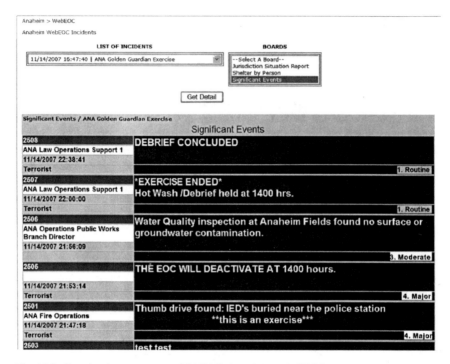

Fig. 14.3 Situational report screen – WebEOC viewed through EVOC

In the end, EVOC was well received at the Golden Guardian exercise in Anaheim. It sped communication and collaboration throughout the demanding drill, helping dozens of teams work together across both disciplines and jurisdictions.

Future Plans for EVOC

During emergencies like the Windy Ridge wildfire and exercises, such as Golden Guardian, we have come to appreciate EVOC's flexibility and effectiveness, as well as the way it accelerates information sharing and breaks down communications barriers both within and across jurisdictions. The system has already expanded to include numerous communities within Orange County. The cities of Anaheim and Fullerton leverage the full capabilities of EVOC, while five other municipalities (Garden Grove, Orange, Huntington Beach, Newport Beach, and Fountain Valley) use EVOC to display CAD information, as well as vehicle tracking in some cases, with fuller participation in the works.

As for future plans, we would like to leverage EVOC even more extensively for our daily operations in Anaheim. Currently, it is still seen more as a tool to manage critical incidents and major events such as marathons and baseball and hockey playoff games. Outside of these situations, on a daily basis EVOC is typically most helpful for people involved in planning and in daily management of resources – the Fire Department's planning team and battalion chiefs, for example, or the Police Department's desk sergeants. But we would like to see EVOC used much more extensively. The outdoor wireless capability will be a key factor, as more vehicles are equipped with routers for faster, more robust data access over the course of 2008. That represents a major phase in the evolution of EVOC; we believe we will see much greater daily use of EVOC out in the field at that point, as more users increase their familiarity with the system and begin to see the benefits that live data access can provide as they do their jobs day in and day out. And we believe that these new users will follow their intellect and inquisitiveness to discover even more ways we can make the system useful to them.

To further extend the base and improve the user experience, we are drawing on feedback from our steering committee for EVOC. It is a broad-based group that includes members from the City Manager's office, the Information Systems department, the Police Department, the Fire Department, the public works and public utilities departments, the information office, and the city planning department. Anaheim's UASI grant administrator is also a member, as well as representatives from other participating Orange County municipalities. The steering committee, using their own observations and garnering input from their departments, is helping us find ways to apply EVOC's capabilities that we would not have predicted and which we believe will prove extremely useful for daily operations. From an information standpoint, there is an endless amount of data that can be provided and made part of the backbone of EVOC. There remains a great deal we can do to expand the data set, while still keeping information accessible, to make the system a fuller response tool for first responders as they arrive at certain sites. For example, more robust access to building plans would be helpful for evacuation purposes, so first responders could have that information on their handhelds as they arrive on the scene.

We will also begin using the information aggregated through EVOC to do more proactive, predictive public safety work as the system enters its next phase of evolution. We would like to use the historical database to detect certain kinds of patterns and to provide more proactive monitoring that will enhance our responsiveness to public safety needs. We believe that EVOC can also help us work more effectively with the community, an objective championed by Anaheim Police Chief John Welter, among others. He sees this as another way EVOC can help us break down barriers, by encouraging community involvement and communication, and ultimately providing the community better service. What a great tool for a police officer to be able to use when working directly with the public. An officer can take his or her laptop into a resident's house and pull up the community on EVOC, showing the number of crime calls from the neighborhood, photos of nearby vandalism, and the date and location of the next community meeting. The fact is community members have the right to know about the crime going on in their neighborhoods. We can educate them on how to help make their neighborhoods safer and change the conditions in that location – in other words, we can help them see what their active role could be in crime prevention in their community. As collaboration develops between a neighborhood's residents and its public safety partners, residents will not only be able to see the problems that exist in their area, but can also see what has been accomplished through the partnership and be aware of the successes that occur.

In addition to using EVOC to collaborate more directly with the community, we also plan to establish more partnerships with private facilities. Among other possibilities, we would like to create means by which, in the event of an emergency, we can essentially flip a switch and have secure access to on-site video feeds from these locations. If we could access footage from bank cameras during a robbery, for example, what a tremendous help that would be for positioning resources and responding to the situation as successfully and safely as possible.

Furthermore, in working closely with DHS, we have become keenly aware of the importance of information sharing regionally, and we would like to see regional use of EVOC expand. The portal application makes it easy to securely add municipalities. Starting from a standard template, participating cities can have custom pages developed to meet their individual needs. Their city page is just one click away from the main landing page that depicts the Orange County area as a whole, and each city can decide how much information they want users outside of their organization to access on a daily basis. When events cross jurisdictional borders, switches can be flipped to allow greater access for other authorized EVOC users. Viewing and listening to a neighboring jurisdiction's real-time communications first hand during a cross-jurisdictional event can provide invaluable information, and it represents another opportunity to knock down silos that hinder emergency response. EVOC can help us transcend similar barriers that exist between levels of government too – with organizations such as DHS, for example, eventually being able to see what is happening in Anaheim, or the California Department of Forestry communicating through EVOC as it responds to a fire. All of this can be done securely, as well. Just as the individual police officer in the field does not have access to all the information in EVOC, the same would be true multiple jurisdictions operating through the same system.

We are also excited about integrating new and enhanced technologies through EVOC in the future. Reference software that provides information about chemical reactions has recently been integrated into the system and chemical plume mapping will soon be integrated as well. For the longer term, we are looking into using infrared to highlight hotspots during wildfires. Because of the wind and smoke during a wildfire, it can be difficult to get line of sight to the worst parts of the fire. Data gathered from infrared sensors and channeled through EVOC would allow the field units to see where the hotspots are. It would provide an innovative solution to an extremely troublesome problem.

On a more immediate basis, we plan to bring more cameras online, locating some of them on fire department vehicles themselves. With the cameras available on-site, fire department officials can assess the situation much more rapidly. With real-time footage streaming live from multiple angles, officials would have the information to make decisions that otherwise require them to physically relocate to the site. Viewing video from their desktops, they can decide whether to assemble an executive team or to activate an emergency operations center, for example. We also plan to improve transmission speeds and video transmission quality for greater image clarity. High-quality streaming video, along with all the other information available through EVOC, means that officials off-site have an instant briefing that provides all the information their senses can pick up; then they can discuss the incident more effectively with the field commanders by bringing their own full awareness of the situation to the decision-making process. That way, everyone sees the same picture and has the same starting point.

Conclusion

Over the years we have learned a great deal as EVOC has come into its own. A key lesson has been the importance of reaching out to the private sector to form a strong technology partnership. Government's first response, particularly in the area of public safety, is often to keep systems development internal. However, I do not think we would have EVOC, certainly not a solution of the caliber of EVOC, without tapping into the innovation and creativity of a private sector partner like EDS. It put us in the position of being able to fully vet through a team of technology professionals how best to accomplish things. Our successes with EVOC would not have been accomplished without the participation of a private partnership, a situation, which I believe would be true of any municipality.

We are also very fortunate for all the help from the US department at Homeland Securities. Early in the development process, we made sure to consistently brief the DHS team, especially those responsible for the grants. With that, we built an excellent participatory network. We wanted to be sure everyone clearly understood how we were spending our money, what our spending priorities were, and the value we were getting. Through that process we received feedback from DHS and developed a greater understanding of the issues on the regional, state, and federal levels, which has been a great benefit to us.

We have been very pleased with what we have been able to accomplish with EVOC so far. We are seeing improved secure data flow for incident management and faster collaboration and response. Our users are responding to the system's ease of use, as they learn quickly how to select, filter, and organize the data viewed so that it serves their needs, curiosity, and interests. Interoperability is a strong and growing component as it allows secure collaboration with other jurisdictions. And reduced reliance on a brick-and-mortar EOC also represents a major step forward.

In the days and years ahead, we anticipate leveraging EVOC to extend and further accelerate situational awareness, collaboration, and action. In an ever-changing world, with issues of terrorism and other threats never far from our minds, it is critical to continually evolve and be prepared. EVOC has enhanced our ability to respond and is a tool that can be modified and changed as we move forward. EVOC is not static. The ability to add or grow the system is there, allowing us to continually evolve our preparedness.

Notes

1. The original iteration of EVOC presented users with a single-screen view that showed all of the city's traffic and security camera feeds, as well as other information, in a three-dimensional simulated "situation room" environment. It used Microsoft BizTalk Server to aggregate data from a subset of critical information systems. This approach took quite a bit of bandwidth, however, and tended to function slowly. In addition, it required users to load special software; consequently, employees could not access the application from anywhere but their city-provided desktop or laptop computers. As a result, the city and EDS decided to shift strategies and move to a browser-based, graphical ("points-on-a-map") view that aggregates data via Microsoft SharePoint portal technology.
2. To provide a little more technical background, EVOC is actually composed of three technology layers. First, the graphic interface that users see is simply a standard web browser. We chose to use a browser-based interface for its ease of use. In the middle of EVOC is a database. Instead of connecting the user interface directly to the information, we chose to use a database as a staging layer in between, partly because it is easier to connect the interface layer into the database instead of a back-end system. But it also gives us the ability to gather intelligence. Because of the database layer, we can send out major alerts or advisories based on the events in the database. Then as things become inactive in the database, we siphon them off into a historical database, which will help us with predictive analysis. The third part of EVOC is the source systems. We use XML to transfer data from back-end systems to EVOC for some data sources; a few others, like camera feeds and radio transmissions, connect directly without using XML. In these cases there is no staging database, just a direct connection from the back-end system data to the device.

Chapter 15
How a Midwestern "Digital City" Serves and Protects the Public

Frank A. Pasquale

Abstract Bellwood in 2005 created an integrated wireless surveillance network focused on 2.5 miles of public streets, sidewalks, and alleys. The system has both audio and video and can focus on sounds of breaking glass or gunshots. Cameras were also installed at intersections to catch red light runners, illegal right on red turns, violators of railroad crossing signals, and even overweight trucks. The system has reduced 911 calls, general calls for service, and such property crime as auto theft.

When a political candidate is elected by voters to serve in public office, regardless of the size of the city or town, they are legally and ethically obligated – and entrusted – to take full responsibility for the municipality's operation and future. Since being elected mayor of the village of Bellwood in 2001, I have been committed to the general principles of managing the village's operations, growth, and finances with a spirit of cooperation and open communication.

With that philosophy as a cornerstone, the village of Bellwood, which is located just 13 miles west of Chicago's renowned Loop business district, boasts of a number of amenities that make it attractive to residents, businesses, and visitors alike. Among those benefits and attractions is convenient transportation, as the village is located at the juncture of the well-traveled Eisenhower Expressway and the Tri-State toll. Bellwood is easily accessible from all directions and commuting to Chicago is easy. O'Hare Airport, known for decades as the world's busiest, is only 10 miles away.

In other words, Bellwood is the quintessential "crossroads town" that each day is a temporary host and destination to thousands of commuters, business owners, residents, and out-of-town consumers. For those reasons, public safety and security always have been a top priority.

When you consider a town's prominent geographic location – as in the case of Bellwood – it makes sense that we devote ample resources to creating and

F.A. Pasquale (✉)
Mayor, Bellwood, IL, (2001–present),
http://www.villageofbellwood.com/html/mayor_s_page. html
e-mail: fpasquale@vil.bellwood.il.us

S. Hakim, E.A. Blackstone (eds.), *Safeguarding Homeland Security*,
DOI 10.1007/978-1-4419-0371-6_15, © Springer Science+Business Media, LLC 2009

maintaining a comprehensive plan for the safety of our 21,000 residents (more than three-quarters of whom own and occupy their residence), business owners, and our 50-person police department. We are proud of the fact that Bellwood is the most technologically advanced municipality in Illinois due to our

- Village-wide integrated wireless Internet access;
- Integrated wireless camera security system;
- Automated traffic law enforcement system that works seamlessly with the village's police officers and police department command staff, the latter of which can access the network and the images it captures via the Internet from anywhere in the world.

One Village's Response

With public safety an enduring top priority of my administration, in March 2005, Bellwood proudly became the first suburb in Illinois to install a state-of-the-art integrated wireless surveillance network throughout our boundaries – creating, in effect, a virtual gated community. The initiative represented a prime example of how forward-thinking plans, especially in the area of public safety, can benefit residents, business owners, village employees, and law enforcement staff. This bold, cost-efficient initiative was a prime example of the "good government" all public officials strive to operate, and a win–win proposition for everyone – except those intent on breaking the law.

Our integrated wireless surveillance network is designed to be an effective, state-of-the-art tool to enable us to re-allocate our police officers for the most efficient patrol of the public way. The cameras in the network are exclusively focused on the village's two-and-a-half miles of public streets, sidewalks, and alleys. They also are aimed at the exterior of our more than 300 local businesses.

Working closely with a qualified technology contractor, we designed the network to be implemented in phases, the first featuring 21 strategically placed cameras throughout the village that are equipped with high-tech microphones that can instantly focus the camera on such discernible audible sounds as breaking glass, trains, auto alarms, and gunshots, among other occurrences. As of July 2006, 39 integrated wireless cameras have been deployed throughout the village, with plans to install 100 cameras by the end of 2006.

Based on ample research and the expertise of Current Technologies Corporation, the information technology, consulting firm that provided the technology, we knew that the network would immediately improve the safety of our police officers who respond to emergency calls. Our expectation was that these integrated cameras would assist our police department in more efficiently monitoring criminal activity and improve officers' response times to emergencies.

We made sure that our coordinated public relations and communications efforts emphasized the fact that the surveillance network would not replace or displace any officers in the Bellwood police department, but rather improve officers' ability to concurrently monitor the area in which they are located and other areas of the village via integrated video surveillance. We anticipated – and effectively addressed – the notion that the cameras represented an intrusion from so-called "Big Brother." We stressed to our residents through the local media and our own publications that courts at the local, state, and federal levels repeatedly have ruled that citizens cannot expect privacy in public.

The New Surveillance

Bellwood's squad cars already were equipped with a mobile data terminal (MDT) that could be used to receive and broadcast video feeds from a wireless camera installed to monitor a public area selected by the police officer. All of our police officers were individually trained on the user-based surveillance system, which features cameras equipped with 360° viewing capability and up-close optical scan to aid the officers in gathering important details while responding to the scene of an emergency or call for service.

When the new surveillance system debuted, the Bellwood Police Department was located at the village hall and was equipped with six monitors in the dispatch center that enabled staff to observe activity in the village 24 h each day, 7 days a week. To further enhance officers' mobility, surveillance and response times, selected police officers, and the department's command staff were granted access to handheld devices that could receive images from a selected wireless camera.

During the project's first phase, approximately 60% of the village's public way was covered by the cameras. We told residents, business owners, and the Chicago-area media that within 2 years the entire village's public areas would be covered by the system that was expected to cost only $1 per hour per camera over 3 years. Based on our detailed plans and budgeting, the initial $200,000 cost of the surveillance network would be significantly offset by fines generated from our automated traffic photo enforcement system (details of which will be provided later).

We could not have been more pleased with the reaction from residents and business owners who not only understood the importance of public safety, but were gratified that the village took a step forward and paid more than just lip service to an important, quality-of-life issue. As previously stated, Bellwood is a quintessential crossroads town that each day is a temporary host and destination for traveling commuters, business owners, residents, and consumers. For that reason, public safety and security are one of our top priorities. Our integrated wireless surveillance system and automated traffic law enforcement system are in response to residents' continued requests that we do more with our limited resources. We are committed to taking proactive approaches to traffic safety awareness and enforcement.

On the public relations front, virtually every television network in Chicago – including two popular Hispanic television stations – news radio stations, and mainstream and community newspaper reporters attended the March 2005 press conference. We demonstrated the new surveillance system, made available to newspaper photographers an MDT-equipped squad car, and facilitated on-site interviews with representatives from the village (including a bilingual employee for Hispanic television) and our technology consultant.

Within the first 6 months of the installation of the first camera in the village's integrated wireless network in March 2005, we had completed one-third of the plan to install 70 cameras. At that point, the strategic decision to implement a wireless surveillance network was reinforced through real-world evidence. Within those 6 months and compared to the same 6 months in 2004, Bellwood had experienced a

- 21% decrease in 911 calls;
- 16% decrease in calls for service;
- 20% reduction in property crimes.

To further reach our residents and business owners with an unfiltered message about the new system, we included a complete presentation of the network in the village's monthly bulletin and quarterly newsletter, both of which are mailed to constituents and can be picked up at various locations throughout the village.

Praise from Constituents

The ultimate barometer of the success of introducing technology-based law enforcement and traffic safety initiatives is in the acceptance – or rejection – from your constituents. The residents and business owners in Bellwood have embraced our efforts and even saw fit to express their support in writing. For example:

Dear Mayor Pasquale:

"I want to relay the comments of several of my church members concerning the Village's efforts to provide more security for the residents of Bellwood. They have, universally, expressed their support for your efforts to extend the reach of Bellwood police in doing their job to keep our streets safe. They have heralded Bellwood's installation of surveillance cameras throughout the Village as a creative use of modern technology to address 21st century problems."

Deliah Jones, Pastor

Logos Evangelistic Church

Dear Mayor Pasquale:

"Thank you for your efforts to make Bellwood safer. While a lot of politicians talk about reducing crime, it's refreshing to find a municipal leader who is willing to 'think outside the box' in doing something about it. As a business person, I know that safer streets will increase foot traffic to my clinic. Curtailing crime is a win-win situation for all of us."

Raj Khanna, M.D.

Medical Director

Advanced Occupational Medicine Specialists

Dear Mayor Pasquale:

"I want to thank you for standing up for the citizens of Bellwood. I was so happy to hear the news that crime in our great town is on the way down but I am not surprised. With all the publicity about Bellwood becoming the first community in Illinois to maintain video surveillance of all Village streets, what criminal would want to practice their trade here?"

                                                        Janet E. Flores

Equally important was the consistently positive response we received from our police officers who value new resources to do their jobs faster and safer.

Taking the Next Step

Armed with empirical and anecdotal evidence, we endeavored to expand our commitment to technology and public safety. In December 2005, the village held another press conference to demonstrate the newest advancement in our integrated wireless surveillance network, this time geared to identifying speeding motorists, many of whom routinely use the village as a pass-through to reach such other west suburban Cook County, IL, towns as Hillside, Oak Brook, Rosemont and Westchester, and of course, O'Hare Airport.

Although the legislation needed to legally validate this program ultimately was not passed, it enabled us to significantly raise residents' awareness of our commitment to traffic safety and law enforcement. It also was the precursor to future legislation that in July 2006 enabled Bellwood to become the first suburb in Illinois to use cameras to detect motorists who disobey traffic signals, e.g., running a red light and making an illegal right turn on red.

Designed to detect vehicles that disobey red lights and make illegal turns on red, the automated traffic law enforcement system focuses on a vehicle's license plate, which is automatically photographed and a warning issued to the registered owner. The system represents the next phase in our groundbreaking project as the first suburb in Illinois to install a complete state-of-the-art integrated wireless surveillance network throughout our entire village. The system only takes a photograph of the motorist's license plate – and not the driver – which eliminates any possibility of racial profiling, which the village does not practice or condone.

Because Bellwood residents, like all others, want to protect their privacy and prevent unlawful intrusions, it was important for key members of my administration to sing from the same hymnal and stress that the automated traffic law enforcement system to catch "red light runners" was not a tool to trap residents. Instead it is designed to change motorists' behavior and emphasize that everybody wins – drivers, pedestrians, and police – when drivers obey the law.

Introducing Red Light Technology

The village's multi-faceted plan to become the first "digital city" in the entire state took another major step forward in May 2006 when the Illinois General Assembly approved and Illinois Gov. Rod. R. Blagojevich signed a traffic safety measure designed to make the state's roads safer by giving municipalities in eight counties – including Cook County, home of the village of Bellwood – the ability to use automated photo enforcement at traffic signals to detect motorists who disobey those signals.

The governor signed House Bill 4835, which authorized counties in northeastern Illinois and the Metro East area to use a networked surveillance system to issue citations to motorists who run red lights; make illegal right turns on a red traffic signal; and violate railroad crossing warning gates and signals. The ticket is classified and handled similar to a parking violation, and not a moving violation, which means there is no adverse affect on motorists' insurance rating or driving record.

Our first camera, installed at an intersection adjacent to a local elementary school that is easily accessed by vehicles exiting the always-busy Eisenhower Expressway, was tested for several weeks. The testing began after a mid-July 2006 press conference to alert the media and public. During that period, warning notices were sent to drivers photographed disobeying the traffic signal. The village began issuing actual citations in late August 2006.

Now motorists caught running a red light, making an illegal right turn on red or violating a railroad crossing warning gate or signal receive a citation by mail within 30 days. If not paid or successfully contested by the vehicle's registered owner within 90 days, the $100 fine doubles to a statutorily mandated $200. The owner's driver's license can be suspended after five unpaid violations.

"Too many drivers think that running a red light isn't a big deal or that they won't be caught. It is a big deal because it's dangerous and now, with photo enforcement, they will be caught," said Gov. Blagojevich at the time he signed this important bill.

The legislation called for the Illinois Department of Transportation to work with local governments to establish locations where the photo enforcement for red lights is installed; the agency continued to monitor and analyze crashes at those locations to determine the bill's effectiveness.

An added benefit of the integrated wireless system is the ability of the surveillance cameras to help our officers identify trucks at multiple locations that appear to be overweight. Those trucks' loads can be the source of minor mishaps and major accidents, as well as a constant drain on the structural integrity of our streets. Police officers who have been trained to detect trucks that might be overweight can review images sent by the surveillance camera and, if necessary, can go to the scene to further evaluate the truck's load and safety.

My concern about the incidence and implications of traffic accidents, and in particular, accidents that result from traffic violations (e.g., running a red light) was why I lead the charge for the legislation that approved the automated traffic law enforcement system. The legislation, which was effective upon the governor's signing, also was influenced by the loud voices from my constituents and others who wanted to see the same type of change.

In addition, Bellwood residents and I were equally concerned about motorists who disobey railroad crossing warning gates and signs after that type of accident occurred in Elmwood Park, IL, on the evening before Thanksgiving 2005. Moved by that unfortunate accident, I was instrumental in raising awareness of the issue, which lead to the Illinois General Assembly's passing of the legislation. Sixteen people were injured when a metro express train crashed into several cars trapped in rush-hour traffic at that suburban railroad crossing.

The automated traffic law enforcement system, in conjunction with the integrated wireless camera system, was another important step in transforming Bellwood into the most technologically advanced suburb in Illinois; a virtual "digital city" that uses a vast integrated wireless computer network in virtually every facet of Bellwood's operations.

More Plans for Technology

Our plans called for Bellwood to be equipped with new surveillance cameras, personal computers, and mobile data terminals for police, fire, and other emergency vehicles, all of which will be Wi-Fi capable. Wireless LAN technology, commonly known as Wi-Fi, has become accepted globally as a prevalent method of wireless broadband Internet access.

In addition, in fall 2006, the village moved into a new $2.5 million regional 911 emergency center in nearby Leyden Township. The center, whose operations enabled Bellwood to become the first municipality outside of Chicago to introduce a 311 telephone system as a one-stop destination to allow our residents to access to village services and non-emergency police services, was funded in part by fines generated through the automated traffic law enforcement system. The project was a collaboration with Norcom, which serves as coordinating agency for a network of 11 suburban community police departments.

What We Have Learned

On the road to becoming the first "digital city" in Illinois, my administration has gained an even greater appreciation for listening to residents' and business owner's concerns and suggestions, and those from our law enforcement staff. We have learned the value of preparing an accurate message in advance of unveiling a new plan. We have gained an even greater appreciation of the value of the media in getting the word out to the people we serve.

When you have a positive story to tell and beneficial changes to make, it is critical to inform your constituents. For example, at the onset of my administration in 2001, I inherited 13 administrative officers in the police department; those officers were not being deployed to our streets. Fast forward to 2006, and as a result of implementing new surveillance technology and a shift in the department's culture and structure, there were only four administrative police officers working from our police department, which effectively put more officers on the street. Our expanded capability to efficiently and effectively provide around-the-clock virtual monitoring of our streets was made possible by the new surveillance system.

As a result of the new command and control center, fewer officers were needed at the village hall to receive emergency calls and dispatch fire and police personnel.

Those significant changes help lead to a 14% reduction in the village's total crime index in 2005 compared to 2004. Such positive stories must be told.

Moreover, the introduction of our integrated wireless surveillance network is largely responsible for nearly 1,300 fewer calls for service from January to June 2006 compared to the same period in 2005. The proof is in the pudding as the village recorded a 14% decrease in narcotics-related offenses, a 20% drop in thefts (excluding burglary and robbery), and a 17.5% decrease in auto thefts from January to June 2006 compared to the same period in 2005.

With respect to budgeting and administration, we have gained valuable insight into how the recycling of funds generated by these fines is an ideal method of ensuring the most efficient and effective spending and allocation of revenue. When you are able to generate revenue and concurrently protect the public and support your law enforcement activities, you promote top-quality budget management and heighten constituents' awareness of the correlation between the two.

In an ideal scenario played out over time, Bellwood's coffers will experience a continual decline in fines generated from the integrated wireless surveillance system and the automated traffic law enforcement system as the systems focus on deterrence and behavior modification and continually prompts motorists (and pedestrians) to obey the law.

Ideally, we will experience a reduction in the number of motorists who disobey red lights, make illegal turns on red, and violate railroad crossing warning gates and signals. Equally important, criminals will take their activity elsewhere for fear of being apprehended – quickly – by Bellwood's finest.

We hope to record and respond to fewer incidents of graffiti tagging on public and private property and to fewer overweight trucks burdening the village's streets. This new technology enables us to more efficiently and effectively allocate our resources to help our police officers practice prevention and investigation, and to solve crimes. At the same time, more routine but important police department responsibilities, such as writing traffic tickets, are being met and improved with the aid of integrated wireless computer technology.

Our hopes and plans are equally numerous. We have successfully used computer technology to become the first "digital city." As an elected official, I have acted on my charge to prioritize public safety and security by merging that responsibility with computer technology. We want to build on our status as the most technologically advanced municipality in the nation. We have started with village-wide integrated wireless Internet access, an integrated wireless camera security system and automated traffic law enforcement system to support our police department command staff and police officers. By doing so, and becoming a computerized "digital city," we hope to become a model for other municipalities to follow for years to come.

Chapter 16
Hurricanes and Modern Communications Infrastructure

Barry H. Axelrod and James V. Mudd

Abstract Hurricanes Charley and Wilma showed how fragile the communication network was in times of disaster. Breakdowns occurred in the public switched network, cellular, and the Internet. In response to that experience, Collier County improved its public safety radio system by adding more automotive radios which are less reliant on antennas, developed a private optic data network, improved the connectivity between the private data network and the Internet, and improved the telephone system through reduced reliance on one central office. It also enlisted volunteers who are "ham" radio users to provide communication during an emergency. The latter are least reliant on any infrastructures.

Collier County was part of the disaster declarations for Hurricane Charley in August 2004 and for Hurricane Wilma in October 2005. The County has a full-time population of 325,000, but being a winter paradise located in extreme southwestern Florida (the seat of Collier County, FL, is Naples), it attracts a peak seasonal population of about 450,000. Hurricane Charley was a very compact storm whose landfall was some 50 miles to the north of Naples, devastating the town of Port Charlotte. Although Collier County was the point of landfall for Hurricane Wilma, the exact landfall location was extremely lucky and favorable, hitting about 20 miles south of Marco Island in the almost unpopulated Everglades before cutting north-northwest into more populated areas. Wilma was a large storm that strengthened as it crossed the Florida peninsula and did more damage on the east coast of Florida than it did at its landfall point in Collier County, although there were fatalities in the city of Immokalee in Collier County. Both of these storms turned out to be primarily "wind events" for us, as there was minimal flooding due to rain and storm surge.

During Hurricane Charley, the structural damage to buildings was not as severe as the damage to infrastructure and services. The wind damage due to Hurricane Wilma was much more pronounced in Collier County due to its proximity and size, along with some tornado activity.

J.V. Mudd (✉)
County Manager, Collier County, FL, (2002–present)
e-mail: jamesmudd@colliergov.net

S. Hakim, E.A. Blackstone (eds.), *Safeguarding Homeland Security*,
DOI 10.1007/978-1-4419-0371-6_16, © Springer Science+Business Media, LLC 2009

These two storms were a humbling "wake-up" call for this community. Before these storms, the last hurricanes to visit upon this area were some 40 years prior. Although all of the emergency management professionals and first responders were well trained, hardly anyone had actually experienced a hurricane and recovery operations. Although plans were in place and everyone knew their responsibilities, our excellent response benefited from the fact that our homes were largely left intact allowing our responders the peace of mind for their family's well-being and the ability to "shelter in-place." We were able to focus on providing services to those who had been directly impacted.

The major technology lesson learned from these storms involved the communications infrastructure services. Collier County uses several different kinds of communications systems. We have an 800 MHz trunked Public Safety Radio System (PSRS), which is used countywide by all police, sheriff, fire, EMS, and city/county field staff. Traditional wired telephone service is the primary means of communications for government office staff. Mobile office staff and field staff use cellular telephones, and the county has a private data network, which connects staff computers to the Internet. The county also provides a television feed to the local cable television franchises and streams the TV station on the Internet.

Because of the ubiquitous nature of cellular phones, the Internet and e-mail, we have now built services, some of them "mission critical," that depend on the availability of these telecommunications and data communications networks. So the truth is that the public telephone system is more fragile now than it was 30 years ago, and we depend on it more now than we ever have. This was confirmed during our hurricane experiences in 2004 and 2005. In fact, every one of our communications infrastructures failed to some degree during the hurricane periods.

First, a little more background on Collier County is in order. The county encompasses 2,025 square miles which makes it one of the largest counties (geographically) east of the Mississippi river, although much of that land is federally controlled Everglades. There are no large cities in Collier County and about 250,000 of the full-time population live in unincorporated areas. Accordingly, Collier County is not one of the 20 top metropolitan areas in the country and gets no special attention from the State or Federal Government with respect to homeland security or FEMA funding. We are in a low-lying area prone to hurricanes. The highest elevation in the most populated part of Collier County is less than 12 feet above sea level. Collier County has inland borders with Miami-Dade County and Broward County to the east and with Lee County (Fort Myers) to the north.

Hurricane Experience

During Hurricane Charley, the PSRS sustained the expected kinds of wind damage, which is largely unavoidable: some damaged antennas and some antenna alignment issues. During the storm period, there were areas where radio system users could receive but not transmit. These issues were corrected within 24 h after the winds died down.

We also had a problem with electrical power. While our power generation equipment at the radio sites performed flawlessly, the power outages lasted upwards of 14 days at some of our remote locations. The fuel tanks on site had only enough fuel for 3 days. Although we had adequate contracts for generator fuel deliveries, gaining access to some of the remote locations due to downed trees in the first 3 days following the storm was not possible.

In Hurricane Wilma, the megawatt generator that provided back up power to most of the government headquarters facilities, including the control point for the PSRS failed. This caused the PSRS to go into backup mode, which resulted in degraded performance. Provisions for a secondary generator for the control point have been made.

All of the cellular telephone services that serve the Collier area failed, more or less completely at some point during the storm periods. The causes of the failures, which the carriers disclosed to us, ran the gamut, including everything from loss of electrical power (no generators, generator failures, etc.) to system overload. Most users of cellular phones had the same experience – no incoming or outgoing service at their location. During both hurricanes, Internet connectivity was maintained although it was unstable for a short period during peak storm activity.

The most serious outages during Hurricanes Charley and Wilma were telephone related. During Charley, our telephone service provider had a failure near Orlando, which effectively cut south Florida off from the rest of the country. In our own phone system, we had facilities that could receive but not make calls, we had facilities that could make but not receive calls, and we had facilities whose service just failed.

The investigation into these failures took several months. We found that the phone system had indeed become less robust over time. In order to understand the findings, some background in how the phone system works is necessary.

About 30 years ago, every home had copper wires that directly connected it to the local telephone central office (CO). These copper wires provided power along with communications capabilities to the rotary or touch-tone phones in the home. Great banks of batteries back at the CO supplied the power. The only way your old telephone would not work was if the copper wire was physically broken. As long as the wires were connected to the CO, you had a dial tone.

Today, a very small percentage of homes are directly connected to their CO. This is the result of the competitive storm unleashed by deregulation during the 1980s. The phone companies had to figure out how to continue to provide voice services (and deal with the emergence of cellular telephony) and to enter into the new markets of cable TV and Internet services. In order to stay competitive, the phone companies replaced most of their copper lines with fiber optics that can carry high bandwidth data services. This led to the situation where we are today; almost all home phones require grid power to operate. As telephone lines started to be used for computer communications through modems in the 1980s, the national telephone system literally ran out of capacity. Up until the rise of home computers, the population of a given area purely determined the phone system's size. In the late 1980s in areas like San Jose, CA, this formula no longer worked. The population in that area had almost one computer for every three people. This was further aggravated by the fact that the average time that a computer was on-line was many times greater than the average time of a voice phone call. The phone system had to find a way to expand. They did this by creating Remote Central Offices (RCO's). RCO's served the same function as CO's, but they are much less expensive to build. RCO's may or may not have permanent electrical generators like CO's do. They may be located in malls or apartment buildings, or they may be purpose built like CO's are. Beyond this, in order to provide high-speed Internet services like DSL, each RCO served many Digital Loop Cabinets (DLC's). DLC's are the boxes we are now accustomed to seeing in our neighborhoods every few blocks. In Collier County, the local phone provider has about 8 CO's, 30 RCO's, and 300 DLC's. Copper wires to our local DLC now connect most of our homes and offices. DLC's do not have electrical power generators and only have battery backup for a short period of time.

The impact of all this is that the public phone system has gotten more fragile. Now even if your home never loses power, if your DLC has lost power, your phone service will fail after the DLC's batteries run down (about 8 h). This is in addition to the "normal" hurricane-related interruptions caused by line cuts due to downed power lines.

Actions Taken

Public Safety Radio System

As a result of our experience, the components of the system we keep on hand for spare parts have been adjusted and more mobile radios (automobile installed) have been purchased as they have more transmit power and perform better than handheld radios in areas of degraded antenna performance. Also, the on-site fuel storage has been enlarged to last 5 days. As noted earlier, provisions have been made for a secondary generator for the system's control point.

Data Network

The county has made a significant investment in a private fiber optic data network. The network has been designed with business continuity needs in mind. All facilities which have been designated "business continuity facilities" are on the backbone of the fiber network. Care has been taken to eliminate the intermediate need for electrical power. Power is only provided at staffed locations, which have redundant power systems. Two Internet service providers that utilize totally diverse infrastructure serve the private network.

The connectivity between the county's data network and the Internet has also been hardened. We have diversified with two ISP's using separate provisioning infrastructure and will be looking into a third ISP with yet another provisioning scenario in the near future. The internal network is being upgraded to provide multiple bridging locations to each ISP to further enhance Internet availability.

The bureau of emergency services has a mobile command unit, which has our first satellite communications system. Even with a low bandwidth service, this will enable critical e-mail and voice communications with global reach.

Telephone System

In order to make our PSTN connectivity as robust as possible, we have made arrangements with our local carrier to provision all of our services directly from multiple CO's. They have collocated equipment at three of our hardened facilities and extended their synchronous optical network (SONET) to those facilities. These three locations also have redundant PBX equipment which bridges between the PSTN and our own private fiber data network. The phone service for all of our facilities that are on our internal fiber data network is internally provisioned as voice over IP (VoIP). As long as any location on our data network remains connected to any one of our three SONET locations, PSTN service at that location will be available. The project to complete these changes is still in progress.

Additionally, we now have about 20 satellite phones for deployment in emergencies. We have chosen units, which do not depend on any ground-based network support. We maintain low-volume contracts, which charge only for talk time. We deploy these units to critical disaster recovery facilities. No operator licenses are required.

Amateur Radio

Amateur radio is the only method of modern communications that requires no infrastructure. An operator in the field with a handheld 2-meter radio will have line of sight communications to another operator. To ensure we can maintain communications, we assign licensed "hams" to critical disaster recovery sites. The hams are assigned the "storm shift" for hurricanes – they are rotated so that they can deploy to their assigned facility as the winds start rising, but before conditions become unsafe for travel. We have designated all water plants, wastewater plants, and fuel and equipment depots as critical disaster recovery sites. We have a program in place, which provides equipment for each ham who agrees to respond as directed during an emergency. To date, we have about ten volunteers in the program.

Conclusion

Collier County has placed a high priority on the ability to maintain communications under emergency conditions. Maintaining command and control internally, maintaining communications with state and federal agencies, and maintaining contact with our citizens will enable the coordination of local resources for the best and most efficient emergency response.

Chapter 17
The First Line of Defense: Cities Using Technology in Homeland Defense

David N. Cicilline

Abstract The city instituted a wireless communications system that allows data, pictures, and other information to be provided to officers on patrol and fire fighters in transit to an emergency. The sophisticated system allows personnel to view traffic cameras so they can often determine the situation before arriving on the scene. The system allows patrol, officers to have access to wireless data system providing information equivalent to that at the station. It permits reports to be completed by officers in the field.

When the first alarm sounds, it does not ring in the State House or the White House. It rings at our city police or fire stations. This simple fact – often quoted by the nation's mayors – drives home the point that the first line of defense is at the local level, whether it is an accident, a natural disaster or an act of terrorism.

Cities are increasingly on the front line of major issues – from energy conservation to environmental protection to gun safety measures to homeland security. The chief executive's policies and actions are having an increasing impact beyond the borders of his or her city. A visit to the web sites of the US Conference of Mayors, CEOs for Cities, National League of Cities, or Mayors' Urban Design Institute affirms this trend. It also reveals the collective effect we, as mayors, can have around these critical issues.

After September 11th, the nation's priorities were clarified in an instant. We were reminded that homeland security must always be our most urgent responsibility. When legions of courageous firefighters, emergency workers, and police officers streamed into a World Trade Center on the verge of collapse, it became clear who bore the greatest burden in search and rescue and search and recovery efforts.

America's cities have responded. They have become increasingly sophisticated in ways of protecting our nation, our infrastructure, and our people. The adage –

D.N. Cicilline (✉)
Mayor, Providence, RI, (2003–present), http://www.providenceri.com/government/mayor.php
e-mail: mayor@providenceri.com

S. Hakim, E.A. Blackstone (eds.), *Safeguarding Homeland Security*,
DOI 10.1007/978-1-4419-0371-6_17, © Springer Science+Business Media, LLC 2009

"Hometown security is homeland security"– is truer than ever. A well-equipped frontline of police, fire, and emergency management personnel is a critical link in this country's chain of protection. Experience has demonstrated that preparation and technology are the two critical priorities in securing that protection.

The first anniversary of 9/11 was also the day after I was elected Democratic nominee for Mayor of the City of Providence, and it was a poignant symbol of the responsibilities that lay ahead. Since taking office in January 2003, my administration has steadily gone about the important work of building a strong, local homeland defense system. We have established the Providence Emergency Management Agency and Office of Homeland Security, created an emergency operations center and emergency operations plan, funded a fully operational mobile command center, created MEDS and MMRS plans, conducted 10 drills on everything from port security to IED response, with participation by all levels of government, and we have hosted *Prepare Providence* days to educate and prepare our residents for any type of emergency.

Technologically, we have established a three-phase effort to upgrade our infrastructure. In Phase I, we replaced all dispatching software. In Phase II, we acquired and made operational the citywide Motorola MESH network – a technology that is the main subject of this chapter – which allows for the transmission of visual and other data, through a city-owned and operated network of 469 wireless routers using a proprietary 2.4 GHz spectrum. In Phase III, we are completing the installation of an interoperable 800 MHz radio system, which replaces our existing VHF and UHF radio system with new 800 MHz portables and allows for full interoperability within the city and among other agencies, state and federal. This will augment the MESH network.

The combination of these initiatives will give us "border-to-border" interoperable voice and data coverage, which is far beyond the capabilities of any other city in our state, and a first for any mid-sized city in this country. We understand that a fast, accurate response and interoperability are key to any successful emergency response or homeland security effort.

About Providence

In Providence, an 18.5 square mile city of 175,000 residents – which swells to double that on any given weekday and a metro economy that ranks 37th in the nation – the risks are serious and our role within the northeastern region significant. A 2006 fire at a fuel distribution site in the Port of Providence – which posed a vast threat to the city and its residents, and where officials from state, federal, environmental, and local public safety officials could not adequately communicate – underscored the importance of the new MESH network and 800 MHz system.

We are the second largest and fastest growing city in New England, the largest city between New York and Boston, located adjacent to Interstate Route 95 and intersected by Interstate 195, and, a hub for Amtrak, Providence Worcester Rail

Road, and public bus transportation. We are bordered by Narragansett Bay and home to the Port of Providence – one of the busiest shipping ports in the Northeast, which receives and stores hazardous materials. We are also the seat of government for the state, and the financial, cultural, and educational center of Rhode Island.

Providence is also home to and responsible for the protection of other critical infrastructure – facilities that are considered high-risk targets. They include eight hospitals – one of which houses the only Level 1 Trauma hospital in the region, five colleges and universities, and numerous research facilities, a large downtown retail center, the state's major convention facilities, and an arena for major events – which draw hundreds of thousands of visitors annually; and, the Providence Hurricane Barrier, which protects hundreds of acres of property and hundreds of thousands of residents, workers, students, and visitors.

These great assets can also be vulnerabilities, making it incumbent upon us to be as prepared and vigilant as possible.

MESH Network

One of the most unique and effective resources we have available to us is the Motorola MEA Network, a 2.4 GHz Mesh Enabled Architecture Solution – commonly known as the MESH Network. It improves our responsiveness to emergencies and homeland security threats by providing high-speed data, video, and location services to mobile users and people in the field.

The MESH networking technology allows users to wirelessly access "critical broadband applications seamlessly any time and anywhere" (courtesy Motorola) and it delivers real-time data to detect, prevent, and respond to an emergency.

The MESH network allows public safety vehicles to be used as "desks," where reports and other forms may be accessed, completed, and submitted by officers in the field and even in moving vehicles, without actually having to return to the Public Safety Complex to work.

MESH allows for a better communication flow among officers and between headquarters and the street. Pictures, images, blueprints, maps, and video are all available on the MESH network, through a laptop computer mounted to the dashboard of the vehicles – providing mug shots of known suspects, image captures of suspects from surveillance cameras, flash sheets, detail lists, special notices, wanted posters, missing, and suspicious persons' reports; they are available to every recognized public safety official, at all times. Even live video feeds from strategically placed MESH-enabled cameras, and links to other live video such as the Rhode Island Department of Transportation's traffic management center, can be made.

For firefighters and emergency personnel, MESH empowers them with medical record data on patients they may be working on, on hospital, and bed availability, and in blueprints about buildings they are about to enter – with critical and instantaneous information about floor plans and the storage of flammable and toxic chemicals – essential to saving the lives and property of those affected and surrounding areas, and in protecting the well-being of firefighters who risk their lives on the scene.

Presently, 600 police officers using 200 vehicles, 500 fire personnel and 25 vehicles, 75 communications' staff and vehicles, 4 Providence Emergency Management Agency and Office of Homeland Security staff and 1 vehicle, are making use of this new MESH technology.

In the months ahead, we will expand the MESH to include vehicles used by other municipal agencies such as the Department of Public Works and the Department of Inspections and Standards.

MESH also allows for easier maintenance of vehicle computers and better technical support for the end user. I/T representatives use the MESH remotely to repair the car's computer software if a problem arises.

How It Works

The MESH enabled architecture is a secure, wireless, and roving network that allows police and fire officers on the street to access all the information they need and perform all the jobs they would do at their desks, but while they are in their vehicles and on the street. The actual infrastructure consists of wireless modem cards, MESH wireless routers, Intelligent Access Points (IAPs), and vehicle-mounted modems. Because of the high number of routers and IAPs throughout the city, we are able to guarantee a high degree of availability that responds to changing network loads (dynamic routing) and resists interference.

It is a self-forming network: devices discover, build, and maintain their own routing tables in real time. It is self-healing, automatically dealing with network congestion and node failures. It has a multi-hopping routing process to move capacity to where it is needed. It has the ability to work despite the line-of-sight issues common with other wireless networks. It has a towerless infrastructure, which saves our taxpayers money on expensive real estate purchases. It supports industry standard Internet protocol, which makes it highly accessible to other agencies upon need. And it allows networks to be established between users (peer-to-peer networking) without special infrastructure.

The MESH network also assures highly secure communications, with a high degree of survivability in the event of temporary problems, even and most importantly, when fixed infrastructure is down.

The MESH network is a model of practical innovation and is an incredible tool for our city's law enforcement, public safety, and homeland security officers. Each day, officers identify new and useful ways for making use of the MESH network.

One officer recently asked for a list of all stolen vehicles in his district. Armed with that dashboard data, he was able to trace a number of these stolen vehicles to hotspots in his district. We are only just beginning to realize its full potential.

What Precipitated the Move to MESH

There was a confluence of two events that brought us to MESH: in June 2005, Cingular – the former wireless carrier for the city – decided it could no longer provide service. The carrier indicated it could no longer upgrade what it considered out-of-date equipment and could not support software applications we envisioned within the foreseeable future. We also had new public safety mobile-applications software, known as *New World*, which could work with our low-speed mobile data network (CDPD) but would require a second implementation project when CDPD was replaced.

Then, there was also the issue of cost. We understood that to continue to lease equipment and to implement this new software with new equipment would be prohibitively expensive –a cost taxpayers would be unlikely able to bear.

At the same time, we were working with Motorola on our 800 MHz interoperable radio system acquisition – which was the provider of interoperable services throughout the state. They proposed a system that could address our communications needs, while giving us both the ownership and the ability to custom build our own system.

That system – MESH or Motorola's MEA Network, a 2.4 GHz Mesh Enabled Architecture Solution – would provide public safety officers the same level of service in the field that they currently receive at their desks, and actually *increase* their efficiency and collective impact, by allowing them to remain on the streets and in the neighborhoods for greater lengths of time. It would also allow them to make greater use of the more sophisticated software –New World – that we own.

In August 2005, we announced the purchase of the $3 million state-of-the-art MESH networking communications system for our public safety departments, and as of the fourth quarter of 2006, we have completed its installation.

In this post-9/11 world, the MESH network gives us the most up-to-date technology in a time when it is most needed. It is one of the most effective resources in our emergency management toolbox and critical to all communications, law enforcement, and firefighting services.

The Comparison Between Old and New systems

With the MESH network, our personnel are now able to access large amounts of electronic and visual data, in a moment's notice, anywhere in the city – and to communicate or transmit data back through the pipeline, without delay.

With our former CDPD mobile wireless data communications system, we endured low-speed transmissions of 19.2 Kbps and text capability only, and it was only a one-way transmission from the headquarters. Because of those limitations, data were transmitted at a fraction of the speed of a home dial-up modem, and more often than not, had to be augmented with voice contact through radios.

Our new level of broadband is at 1.0 Mbps it facilitates text, image, blueprint, map, video, and voice capability, and we are poised to leverage advancing digital technology. Initially dedicated to law enforcement personnel, it will eventually be expanded to several other key city departments. It enables mobile personnel to access IT applications wherever they are in the field, even in moving vehicles. None of this capability existed previously.

Additionally, although the MESH only extends to the city's border, the fact that it is an IP (Internet protocol) network enables it to communicate with other agencies and other communities instantly upon need.

Funding for the MESH network was made possible through grants from the US Department of Homeland Security and the US Department of Justice COPS (Community Oriented Policing Services) program. It has been fully operational since the fourth quarter of 2006.

In the words of those who use this system, it works:

- "It puts the power of our best crime fighting software on the dashboard of every car," said Police Chief Dean Esserman.
- "If we get a call for a structure fire, this will allow us to download the floor plans right to the fire truck en route," said former Fire Chief David Costa. "The bottom line is it will make us faster, and speed saves lives."
- "It allows us the ability to instantly view in real time the scene of an emergency incident from Emergency Operations Center (EOC) so that critical decisions can be made to effectively mitigate the incident," said PEMA Director Leo Messier.

As the Mayor of this capital city, there is no greater responsibility that I bear than ensuring the safety of those who live, work, study, or visit here. And while there are never guarantees in life, the MESH network gives us an added measure of confidence that Providence is as prepared as it can possibly be.

Chapter 18
Full Interoperability for All South Dakota Public Safety

M. Michael Rounds and Otto Doll

Abstract South Dakota developed a statewide radio system that allows its more than 14,000 public safety officials (local, state, federal, and tribal) to communicate with each other. The digital, trunked system permits voice and data transmission in a cost-effective manner. The trunked feature ensures efficiency because the computer searches to find the first available channel rather than dedicating a particular channel to a particular user.

Several Radio Frequencies in Use

State Radio in South Dakota had its inception in the 1940s with a low-band (39 MHz) system consisting of a few towers that were tied together with radio (RF) links. The low-band radio frequency offered the greatest range and required the least number of stations.

In the early 1960s, a plan was drawn up and implemented for a statewide communications system interlinked by a microwave network. The network would serve only state government agencies.

The 1970s saw the development of the Department of Transportation (DOT) VHF high-band (150–170 MHz) system. This was put in place primarily as a means for the DOT engineering staff to have a communications system within their own organization. The high-band frequencies allowed for a quieter radio operation and for the ability to "repeat" the signal, vastly extending the range vehicle to vehicle.

The forest fires in the late 1980s prompted the building of a State Division of Forestry high-band system in the Black Hills in southwestern South Dakota. Constructed primarily for fire and emergency response, the system allowed for handheld radio operation during fire fighting.

M.M. Rounds (✉)
Governor, The State of South Dakota, (2003–present), http://www.state.sd.us/governor/
e-mail: sdgov@gov.state.sd.us

S. Hakim, E.A. Blackstone (eds.), *Safeguarding Homeland Security*,
DOI 10.1007/978-1-4419-0371-6_18, © Springer Science+Business Media, LLC 2009

The Department of Corrections (DOC) facilities also had communications come on-line in the 1970s–1990s. The Sioux Falls correctional units were the first to get an in-house system with a UHF (450–470 MHz) repeater system. The UHF frequency allowed for communications in a campus type situation. Systems at Springfield, Custer, and Pierre followed.

The 1990s saw communications systems developed at some of the major park and recreation areas in the state. Lewis & Clark, Oakwood, Farm Island/West Bend, and Newton Hills all had UHF systems providing portable (handheld) radio coverage.

By 2000, the state government radio infrastructure consisted of 43 towers, 22 transmitter sites, and a microwave interconnect system. State government used 1,929 mobile (vehicle) radios and 618 portable (handheld) radios on low-band, high-band, and UHF.

Local public safety agencies used more than 5,000 mobiles and 3,500 portables on numerous low-band, high-band, UHF, and 800 MHz systems across the state. Federal government agencies often used VHF and had an internal mandate to be completely on narrowband (a more efficient frequency use) by 2005.

Agencies Cannot Talk When Most Needed

The low-band frequency in use from the 1940s has a number of fundamental problems. Low-band is the most prone to "skip" (radio signals bounce off the atmosphere to interfere with other radio systems) and to RF interference from computers and other electronic equipment.

As other local, county, and federal agencies developed communication systems for their needs, the move was made to other frequencies such as VHF high-band (150–170 MHz), UHF (450 MHz), and to a limited extent 800 MHz. These frequencies offered a much cleaner signal and proved more flexible in operation. Unfortunately, these moves to different frequencies caused an inability to talk between agencies. For example, a snowplow operator on VHF could not talk to a sheriff on 800 MHz.

State government saw the critical need to solve the dilemma of different agencies unable to talk when needed most – whether passing on the road, during an emergency (such as the Spencer tornado), or fighting fires (such as the Jasper fire).

Legislature Took Action in 1999

House Bill 1292 was signed into law directing eight state agencies to integrate their radio telecommunications functions and facilities into a single cohesive network. South Dakota Codified Law 34-45-33 also put all state radio infrastructures and the three state government dispatch centers, under the Chief Information Officer's (CIO) control.

Funding Found

A $7,000,000 COPS grant from the US Department of Justice, a $4,000,000 appropriation from the 2001 legislative session, another $3,991,200 COPS grant, a $1,156,000 highway safety grant ,and $1,431,354 in state agency funding allowed the governor to begin the process. These funds were used to buy the radio system infrastructure, and mobile and portable radios for state government and local public safety agencies. Ultimately, $28 million dollars were raised to buy 7,890 radios, RF equipment for 35 towers and a central network switch.

Local mobile radios were issued to 232 fire departments, 107 police departments, 65 sheriff's departments, all ambulance/EMS entities (including air ambulances), all emergency managers, and all emergency care medical facilities.

Motorola's VHF Solution Best for South Dakota

After a lengthy evaluation process, a Motorola VHF (150 MHz) digital trunked system was chosen as the best fit for South Dakota based upon the following criteria:

- Compatible with 73% of existing local mobiles in the state and all federal users.
- Direct compatibility with federal users on VHF.
- No usage fees for local agency use.
- Many radio dealers in state.
- Uses existing state and federal facilities (towers, buildings, etc.).

One Frequency Ensures a Smooth Transition to the Statewide System

The state's radio system solution allowed existing analog VHF users to communicate on day 1 – at a minimum through the statewide mutual aid channel. All proposed radios could utilize any VHF system – whether new, existing, analog, or digital. Ultimately, using one frequency ensures radio communications anywhere in South Dakota. Additionally, VHF allows the easiest, less costly path of local agency migration into the digital world.

For those operating on UHF (450 MHz) or 800 MHz, the state used cross-band repeaters to allow access to the mutual aid channel in their area during transition to the statewide system. The local agency had the responsibility to install and maintain the repeater equipment (Fig. 18.1).

Digital Radios Outperformed Analog Radios

Digital radios convert spoken voice into a stream of data bits (0s and 1s), which is sent over the air on a radio wave. Analog radios convert spoken voice into a modified frequency format, which is sent over radio waves.

Single Frequency Statewide
VHF – Highband – 150 Mhz

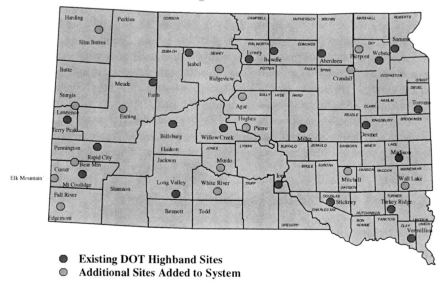

● **Existing DOT Highband Sites**
○ **Additional Sites Added to System**

Fig. 18.1 Highband locations

Digital radios outperformed analog radios by offering superior voice quality, signal range, and security. Since the digital radio actually is a computer, the radio can "digitally" fill in missing or garbled transmissions, thereby extending the radio's range of clear signals. Digital audio provides a more constant level of quality audio – the dark area in the diagram below:

Data, Not Just Voice, Travels the System

The system, since October 2005, allowed state and local radio users to transmit data in addition to their normal voice communications. Now information flows to the state's public safety officials with laptop computers in the field.

Trunking Technology Ensures Optimal System Performance

A trunked system was chosen because many users can share a limited number of radio channels by utilizing the first available channel for each conversation. By not having dedicated channels, a trunked radio system allows the radio to "hop" from channel to channel to find an open path, thus more efficiently using the channels at a site. This trunked technology allows the following:

- More efficient use of radio channels (supports up to 100 radio users per channel), thereby lowering system costs.
- Communications with anyone, anywhere in the state – from mobile users to portable users to dispatchers.
- Complete autonomy for each talk group (a predefined group of radio users who can privately communicate with each other). Radio service can be made to follow the radio anywhere in the state.
- Enhanced system management to ensure high availability, reliability, and serviceability.
- Bridging from analog to digital technology. New radios can access old systems, while old radios can access the new system through mutual aid.

The communities in South Dakota benefit with a VHF digital, trunked network by getting improved federal–state–local communications, improved emergency response, standardized communications, modern communications facilities, and data communications.

The radio system went live on October 23, 2002. Local agencies received 5,567 radios to bring all policemen, sheriffs, firemen, emergency managers, emergency medical personnel, and transit bus drivers onto one radio system with state government public safety personnel.

Radio System Coverage Best It Can Be

The state's radio system guarantees mobile coverage as shown in Fig. 18.2.

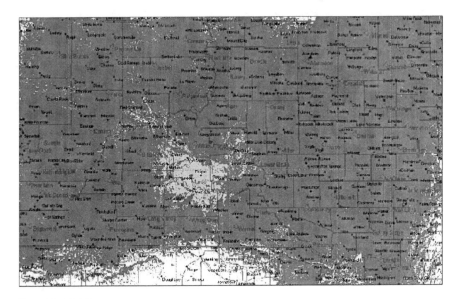

Fig. 18.2 Mobile coverage

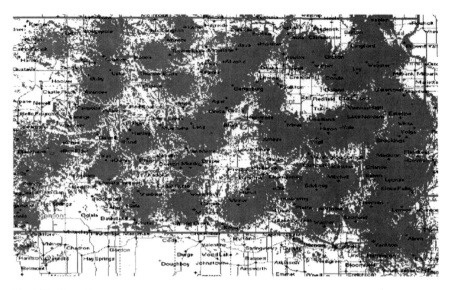

Fig. 18.3 Portable coverage

Portable coverage is never as extensive as mobile coverage but the state has engineered extensive coverage in the Black Hills and major population centers (Fig. 18.3).

Digital Radios Act Like Computers

A trunked radio is basically a computer with a receiver and a transmitter attached. Digital radios send and receive voice and data digitally – sending 1s and 0s through the air rather than analog audio waves. Digital radios convert the signals back to analog to play over the speaker. Each radio has a digital address much the same as a computer on a network. This address identifies the radio to the central network controller, which then directs a given transmission to those users listening to a particular talk group. Radios can search across talk groups and the radio user can easily switch between the primary talk group and any other talk group, such as the statewide mutual aid channel.

The mobile/portable radios for use on this system also accommodate all conventional (non-trunked) VHF channels. This allows communications on both old and new radio systems with a single radio, thereby allowing local agencies relatively easy migration from their older conventional systems. All radios are "data ready" and APCO 25 compliant (the federal government's standard), operate in the federally mandated narrowband (12.5 MHz) and have built-in security features.

Radio System Works Like Telephone System

In a trunked radio system, there are no dedicated channels for any one user. The channels at all sites are available for use by all users and are linked together by a control computer located in Pierre. As the microphone push-to-talk (PTT) button is depressed, an open channel is selected and a communications path is set up between those users in the talk group. This eliminates the need to wait for an open channel (as is the case on a dedicated repeater) and allows for a much more efficient use of the frequency.

With all radio sites (at various towers) across the state linked together through the central controller in Pierre (the geographic center of South Dakota), radio users have access to the system anywhere in the state. Radio users can communicate across the state simply by speaking into the microphone, just like the public telephone system.

The state has engineered its radio sites to have a minimum of four trunked channels. One is used for control purposes (to run the system), leaving three channels for handling radio calls. A trunked channel can support between 75 and 100 radio users. (Keep in mind the average radio conversation is between 5 and 10 s. With three radio channels available at 180 s per minute, the likelihood of conversations bumping into each other is slim, even if a large number of users are under way.) If traffic on the radio system exceeds capacity, then the state adds channels at the problem sites.

In addition to the trunked channels, there is an overlay of "mutual aid" channels. These conventional VHF channels are placed at 49 sites statewide. These channels allow anyone with an older conventional VHF radio to communicate with those on the new system. These channels are conventional repeaters and operate only in the coverage area of those repeaters – not across the state. All state radios are equipped with these frequencies. State radio dispatch monitors these channels around the clock.

A data channel, in addition to the channels mentioned above, is also placed at each site. This is a dedicated data channel that allows the use of mobile data terminals (MDTs) by law-enforcement or other agencies. The data speed is at 9,600 bits per second.

State Will Maintain a State-of-the-Art Radio System

The radio system and network are supported by the State of South Dakota via the Bureau of Information and Telecommunications' (BIT) State Radio group. The state maintains the towers, repeater equipment, central controller, and transport equipment. Local users are responsible for maintenance and repair of the mobile and portable radios in use by those agencies and any related control equipment (console/dispatch) used.

Talk Groups are Facilitated

Agency groupings (talk groups) have been established with the cooperation of local users. These talk groups allow private conversations within that talk group, similar to that of a dedicated channel. The system is "fleet-mapped" to connect the members of a talk group regardless of their location within the state. Multiple talk groups (up to 256) can be programmed into the radios and can be scanned between groups.

New Radios Can Be Used on Existing Radio Systems

The radios being utilized for the system are capable of talking on both existing analog systems and the new trunked system. The state asked local agencies for an accurate channel plan of their current radios. The channel plan was programmed in their new radios prior to shipment.

State and Locals Can Make Radio System Succeed

A memorandum of understanding was reached with all local public safety organizations. The state only needed the following from local agencies:

- The desired channel plan to have programmed into agency radios.
- Identify local, district, and regional communications needs – this drove the development of agency talk groups.
- Follow grant process to request mobile and portable radios from the various funding sources established by the state.
- Participate in the radio system.
- Consider offering their local assets (towers or frequencies) to the state system – such as Marshall County and Bon Homme County did.

Easier, Least Costly Migration Path

With the majority of local radio users in the state operating on VHF, access to the state system is gained by simply programming the mutual aid channel into their current radios. The mutual aid channel allows communications with all state users and dispatch centers. This allowed the local entity to phase in new state-supplied digital radios on their own schedule. Besides working on local agency systems, these new radios offer more capabilities on the state system.

For those operating on UHF (450 MHz) or 800 MHz, the state offered a crossband repeater that allows access to the mutual aid channel in their area during the transition phase. The system operator had the responsibility to install and maintain the repeater equipment.

Low-band (39 MHz) users continued to have a government (39.1) station available in their area to access State Radio (SRC) dispatch during the transition phase.

Dispatch centers had many options to connect into the new radio system:

- An inexpensive VHF control station connected to the dispatch equipment allowed access to the local mutual aid channel.
- Digital trunked control stations were connected to console equipment to allow access to particular talk groups. Initial state dispatch talk groups alignment is around tower sites (geographical), allowing a local dispatch center to monitor dispatch-related traffic only in their area. An example would be the Mitchell SRC talk group. Davison County would only need a single control station to monitor all traffic to and from the SRC dispatch center within the county. Additional coverage areas could be added as needed.
- A digital trunked base can be set up in the center that allows access to all authorized talk groups.
- A direct connection to the central controller was also an option. This allows backup of any connected site by any other connected site. This option requires particular dispatch equipment, and a transport to the master site in Pierre.

State Continues to Expand System

Governor Rounds saw a need to improve and expand upon South Dakota's Statewide Radio System. Through the acquisition of Department of Homeland Security grants, more tower sites were built to improve further the portable coverage – the system now has 56 towers, 400 voice repeaters, and 298 licensed frequencies.

Federal agencies have been integrated into the system – the BIA (Lower Brule first), BLM (Custer Grasslands), FBI, FF&W (Sandhill), ND National Grasslands, NPS (Mount Rushmore fire crews), US Marshals, and WAPA are on the system.

In 2003, the state sponsored a user-driven program to develop protocols for system use and a training program. Completed in 2004, DVD-based training was sent to all county emergency managers for distribution within their counties. A web-based training site was also established.

The ability for data communications was added in October 2005. The system now has 35 data stations.

One-of-a-Kind System

Over 14,000 local, state, federal, and tribal public safety officials currently interoperate over a single statewide radio system. No other state in the nation has such a ubiquitous radio communications system – with all public safety officials able to talk to one another. Only in South Dakota!

Chapter 19
Evolutionary Planning for the Technology Revolution

Bill Baarsma

Abstract Tacoma, WA, was instrumental in creating a regional law enforcement agency, the Law Enforcement Activity and Data System (LEADS) program. It employed a state-of-the-art information management system that integrates law enforcement, the jail, courts, prosecutors, and state repositories while conserving resources. Through technology development, LEADS allows officers to be more effective through both the reduction of time-consuming administrative tasks and by significantly increasing access to critical information for investigations and community awareness.

Introduction

Law enforcement, like many government agencies, struggles with the rapid deployment of technology. It is generally accepted that technology will significantly improve how we conduct business. Planning, funding, and implementation create a true dilemma for most government agencies since the technology revolution, by its nature, demands rapid change. However, government is generally designed to work in an environment that will only support evolutionary change over time. Our hope is that government will eventually find a way to respond more quickly to our future business environment, but for now it is safe to say that government is slow to respond to change – especially when those changes require significant funding, planning, and/or involve coordination with multiple jurisdictions. In addition, technology providers continually add to the problem by constantly updating, enhancing, and changing their products to meet increased user demand. Government often spends hundreds of thousands of dollars or more to buy the "latest" and "greatest" technology, only to be outdated months, weeks, or days down the road.

This chapter will share our experience and success with implementing law enforcement technology solutions in the City of Tacoma and Pierce County.

B. Baarsma (✉)
Mayor, Tacoma, WA, (2002–present)
e-mail: bill.baarsma@cityoftacoma.org

S. Hakim, E.A. Blackstone (eds.), *Safeguarding Homeland Security*,
DOI 10.1007/978-1-4419-0371-6_19, © Springer Science+Business Media, LLC 2009

Background

In the mid-1970s, the City of Tacoma was fortunate to have the foresight to partner with Pierce County to form a combined law enforcement support services department using Law Enforcement Assistance Administration (LEAA) funding. An inter-local agreement created a five-member Executive Board made up of the Tacoma City Mayor, the Pierce County Executive, the Tacoma Police Chief, the Pierce County Sheriff, and a citizen appointed by the four public officials. The newly formed Law Enforcement Support Agency (LESA) was initially responsible for police dispatch services and later expanded to include E911, police records management, and information technology.

LESA's customer base, now a force of 14 law enforcement agencies, serves a critical geographic area of Washington State and a diverse population of approximately 773,500 in urban, suburban, and rural areas – including Mount Rainier. The Pierce County community is a hub of international travel and commerce (via the Port of Tacoma, the bustling I-5 corridor, Puget Sound, our proximity to the Canadian border, and our position as a Pacific Rim state), as well as being part of the state's military core with both Fort Lewis and McChord AFB located within the county.

LESA's facilitation of the Law Enforcement Activity and Data System (LEADS) program created a state-of-the-art information management system that integrates law enforcement, the jail, courts, prosecutors, and state repositories – agencies that often vie for resources. Through technology development, LEADS' innovations allow officers to be more effective – through both the reduction of time-consuming administrative tasks and by significantly increasing access to critical information for investigations and community awareness.

But, how was this accomplished?

Established in 1997, a consortium of agencies including LESA, Tacoma Police, Pierce County Sheriff, and Puyallup Police, developed a strategy for a fully integrated law enforcement system. The goals of the program were – and are – to increase community safety, speed the justice process, and effectively use resources. An interoperable program such as this, allows agencies to analyze and research crime across multi-jurisdictional boundaries, while also providing agencies the ability to team-up for the development of new tools without the risk or cost of surmounting major technological challenges alone.

By the mid-1990s, we realized that for law enforcement to fulfill its public safety responsibilities, it would have to more effectively use its resources and be able to access current, complete, and accurate information in a timely fashion. On behalf of its member agencies, LESA embarked upon perhaps the most ambitious effort seen in law enforcement at that time.

At a time when many police departments were beginning to purchase and pilot expensive technology without a long-term strategic direction in mind, LESA took a step back and decided to plan first, then implement – to ensure taxpayer money and law enforcement time were not wasted. What developed was the LEADS 2000 Strategic Plan.

Plan, Plan, Plan

The objective of the LEADS 2000 Strategic Plan was to define the current and future business and technical environment for providing law enforcement services. This was to be accomplished through the redesign of business processes and the use of information technology. These improved processes were to be facilitated by technology for data capture, access, and distribution. The plan addressed the overall direction for law enforcement information management and identified initiatives and tactical projects that would help achieve the desired environment, as well as establish a plan to replace all current information systems – most of which were not Y2K compliant.

Originally published in 1997, LEADS 2000 established a vision and defined how the future would look if all of the envisioned changes were fully implemented. It described how key operations and support staff would do their work, the overall business environment, and the functional technology environment that would be in place.

The planning process encompassed strategic and tactical components. The strategic component recognized the current environment and established the overall purpose for the plan, goals, future vision, and major action areas as a framework for more detailed planning. The strategic component developed a migration strategy to move the organization toward the vision and organized specific projects into action plans. It also listed major action areas, or initiatives required, in order to realize plan goals. Then, a multistage implementation strategy outlined the parameters that were identified and the decisions that influenced the plan.

Each stage of implementation included a tactical plan that estimated human resource and financial costs, and the sequencing of stages and activities over time. This section also identified required management actions to help ensure organizational acceptance of the changes in technology, workflow, structure, and job responsibilities.

But, the late-1990s were influenced by a number of challenges and opportunities, creating an increased sense of urgency and risk for this planning effort. Among the challenges, aging systems originally designed to address specific functions were not Y2K compliant. Business processes and practices were not satisfying the need for convenient and timely access to accurate information – for law enforcement, criminal justice, and public use. Furthermore, customers and taxpayers were increasing pressure for improved services.

Yet, several opportunities compelled further exploration. The federal COPS MORE (Making Officer Redeployment Effective) Grant was specifically directed at improving law enforcement effectiveness, and the idea of integrating law enforcement and criminal justice systems was gaining support for the potential benefits to deliver information on a regional community basis while sharing the cost of new technology. Technology advancements alone provided opportunities for significant changes in critical criminal processes and services.

These challenges and opportunities combined to create a compelling case for action to dramatically improve products, services, and systems for the law enforcement community.

As planning progressed, it became apparent that the desired process and technology improvements required a multi-year, multi-million-dollar effort comprised of various projects. Additionally, LEADS 2000 needed to be supportive of the various business plans already in place or under development by the constituent agencies.

The obvious risks for this type of project were well documented. The public sector was spending millions of taxpayer dollars on numerous attempts to improve government services by implementing technology solutions. The original intent was to implement LEADS 2000 in four stages over 4 years at a cost of approximately $14 million.

In 2000, midway through stage one, we realized that we were not going to meet our goal of implementing LEADS in a "revolutionary" manner. Instead, we would have to settle for a more evolutionary approach. Factors that entered into this decision included the following:

- Only one-fourth of the funding was obtained through the COPS MORE Grant. Local funding was not appropriated to complete the projects in stage one.
- There were significant delays in delivering core vendor-provided software.
- Budget reductions and overdue appropriations affected the ordering of necessary hardware.
- There was insufficient IT staff to support all the work needed to develop, implement, and maintain the new environment – or to convert legacy applications for Y2K.
- The dot-com era was attracting IT staff to the private sector, leaving the remaining and dwindling staff to accomplish all the work.
- Fragmented project management added to project delays.
- A lack of customer confidence in LESA's ability to implement LEADS continued to escalate.

In 2001, LEADS was "rebooted" to address the above issues, and by 2002 we were back on track with the LEADS Strategic Plan. This time around, the plan would focus on objectives that would implement the first two stages and restore customer confidence in the project.

The "Rebooted" LEADS Plan

It was apparent that the LEADS Strategic Plan should not be expected to remain unchanged over its life. The plan has been – and is – adjusted biennially in response to changes in business direction and priorities and to include wisdom gained through completed projects or projects under way. Updates are logically tied to existing budget development processes to ensure coordination with appropriate fiscal and resource planning efforts.

The "rebooted" LEADS plan also identified 13 critical success factors (CSFs) – all of which needed to be in place to ensure success. These CSFs are considered and factored into every initiative and project:

1. *Participants must have a shared vision.* Stakeholders' view of the future throughout all levels should have a common sense of purpose. Without a shared vision there would be differing objectives, desired outcomes, and expectations.
2. *Participants must have an enterprise view.* In the highly interactive and inter-dependent law enforcement environment that surrounds LEADS, the ability to realize significant improvements depends on the willingness of all participants to seek solutions that are in the best interest of the enterprise – in this example, of the criminal justice enterprise.
3. *The strategic plan should be driven by executive sponsorship.* Change is accomplished through a well-designed plan and with the commitment of all affected parties. Senior law enforcement executive staff should understand and agree to support the plan – the shared and common vision. Commitment should also come in the form of providing leadership for defining and implementing change.
4. *A structured program management approach must be in place.* All aspects of the program management methodology are designed to recognize the changes that will be introduced into member agency business processes and to ensure plans for the successful implementation and ongoing support of LEADS.
5. *The plan must satisfy business needs.* To be successfully implemented, each project in the plan should be clearly focused on satisfying the business needs of participants. Automated systems simply enable changes in processes and work-flow. If enabling these systems becomes the focal point, the LEADS program and participants could lose sight of the business needs and anticipated benefits.
6. *Establish realistic expectations.* Each participant contemplates the magnitude and rate of change it is willing to undertake and sustain. Expectations should be high, but not unrealistic. Establishing challenging but realistic expectations will help lead to a healthy evolution of system improvements and additions that achieve results without parayzing an organization.
7. *Establish performance indicators.* To ensure progress is made toward the shared goals, performance indicators should be established and regularly measured.
8. *Business processes must be owned.* Those who are responsible for the business processes in question must drive change. These are clearly identified process owners who are responsible for the operational processes being changed.
9. *Participants must commit resources.* Each organization should be willing to commit resources to further projects. It is particularly important to devote human resources whom senior executives and process owners will empower to design and implement new processes and systems. Investing adequate and appropriate resources is critical to accurately represent all perspectives and to produce high-quality results.
10. *Prepare for change.* Appropriate effort should be invested to ensure everyone affected by a change is prepared to work in the new environment. This includes

changes in job duties, organization and reporting structures, business processes, and technology infrastructure.

11. *Provide technical and operational support.* Participants should provide both technical and operational supports to maintain the LEADS environment.

12. *Cultivate training.* LEADS will develop standard, comprehensive training guidelines and documentation to ensure consistency and commonality in the use of the shared systems. Participants should be prepared to contribute to the development of training programs and to provide customized training (if needed) to their users in the context of each agency's unique requirements.

13. *Maintain communication.* Deliberate and frequent communication with all participants will ensure personnel are kept informed of the plan, the purpose, the implementation, and the progress. Numerous communication methods, appropriate to the needs of specific audiences, are required to make certain it is the right communication at the right time.

For each CSF, the LEADS Strategic Plan provided answers or actions to be taken. The CSFs combined to form the foundation of the LEADS program.

First, the LEADS program became – and is – a consortium effort comprised of LESA, the Pierce County Sheriff's Department, Tacoma Police Department, Puyallup Police Department, and the Lakewood Police Department. With agency ownership, each stakeholder within the scope of the plan is able to embrace the plan's mission, goals, and philosophy as part of a shared vision for the future. The senior executive within each agency acts as a sponsor for plan implementation and supports the importance, priority, and benefits of impending changes or improvements.

To facilitate the plan, a LEADS-specific program manager was hired and a program organizational structure was established to manage the program over time. Each agency in the consortium assigned its own program manager who represents and is responsible for agency-specific planning and implementation. The agency program manager provides program oversight and acts as the agency voice on the Program Management Team (PMT), a group comprised of consortium program managers. The PMT focuses on law enforcement and criminal justice business needs, ensures that the manual and automated systems are coordinated and integrated, and deals with computer technology matters, as well as resolves issues regarding policy, direction, priority, and funding.

We are careful not to rush to introduce new technology without clearly defining how that technology supports our business priorities. Rushing technology could dilute the focus on business requirements. The consortium understands that individual agencies may evolve at different rates of change over time, so plans develop accordingly.

An action plan builds upon the implementation strategy and objectives, integrating all associated activities into an organized plan of action with specific tasks, deliverables, and a timetable for completion. The action plan applies the decisions, parameters, and priorities identified during development of the migration strategy. It then outlines the activities and human resources required.

Performance indicators are then identified for each project under the LEADS plan and are consistent with plan objectives and performance audit recommendations adopted by member agencies. For every new project, a complete workflow analysis is completed, showing current processes and procedures. All work is then reviewed and approved by those responsible for the business process.

The consortium's shared vision necessitates the allocation of limited resources for the program's operational needs and priorities. Resource limitations of all participating agencies do, however, affect tasks associated with designing project specifics covered under this plan. Unfortunately, this is an all-too-real situation that must always be taken into consideration. Agencies' standard budget processes provide funding, with supplemental funding through grants when possible. Each agency and the LEADS strategic planning effort have the ability to significantly influence the magnitude and rate of expenditures.

Each organization within the scope of this plan works to establish a receptive environment for change. Each organization understands and accepts the role and responsibilities it has in this shared environment. Consortium agencies work together to agree on and enforce minimum standards in order to protect the value of the information we share. A Consortium Training Committee was formed to assist with this and to develop LEADS training materials, as well as on-line training video presentations. Additionally, to smooth the path of progress, a simple-to-follow communications plan was developed to include newsletters, presentations, and online services.

Planning Produces Results

Of LEADS' current 100-plus computer programs and support systems, significant improvements to the city and county's justice system were made possible through mobile electronic reporting – providing more timely, accurate, and complete reports – and the speeding of the justice process by which reports are submitted by the officer to supervisors, records, and to the prosecutor's office in time for arraignments. The program converted an archaic system of handwritten reporting, copying, and delivering to an electronic report that is electronically distributed through the proper channels.

Over the last 4 years, the LEADS consortium deployed a wireless electronic police reporting system using capture and retrieval technology into a broad-based production environment and integrated that functionality into other criminal justice systems. One such example is Tracking, Review, Approval and assignment, Case control, Electronic Distribution (TRACED), a well-thought tool to automate the workflow of all formal reports from dispatch to review, approval, assignment, and distribution. TRACED ensures that "no report is left behind"; it provides an audit of all calls an officer responds to that requires documentation and possible investigative follow-up. More importantly, TRACED controls how well agencies keep track of situations in their jurisdiction and, combined with the standardization of data captured via electronic reporting, creates the power to see crime trends

– despite limited resources. Communities can now be better informed and agencies are more responsible to the communities they serve – thus, the data have become meaningful.

The LEADS program has already made significant progress and achieved some of the plan objectives, but true to its nature, the LEADS Strategic Plan must continue to be reflected upon in order to effectively evolve. A series of interviews were conducted in January 2006 with LEADS consortium program managers to determine the benefits realized through 2005, the lessons learned, and the recommendations for improvement as LEADS progresses.

It is apparent that a high level of satisfaction for the program exists today. The struggle and frustration to implement new information systems and new automated business processes has given way to a desire to complete the original LEADS vision as soon as possible. Performance measures indicate that LEADS is closer to meeting its goal of providing timely, complete, and accurate information; providing a mobile information environment equal to any office; and, automating time-consuming administrative tasks.

The program's results, though difficult to measure, can be shown in timelier report processing. For example, in 2005, officers submitted 75% of all arrest reports within 4 h of arriving on-scene. In the same year, field supervisors reviewed 78% of all arrest reports within 4 h of an officer's submittal. This is a dramatic change from before LEADS, when reports were hand-written; it was difficult for officers to submit arrest reports before the end of their 8-h shift – and sometimes days passed before reports were submitted.

Results are also shown by the change in focus – from a data entry atmosphere to one of accuracy by way of report validation. TRACED allows supervisors and the records division to return reports either for further review or for compliance with IBR (incident-based reporting) rules. These processes ensure reports meet agency standards for completeness and accuracy. In 2005, there was a 23% increase in the number of further action required returns by sergeants, which means supervisors can focus on accuracy rather than "cleaning out their in-boxes." Additionally, the records division showed a 48% decrease in the number of returns for coding errors, meaning reports are being submitted more accurately.

Managing the Winds of Change

Consortium agencies take on a hefty dose of responsibility on their end to effectively use technology and make changes work. Responsibility comes in the form of communication (alerting officers and staff to changes and new applications), customized training, and additional IT support.

Program Management Team communication within the team and to their respective agencies continues to improve – providing project status to the command staff, technical updates, and training to the end user. While inter-department communication has improved, program managers are still challenged by intra-departmental communication, which can break down at times when business process change involves multiple departments.

Additionally, agency program managers continue to compete for limited resources to conduct user training. The amount of officer training time needed to meet annual requirements puts LEADS training toward the bottom of the list. Training alternatives are pursued to ensure maximum benefit from the systems currently in place and for those scheduled for implementation. In general, end user computer skills have been adequate for the current environment, but additional training is recommended to increase awareness and, thereby, maximize employee effectiveness.

As new technology was implemented, we realized the need for some agencies to upgrade equipment in order to take full advantage of new systems. LEADS systems have been operationally critical and complex, with many dependencies. System architecture needs to take into consideration current and future business needs; therefore, there is a need to move from a concept to a formal design. Scope creep must be controlled – though changes should be allowed when they will have measurable benefit. To achieve this, agencies must assign the appropriate staff to focus groups to guarantee that the appropriate product is developed. Then, realistic timelines should be considered, as should the number of projects being scheduled for the year. Project delays impact IT staff, agency plans, and policy, as well as future projects.

Planning for the Future

As LEADS progresses and the strategic plan evolves, new visions for the future emerge. The challenge is to remain focused on critical path projects that complete core functions. Additionally, the availability of these automated functions will require a rigorous review of the participants' organizational structures, job descriptions, and classifications, as new work processes and workflows are enabled by new automated systems.

Emphasis is being placed on "real time" information to mitigate crime. A new mobile environment that introduces map displays can provide easy access to a variety of law enforcement and administrative applications. Information will be proactively analyzed and officers will be alerted to crime trends as they develop – and be able to respond appropriately.

This functionality will be closely tied to other resource management and can provide information on all of an organization's resources (personnel, facilities, equipment, vehicles, technology, etc.). Standard reports and analyses will provide key measures of efficiency. (For example, the ratio of the number of cases assigned as compared to the total number of cases investigated by type of crime, and the ratio of the number of cases solved to the number of cases actually assigned.) Analysis will focus on supporting strategic and tactical planning and the application of resources for an organization, as well as business forecasting and planning based on historic trends and future projections.

At the same time, budget restraints are forcing law enforcement to accomplish more with less – less money, less staff. Force multipliers are being explored in the form of mobile wireless video, dynamic "quick" reports, and citizen self-service applications – for both the case inquiry and the reporting of minor crimes. The latter is part of a coordinated public service delivery strategy to provide services to the community efficiently and effectively.

The LEADS program will continue to evolve over time to fulfill current and future business needs. As improvements and innovative applications are developed and implemented, new challenges and opportunities arise. That evolution is both an anticipated and a necessary part of the LEADS program. Further, there will be a point in the near future when all of the objectives and goals *originally envisioned* will have been either achieved or discarded as being unworkable.

The transition from an original vision to a new and updated one must be viewed as a process not having a distinct ending point and a specific beginning point. The plan's progress and advancement should be viewed realistically as a continuum.

Chapter 20
History of Regional Unified and Integrated Public Safety and Public Service Communication and Transportation Systems

Will Wynn

Abstract This chapter describes the detailed history of the processes of integrating the public safety agencies in the City of Austin and Travis County. By integrating and upgrading the systems, the City of Austin and Travis County are better able to coordinate their activities and protect the public. A combined Communications, Emergency, and Transportation Center was also developed.

Background and Statement of the Problem

At the start of the 1990s, the City of Austin and Travis County public safety agencies were starting to feel the effects of population growth and increased demand for services. Efforts undertaken by the City of Austin and Travis County public safety agencies to share resources and work cooperatively were frustrated because each agency involved had its own separate radio and dispatching system. When law enforcement officers were assisting one another, each could have completely different information about the incident. Fire service agencies were reluctant to ask for assistance because they could not communicate by radio. Large emergency incidents, both planned and unplanned, often times had several persons in charge because radio systems did not interoperate.

These limitations were compounded by the high rate of population growth that the City of Austin and Travis County were experiencing during the 1990s. During this decade Travis County and the City of Austin had one of the highest rates of growth in the United States. Population growth always leads to an increased demand for public safety agency services. As this demand for services increased, both Austin and Travis County began to experience space constraints at their existing communication facilities.

At the same time, the Federal Communications Commission (FCC) began an initiative in the 1990s to move public safety and public service agencies into one

W. Wynn (✉)
Mayor, Austin, TX, (2006–present), http://www.ci.austin.tx.us/council/wynn.htm
e-mail: william.wynn@lpbenergy.com

S. Hakim, E.A. Blackstone (eds.), *Safeguarding Homeland Security*,
DOI 10.1007/978-1-4419-0371-6_20, © Springer Science+Business Media, LLC 2009

segment of the radio spectrum. This initiative would require all the public and public service agencies in Austin and Travis County to replace all existing radio systems.

Forming the Coalition

Initial discussions between the City of Austin and Travis County quickly led to the recognition that regional cooperation would control costs and improve service provision by using shared systems. Elected officials for the City of Austin and Travis County recognized that regional cooperation would be painful for all involved. However, the benefits of regional cooperation (resource sharing, improved service delivery, and real-time communications between involved agencies) would be well worth the effort.

The City of Austin took the initiative to form a team with membership from all the governmental bodies in the Austin, TX, area to assess the communication needs of the City of Austin, Travis County, school districts, small cities, and state agencies operating in the area. The City of Austin hired a consultant firm to work with the team and develop a requirements document, which identified each agency's individual communication needs and its needs to communicate with other agencies.

The Public Safety and Public Service Communication Needs Assessment Report was presented to all the governing bodies of all the public safety agencies in Austin/Travis County. The Public Service Communications Needs Assessment Report identified four main areas of need: Voice Radio, Dispatch – both systems and facility, Mobile Data, and Transportation Management (RDMT). The vision for these initiatives was to cooperatively plan and implement a unified and coordinated communications and data management system to meet the identified needs.

In order to facilitate the development and implementation of the identified communication needs the RDMT Team and Executive Committee was established.

In March 1996, the City of Austin, Travis County, Capital Metropolitan Transportation Authority (CapMetro), Texas Department of Transportation (TxDOT), Austin Independent School District (AISD), small cities in Travis County, and 13 County Emergency Service Districts passed a resolution to cooperate with other participating governments to plan and develop a regional unified public safety wireless emergency communications system.

The City of Austin was the managing partner in each of the projects identified. An RDMT Project Office was established in 1997 to manage the requirements, procurement and implementation of the array of projects identified through the needs assessment. For each project there was a Phase I, Comprehensive Needs Assessment; Phase II, Design; and Phase III, Implementation. After completion of the Implementation Phase each project transitioned to operation and maintenance, using a long-term intergovernmental agreement between the participating partners.

By the end of 1998, Phase I and a suggested design for each initiative had been completed. At this point, the elected officials of each entity committed to provide the necessary funding to support the four projects. Based upon this commitment, the project office expanded and requests for proposals (RFP) documents were issued.

The RDMT team members representing the participating entities worked through the evaluation and selection process and by early 2000 implementation for all projects had begun. In all cases, the decisions on vendor selection were unanimous.

Details of the Individual Integrated Projects

Regional Radio System

In the fall of 1992, the Federal Communications Commission proposed what came to be called "refarming" (or "narrow banding") of existing VHF and UHF frequency bands. It was predicted that those public safety agencies operating radio equipment in these bands would eventually have to purchase either narrowband radios or move to an 800 MHz trunked technology. In 1993, the City of Austin reached out to Travis County, and a number of other local jurisdictions, in an effort to bring together an Austin/Travis County Radio Coalition. The focus of this coalition was to explore the possibility of implementing a joint radio system, as many local agencies were operating as "radio islands" and were often not able to interoperate with one another during times of mutual aid, or major critical incident responses.

A team made up of participating agencies was formed to document system requirements for the Regional Radio system and produce a request for proposal document. The RFP was issued in June 1998 and two vendor responses were received: one from ComNet-Ericcson and the second from Motorola. The team reviewed the responses and recommended Motorola as the preferred vendor. Contract negotiations with Motorola began in May 2000 and were completed in November 2000 and included the final statement of work, tower site configurations, technical systems, terms and conditions, test and acceptance plan, training plan, and final pricing.

The Austin City Council voted to authorize execution of a contract with Motorola on November 30, 2000. The City of Austin, Travis County, the Austin Independent School District, the Capital Metropolitan Transportation Authority, the University of Texas, and the Texas Legislative Council executed the inter-local agreement between the six Regional Radio System partners in April 2001. The purpose of the inter-local agreement was to fund the procurement and implementation of the facilities, hardware, software, and engineering services for a unified and integrated Trunked Voice Regional Radio System (RRS) for Public Safety and Public Service agencies.

Preliminary design work had started in spring of 2001 and by February 2003 the installation of towers and network system equipment for the radio system was completed. Beginning in August 2003 agencies of the participating governments began the process of transitioning to the new system. This transition, of over 4,000 portable radios and 2,500 mobile radios, was completed in the summer of 2004.

Coverage Testing consisted of portable and mobile radios each being tested in every 1-mile grid established for the entire Austin/Travis County area with additional testing using one-fourth mile grids for critical coverage areas defined as Lake Austin, Lake Travis, Downtown/University, and Barton Creek Greenbelt. Testing was also done for in-building coverage. In all cases performance was higher than the "95% countywide coverage to portable radios worn at hip level inside light-construction buildings requirement" in the contract.

In April 2004, the partners approved the Inter-local Agreement for the Operation and Maintenance of the Region Radio System. This agreement detailed the organizational structure and funding support for the operations and maintenance of the Regional Radio System. It also details a process for the original partners to sponsor additional governmental agencies to become "Associate" users of the Regional Radio System.

In 2005, a grant of $6,000,000 was awarded to the City of Austin by the US Department of Justice, Office of Community Oriented Policing Services (COPS), which allowed Williamson County located north of Austin, to provide the $1,850,000 match to the grant and expand the Regional Radio System throughout that county. This will be completed by late 2008. In September 2007, the City of Austin was awarded another COPS grant – this one for $4.8 million – to extend the Regional Radio System to Bastrop County and its municipalities and the City of Lockhart in Caldwell County. Both entities will be putting up the required "match" for the grant. Both COPS grants are being project managed by the City of Austin.

State Radio Coalition

Based upon the work accomplished by the Regional Radio System, City of Austin Chief Information Officer, Peter Collins, began discussions with other local government agencies in Texas that led to the formation of the Texas Radio Coalition (TxRC) in September 2006.

Texas Governor Rick Perry, Austin Mayor Will Wynn and representatives from multiple jurisdictions throughout Texas announced on April 11, 2007, a partnership between the Governor's Office and the Texas Radio Coalition at a State Capitol News Conference. The partnership was formed so that the TxRC could work with the state in the planning of a seamless statewide interoperable wireless communication system for federal, state, and local public safety agencies. This coordinated effort will allow public agency first responders to better communicate during joint operations, thus avoiding potential delays in providing aid to the public.

The TxRC is a voluntary association of Texas government entities, agencies, and organizations. These representatives have come together in a cooperative effort to facilitate the planning, developing, and financing of a statewide interoperable public safety wireless communication system, consisting of existing and future local and regional wireless communication systems which are under local control.

Membership in the TxRC is open to representatives of federal, state, local, and tribal government agencies; public safety, health, and emergency management organizations; critical public utility and transportation entities; and other organizations, which are or may become involved in critical incident responses, or government agency responses to calls for assistance from the public.

Current participants include representatives of governments or emergency service response organizations that geographically encompass the majority of Texas' population in the following areas: Houston/Harris County and eight surrounding counties, Dallas-Fort Worth-Arlington, San Antonio/Bexar County, Austin/Travis County/Williamson County, El Paso/El Paso County, Midland area, Texas panhandle, East Texas to Waco, Bryan/Brazos County/Washington County, southeast Texas, the Middle Rio Grande Development Council area in southwest Texas along the border with Mexico, the Lower Rio Grande Valley, and the Lower Colorado River Authority service area ranging from central Texas to the Gulf Coast.

In cooperation with the Texas Association of Regional Councils (TARC), all 24 Texas Councils of Governments (COG's) have been invited to participate to maximize representation from all parts of the state. The TxRC has not endorsed any particular radio communication equipment or products, as it has elected to remain "vendor neutral".

The TxRC is partnering with the US Department of Homeland Security (DHS) and the Texas Homeland Security Office to achieve the above-stated goal, in keeping with standards set by SAFECOM (the communications program of the Department of Homeland Security's Office for Interoperability and Compatibility) and the Texas Governor's Division of Emergency Management. TxRC has been tasked by Texas Homeland Security Director to update the Texas Statewide Communications Interoperability Plan (SCIP) to meet the current DHS Statewide Planning criteria.

Computer-Aided Dispatch

The computer-aided dispatch (CAD) Project was another of the projects included in the RDMT Program. The CAD project was initiated because the Public Safety agencies in the City of Austin and in Travis County recognized in the need to upgrade current dispatching processes and systems to meet growing demands, support sharing of resources, and take advantage of the benefits of new technologies.

The vision for the CAD system was an integrated, shared, regional dispatching system that would provide a very high level of interagency cooperation and information sharing. The main goal for the multi-agency system was to provide a high degree of interagency situation management, facilitate resource sharing while maintaining data security required by law enforcement agencies. The CAD project team undertook to research state-of-the-industry computer-aided dispatch solutions.

The project objectives and goals were the following:

- Update old CAD systems with a modern, state-of-the-industry solution.
- Obtain a CAD system that would provide a high degree of interagency situation management, secure data sharing, and secure resource sharing among the participating agencies.

- Increase the value of the new CAD system by securely interfacing it to other computer systems for data interchange and increased functionality.
- Select a CAD system that would employ the latest in hardware and software technology so that the needs of each coalition member would be met for the next 10 years.
- Procure a CAD system that would assure system availability of 99.9%.
- The CAD Project Team envisioned a software system that allowed selective data sharing among the various governmental agencies in the coalition though a secure network.

The overall goal of the CAD Project was for the Contractor to install and implement the VisiCAD Software, system interfaces and modifications, and the hardware infrastructure for a state of the industry regional computer-aided dispatch system for the City of Austin Fire, Police, EMS, the Travis County Sheriff's Office, Travis County Constable, Austin Bergstrom International Airport Police, Austin Park Police, and the Texas Department of Transportation.

The CAD project followed the same processes established by RDMT: work cooperatively to gather requirements, develop and issue a request for proposals (RFP), evaluate the responses and recommend a vendor. The CAD Project Team was comprised of voting members of each participating government agency. In addition to the voting members, the CAD Project Team had resource members who did not vote, but provided input into the CAD Project processes and decisions. All decisions were made with full agreement among the voting members.

Four vendors responded to the Request for Proposals. After review of all proposals, live demonstrations of the required functionality, and many meetings to discuss the proposals, the CAD Team selected the TriTech VisiCAD system. The RDMT Executive Steering Committee approved execution of the contract in March 2001. Austin City Council approved the contract in late March and their governing bodies approved inter-locals with the partners shortly thereafter.

Implementation of the CAD system began in the fall of 2001 with the execution of the contract. Like other RDMT projects, the CAD project followed the RDMT implementation process, which was based on material taken from the Project Management Institute and from the Software Quality Institute. These phases were design/prototyping, functional testing, system testing, operational testing, and completing with system acceptance.

After successful completion of system testing phase, a go-live date would be established and the process for moving agencies to the new system begun. In the case of the CAD system, a phased approach was taken; bringing on one agency at a time, followed by a period of monitoring and stabilization. Once all the agencies had been migrated to the new system, the operational testing phase began. This phase consisted of monitoring system performance and tracking end user functionality issues for a period of 6 months.

During operational testing, the agencies met daily to monitor progress and track incident resolution status. The CAD contract specified the criteria to meet for successful completion of operational testing. The project team and vendor team met on a daily basis to monitor progress toward the criteria and would make task adjustments as needed. For the CAD system, these criteria were met in the summer of 2004.

Mobile Data Computer

The mobile data computer (MDC) Project was also a RDMT initiative made up of City of Austin and Travis County Agencies including the Austin Police Department, Austin Fire Department, Austin/Travis County Emergency Medical Services, and the Travis County Sheriffs Department. The MDC Project was co-managed out of the RDMT office by the Regional Radio Project Manager and the Computer-Aided Dispatch Project Manager.

The City of Austin and Travis County Agencies had been using a text-based system for mobile data functions. This system provided basic messaging functionality, records checks, and limited access to incident information. As the CAD project began moving forward, the RDMT team recognized a number of limitations in the current mobile data system.

The current system had to be constantly refreshed and did not provide quick access to prior incident history, hazmat information or caution notes. There was no mapping capability nor did it have automatic vehicle locator functionality. A major concern was this system provided no ability to share information among all agencies; consequently information during joint responses had to be relayed by phone either by dispatch or the communications supervisors, which posed challenges when coordinating response logistics.

As an extension of the computer-aided dispatch (CAD) system, the coalition sought a mobile data computer solution that consisted of the hardware and software application that would seamlessly extend the Tri-Tech computer-aided dispatch systems to in-vehicle computers.

The coalition discussed this need with the CAD vendor (Tri-Tech) and determined that the VisiCad Mobile software currently had the functionality to meet the coalition requirements. Specific functionality included the following:

- The ability to manage calls while in the field empowers personnel to instantly view calls and assign the closest unit to the call.
- Integrated mapping provides field personnel with immediate visual ability to view the incident location and then determine their current location with respect to the incident.
- Easy touch screen capability enables the ability to view the specific incident address and see the detail or view multiple identified incidents within a specific area.
- Full messaging functionality facilitates sending messages between field personnel, dispatchers, and administrative personnel. Messages are easily seen with both visual and audible alerts. It also provides the ability to send a message to

a specific individual or unit even though they may be off duty. Similar to e-mail, the recipient logs in to retrieve their message.

- Reports submission is no longer a tedious task. They can be easily attached to a message in the mobile application and sent for review to the desktops of appropriate personnel. This streamlines the review process and ensures that designated personnel receive the necessary reports in a timely manner.
- Automatic vehicle locator (AVL) enhances safety out in the field with an easy push of the emergency button; dispatch confirms the location of the unit, broadcasts it to other field personnel and the location is then easily mapped directly from the emergency dialog.
- Field personnel have turn-by-turn directions to the incident location.
- Integrated query forms to provide incident, driver license, vehicle registration, warrants, and local records management checks.

In assessing the bandwidth and infrastructure to transmit all the CAD information over the air to the mobile units, the coalition looked at either upgrading the existing private system or using a service provided by a broadband carrier. The assessment determined that the service provided by broadband carriers would meet the coalition needs for bandwidth, reliability, and coverage.

The mobile data computer has provided the City of Austin and Travis County Agencies with seamless integration and allows field personnel with unparalleled access to information they need. Unlike the previous solution, which had to be manually refreshed to view the latest information, mobile data computer continually shows incident details and unit locations as they occur.

Since the implementation of upgraded mobile data computer, the business process has significantly improved in several ways:

- Field personnel safety is enhanced, as supervisors now know the location of their units.
- The ability to share information among agencies provides more coordinated response logistics
- Has proven to be a very effective resource management tool that enables a more effective way of managing personnel and resources to proactively respond to a call.
- From an administrative perspective the decrease in response times, even seconds, further enhances field personnel safety while having the added benefit of increased safety for the public.
- Integrated mapping capability has enhanced field personnel's ability to allocate the right resource, quickly locate addresses, and respond to calls in various types of situations.
- The use of commercial wireless networks means that the housekeeping is taken care of by automatic software and GIS updates.
- GIS and preplans are updated automatically without a technician needing to gain access to each unit.

Primary users of mobile data computer functionality are the City of Austin Police Department, Austin Fire Department, Austin/Travis County Emergency Medical Services, and the Travis County Sheriff's Department. There are current discussions to expand the system to Travis County Constables, other cities in Travis County, and County Emergency Services Districts.

Combined Transportation, Emergency and Communications Center (CTECC)

This initiative had the following two goals:

1. Replace the then City of Austin and Travis County Emergency Communications Centers, as well as the City's Emergency Operations Center.
2. Provide the data center infrastructure required for regional emergency service systems, fully integrating public safety, intelligent transportation management, and public service operations.

The City of Austin and Travis County Public Safety Departments working with the Texas Department of Transportation and the Capital Metropolitan Transportation Authority were participating governments that implemented CTECC. The involved governments/agencies were looking for a regional approach to multi-jurisdiction issues, integration of related systems, coordination of response resources, expedite rescue efforts, reduced costs, seamless exchange of information between agencies, and improved safety of public and personnel.

The coordination and communication between agencies for the Regional Radio System laid the groundwork for the trust, which was required to proceed with a jointly owned and operated combined communication center. Between June and September 1997, there was extensive input from all possible participating agencies and entities through their representatives to the CTECC Project Team.

In April 1998 the CTECC partners agreed to execute an Inter-local Agreement for the purposes of cooperatively planning, developing, potentially funding, and operating CTECC. The inter-locals outlined joint ownership with percentages based on square footage for each partner and their proportional share of multi-use areas. The City of Austin was designated the managing partner.

The evaluation team for responses to the RFQ included 16 representatives as representing the participating governments and agencies:

- City of Austin Police, Fire, EMS, Office of Emergency Management, Information Systems, and Public Works;
- Travis County Sheriff, Emergency Services, Constables, Office of Emergency Management, Wireless Coordinator, and County Fire Departments;
- TXDOT District Operations Engineering and the Traffic Operations Division;
- Capital Metropolitan Transportation Authority.

The Project Team worked together to develop the request for qualifications (RFQ), which was sent to over 242 firms. On October 27, 1997, 38 firms attended the mandatory pre-proposal conference. Of the firms attending, 8 submitted qualifications statements.

CTECC's design includes commercial power from two separate substations, backed up by two megawatts of power generation on-site; water storage on-site; telephone service from two central offices backed up by direct phone lines and satellite phones; radio communications; and, a facility that is shelter rated for a F2 tornado. The facility was also designed with an automated security system with both perimeter and interior coverage.

The building includes a total of 79,667 square feet of which there are 74,002 square feet in the main building. The main Operations Floor for dispatching operations is 13,000 square feet (1/3 acre) with 111 consoles/workstations. In addition, the joint Emergency Operations Center (EOC) has another 4,200 square feet that is utilized when disasters strike. Both the main operations floor and the EOC have raised floor to facilitate air quality, flexibility of design, and thermal comfort.

The Combined Transportation, Emergency and Communications Center was mandated by the City Council to achieve the silver certification for Leadership in Energy and Environmental Design (LEED). The US Green Building Council for the Department of Energy developed this certification. CTECC was the first government owned building in Texas to receive a silver certification.

Agencies began moving operations into CTECC in May 2003. All participating agencies had completed move-in by February 2004. Prior to move in all partners participated in the development of standard operating procedures. These procedures deal with general office management, facility maintenance, building security and emergency procedures, IT system security and support, CTECC administration including management structure and budgeting. The CTECC Operating Board, which is made up of director levels from each of the nine agencies, approves the SOPs and the CTECC General Manager is responsible for their implementation.

During any typical shift there are approximately 150 staff onsite, and during an Emergency Operations Center deployment an additional 75–100 may be added from up to 50 additional agencies. Agreed upon procedures are critical for successful operations.

CTECC is the location where the integrated pieces of the varied communication systems are brought together. Both the integration of the communication systems and the co-location of the different agency staffs at CTECC promote ongoing collaboration and identification of additional opportunities for more integration.

This process of working together provided a better understanding of cross-jurisdictional dynamics among agencies and a greater understanding of needs and issues faced by various agencies. This understanding has lead to an increased incident coordination resulting in faster response times for agencies and faster response for requests for assistance between participating agencies. The addition of transportation coordination is helping to reduce congestion on roadway corridors and improve response routing. The interaction of the agencies working together at CTECC provides opportunity to continue improving integration and information sharing.

Regional System Operations

Governance of these systems and facilities is handled similarly. Each system has a governing board and an operating board. Each system has operations/support staff that is responsible for ensuring the system meets performance standards and address and resolve problems. Each system looks to expand capability and improve technology annually.

Normally, the governing boards of each system or facility meet once or twice each year. These meetings focus on budget and policy issues for the respective system. An example was a Regional Radio Governing Board meeting called to discuss the possibility of linking/joining the Regional System with adjacent counties. The operations staff and vendor briefed the board members by listing the pros and cons of the proposal. Impacts on current performance, budget, and support were discussed. The benefits of improved interoperability, common talk groups, and better sharing of public safety resources were also explained. Support staff along with selected members of the operating board presented the information and answered governing board questions. The result was the approval by the Regional Radio Governing Board to move forward with the linkups to adjacent systems.

The primary focus of the Operations Boards is the day-to-day operations of the systems. Topics like planned maintenance, testing, and installation of patches and functionality enhancement requests are reviewed and prioritized. The Operations Boards also discuss and plan version upgrades for the systems that are needed to keep them current.

A recent Operations Board meeting for the computer-aided dispatch (CAD) system covered the status of the deployment of a new version of the mobile client, status review of current issues, and discussion of a new enhancement for adding pre-plan information to the system.

From a budget perspective the budget for all the systems falls under the budget of CTECC. The budget for CTECC contains all the costs for operating the facility and for supporting the systems that are housed there. The budget is organized so that governing board members for CTECC and for the respective systems can see the overall budget picture and the budget status for the individual systems.

The budget process for the regional systems is that each year the governing board for the system or facility meets to review the current year's budget and develop the budget for the coming fiscal year. When the governing board has finalized the budget for the system or facility, each of the partners (City of Austin, Travis County, Austin Independent School District, Texas Legislative Council, Capital Metro, Texas Department of Transportation) knows the budget responsibility of their agency. That figure is then included in the agency's budget request to their elected officials and included as part of that agency's annual budget.

For example the operational costs for CTECC are shared as follows; City of Austin – 63.110%, Texas Department of Transportation – 21.330%, Travis County – 14.060%, and Capital Metro – 1.500%. For the current fiscal year, the governing board of CTECC recommended budget was $11,353,455.00. The City of Austin is responsible for $7,165,165.45; the Texas Department of Transportation is responsible for $2,421,691.95; Travis County is responsible for $1,596,295.77; and

Capital Metro is responsible for $170,301.83. These amounts were included in the respective budgets and approved by the elected/appointed officials for the respective agencies.

For all the regional systems, the City of Austin has been asked by the partners to act as the managing partner. Thus all the employees responsible for supporting and maintaining these systems are City of Austin employees. The City of Austin is responsible for ensuring the agreed upon staffing levels are fulfilled. In some cases, the partners are asked to participate in reviews of support staff applicants, however, the final decision is left to City of Austin.

For each regional system, the City is required by the governing boards to designate one person as the responsible person for that system. This person answers to the Chief Information Officer of the City of Austin and is also accountable to the respective governing board and operating board to ensure that performance objectives are met.

In the case of system expansion, the governing board of the respective system meets to discuss the scope of the expansion and review the cost estimates. The expansions are shared based upon the existing participation percentages or a new formula that is developed by the partners. The governing board members then meet with their respective elected officials to assess funding and support for the expansion. Next the governing board meets again to finalize agreement on participation and funding for the expansion. As managing partner, the City of Austin is responsible for implementing the system expansion to the satisfaction of the members.

A recent example of this expansion was the linking of the Regional Radio System with the radio systems of adjacent counties. For example Williamson County, the next county north of Travis County, was added to the Regional Radio System. The common border of these two counties is approximately 40 miles and a portion of City of Austin lies in Williamson County. Numerous incidents take place along this border and response improvements would be greatly facilitated by having a common radio system.

To improve interoperability, discussions were initiated by some of the public safety departments with their counterparts in Williamson County to assess interest in linking the Regional Radio System with the William County radio system. The same vendor (Motorola) manufactured both systems, so the first effort was to determine the cost of establishing this link. The total cost was determined to be $7,000,000.00.

While the cost determination was being developed, Regional Radio System and Williamson County staff identified potential grant funding sources to cover the majority of the costs. In this particular case, the City of Austin staff was able to identify a matching grant opportunity. With support of elected officials, applications for grant funding of this expansion were submitted and received the support of the respective agencies. The net effect was that for a little less than $1,000,000 of local funding shared among the partners (including Williamson County) the two systems were able to establish a link (with failover redundancy) that improved coverage for the Williamson County Public Safety agencies while providing enhanced interoperability for Regional Radio System users.

Regional System Yields Benefits

Below are just a few examples of how a regional approach has benefited the citizens of central Texas. Austin Fire Department now dispatches all the fire departments in Travis County. In the past this would not have been possible because of all the different radio systems that were in use. This has allowed the closest available fire unit to be dispatched, regardless of political boundary.

A recent example was a house fire in northern Travis County. The fire department with jurisdiction is Travis County Emergency Services District #2 (TCESD #2). At approximately 4:00 a.m. in the morning, Austin Fire Dispatch received a report of a house on fire Golden Flax Street. The regional computer-aided dispatch system recommended dispatching units from both Austin Fire Department and TCESD #2. The dispatcher handling the call initiated the dispatch and assigned a common Regional Radio System talk group to the incident.

The first arriving units reported heavy fire on the first floor. Through the Regional Radio System, all units responding were able to communicate to coordinate their actions to quickly control the fire. Because units from both Austin Fire Department and TCESD #2 were dispatched, some TCESD #2 resources were able to remain available to respond to two other incidents that occurred while units were handling the structure fire.

Home football games for the University of Texas at Austin normally attract nearly 90,000 people. With this size crowd, law enforcement and emergency medical services are in great need of reliable communications. With the implementation of the Regional Radio System, the University of Texas Police Department (UTPD) has been able to greatly improve communications at these events by assigning a talk group to the public safety staff in designated geographic areas of the stadium. This coordination ensures that all public safety staff in the area of a stadium incident is notified. The net effect has been significantly reduced radio congestion and noticeably improved voice radio communications. This also allows UTPD to continue with normal operations to respond to other events on the campus.

During the evacuations for Hurricane Rita, the Emergency Operations Center (EOC) at CTECC was activated to manage the influx of the tens of thousands of people that left the Texas Gulf Coast for the safety of Austin (approximately 200 miles inland). The logistical, audio/visual, physical space, telephone, and radio capabilities of CTECC allowed city, county, state, school officials to work together seamlessly to route evacuees to the closest available shelter space. This required almost ballet like coordination among shelter managers, school officials, and city and state transportation staff to continually change directions for arriving evacuees. In later debriefings at a regional and state level, the Austin/Travis County effort was repeatedly cited as an outstanding example of coordination and effective resource management to ensure evacuees had a place to stay when they arrived in Austin.

At the Combined Transportation and Emergency Communications Center numerous examples of the regional systems and regional approach can be found.

The Texas Department of Transportation (TxDOT), City of Austin Traffic Signals Group uses their traffic camera systems to more quickly identify problems and provide the appropriate response. Examples include identification of debris in the roadway, pedestrians attempting to cross freeways, and views of traffic collisions. This additional information allows for the dispatch of the most appropriate public safety resources to incidents.

Recently a Capital Metropolitan Transportation Authority (CapMetro) Bus was behind a collision on a major freeway during rush hour. Working with the CapMetro dispatchers, Police and Emergency Medical Services (EMS) dispatchers were able to have the CapMetro bus block traffic allowing the ambulance to arrive at the scene more quickly. This was only possible because the EMS, CapMetro, and Police dispatchers were in the same facility.

For a warehouse fire located near a busy roadway, TxDOT traffic cameras were able to view the incident. This information was relayed to the incident commander, alerting him to several potential hazards associated with this incident.

Austin Police Department (APD), Travis County Sheriff Office (TCSO), Austin Fire Department (AFD), and Austin-Travis County Emergency Medical Services (A-TC EMS) receive calls of accidents at major intersections. They will get numerous calls with different interpretations of exactly where the accident is located. With the help of TxDOT and their traffic cameras, they can search that section of the roadway from the Ops Floor, determine where the accident is and the appropriate response. There have also been times when TxDOT techs are watching traffic feeds and actually see accidents happening. They are able to immediately notify law enforcement and medical personnel of the accident and provide camera coverage during the response.

During ice storms the TxDOT cameras provide dispatch with real-time road conditions of the specific parts of the roadway. This allows them to make routing decisions for each area. With a number of factors impacting the exact point at which any portion of the roadway reaches the freezing point, this provides more information and additional safety for the service providers

As a result of implementing the shared computer-aided dispatching (CAD) system, the Austin Fire Department is now providing dispatch services for all County Fire Departments in Travis County. This is only possible through the use of a common base map, mobile data devices, and the regional radio system. The Austin Fire Department can now send the closest fire engine to any emergency in Austin and Travis County, providing quicker response.

Recently, the users of CETCC held a debriefing covering several recent small aircraft accidents. One of the very positive items was "Being at CTECC for this event was a HUGE help. In the first several minutes of these incidents A-TC EMS was able to communicate directly, face to face, with the TCSO call-takers and supervisors allowing us to narrow down the specific location and exchange information very quickly".

And finally, in a recent exercise with SafeCom, a vendor assessing interoperability for the US Department of Homeland Security (DHS), our area achieved a Regional Communications Interoperability Level 6 rating, the best in the country.

Emergency incidents do not recognize political or governmental boundaries. The closest ambulance, fire engine, or law enforcement officer to an incident might be just across the boundary and can more quickly respond than one belonging to the organization having jurisdiction. Sharing resources based upon geography continues to prove its benefits for the citizens of Austin and Travis County.

Chapter 21
Interoperability in the City of Tampa: A Partnership with the Department of Homeland Security

Pam Iorio

Abstract Tampa was the focal city for developing a prototype interoperable communications system for the Tampa metropolitan area, the fourth largest metro area in Florida. The regional cooperative effort decided that police, fire, and emergency management had sufficiently different requirements that separate but interoperable systems were most appropriate. The regional effort also led to a joint operations center which was tested during the January 2008 Gasparilla Festival which attracts crowds in excess of a quarter million to a water and street parade. The multiple systems in operation provided a single view to the field commanders in the joint operations center, and they worked so well that the regional cooperative now has applied for a federal grant to move from development to full implementation.

City and county governments quite often face unique challenges implementing and managing technology projects utilized for daily operations. However, the most problematic are the challenges these entities face in the administration of homeland security projects that are regional or multi-jurisdictional in scope and size. All too often valuable projects are lost to turf wars over issues such as ownership of the project, governance structure, the lack of large technical staffs within the local government, and the impracticality or unwillingness of the technology companies to deploy open architectural systems.

Communications (both voice and data) are usually cited as the first problem during any man-made or natural disaster, which in turn leads to the breakdown in the command and control model used by public safety agencies. The Tampa Bay Urban Area Security Initiative (TBUASI) program addressed issues early on related to design, development, implementation, sustainability, and the governance of technology projects purchased for the purpose of homeland security to support an integrated multi-jurisdictional program of prevention, protection, response, and recovery. The Urban Area Working Group (UAWG) serves as the focus point for the region's collaboration with DHS and as a governance structure for the public safety disciplines.

P. Iorio (✉)
Mayor, Tampa, FL, (2007–present), http://www.tampagov.net/dept_mayor/
e-mail: pam.iorio@tampagov.net

S. Hakim, E.A. Blackstone (eds.), *Safeguarding Homeland Security*,
DOI 10.1007/978-1-4419-0371-6_21, © Springer Science+Business Media, LLC 2009

DHS identified the City of Tampa as the "core city" for the purpose of homeland security grants. This geopolitical entity, consisting of Pinellas and Hillsborough counties and cities of Tampa, St. Petersburg, and Clearwater, has been tasked by DHS with managing the development of strategies and programs related to the procurement and distribution of equipment, training courses, conduct of exercises, and planning functions for the prevention, protection, response, and recovery from terrorism. The distribution of millions of dollars to local jurisdictions in association with the 2003 Urban Area Security Initiative (UASI) II program from the Department of Homeland Security, Office for Domestic Preparedness (ODP), was focused on closing equipment gaps of first responders.

Early on, the UAWG formulated an Urban Area Homeland Security Strategy (UAHSS) as a regional effort with the participation of two large counties (Hillsborough and Pinellas) and three cities with populations in excess of 100,000 (Tampa, St. Petersburg, and Clearwater). Pinellas County's population density of 3,292 residents per square mile is the highest in the State of Florida. Hillsborough County is one of the largest counties with 1,266 square miles with a population of 1,157,738. The Tampa–St. Petersburg–Clearwater is the fourth most populated Metropolitan Statistical Area (MSA) in the State of Florida.

The diversity of the metropolis would normally compound the ability to manage a technology program in which the local and national focus is on the equipment of first responders; but this was not the issue for the Tampa Bay region. In 2003, the representatives from the jurisdictions identified the inventories of the various specialty teams and the homeland security/emergency management capabilities of the region as a priority, but also identified the need to share data and voice communications during a catastrophic event as an equal priority and established a 5-year plan to accomplish that.

The need for strategic implementation procedures for technology projects preceded the 2005 release of the National Incident Management System (NIMS) doctrine and requirements, implementation of the National Infrastructure Protection Program (NIPP), as well as the 2006 identification of seven National Priorities by the Department of Homeland Security. Throughout the planning process, the Tampa Bay Urban Area has been able to maintain progress for each technology project and ensure compliance with the needs and demands of the multi-faceted homeland security grant programs and national policies.

The first Technical Assistance (TA) request made by the Tampa Bay UASI to the Office for Domestic Preparedness (ODP) was for the support and assistance of the Interoperable Communications Technology Assistance Program (ICTAP). As the various federal elements were developing, following the President's approval of the 2002 National Strategy for Homeland Security, the Tampa Bay region identified the ICTAP Office as best suited to provide independent guidance and subject matter experts, removing many of the normally occurring interpersonal barriers of "turf wars" and "firewalls" among the various technology and communication managers.

In 2002, Department of Justice (DOJ) and ODP selected the City of Tampa to pilot a technology program for enterprise risk management. This system allowed the Tampa Bay region to identify its critical infrastructure and key resources and assign a weight to the risk and value of this infrastructure to the community and nation for prevention, protection, response, and recovery missions. The award for the system, known by the commercial product name of Site Profiler, provided the City of Tampa many lessons learned. Rather than multiple single-agency-licensed systems that were not connected or were isolated behind firewalls, a single license was negotiated to encompass the region. This was the first system identified as being best suited for regional deployment. The City of Tampa Technology and Innovation Department were identified as the location to host and support the application.

Design of the Regional Technology Program

From the Site Profiler project, the leadership of the Tampa Bay Urban Area recognized that several issues would need consideration in further designing and building out the regional technology program. First, homeland security technology programs must be comprehensive in the types of software programs purchased, next, they must be broad enough to recognize each discipline as having varying needs and finally, it is improbable that one product can or will be the solution for everyone. Additionally, the technology program must recognize the varying levels of technology that reside with the individual jurisdiction; in calendar year 2004, many jurisdictions were using Windows 1995 and Office 1997, while others had begun the migration to Windows 2000 and XP. The selection of software programs to support the homeland security mission must be able to work within the varying operating systems. The initial implementation of the Site Profiler system introduced a Red Hat Enterprise Linux Operating System to the city's technology office and put a demand on the office to learn how to operate, maintain, and troubleshoot a new operating system simultaneous to the expected field deployment and use by the Tampa Police Department.

Through the ICTAP Office, the Tampa Bay region obtained contractor support from the Space and Naval Warfare (SPAWAR) Office in San Diego to conduct an assessment of the current technologies and operating systems deployed across the seven technology offices (each county sheriff's office maintains an independent technology office from the resident county). The ICTAP authorized SPAWAR to conduct a feasibility study to create a regional data center to link all seven technology offices through existing fiber optic and wireless networks. The concept behind the Data Center Project was to both enable the sharing of data in real time and more importantly have the ability to be the back-up servers and provide the immediate off-site server to minimize disruption and maximize recovery efforts following a catastrophic event.

Through Joint Application Development (JAD) sessions, the user requirements for the primary first-responder disciplines (law enforcement, fire and emergency medical services, emergency management and public health) and the base functionality requirements for each system were developed. With the user requirements identified, the functional leads were tasked to identify commercially available software solutions.

With the City of Tampa involved in the pilot project for Site Profiler, managing two or more developmental systems would have been overly taxing on the first responders and technology staffs.

The systems selected had to have with the ability to migrate legacy data or accept data sets in commonly available formats such as Microsoft Excel. The UAWG required the jurisdictions and disciplines to commit to the identified solutions for the life span of the project, recognizing that there would be successes and failures during the development and implementation of merging technology systems to meet the new and growing demands of homeland security management.

For law enforcement, the primary system functionality was to consolidate, share, and identify records that normally would reside in disparate systems, such as jail records, police reports, traffic tickets, vehicle impounds, and field interview reports. The functionality was driven by the requirement of daily use by all law enforcement officers, especially those on street patrol, the first line of defense in the prevention of a terrorist incident, but also to handle their daily interaction with mobile criminals who do not respect jurisdictional boundaries. Each county sheriff's office maintained the booking records for every person arrested in that respective county; and each police department maintained its own record management system for police reports, vehicle impounds, and field interview reports. Also, the law enforcement users identified the need to have an analytical tool to not only search across records but also populate the list with a scored outcome to provide the user access to the highest matching response versus a random list of responses. The selected system was Knowledge Computing Corporation's Coplink program, referred to as the "Google for Law Enforcement." Coplink is Microsoft Windows based, using a Microsoft Sequel Database and Java Application.

The law enforcement community had identified a need for a system to manage daily tactical events and the multitude of special events. The requirements described a system that is to be user friendly, Internet based, and can expand and contract depending upon the situation. The system selected had to comply with the Department of Homeland Security requirements found in Homeland Security Presidential Directives five and eight, the National Incident Management System (NIMS) and National Preparedness Goal. The selected system was Convergence Communication's E-Sponder program that is Microsoft Windows based and built upon Microsoft Office SharePoint Server (MOSS).

The fire and emergency medical services discipline had not invested in technology management programs outside of the dispatch and communications center for Computer Aided Dispatch (CAD) prior to the initiation of the UASI grant program. The emergency management agencies had "home-grown," or limited tested, systems to manage a catastrophic event and capture dispatched resources.

A commercially available system was identified that would provide the ability for dispatched information to be transmitted to fire vehicles and provide the information displayed at the dispatch console to the responding units, as well as provide real-time global positioning system (GPS) map overlays that would provide the units with direct routes and locate nearby fire hydrants. The GPS capability was also a requirement for the dispatch center to track and locate the closest available unit for emergencies.

The Fire discipline was also seeking a method to provide an electronic format for pre-incident fire planning for high hazard locations. One internal process assessment of fire surveys and pre-incident fire planning found instances of up to four units within one fire department conducting various site surveys on the same site within weeks and sometimes hours apart. It was decided not to purchase and implement a new system for fire safety inspections. Through a review of identified work processes and procedures on a typical fire inspection, it was determined that the critical infrastructure system purchased for the police department required the same information on each site and could be shared unilaterally. By combining the critical infrastructure assessments with the fire inspections into a single software solution, the only modification for the vendor was the creation of a report-generating tool in any required format. This also increased city efficiency through the removal of redundant surveys and data input. Data fields and report generations were developed in the existing Site Profiler system to maximize data collection, usage of systems, and sharing of resources across disciplines that normally would act independently.

Emergency management agencies determined an available commercial system used in a majority of counties within Florida was the best solution for the management of catastrophic events. The commercial product was required to have the ability to connect the three systems to be purchased for the two county emergency management offices and the City of Tampa. Having the ability to provide live "looks" into events in the county environments, as well as the ability to be a back-up to each other, was an absolute requirement the emergency management community was not willing to negotiate. The selected system was NC4's E Team, which is a Microsoft Windows-based system that is built upon a Lotus Domino database.

With the wide variation in user requirements across disciplines, the strategy employed was to not hinder a discipline's operations by forcing a joint use of a system that does not meet the full user need. Instead the discipline-specific systems were authorized for purchase through the homeland security grant programs with the vision of seeking a bridge or data-sharing ability to minimize duplication of data input and allow incident commanders to obtain the best single view of an incident.

Implementation

Through the efforts of the Science and Technology Directorate of DHS and the ICTAP Office, the Tampa Bay Urban Area was identified as the recipient for a pilot project, titled "Tampa Bay Safety Net." The concept for the Tampa Bay Safety Net project was created through the results of the original JAD sessions to provide a web-based link to each system and generate a report based upon the inquiry generated in the discipline-specific system. The project was jointly developed with DHS Science and Technology, the ICTAP Program, and the Tampa Bay Urban Area.

The DHS approach is to not identify the linked systems by proprietary name, but by the type of data sets (i.e., Red Hat Linux, Microsoft Sequel Server, etc.) to allow for the concept to be cost-effective and replicable in any Urban Area with similar or like problems of disparate data systems. The local first responder community can now have information extracted from any of the deployed systems to the requesting system without the need to have access to all systems, intimate knowledge of each system, or the ability to remember multiple passwords during a time of crisis.

For each data set identified, a variety of obstacles were identified. The primary concern was the access to systems that reside behind jurisdictional firewalls and the willingness of technology projects to allow an outside entity in to extract information. An additional concern was the proprietary components of the commercial systems and the ability to extract data without compromising copyright and proprietary intellectual property of the companies.

To minimize concerns of outside access into a normally closed system, the DHS proposal included the installation of appropriate software and hardware solutions to segregate the closed city or county system for outside intrusion and to also allow for the maximum access to data.

The Tampa Bay Safety Net was commissioned by DHS in calendar year 2006 and the development and implementation began in 2007. The project was developed in a spiral model, combining elements of both design and prototyping-in-stages; proof of concept occurred in January 2008 at the City of Tampa Gasparilla festival.

The executive leadership for the TBUASI has historically the Gasparilla Day Parade as the proving grounds for all plans, processes, and equipment. This event is a 1-day water and land parade that attracts crowds in excess of a quarter million. It covers over 20 linear miles of city streets. It is inclusive of 2,000–3,000 personal watercraft. The parade participants include over 50 crews, 115 floats/vehicles, and 8 marching bands. Over 1,200 law enforcement officers from around the region assist in providing security; multiple tactical teams are pre-staged on or near the parade route, 60 fire rescue personnel, and 100 health/medical workers are assigned key posts along the parade route. It is an all-hands event for the City of Tampa and the Tampa Bay region. It is as close to the operational deployment a city may experience post-disaster. Any item tested in this environment is truly at the mercy of the unknown experiences and situations first responders face and must prove its mettle and worth.

During the event the Joint Operations Center was able to provide executive summaries and real-time situational views to field commanders through a single view from the multitude of systems in operation. Just prior to the event, a question was asked of the DHS provided vendor, Raytheon Corporation, about the ability to bring disparate video feeds. Within a short period of design and testing, the video feed from both the Hillsborough County Sheriff's Office and Tampa Police Department aviation units was streaming to the workstations in the Joint Operations Center. The request to DHS, to design, and deliver a repeatable system that was scalable, portable, and flexible was proven among the many pirates of Jose Gaspar invading Tampa's streets and for the multiple disciplines and jurisdictions providing safety and security.

Conclusion

The vision of the Tampa Bay Urban Area is to provide a comprehensive approach to the management of catastrophic events as defined by the National Response Plan (NRP), through shared resources for first responders. These resources certainly take the form of front line equipment, but also include the management and development of technology programs as a vital component.

Though the Tampa Bay Safety Network is in the infancy stage, the comprehensive steps to purchase, implement, and develop discipline-specific systems have provided a framework of success. Success was defined not just by the ability to prevent, protect, respond, and recover from an event, but also by the willingness of multidisciplinary and regionally applied programs to cooperate and work together.

The value added by the Tampa Bay Safety Net project was so highly rated by the Urban Area executives; it was included in the fiscal year 2008 UASI Grant application to DHS to move from development stage to production stage. It is anticipated the cost for the production model for the nine counties that encompass not only the urban area, but Regional Domestic Security Task Force (RDSTF) will be $1.3 million.

While there is always more demand for resources and higher government accountability and efficiency, the City of Tampa, the Tampa Bay Urban Area, and the Department of Homeland Security have demonstrated the talent and vision to take on tough challenges in adopting and using new technologies for the safety and security of the nation.

Chapter 22
Capital Connections: Washington's Public Safety Communications Suite

Anthony A. Williams

Abstract Washington, DC, created a broadband wireless interoperable network which allows transmission of audio, video, and data. The system was used during the July 4, 2006, celebration in part to test emergency evacuation routes. The District also developed a regional interoperable network. It also created a private fiber-optic network to increase capacity and reliability of public safety and governmental communications. A unified communications center was established using the most advanced technology. The center can sustain usage for 3 days in terms of food, power, and other critical elements. Redundancy was built into the system so that when flooding took out part of the 911 emergency response system, the alternative portion immediately became operational. The current public safety communications center also serves as a backup. The center was purposely located in a depressed area and to help stimulate the ward's economic development.

Introduction

Since September 11, 2001, homeland security has been a forefront concern for national and local leaders – particularly those like me who serve cities that were targets of the attacks. But homeland security threats are simply additions to the public safety challenges our first responders confront every day. In any big city, every day or more, someone has a heart attack, someone is robbed or assaulted, or somewhere a fire erupts – and each time our 911 dispatchers must send police, firemen, or emergency medical technicians to answer a desperate call for help. In Washington, DC, the nation's capital, our first responders also face the special challenges of marches, demonstrations, and protests many times each year. And as the hub of a vast and growing multi-jurisdictional metropolitan region, Washington plays a leading role in interstate policing and in regional response to emergencies of all kinds.

A.A. Williams (✉)
Mayor, Washington, DC, (1999–2007)
e-mail: awilliams@fbr.com

S. Hakim, E.A. Blackstone (eds.), *Safeguarding Homeland Security*,
DOI 10.1007/978-1-4419-0371-6_22, © Springer Science+Business Media, LLC 2009

From the beginning my administration was committed to making technology a vital partner for our first responders in meeting all their public safety challenges, both ordinary and extraordinary. Effective communications are the bedrock of public safety technology. So one of the first technology investments my administration planned was a multi-faceted, state-of-the-art communications infrastructure to support day-to-day public safety communications as well as emergency preparedness and response in the District and the surrounding region.

In 1999 my administration partnered with our local governing body, the District Council, in passing legislation to create the District's first technology agency, the Office of the Chief Technology Officer (OCTO). I tasked the leader of our new technology agency – the District's first Chief Technology Officer, Suzanne Peck – with assessing the current and future needs of first responders and the District as a whole in public safety communications. Suzanne and her agency outlined a broad and visionary suite of programs that considered the District's multiple roles as a municipality, as a regional center, and as the home of the federal government. Several of the programs are designed to do double duty, serving strategic goals beyond public safety – such as economic development and substantial cost savings for the city.

Getting It Together: A Comprehensive Public Safety Communications Suite

OCTO's public safety program encompasses both wireless and wireline communications and a centralized communications center for local public safety communications and regional emergency response.

The wireless component of our public safety communications program has delivered a state-of-the-art local wireless infrastructure with regional interoperability, as well as a policy initiative to help first responders around the nation benefit from advanced wireless public safety tools.

The program's foundation was a comprehensive upgrade of the District's *public safety radio*infrastructure. For day-to-day policing and emergency response, the radio is as indispensable as the policeman's gun or the fireman's hose. When police need backup at a crime scene, when firemen find smoke inhalation victims who need medical help, when an officer is shot or injured on duty, the call to other first responders must go through – and fast. Minutes lost in calling to a dispatcher instead of straight to a fellow officer may mean lives lost.

At the start of my administration, our radio network was in bad shape. There were coverage gaps all over the city – particularly in historic buildings, like our own District government center, the John A. Wilson Building, where beautiful marble walls pose powerful barriers to wireless signals. In addition, we had two separate, un-interoperable systems for our police (operating on the 800 MHz band) and our fire/EMT personnel (operating on the 460 MHz band), so police and fire/EMT responders could not communicate directly. And neither of these networks worked underground in our vast regional Metro subway system, a crown jewel of regional transportation but a prime potential target for terrorist attack.

The District's radio upgrade, a 2002–2004 partnership between the OCTO and the District's Metropolitan Police Department (MPD) and Fire/Emergency Medical Services (FEMS), set out to correct all of these problems. The project transformed the city's wireless infrastructure from a four-site network to a ten-site network supplemented with 63 Vehicular Repeater Systems, ensuring outdoor and in-building coverage in every corner of the city. The project extended coverage for the first time throughout the 300 miles of tunnels in the Washington Metropolitan Area Transit Authority (WMATA) subway system in the District, Maryland, and Virginia. The project also increased efficiency by expanding the number of channels on which firemen and police officers could talk from 32 to 100, enhanced audio clarity by migrating the police force to digital communications, and strengthened communications security by providing encryption capabilities for the police fleet. Equally important, the upgrade project integrated the city's pre-existing 800 and 460 MHz radio systems to provide interoperability between all of the city's public safety and emergency management agencies and federal and regional partners.

But our wireless voice upgrade was just the beginning. As we planned the voice project, we also probed the growing capabilities of wireless broadband data. Broadband wireless networks offer the bandwidth necessary to support an extensive arsenal of next-generation public safety applications, such as remote video surveillance, chemical and biological weapon detection, bomb squad support, in-ambulance pre-admission screening, and others. Applications like these not only strengthen day-to-day policing and emergency response, but also could be vital in responding to the special challenges we face as the nation's capital and the regional hub – citywide political demonstrations, region-wide natural disasters, or the possible next terrorist attack. To harness these next-generation tools for our first responders – in the city and the region – we decided to develop the nation's first high-speed, broadband wireless public safety network.

By summer 2004 the District developed a pilot citywide wireless broadband public safety network that we call the Wireless Accelerated Responder Network (WARN). WARN consists of 12 sites, with 36 antenna sectors, operating under an experimental license approved by the Federal Communications commission (FCC). The network provides the wireless "transport layer" for applications such as access to law enforcement and public safety databases, criminal record and motor vehicle queries, remote surveillance, chemical/biological weapon detection, bomb squad support, helicopter video transmission, in-ambulance pre-admission screening for emergency patients, and other uses critical to preventing attacks and responding to emergencies swiftly and effectively. WARN is available for use by District agencies and federal and regional partners throughout the District of Columbia and the National Capital Region (NCR), and it facilitates coordination and collaboration among multiple jurisdictions in regional events.

With this network, first responders have been able to use full-motion, high-resolution video monitoring and other bandwidth-intensive monitoring tools to immediately share time-critical information about day-to-day incidents and emergency events throughout the Washington, DC, region. On-demand wireless access to large centralized databases, coupled with the capability to integrate real-time ground and/or air video feeds with stored pre-plan data, has yielded significant incident command and control capabilities for police commanders and for battalion chiefs in the Fire Department.

During the 2 years since we launched WARN, the network has been used by both local and federal public safety agencies for a wide variety of events and operations. For example, WARN provided streaming video from various federal and District vehicles for the 2005 Presidential Inauguration. FEMS, one of the network's largest daily users, relied on WARN in responding to a major local emergency, a mercury spill at Cardozo High School, in March 2005. District public safety agencies used WARN extensively during International Monetary Fund demonstrations in spring and fall 2005, and our Emergency Management Agency (EMA) utilized the network for video overview and Internet access for Hurricane Katrina evacuees sheltered at the DC Armory.

WARN has also been used extensively by District and federal agencies collaborating to ensure safe and efficiently managed national Fourth of July celebrations in 2005 and 2006. The use of WARN during the 2006 celebration illustrates the network's versatility and its effectiveness in promoting multi-jurisdictional coordination. The United States Park Police (USPP) hosted the Fourth of July Multi-Agency Communications Center (MACC) at their Anacostia Operations Facility. The USPP, the District FEMS, EMA, and Department of Transportation (DDOT), the federal Public Health Service, National Park Service, Weather Service, and Smithsonian, and the regional WMATA Transit Police and Red Cross shared the MACC and collaborated in managing the Fourth of July event. Throughout the day all of these agencies used WARN to view video transmissions of the Fourth of July celebration – a parade, a fireworks display, and the movement of people and vehicles to and from the national Mall – from the FEMS command vehicle and helicopter video transmitted by the USPP command bus. WARN allowed the MACC users to monitor crowd size, crowd distribution, parade progress, and the effects of a severe late afternoon thunderstorm. DDOT also relied on WARN to monitor traffic cameras throughout the city as part of a successful effort to use the Fourth of July celebration to test emergency evacuation routes.

Throughout 2005 and 2006, WARN steadily added users. As of late 2006, about 20 District, federal, and regional agencies use WARN. The most frequent WARN users include public safety officers in eight District agencies (MPD, FEMS, EMA, DDOT, the Office of the Chief Medical Examiner, the Department of Corrections, the Department of Youth Rehabilitation Services, and the Department of Health), four federal agencies (the USPP, Secret Service, Federal Protective Service, and Department of Homeland Security), and the regional WMATA Transit Police.

The District has shared information about WARN's design, operations, and results with the public safety community, researchers, policy makers and the public through newsletters, presentations at public safety organization meetings, trade papers, press conferences, and Capitol Hill briefings. A demonstration of the network appeared on Washington's WRC-TV as a story about safety and security preparations for the 2005 Fourth of July event. As a result of this program of information sharing and demonstrations, WARN now offers a model to other regions that seek enhanced and scalable public safety wireless systems.

The District's WARN network is a pioneer initiative in demonstrating broadband public safety applications, but it is just one prong of the District's two-pronged wireless broadband strategy. Wireless broadband applications are spectrum intensive, and we quickly discovered that current spectrum allocations do not provide sufficient bandwidth for public safety agencies around the nation to support advanced broadband applications. Without adequate spectrum, wireless public safety broadband will not progress much beyond the regional demonstration we have in WARN. WARN itself would not be possible without the FCC experimental license that grants the necessary spectrum. So as the nation's capital, the District decided to take the lead in seeking more spectrums for public safety nationwide.

To secure the needed spectrum allocation, the District founded and is leading the Spectrum Coalition for Public Safety, now a national coalition of over 30 states, counties, cities, and public safety associations. The coalition is pursuing federal legislation to secure spectrum dedicated to wide-area broadband wireless public safety applications. The Coalition has already succeeded in winning provisions in the Intelligence Reform and Terrorism Prevention Act of 2004 that will accelerate the designation of dedicated public safety spectrum. In addition, the Spectrum Coalition was instrumental in persuading the FCC to issue an April 2006 Notice of Proposed Rule Making proposing expansion of public safety data channels. If finalized, the rulemaking would allow spectrum originally planned for wideband data to be used for broadband data, permitting deployment of bandwidth-intensive advanced public safety data applications throughout the United States.

The final element of the District's wireless communications program addresses a key need highlighted by the events of September 11, 2001, and expressly recognized in the 9-11 Commission recommendations: regional public safety communications integration, including wireless interoperability. The National Capital Region (NCR) that rings our city – within and beyond the famous "Washington Beltway" – encompasses 18 jurisdictions. Any major natural disaster or terrorist attack will demand coordinated response from many if not all of them. Here again, as the nation's capital and the region's geographic center, we felt it incumbent on us to play a leading role.

Spurred by the federal DHS, the NCR jurisdictions have collaborated to launch the NCR Interoperability Project (NCRIP) to develop a secure communications infrastructure that will facilitate comprehensive inter-regional data sharing throughout the NCR and between the NCR and federal and other State agencies. OCTO is one of the jurisdictions leading the NCR interoperability effort. The NCRIP consists of the following three projects:

- A dedicated network of local government-owned Institutional Networks (I-Nets) interconnected into a redundant, secure, high-capacity network.
- A Regional Wireless Broadband Network (RWBN) to establish comprehensive field access for emergency responders on the combined network.
- A Data Exchange Hub (DEH) to enable the exchange and sharing of applications and data within an interoperable framework.

When the NCRIP project is completed, first responders throughout the region will be able to exchange data and applications in real time. As a result, NCR emergency managers will be able to coordinate their response to regional emergencies and deploy emergency responders rapidly and efficiently to save lives.

The NCR region's efforts to achieve advanced regional interoperability recently won high praise from the federal DHS. In late 2006 DHS assessed interoperable communications capabilities in 75 Urban Area Security Initiative (UASI) areas nationwide, using an exhaustive, peer-reviewed process. The assessments addressed three elements of interoperable communications – governance, standard operating procedures (SOPs), and usage. Of the 75 areas evaluated by DHS, only the NCR and 5 others received the highest score of "Advanced Implementation" on all three dimensions of interoperable communications.

Wireline communications are as critical as wireless capabilities in a comprehensive communications suite. The wireline component of the District's public safety communications infrastructure is DC-NET, a now substantially completed state-of-the-art fiber-optic voice and data network that provides telecommunications and data services for the District government, replacing our leased T-1 lines.

DC-NET was originally conceived in 1999 primarily to meet two strategic needs related to general communications and cost containment. First, we saw a need for a high-speed citywide data communications network because of the growing demand for advanced data services, data transport services, and wireless. Second, a history of service installation delays, barriers to access to the city's data, and billing errors and over-billing by telephone carriers created a strategic need to consider alternative sources of data and voice telecommunications services.

But then the September 11, 2001, tragedy highlighted the public safety/homeland security need for the DC-NET project. That day saw crippling voice communications failures as our commercial lines were overloaded and it was impossible to make outbound telephone calls from anywhere in the District government. From that day on, we knew that, as the nation's capital, we would be a prime target for possible successor attacks and that our voice and data communications could never fail again. We had to secure dedicated bandwidth to free District communications from contention with commercial users. A private government network with virtually unlimited bandwidth, capable of supporting the most advanced public safety tools, became essential to meet the city's homeland security needs. DC-NET provides that strategic capacity.

The DC-NET network itself consists of several overlapping rings of fiber. We leveraged our cable franchises to get substantial amounts of this fiber donated by the franchisees, and we laid the rest underground in the conduit systems of our local electric utility company and the city's largest commercial telecommunications carrier. DC-NET's high-level design began in 2002, and its basic Synchronous Optical Network (SONet) rings were built by 2004.

Functionally, DC-NET is designed to connect all District offices and schools, libraries, police stations, firehouses, and other facilities. DC-NET provides all the voice and data services District government customers now use – telephone, voice mail, e-mail, Internet access, and access to computer applications. As of September

2006, DC-Net is providing over 13,000 phones and 70 high-speed data circuits at 165 DC government sites; it will serve a total of 400–600 District government sites when completed in 2009.

DC-NET ties the District network of buildings and systems to the national communications network through a contract with a private telecommunications carrier, so that DC-NET does *not* get the District of Columbia into the telephone business. DC-NET simply connects District government facilities and systems, while our contracted commercial carrier performs all other telephone services.

Operationally, DC-NET is designed for maximum reliability and capacity.

DC-NET increases the reliability of our voice and data services through "virtual private networks" that separate secure data traffic from regular business traffic, and through a "self-healing" ring design that allows instantaneous re-routing of communications in the event of any physical breaks in the cable. This feature was recently tested when a dump trunk snagged DC-NET cable, pulling hundreds of feet from the telephone poles where it was mounted. The DC-NET system instantly and automatically re-routed all communications traffic around the break with no interruption in service.

DC-NET's fiber-optic technology provides virtually limitless capacity – essential to meet growing city telecommunications needs, support high-bandwidth services like video streaming and, of course, key to maintaining city government communications in emergencies. Today, though we are already serving almost half our planned District government voice subscriber base and carrying 30–40% of the city's data traffic, we are using only about 5% of the network's capacity. In addition, the network is highly scalable. If at some point in the future we find additional uses for DC-NET and approach 75–80% usage, we can readily switch network components to multiply the network's capacity exponentially.

DC-NET's dramatic increases in reliability and capacity are the network's most important strategic public safety contributions, ensuring that government communications will stay up and running in the event of another terrorist strike or a major natural disaster. In addition, DC-NET is or will be playing several important specific public safety roles. Today, DC-NET provides backhaul for the District's public safety radio and wireless networks (discussed above). DC-NET also supports the communications infrastructure for the District's Integrated Traffic Management System (ITMS), which controls traffic lights and cameras and will monitor traffic and evacuation routes in emergencies. The network supports our new E9-1-1 public safety communications network (discussed below); virtually every 911 call traverses DC-NET. In addition, DC-NET provides the communications backbone for the Unified Communications Center (discussed below), the city's new, central public safety, and homeland security communications center.

DC-NET's strategic purposes, along with public safety and day-to-day municipal communications, included achieving cost savings. From design in 2001 to near completion today, DC-NET's detailed budget and financial plan has always contemplated significant cost savings over what we have traditionally paid for leased commercial telecommunications services. We have consistently projected an annual savings of about $10 million once the network is complete in 2009 – savings that will first repay the project budget and then will be applied to reduce District agencies' ongoing telecommunications costs.

The last major component of our public safety communications suite is the Unified Communications Center (UCC), a new, purpose-built public safety communications center.

The UCC was planned early in my administration with the primary purpose of addressing a series of weaknesses in our public safety call-taking and dispatch functions and implementing best-practice solutions from other jurisdictions. First, the District had only one Public Safety Answering Point (PSAP) – with no backup PSAP. Second, the existing PSAP location was insecure and just plain unpleasant: the building was poorly shielded from possible intrusion, and its antiquated air conditioning system often failed on the steamiest summer days. Third, suboptimal conditions prevailed in our call-taker and dispatch workforce. The police and fire/EMS departments had separate call-taker and dispatch units, so precious time was often lost in transferring calls from one group to another. The age and lack of amenities in the PSAP facility, combined with the absence of career paths for the civilian call-taker/dispatchers in otherwise uniformed departments, made it difficult to attract and retain highly motivated employees for these critical jobs. Fourth, the E911 communications network supporting the PSAP used outdated analog technology that could not process call data as fast or as accurately as newer digital technology.

To solve these problems, we decided to follow a path blazed by other leading public safety jurisdictions like Atlanta, Chicago, Dallas, Miami, and San Francisco: consolidate and civilianize the call-taker units into a single agency staffed by "universal call-takers" with career paths to agency management, transform the existing PSAP to a backup PSAP, and relocate the new consolidated agency to an attractive new primary PSAP facility equipped with strategic amenities and up-to-date technology.

This new facility was the UCC, a new primary PSAP where the District would consolidate public safety call-taking and our 727–1,000 citizen service call center. Planning for the UCC long pre-dated our work to site the District's new baseball stadium in one of our least advantaged wards, Ward 8. At the time we designed the UCC, Ward 8 sorely needed investment to attract new businesses and create new employment opportunities. The 70,000-plus residents of the Ward lacked local job opportunities, entertainment venues, and retail; there was not even a single full-service grocery store in the Ward. So we decided to use the UCC as an anchor to spur economic development and community revitalization in this part of our city.

Then – as with DC-NET – the events of September 11, 2001, intervened to place a new homeland security emphasis on the UCC. With its Ward 8 site on a high bluff far from the center of the District, the UCC was well suited to serve as an emergency management center. So the UCC was planned not only to consolidate public safety call-taking but also to consolidate the emergency communications functions of all District first-responder agencies, along with the DDOT traffic management function, which guides evacuations as well as day-to-day traffic control. The UCC was also designed to serve as the District's Emergency Operations Center and the Regional Incident Communications Command and Control Center (RICCC), during major local, regional, and national events. As the RICCC, the UCC will facilitate and coordinate communication among local, state, and federal authorities for effective and timely response to regional and national emergencies.

The 138,000 square -foot UCC incorporates state-of-the-art call center technologies – an automatic call distributor/intelligent workstation telephony system for automated call distribution and tracking, computer-aided dispatch, voice logging systems to record call-taking and dispatch operations, LAN/WAN Infrastructure to connect the UCC systems to the DC Wide Area Network and our government fiber-optic network, DC-NET (described above), and a web-based incident tracking and notification system. All systems are fully redundant and fully integrated with the Public Safety Communications Center, which is our new backup 911 center. The UCC building "shell" is designed to GSA security standards, with features such as a 100-foot setback and berms, blast- and bullet-resistant glass, monitors and security cameras, controlled access, security check points, turnstiles, bollards, and tamper-proof exterior windows and doors. The facility is also equipped with a 72-h self-sustaining capacity – enough food, water, fuel, and power to last through a 3-day emergency lockdown.

The UCC is also a citizen-centric center equipped with amenities designed to attract the most capable call center employees. It provides an 11,000 square foot child development center, an exercise facility, stress reduction rooms, a cafeteria, and a terrace retreat overlooking a broad vista of the nation's capital.

Finally, the UCC links to state-of-the-art public safety communications technology. Simultaneous with the completion of the UCC in 2006, we have revamped our E911 network infrastructure. The District's new E911 network replaces our legacy analog network, managed by the incumbent phone company, with proprietary digital technology that significantly boosts the speed and accuracy of call data processing. The new network is the largest fully digital E911 network in the United States. It is also fully redundant. All telephone carriers, both wireline and wireless, have connected their systems to the PSAP at two separate locations that are linked via the District's DC-NET fiber-optic network (described above). If a carrier loses one circuit, it will still be able to route E911 calls to the District via the secondary circuit. Since the DC-NET fiber-optic network is fully redundant, if one entire site goes down, the other site will process all calls. The network's redundant configuration passed its first test in June 2006, when flooding disabled part of the District's E911 hardware, along with 13 carrier circuits. Our new network automatically rerouted calls to the PSAP via the redundant connection.

The UCC officially opened on September 26, 2006, with a ceremony featuring US Homeland Security Secretary Michael Chertoff, Virginia Governor Tim Kaine, DC Congresswoman Eleanor Holmes Norton, and other dignitaries. In his remarks, Secretary Chertoff honored the District's achievement by expressing his strong "operations center envy" for the new, state-of-the-art facility.

Today, we can also credit the UCC with meeting our goal to help spur economic development and foster opportunity in Ward 8.

Throughout the building of the facility, OCTO provided construction jobs for Ward 8 residents and summer internships for students at the local high schools,

Anacostia and Ballou. The completed facility has created new job opportunities in call-taking, food service, and maintenance. Community residents are also eligible to use the UCC's round-the-clock childcare facility.

In addition, the plan for the UCC at the start of my administration stood as an early vote of confidence that helped to attract other businesses and development plans to the Ward. A beautiful new community center and theater now stands not far from the UCC. Art galleries are opening nearby on Martin Luther King Drive. The Ward's first grocery store will open in 2007. In 2006 the District Council approved the building of a publicly financed baseball stadium, slated for completion in 2008, and now developers have proposed a privately funded soccer stadium in Ward 8 as well.

Getting Over the Hurdles: Obstacles and Challenges

The District's public safety communications suite has been a very ambitious undertaking. With such broad ambitions come significant challenges. To bring our communications programs to fruition, we had to surmount a variety of obstacles – historic, political, and operational. Here are just a few examples.

One of the first challenges for our public safety communications programs derived from the strategic siting of the UCC. Chosen for purposes of physical security and economic development, the UCC's Ward 8 site is also part of the historic St. Elizabeths campus. Before we could break ground on the facility, we had to resolve historic preservation issues surrounding several dilapidated structures on the site that dated from the late 19th and early 20th centuries. Originally federal historic preservation authorities were reluctant to permit any changes in the historic structures on the site – even though the locations of some structures presented obstacles to the UCC design plan. To resolve these problems, OCTO partnered with the District's planning agency to negotiate a solution with the federal government. After lengthy discussions, the District and federal parties agreed to a plan under which the District could relocate two cottages, provided we restored the cottages and stabilized a historic barn and stable located next to the UCC site.

The UCC also faced political challenges from the Ward 8 community. Early in the project planning phase, community associations voiced opposition based on concerns about potential traffic congestion and potential release of fly ash in the soil on part of the site. The neighborhood associations also expressed skepticism about the projected economic development benefits of the UCC.

The OCTO UCC team took several steps to overcome this community opposition. They commissioned an independent traffic study, which concluded that UCC-related traffic would add only modestly to existing St. Elizabeths traffic. They commissioned testing of the fly ash by a highly reputable environmental consultant, who found the ash to be non-hazardous. But in addition, they decided to construct the building itself on natural/undisturbed soil, while placing surface parking and landscaping over the fly ash to contain and seal it. Throughout the planning, design, and construction of the UCC, they conducted extensive community outreach to inform and involve the community in the project. During the outreach process, they committed to a package of specific community benefits including job opportunities during construction; job opportunities in the completed facility in call-taking, food service, and maintenance; and opportunity for community residents to use the childcare facility at the UCC. As described above, we delivered on these promises, providing construction jobs and internships during the building of the facility, other job opportunities at the finished facility, and opening the childcare center to local residents.

A major operational challenge to our public safety suite arose in 2004, when the DC-NET team began transferring, or "porting" District government telephone numbers from the incumbent local exchange carrier (ILEC) to our contracted carrier. Through the contract carrier, we obtained the ILEC's "customer service records" (CSRs) for the District government. Although we had anticipated some mistakes, the CSRs proved to be much more inaccurate than expected – containing, on average, about 35% errors. For example, the office of one of our OCTO executives for the last 6 years had been in 441 4th Street NW, but the ILEC 's records showed his phone to be located across the street at 300 Indiana Avenue NW. There were thousands of such errors, and every one had to be resolved, building-by-building, before the team could proceed to convert, or "cut over" District phones to DC-NET. The DC-NET team had to conduct a physical survey of every telephone, every wire, and every wall outlet in the District and had to call thousands of telephone numbers to ask the answering employees where they were.

Once the cutover process began, further challenges emerged. Sometimes the ILEC could not assure the DC-NET team that certain telephone numbers would port properly, so the team had to correct errors on the days following each building cutover. In addition, midway in the porting process, the ILEC lengthened the notice period required for placing port orders from 18 to 30 business days, extending the DC-NET cutover schedule by 2 weeks. These problems led to a temporary 5-month delay in the DC-NET telephone cutover schedule. Through sheer hard work (and some contractor overtime), the project recovered the 5 months and completed the telephone cutover on the original implementation schedule in FY 2005.

The broad and ambitious scope of our public safety communications suite has also meant financial challenges – where to get the many millions of capital dollars to fund programs of this scope? Our answers: borrow some and beg for the rest from the federal government.

But even a borrow-and-beg strategy presented serious challenges early in my administration. In January 1999, the District was still subject to a congressionally mandated Financial Control Board, had barely pulled back from the brink of bankruptcy, and still labored under a large deficit in credibility. Our bonds were at junk status, making very large-scale borrowing extremely expensive.

Through the efforts of the Control Board (until its end in 2001), our independent Chief Financial Officer, Dr. Natwar Gandhi, my administration and the District Council, the District restored its budget health from three consecutive GAAP deficits in FY 1994–1996 to nine consecutive GAAP surpluses in FY 1997–2005. Accompanying this transformation was a rapid rise in our bond ratings, first to investment-grade status by 2000 and ultimately to "A" category ratings from all three rating agencies by 2004. With our rapid recovery in creditworthiness and fiscal credibility, we were able to borrow at affordable rates and to convince the federal government to support our public safety programs. Federal homeland security funds have helped the District finance both our wireless program and the UCC.

The operational, political, and historic challenges I have described here are just a few of the hurdles we have faced in building our public safety communications suite. Thanks to the dedication and determination of government employees and politicians, we have surmounted these obstacles and more.

Conclusion

Today, the District of Columbia is near completion of a nation class – even world class – public safety communications infrastructure. Along the way, our public safety communications programs have set the stage for additional benefits in cost savings and economic development. When we started planning these programs in 1999, our vision was ambitious, even audacious – but we have proved that this grand vision could become real. Indispensable to our vision was the foundational act of creating a central technology agency with the expertise to conceive these programs. Indispensable to realizing our vision have been the skill and dedication of our CTO and technology staff, the support of our political leaders, the dedication of our financial leaders to fiscal health and stability, and the partnership of the federal government.

Chapter 23
Information, Leadership and Decisiveness, All in One Room

Richard M. Daley

Abstract Mayor Daley of Chicago established a Joint Operations Center that houses both officials from federal, state, and multiple jurisdictions in the region and the various Chicago's agencies. In addition, Chicago has an incidents Center that deals with more limited cases and is associated with JOC. It has also a mobile unit that can be dispatched to specific sites and has two satellite dishes, mobile radio capacity, Wi-Fi computer access, independent cell tower, and over 100 telephone lines. JOC controls the surveillance cameras spread throughout critical locations and the Intel Cell database that includes floor plans, demographics, and other macro- and micro-information that is needed in emergencies. The JOC deals with large-scale emergencies, pre-planned mass events, and has proven its success.

Introduction

The phrase "Many hands make light work" may be a well-dated cliché, but in the fields of emergency management and Homeland Security, it is a remarkably appropriate phrase. Considering the complexity of emergency response, it is important to have everyone working together. In Chicago, we have worked hard to make preparedness a way of life.

This is a city I have loved since long before I was first elected mayor in 1989. I have seen changes in nearly every facet of urban life, some of them minor and subtle, others vast and all encompassing. We have made broad improvements in public education, in housing, in business, in environmental issues, in tourism, and in public safety.

In Chicago, preparedness is a way of life. With potential hazards ranging from a terrorist attack to extreme weather to a utility breakdown to infrastructure decay, the city has worked very hard, for a very long time, to identify areas of risk, and

R.M. Daley (✉)

Mayor, Chicago, IL, (1989–present), http://egov.cityofchicago.org/city/webportal/home.do

e-mail: erika.zovka@ex.citychicago.org

S. Hakim, E.A. Blackstone (eds.), *Safeguarding Homeland Security*,
DOI 10.1007/978-1-4419-0371-6_23, © Springer Science+Business Media, LLC 2009

take the steps necessary to minimize if not prevent such incidents. But preparedness is not limited to trying to prevent disasters from happening; it also involves being ready to react, with the most efficient and comprehensive response possible, when emergencies do occur.

To marshal such a response, the City of Chicago in 2005 unveiled our Joint Operations Center, a place where big problems are solved through the methodical and efficient solving of small problems.

Our Joint Operations Center

In the most fundamental of terms, the Joint Operations Center, or JOC, is a large room where officials from multiple jurisdictions all can do their jobs in concert. Located in Chicago's Office of Emergency Management and Communications (OEMC), the JOC is in a hardened structure easily accessible on the city's Near West Side. Just steps away from the 9-1-1 operations floor, those in the room have access to up-to-the-minute information about what is happening to the almost three million residents of this city.

But on a higher level, the room represents a deep and abiding commitment, on the part of the city and the numerous city, state, federal, and private agencies that work regularly in the JOC to bring Chicagoans assistance as quickly as possible. City departments represented in the JOC include the OEMC; the police and fire departments; the Departments of Transportation, Streets & Sanitation, Public Health, Senior Services, Human Services, Buildings, and Environment; the Mayor's Office for People with Disabilities, and the Chicago Park District. Outside agencies include the Department of Homeland Security, the Federal Bureau of Investigation, the US Coast Guard, the Transportation Safety Administration, the Chicago Transit Authority, the Chicago Housing Authority, the Illinois State Police, the Illinois Emergency Management Agency, the Red Cross, ChicagoFIRST, and the Building Owners and Managers Association (BOMA), among others. Other city departments or outside agencies can also be invited to the JOC depending on the nature of the incident. In short, if an organization can help resolve an emergency situation, we will find a seat for it in our Joint Operations Center.

This stance stems from a fundamental recognition that the City of Chicago, as large as it is, can still benefit from the assets and abilities of our partners in public safety, whether they are neighboring communities or state and federal agencies. We have worked in advance here in Chicago to ensure that, in the event of an emergency, there will be no time spent debating questions of jurisdiction or determining the structure under which assistance will be rendered. Instead, we will respond with every asset necessary, regardless of ownership, to ensure a coordinated reaction. And, depending on the nature of the incident, an activation of the Joint Operations Center could be at the center of that response.

While the JOC is an important asset in the event of a large-scale, multi-agency emergency, we also activate the JOC for other types of incidents such as severe heat and for pre-planned event such as marches, parades, and major city special events. This brings together the city departments and the outside agencies and gives them an opportunity to work side by side. By working together, all gain a better understanding of each other's strengths, challenges, and resources, so when and if the City of Chicago is called upon to face a true urban emergency, the city, and its many partners, will be ready.

Consolidated Response a Growing Tradition

The placement of the Joint Operations Center in the Office of Emergency Management and Communications was not an accident, but a further step in a long-range vision. Recognizing the importance of seamless emergency response, the City of Chicago in 1998 consolidated the dispatching operations of the Chicago Police Department and the Chicago Fire Department under a single agency, the Office of Emergency Communications. On the 16,000 square foot Operations Floor, built in 1995, call takers answer residents who dial 9-1-1, routing those requests for service to the police and fire dispatchers who send police units, fire engines, and ambulances to addresses across the city's more than 220 square miles.

In the years that followed, the agency further grew into the Office of Emergency Management and Communications and came to oversee Chicago's emergency management planning and homeland security efforts, which included developing emergency response plans that incorporated not only the police and fire departments but also the assets and abilities of two dozen other city departments. In 2005, the OEMC added to its portfolio the newly formed Traffic Management Authority and the city's permit issuing division, consolidating the city's handling of everything from parades and festivals to construction projects and bridge lifts.

Having all of these agencies under a single roof was only part of the process; designing an environment where they could make a habit of working together was the next step. The Office of Emergency Management and Communications opened an Operations Center in 2004 and a City Incident Center in 2005. In each of those centers, the best available technology was installed with workstations for the varied agencies. The Operations Center is staffed around the clock with representatives of the city's Department of Streets and Sanitation and Department of Water Management, as well as an OEMC watch manager and dispatchers who can monitor calls for police and fire assistance. Similar workstations were put in the City Incident Center, where additional supervisors monitor weather and street conditions while using GPS technology to track the routes of garbage trucks and snowplows. Both centers have monitors allowing officials to make use of the thousands of video cameras arrayed around the city and assess traffic movement, crowds, snow accumulation, and event infrastructure repairs. The centers also can access weather-monitoring and tracking systems.

In Chicago, we are extremely proud of our use of modern technology and camera technology in particular. In fact, during a July 2007 visit to Chicago, Michael Chertoff, the Secretary of Homeland Security, praised the city's use of cameras as "a model for the country."

We believe that cameras serve as a force multiplier, bringing the dual benefits of instantaneous intelligence from a scene with the click of a computer mouse as well as archived footage that can be evaluated later. Surveillance cameras have a well-established benefit in the area of homeland security, offering around-the-clock coverage of strategic assets in Chicago while having a deterrent value as well.

Locally, archived footage contributed greatly to the arrest of two men for the murder of a 14-year-old Chicago boy in the summer of 2007. Police detectives were able to examine images taken from two cameras around the scene of a gang-related shooting that left a student dead and from that were able to gather crucial information that led to the arrest and charging of two suburban gang members.

But the cameras are useful in many other ways. Not only have cameras helped us monitor a scene as police secured an office building during a hostage situation, they have given us information during utility repairs, severe weather, sporting events, and public festivals. And the information is immediate; our crews are not getting second- or third-hand information. They are seeing what is happening as it is happening, and it is difficult to imagine better information than that.

The images of the cameras, while valuable and unique, are not the only examples of advanced technology in the Joint Operations Center. We also can access Flight Tracker, a visually driven interface that allows officials to monitor the air traffic in and out of our two major airports, O'Hare International and Midway, on a minute-to-minute basis. We have access to up-to-the-second weather information, not only using computerized map systems but also taking advantage of the direct hotline that links the OEMC with the National Weather Service office southwest of Chicago. The OEMC also operates the city's reverse callback system, which can send recorded messages to as many as 1,000 phone numbers per minute. And we can reach into our Intel Cell, a database that provides critical details in both horizontal and vertical formats.

In simplest terms, our Intel Cell is a long, long list of useful information presented in formats that translate very well for advance planning or the structuring of responses. In the vertical sense, the Intel Cell provides floor plan layouts, demographic data, and contact information for every floor in every building taller than 540 feet in Chicago's Central Business District. In the event of an emergency in or around the building, officials would be able to access and use this information, for example, to direct or prevent an evacuation, depending on the nature of the threat. The data were gathered after I proposed an ordinance requiring high-rise buildings to develop response plans and gather information and to share that with the city. The Chicago City Council approved that ordinance in 2001, shortly after the 9/11 terror attacks.

Beyond this vertical information, the Intel Cell can also deliver an instant snapshot of the city's key assets and relevant infrastructure in map form. Using these data and the interface, officials at our JOC can call up a map of a block, a neighborhood, a city ward or all of Chicago, and identify the location of every water main, gas main, police and fire station, school, daycare center, hospital, park district facility, and city office. This technology also is mated to a "plume modeling" system that, in the event of an emergency ranging from a gas leak or overturned tanker truck to a terrorist detonated dirty bomb, would take into effect the nature of the chemical and the prevailing weather conditions to identify the area most at risk from any fallout. The city could then define the area defined by the plume and use the reverse call-back system to call those in the defined area, advising residents to remain indoors and close their windows until they receive further instructions from first responders.

The availability of the information on the Intel Cell in the Joint Operations Center can be extremely useful in a number of circumstances and to a number of different agencies. With all of those agencies represented in one room, the information can go to the right people almost immediately.

One Night in the Joint Operations Center

Between 7:00 a.m. and 9:00 p.m. on July 3, 2007, people ambled into Grant Park for the City of Chicago's annual fireworks show. Over the course of 14 h, they set up tents, dozed in the sun, threw Frisbees, and sampled food and drink from more than 70 vendors at the Taste of Chicago. They arrived incrementally, a few hundred at a time, until there were an estimated one million people looking up as fireworks rose and burst in the eastern sky over Lake Michigan.

Then, at 9:58 p.m., the 20-min fireworks show having just ended, all of those people tried to leave at once.

Throngs of people began leaving the park, on foot and on bikes, pulling coolers and pushing strollers. Streets that were empty minutes before became a river of humanity flowing west.

The July 3 fireworks show is an annual event for Chicagoans and an annual test for the City of Chicago. It consistently brings a million people or more to Grant Park and Taste of Chicago, the annual festival of food, drink, and music. Held along the lake east of downtown, July 3 challenges emergency response for the police and fire departments, demands a late but thorough cleanup by the street cleaners, brings an incomparable rush of travelers to the public transit system, and fills the streets in every direction with drivers trying to find their way home.

Against this backdrop, the Joint Operations Center is staffed every year for July 3, and the 2007 activation of the JOC for the event brought representatives from the police and fire departments, as well as six other city departments, two train lines, the Illinois State Police, the state's Department of Transportation, the Bureau of Alcohol, Tobacco, and Firearms, the Department of Homeland Security, and the US Coast Guard. So when those million people set off for home, the City of Chicago and the other jurisdictions had ample assets in place to make sure they got there safely.

In the room with its 39 workstations, radio traffic from the central business district dispatcher was monitored, and cameras were redirected to areas where problems were reported. As lines grew heavy and restless outside transit stations, police officers were dispatched. Where pedestrian traffic grew thick enough to interfere with cars, traffic aides were sent. When reports of fights or threats to bus drivers came in, the representatives of various agencies called out to each other with information and suggestions.

The benefits of the Joint Operations Center were crystallized around 11:05 p.m., when the Chicago Transit Authority supervisor reported CTA trains were stopped along the elevated rails due to a power problem. In the space of 90 s, fire and police units were deployed, traffic aides were ordered to respond to transit stations and 911 officials, anticipating cell phone calls from riders aboard those trains, discussed whether to have call talkers tell the riders aboard the trains to remain patient and not try and self-evacuate from the train cars.

At one point, the CTA supervisor, a Chicago Fire Department district chief and a Chicago Police Department Assistant Deputy Superintendent were gathered together, discussing command post-locations and response scenarios, making coordinated decisions barely 10 min after the first report. It was an exchange that likely would never have happened under ordinary circumstances, but because the Joint Operations Center had been activated that evening, it was an exchange both easily executed and extremely effective.

The Extended Joint Operations Center

Technology is a wonderful thing, but made portable, it becomes even better, which is why we in the City of Chicago took steps to make sure that the benefits of the Office of Emergency Management and Communications can be brought elsewhere. We do this using our Unified Communications Vehicle, a $2 million mobile unit with two satellite dishes that features more than 100 phone lines, land mobile radio capability, Wi-Fi computer access, and an independent cellular tower. This vehicle, unveiled in September 2006, gives us the ability to project the abilities and assets of the Joint Operations Center to any location anywhere.

We put this ability to the test on December 31, 2006, when the City of Chicago faced a unique evening. Not only would the city be filled with the celebrations and revelry that comes with New Year's Eve but also the Chicago Bears and the Green Bay Packers would be reviving their decades-long rivalry at Soldier Field. This combination of events brought a combination of concerns, among them crowd control, heavy traffic (some of it bound for the Illinois–Wisconsin border upon the game's conclusion), and not one but two periods of extensive use of the city's public transportation system.

With those concerns in mind, the City of Chicago decided to not only activate the Joint Operations Center for that evening but also set up a Forward Command Post at a location that put personnel close to both Soldier Field and the downtown area. A tennis court in Grant Park – north of Solider Field, east of the Loop, and south of the Magnificent Mile – offered an effective location, and it was there that the OEMC, joined by the Chicago Fire Department and the Chicago Police Department, inflated a field tent alongside the Unified Communications Vehicle. The result was a second Joint Operations Center, equipped with a single large monitor and 24 workstations featuring laptop computers and phones that could use not only the conventional telephone network but also the PAX line system unique to the Chicago Police Department.

The evening passed by relatively peacefully, if not happily (the Bears lost to the Packers that night), but we were pleased with what we were able to bring to the Forward Command Past. I would add that when we returned to the area 2 weeks later, setting up another command post for the Bears' home playoff game against the New Orleans Saints, we were joined at the scene by the Federal Bureau of Investigation's command vehicle in yet another example of multi-jurisdictional teamwork.

Conclusion

The City of Chicago is an amazing place, filled with everything one could hope to find in a true international city. We have museums and theaters, sports teams and parks, two major airports, and a spectacular lakefront. We are a major business center, home to some of the world's largest companies. And we are a city of neighborhoods, where people from all across the world have come to make their homes.

As this rich diversity in our population strengthens the fabric of Chicago, the diversity in our thinking strengthens our readiness. We have worked very hard to build a culture of preparedness here, with Chicago last fall conducting the first large-scale evacuation drill ever held in a major US city. We have used advanced technology in creative ways, and we have engaged in the most fundamental of community meetings, all in the interests of keeping our residents safe and secure. Whether using satellite communications or simply speaking to people in a local meeting place, we realize very clearly that the exchange of relevant information – before, during, and after an emergency – is one of the most important elements of public safety.

We have many assets in Chicago, and an informed and prepared populace is only one of them. We also have the strength of world-class police and fire departments, the most advanced emergency dispatching system in the nation, two dozen city departments ready to contribute to any emergency response and close relationships with municipal, county, state, federal, and private agencies. This group of public servants and like-minded private agencies is capable of working together, quickly and efficiently, to respond to, mitigate, and recover from an emergency in our city.

Ultimately, our Joint Operations Center is one of the strongest assets we have as we use cooperation, collaboration, and communication to make Chicago as safe as any large city can be.

Chapter 24
Beyond an Information Technology Approach to Continuity of Operations: The Commonwealth of Virginia Story

Timothy Kaine

Abstract Virginia developed and implemented a continuity of operations plan for all disasters including a possible flu pandemic. Continuity plans include provision for use of alternative facilities in case a disaster disables the primary department or agency facility. Virginia also created a new Emergency Operations Center with sufficient space to accommodate individual departments and agencies that have had their facilities made inoperable. The Emergency Operations Center has sophisticated computer and communication technology which permits operational management of a disaster. Especially important is the redundancy aspect so that the center is resilient to failure of any individual system.

T. Kaine (✉)
Governor, The Commonwealth of Virginia, (2006–present),
http://www.governor.virginia.gov/ index.cfm
e-mail: ima@governor.virginia.gov

S. Hakim, E.A. Blackstone (eds.), *Safeguarding Homeland Security*,
DOI 10.1007/978-1-4419-0371-6_24, © Springer Science+Business Media, LLC 2009

Introduction

Beyond an Information Technology Approach to Continuity of Operations: The Commonwealth of Virginia Story. For years the private sector has utilized Business Continuity Planning to mitigate financial, operational, and business impacts from hazards. The utilization of procedures developed to resume or restore critical business processes following a disruption further ensures survivability under various conditions. In July 1999, the federal government followed suit, issuing Federal Preparedness Circular (FPC) 65. FPC 65, which was updated in July 2004, provides guidance to federal executive branch departments and agencies for use in developing viable and executable contingency plans for continuity of operations (COOP). COOP planning is the effort to ensure the survivability of essential business functions during a wide range of potential emergencies and events. Today's ever-changing threat environment and ever-present emergencies encompass the need for COOP plans and capabilities.

The public is generally unwilling to overlook lapses in services, even in the wake of disasters. The obligation of both business and government is to provide seamless services, especially those involving public safety and health, in spite of any event. COOP planning is a "good business practice" and the public expects good "customer service" from the government as much as it does from any business.

Recognizing that reliability is the key, Governor Mark Warner's administration expended great effort to establish the requirement that Commonwealth agencies develop COOP plans. Governor Warner issued two Executive Orders: the first required all executive branch agencies to develop and evaluate their COOP plans and the second required agencies to exercise them.

Virginia's COOP-planning strategy consisted of five phases. First, COOP was integrated into the Commonwealth of Virginia Emergency Operations Plan. Second, the scope of evaluation was narrowed to the 45 agencies that make up the Virginia Emergency Response Team (VERT). Third, the Virginia Department of Emergency Management (VDEM) developed a COOP Planning Manual to serve as a standard and as guidance for state agencies. Fourth, VDEM worked with consultants to build an assessment tool that encompassed standards from the National Fire Protection Association, Emergency Management Accreditation Program (EMAP), Federal Emergency Management Agency (FEMA) Interim Guidance to State and Local Governments, as well as FPC 65. Fifth, using the assessment tool, the consultants evaluated each VERT agency's COOP plan.

In the fall of 2005, EMAP Assessors reviewed the VERT agency plans, assessment reports, and the VDEM COOP Planning Manual and awarded full EMAP accreditation. In addition, the VDEM COOP Planning Manual was cited as a "Best Practice." What began as a planning strategy became a strong foundation for a viable statewide COOP program.

Further commitment to COOP came in the form of Section 44-146.18 of the Code of Virginia (2005), which tasks VDEM with providing guidance and assistance to state agencies and local governments in developing and maintaining COOP programs, plans, and systems. Throughout this process it became evident that there was a lack of guidance and information currently available. The COOP Planning Manual was a good start, but agencies and localities needed more, particularly help with relating emergency management concepts to their own functions. As a next step, VDEM developed a State COOP Steering Committee to help guide the process from a multi-disciplined perspective.

The Steering Committee provides the principal inter-organizational forum for discussion of COOP matters. Such matters include dissemination of information, managing inter-agency dependencies, coordinating COOP exercises including inter-agency exercises, accommodating ongoing legal and regulatory requirements, facilitating the overall COOP program and project plans to include the supporting financial/budget plan for the Commonwealth, conducting periodic assessments of statewide COOP capabilities, and reporting the results to the Governor. The committee includes representatives from the Virginia State Police and the Virginia Departments of Accounts, Conservation, and Recreation; General Services; Health; Human Resource Management; Planning and Budget; Social Services and Transportation as well as the Virginia Information Technology Agency.

In addition, VDEM provided training on how to develop a COOP plan using the VDEM's COOP Planning Manual. The training was first offered to the 45 VERT agencies and then continued on to all state agencies. Finally, the training was tailored and offered to two state universities. As COOP gained more recognition, the training became more popular and the demand for access to COOP information and materials was apparent from all sectors of the state and localities, as well as the business community.

To meet this increasing demand, VDEM created the COOP Toolkit, an online resource posted on the VDEM web site: http://www.vaemergency.com. The Toolkit provides one-stop access to a variety of business and government continuity planning resources including the VDEM COOP Planning Manual, COOP Worksheets, a COOP Plan Template, the COOP training slides and videos, lessons learned, information about the COOP Steering Committee, and potential COOP funding sources.

The COOP Planning Manual provides aid in the development and maintenance of COOP plans. The manual reflects FEMA (Guidelines and FPC 65), industry standards, and COOP best practices. It offers both procedural and operational guidances for the preparation and implementation of a COOP plan following a seven-phase process. The seven phases are (I) Project Initiation, (II) Identification of Functional Requirements, (III) Design and Development, (IV) Implementation, (V) Training, Testing and Exercises, (VI) Execution, and (VII) Revising and Updating.

The project initiation phase consists of appointing a COOP coordinator, organizing a COOP team and holding an initial project meeting. Phase II is an assessment of the functional requirements of a COOP plan and consists of identifying essential functions, vital records, systems and equipments, naming key personnel, selecting an alternate facility, and determining the existence of interoperable communications. The third phase of the planning process is when the plan is actually written. During the implementation phase, phase IV, the COOP plan is put into practical effect. Phase V, testing, training, and exercising the plan, is extremely important for employee awareness and readiness. Phase VI, execution, is the actual activation of a COOP plan in part or in whole depending upon the magnitude of the disruption or threat. Finally in phase VII, the COOP plan, a living document, is revised and updated on a regular basis.

The two main tools in the COOP Toolkit are the worksheets and the COOP Plan Template, which coincide with the seven phases of the planning process. Completing the worksheets assists in assembling the information necessary to develop the ten critical elements of a COOP plan. Because every organization has a different mission, each COOP plan will be unique. Merely filling in the blanks on worksheets is not a substitute for a plan that allows for the continuity of an organization during a disruption. The template provides organization for the plan itself. This template, in collaboration with the information gathered through use of the worksheets, assists in completing a cohesive and comprehensive COOP plan specific to each individual organization's mission, needs, and essential business functions.

The COOP training slides and more than 2 h of video provide an overview of the seven-phase process. Presented in modules for convenience, both the training slides and the videos can serve as a good introduction for someone new to COOP planning or as a refresher course.

The COOP Toolkit serves as a resource not only for the Commonwealth but also for other states and local government programs. Between January and May 2006, the COOP Planning Manual was downloaded more than 22,000 times and the training slides were downloaded more than 8,000 times. Requests continue for presentations at professional associations, including the 2006 Virginia Emergency Management Association Conference and the Homeland Defense Journal's Continuity of Government Operations Training Conference. Both the COOP Planning Manual and the Toolkit received an Honorable Mention Media Award from the International Association of Emergency Managers.

In order to maintain the momentum of the COOP program and further Virginia's mission of preparedness, I issued Executive Order 44 (EO 44) in January 2007. EO 44 recognizes COOP planning as critical to the Commonwealth's ability to deliver valuable services to its citizens during and immediately after a disaster. Each executive branch agency, including institutions of higher education, is required to submit an updated version of their COOP Plan by April 1 of each year to VDEM. In addition, the EO requires the Office of Commonwealth Preparedness, in consultation with VDEM to review all executive branch agencies' COOP plans by the first week of December each year.

With the continued support of the Governor's Office and funding allocated from the General Assembly, VDEM organized a project plan and managed five major Commonwealth COOP initiatives between July and December 2007. To support the execution of EO 44, VDEM, in conjunction with the Office of Commonwealth Preparedness and a team of consultants, reviewed all executive branch agency COOP plans, developed two new COOP Toolkits (one for local governments and one for institutions of higher education), developed a Continuity of Government Plan for each of the Cabinet Secretary Offices including an overarching logistics plan, and created a Pandemic Influenza Annex to the COOP guidance.

Each agency and institution of higher education received a COOP Plan Assessment Report that provided them with an overall plan assessment. The assessment report identified strengths and areas for improvement and provided recommendations. The organizations were evaluated on 24 assessment criteria across 13 elements of COOP planning. The criteria were derived from VDEM's COOP Planning Manual, September 2006, Version 3, and the VDEM COOP Plan Template, March 2006, Version 1. A final report was submitted to the Governor's office summarizing the assessment of COOP plans for 109 of these organizations, a 91.5% response rate. This process not only assessed each individual agency's COOP plan, but the overall COOP program.

Institutions of higher education are subject to the provisions of EO 44; therefore, each is required to submit a COOP plan annually to VDEM. While the initial COOP Toolkit provided resources on the overall planning process, it did not fully address the unique situations that make COOP planning a challenge for these institutions. These challenges include having a dependent care population of students for which they must provide emergency functions, preserving their reputation with students, parents, alumni and research partners, and their dependency on research funding and large investments in research facilities and projects, which require unique protection methods. To address these, VDEM, in collaboration with an outside consultant and representatives from public and private colleges and universities, both 2 and 4 year, from across the Commonwealth created an online COOP Toolkit for institutions of higher education complete with a distinct planning manual, worksheets, and templates.

Like the former COOP Planning Manual and worksheets, the resources provide guidance to colleges and universities in the development and maintenance of COOP plans. The major difference in the Toolkits is the template section. For institutions of higher education, the Toolkit has three templates from which to choose. Each institution must decide on the structure of its COOP program and plan. Alternatives are a single comprehensive plan, or a basic plan that provides overall guidance and structure, with a series of divisional or departmental plans that address the specific needs of functional areas. The strategy decided on depends on the size and structure of the college or university, the complexity of its mission and the availability of resources for planning. These templates, in conjunction with the information gathered in the worksheets, will assist in completing cohesive and comprehensive COOP plan(s) to meet each institution's needs.

While no mandate exists requiring localities to complete a COOP plan, VDEM developed a COOP Toolkit for local governments to address the growing number of questions being raised and to assist localities in the areas that make COOP planning a challenge, in particular, the broad range of public works and services they perform on a daily basis. VDEM, again in collaboration with an outside consultant and a committee comprised of representatives from localities across the Commonwealth, including the Virginia Association of Counties and the Virginia Municipal League, developed a COOP planning manual, worksheets, and templates to provide guidance to local governments for the development and maintenance of COOP plans.

In addition, VDEM, utilizing the COOP Steering Committee's expertise, created guidance to assist in COOP planning for pandemic influenza. The online manual, worksheets, and template focus on the efficient and effective management of expected limited human resources. The guidance manual focuses on pandemic influenza, though it can apply to any scenario involving loss of workforce from highly communicable diseases. The worksheets help to gather the raw data needed to develop a pandemic influenza COOP annex. They can be modified to fit the needs of an agency, institution, locality, or department. The template provides agencies and institutions with the basic annex itself. The template, in collaboration with the manual and worksheets, will assist in completing a pandemic influenza annex to a COOP plan.

As part of the Commonwealth COOP program, VDEM worked closely with the Office of Commonwealth Preparedness in the development of Continuity of Government (COG) Plans for each Cabinet Secretary Office including an overarching logistics plan. COG ensures the command and control of response and recovery operations as well as continuance of governmental functions. The COG plans prioritize essential services and functions across each Secretariat and detail appropriate resource assignments to ensure these services and functions are continued during times of emergency. The logistics plan establishes the framework whereby logistics support actions of Secretariat Offices can be effectively integrated and coordinated in the movement between the primary facilities and the Secretariat Offices' alternate facilities.

The Commonwealth of Virginia has led the region and the nation in assisting executive agencies and institutions of higher education develop COOP plans. In 2008, VDEM in collaboration with the Office of Commonwealth Preparedness will continue to promote a culture of preparedness and further enhance the Commonwealth COOP Program through several methods. These include the following:

- Training that focuses on the areas where agencies and institutions need the most improvement;
- Offering continual planning assistance and guidance in COOP plan and program development;
- Revising the current online COOP Toolkit to ensure it continues to reflect current planning standards and the changing needs of the executive branch agencies;
- Training on the newly developed COOP Toolkit designed specifically for institutions of higher education;
- Updating the COOP Toolkit for institutions of higher education as necessary to reflect current planning standards and the changing needs of the institutions.

While COOP remains a relatively new concept to the Commonwealth, the technological capabilities necessary to support a COOP effort have been in development for years. The state realized a new facility was needed to support emergency management operations. With the construction of the new Virginia Emergency Operations Center (VEOC), this initial requirement was met. This facility provides not only redundancy for continuance of emergency operations but also ample workspace for other agencies and personnel required during state emergency operations. External agencies can bring in employees and maintain access to various levels of their own technologies. This access provides a greater opportunity for agencies to provide good customer service during a disaster or emergency. The circumstances under which those services are performed remains transparent to the end users, meaning they are unaware that the service they are using is now being provided from the VEOC, thus making continuity an easier process.

From the ground up, the VEOC was created with a service-oriented architecture. Virginia formed the EOC Planning Committee, which worked closely with state agencies to determine key functions needed in an emergency. This information was critical in designing an architecture that was flexible and scalable enough to support the 45 VERT agencies. The end result was a facility that continues to grow using an open, yet extremely secure platform for COOP and information sharing.

In the VEOC, the WebEOC software package was selected as a critical information management system. WebEOC is a simple tool that serves a very important purpose – it enables information sharing across state agencies and localities during an event. Due to the straightforward architecture of the application, VDEM is able to share real-time information quickly and easily with localities and other agencies, a key component in emergency response efforts. Emergency managers in Northern Virginia, Maryland, and the District of Columbia quickly adopted WebEOC.

WebEOC's architecture allows for integration with other web-based services. Geospatial Information Services provide real-time event location-specific information that is vital to the emergency response planning process. Being able to redirect critical resources to those who need them, where they need them in real time can save time, money, property, and lives.

To support this software and other applications within the VEOC, a completely redundant network was constructed. This network includes data lines that come from two different geographical locations, come from different vendors, and come into the facility at opposite ends of the building. These data lines are managed by redundant hardware with complete failover functionality. Not only is each piece of hardware duplicated but each component that makes up the hardware device is redundant.

The practice of redundancy applies to all hardware components involved with the servers as well. The VEOC architecture is being considered by the Virginia Information Technology Agency as a standard for how redundant enterprise systems should be built. Each application has two servers to support it. These applications are then shared with other servers in a "passive" mode, meaning that applications are not running on the passive servers until the first two levels of redundancy fail. Should a failure of this magnitude occur, the passive servers become "active" and start serving whatever application is required until the failed server can be repaired. During tests and exercises, this process happens in less than 1 h. Finally, a series of portable machines that can be plugged into a satellite-based mobile network have been configured to support WebEOC and e-mail, allowing these two critical functions to operate from not only anywhere in the Commonwealth but also anywhere in North America.

The VEOC is outfitted with Voice Over IP, analog and satellite phones, and cellular repeaters. These technologies ensure that all users maintain full signal strength regardless of provider for every cell phone, PDA and pager in use by state, local, and federal agencies. Finally, to provide constant audio and visual interactions, the VEOC is outfitted with an array of monitors that have redundant cable and satellite feeds, as well as internal computer feeds. With more than 200 computers and 600 network connections available, users have ample opportunity to display vital information anywhere within the VEOC.

Each technology component was designed for continuity in a rapidly changing environment. Industry standards accept a 5- to 12-h restoration timeframe for IT systems considered "mission critical." Systems supported within the VEOC, including WebEOC, e-mail, or any other critical communications system, maintain a turnaround time of 1 h or less.

The Commonwealth places great emphasis on using technology as an integral part of the continuity of operations. Continuous integration of COOP and IT practices, plans, and systems ensures that Virginia's public continues to receive good customer service despite any incident. Virginia continues to employ both these efforts to mitigate against financial, operational, and "business" impacts.

Chapter 25
The Soft Stuff is Still the Hard Stuff

Albert Morales and Todd S. Ramsey

Abstract The chapter details the complications and issues associated with integrating and coordinating the introduction and use of technology for homeland security. The use of a steering committee including both technical and organizational personnel is important for the process. The chapter shows the importance of culture and the role of IT people in educating other team members.

Today's homeland security threats are unpredictable and organic. Natural disasters can occur anywhere at any moment and man-made threats continuously evolve and expand. Terrorism feeds on vulnerabilities. As security is strengthened in one area, terrorists simply shift attention to the next weakest link. Governments need to meet threats on the same relentless terms – continuously adapt processes, exploit new technologies, and capitalize on flexible human resource capabilities. The ability to adapt hinges on the government's capabilities to implement new management systems and new processes entwined with new technologies. In the early 1990s Michael Hammer launched the process re-engineering revolution with the words, "The soft stuff is the hard stuff." Not much has changed. The soft stuff remains every leader's biggest challenge – strategy, complex project management, and culture change. In fact, today's imperative to coordinate preparedness and response – with other people and systems across boundaries of governments, health-care institutions, transportation, utilities, health-care providers, and law enforcement – raises the need to collaborate to an unprecedented level.

Leading-edge technologies are available, reliable, and affordable to combat the toughest security threats. In the forefront are foolproof biometric identification, cross-boundary wireless or broadband communications, massive evacuations guided by the latest advances in GPS, "track and trace" of cargo and people, satellite imagery and mapping, smart video surveillance, wearable computers, traffic management, and many others. With the right advice, technology is not the hard part.

A. Morales (✉)

IBM Global Business Services, General Manager Public Sector Federal Industry Leader

e-mail: albert.morales@us.ibm.com

S. Hakim, E.A. Blackstone (eds.), *Safeguarding Homeland Security*,
DOI 10.1007/978-1-4419-0371-6_25, © Springer Science+Business Media, LLC 2009

Technology is not even the most expensive part. Technology is nothing more than an inert tool until people release and manage its power.

It is a daunting challenge to create, execute, and manage a portfolio of security initiatives, especially those that cross boundaries – across agencies, across horizontal jurisdictions, across vertical jurisdictions, across the public/private divide or all of the above! But, it can be done. The St. Louis Area Regional Response System (STARRS) is an integrated wireless network across 2 states, 8 counties, and 120 cities coordinating police, firefighters, emergency medical services, and government agencies. Previously, responders relied on limited cellular technology and landlines, which are vulnerable to failure. STARRS replaced these systems with an integrated and collaborative wireless communications network that people can count on even when power and phone lines are inoperative.

It all starts with leadership and innovation. Although the origins of cross-boundary initiatives may differ, they share similar characteristics. It may begin with one visionary. It may begin with a simple conversation, a staff recommendation, a legislative mandate, a new technology, or a failure. Whatever the genesis of the innovative idea, the evolution brings stakeholder groups together facing a common threat, sharing a common purpose and vision. One example is the Mid-Atlantic All Hazards Forum, a public–private partnership of Mid-Atlantic governments and private corporations. This grass roots, first-of-its-kind initiative was designed to improve regional homeland security and emergency management, facilitate dialogue among state directors, increase interaction among all of the stakeholders, and generate innovative initiatives. Participating states include Delaware, the District of Columbia, Maryland, New Jersey, North Carolina, Pennsylvania, Virginia, and West Virginia. Private sector, universities, and non-profits, including volunteer and faith-based organizations, also joined. Focusing on all three phases of a hazard (readiness, response, and recovery), the Forum's mission is to help build communication and forge relationships among stakeholders in the Mid-Atlantic region.

Regardless of how a homeland security initiative begins, the hard part is transitioning from idea to implementation. Building a governance scaffold is the first step. Begin by establishing a governing steering committee that accommodates the voices of all stakeholders. Typically, the steering committee domain includes (1) threat assessments, (2) a scan of applicable state-of-the-art technologies, (3) identification of candidate projects, (4) prioritization, (5) selection of projects, (5) funding mechanisms, (6) staffing and deployment of high-performance project teams to manage implementation, and (7) continuous project oversight.

A steering committee is critical to direct, coordinate and align the work of multiple project teams over a portfolio mix of initiatives. However, successful execution boils down to the right skills of experienced project team members. As projects unfold, three key skills – people, processes, and technology know-how – need to be integrated and managed together. For example, a homeland security initiative might include improving communication among local law enforcement, state or federal investigative resources, emergency responders, and transit agencies. Besides representation from each stakeholder on the steering committee, skills of project team members should include expertise in each participating entity's technology infrastructure, expertise in developing workable cross-boundary processes, and expertise in change management to facilitate implementation.

A recurring theme runs through virtually any cross-boundary security project. Most critical infrastructure in the United States is privately owned. Any project designed to shore up vulnerabilities in critical infrastructure will require cross-boundary coordination across public and private sector to include entities such as utility companies, transportation systems, or financial networks. Initiatives that involve public health ultimately involve numerous agencies on both the public and the private sector sides. By their nature, transportation initiatives could encompass any number of disparate entities – rail, shipping, airport authorities, local, state and federal law enforcement, or border security. What are the implications of introducing new technologies across stakeholders given underlying technology infrastructures of each? By what method will new processes be defined? What impact will re-defined roles and responsibilities have on employees of each stakeholder group? Irrespective of the threat and preemptive response to that threat, the challenges are the same.

Build the Governance Scaffold

Fortunately, proven management principles and models are available. The following cross-boundary governance model can be scaled to manage one project across agencies within one government or to manage major regional or cross-governmental initiatives with multiple stakeholders and multiple projects.

One role of the steering committee, with representatives from each stakeholder group, is to exhibit leadership and highly visible sponsorship. It falls upon the sponsors to engender commitment to a compelling vision at two levels. Not only do steering committee members have the responsibility to lead security projects to successful conclusions, but they also need to cascade the vision, goals, and values to their own respective stakeholder organizations to facilitate change that may be necessary as the result of individual project implementations. One hallmark of an effective vision is an understanding that the status quo is not sustainable. Buy in and commitment will not happen overnight. But, it will happen if steering committee members assume proactive leadership roles.

If the initial representative from any of the stakeholder groups is unlikely to be present throughout the full transformation, establish a clear succession plan to reinforce that the program has ongoing support. Otherwise the transformation may stall or the coalition may not survive a leadership change.

Generally, the steering committee facilitates a joint, robust threat assessment, evaluates security exposures based on the magnitude of potential damage, and identifies candidate projects for a security portfolio (see Table 25.1). No plan offers 100% protection from every man-made or natural disaster. Therefore, setting priorities is essential. Once individual projects are identified to include in the portfolio, the

Table 25.1 Likely candidates for security portfolios

Border Security

Related to the movement of people across borders, three key elements stand out: (1) authentication of travel documents, (2) confirmation that the person presenting the documents is the person to whom they were issued, and (3) connecting the individual with his life history to determine the desirability of entry. Similar steps are relevant to cargo shipments. Shipments need to be connected back to the shippers and common carriers, whose trustworthiness can be assessed. Technologies available today such as smart cards and biometrics clearly help to authenticate documents and the people who carry them.

Transportation

Transportation has been a terrorism target for decades. Since 9/11, attention has concentrated on the role of central government agencies, airport authorities, and airlines to protect the flying public and those on the ground from the threat of commercial aircraft hijackings. However, high air travel security in the absence of similar emphasis on regional, land, or sea transportation simply shifts the focus of terrorists. In addition, evacuation planning relies upon coordination of multiple modes of transportation. Central to transportation security are processes and technologies that support identification and authentication. These technologies apply to vehicles, cargoes, and, of course, people, including travelers and employees. The preoccupation with the concept of "trusted" travelers will likely be short lived. Over time, identification and authentication technologies such as smart identification cards and biometric recognition will separate "known" from "unknown" rather than "trusted" from "untrusted" – particularly for travelers. This approach validates trustworthiness at the time of travel for known travelers, cargoes, or even vehicles based on the privileges they attempt to exercise. Meanwhile, unknown entities will likely receive additional scrutiny from inspectors and law-enforcement personnel. This concept requires investment in infrastructure and data management capabilities to support the validation of trust on a transactional basis. The combination of databases that support authorization at the transaction level and identity authentication of people, cargoes, and vehicles can be applied to air and train travelers, transportation of hazardous waste, movement of shipping containers, and many other situations. In the domains of public mass transit and large public areas, such as ports and waterways, are surveillance and site-security technologies, including digital video monitoring as well as many derivative technologies that can be applied to digital media data. Transportation security also links tightly to public health and public safety, given the focus on emergency response to transportation incidents and collaboration among multiple jurisdictions of law enforcement at transportation facilities such as airports and seaports.

Critical Infrastructure

Some degree of protection is delivered by the geographic dispersion of critical assets and the localized nature of natural disasters. Even the most widespread damage from a hurricane, flood, or earthquake may not threaten the viability of a nation's economy. However, a coordinated terrorist attack against known critical points of failure or geographically dispersed critical infrastructure such as transportation systems, utilities, or financial networks could be devastating to a nation's economy in a way that no natural disaster could. Key strategies to minimize risks vary, depending on whether the threat is a physical attack (e.g., demolition of key components in the electric distribution system or petroleum pipeline) or a cyber attack (e.g., denial of service for financial institutions or interference in the national telecommunications network). Security against the former can be aided with closer surveillance, monitoring, and access control; measures against the latter involve the definition and implementation of barriers and careful authentication of access to resources. Although each of these categories involves the collaboration of multiple organizations (e.g., utility providers and their customers or the partners within a financial network), there is less reliance on communication and collaboration in this

Table 25.1   (Continued)

category than there is in the public health or public safety category. Infrastructure protection relies on all asset owners to secure themselves and the critical infrastructure they own and to be ready to recover that infrastructure if it is disabled. Beyond that, the reliance on extended enterprises and collaborative networks that link organizations across countries and industry boundaries places a burden on every organization to expand its relationship agreements to include the definition of mutual protection so that an attack at one point in a network can be contained and isolated, preventing the disablement of an essential element of a nation's infrastructure or economy.

Public Health

Chemical, biological, radiological and nuclear attacks, or the contamination aftermath from other attacks, endanger human as well as agricultural plant and animal health. Geographical targets could be in heavily populated inner cities or in rural agricultural areas where both monitoring and response resources are limited. Combating these threats depends on access to centralized information within national organizations – including university research institutions, pharmaceutical suppliers, and biological/chemical warfare assets of the military – and coordination with local first responders and local medical provider networks. Key to securing public health is connectivity among multiple government and non-government entities. In the past, some linkages existed across these organizations; however, the purpose was generally limited to the collection and sharing of epidemiological information. Today's threats require a higher degree of readiness and joint operational capability. Underpinning new security processes are technologies capable of any-to-any, cross-boundary communications – on a moment's notice. Technologies include (1) the development of bi-directional communication that allows the knowledge in national or centralized organizations to be delivered to a point of need as easily as disease outbreak information is collected today and (2) a shorter cycle time for collection and dissemination of accurate information. Communication and collaboration tools include local and wide-area networking (including wireless networking for field personnel from inspectors to responders), groupware for collaboration across traditional organizational boundaries, knowledge management tools to access and propagate information, and e-learning to allow first responders and providers to stay abreast of threats and recommended response techniques.

Public Safety

Public safety resources – law enforcement, investigative resources, and emergency responders – play critical roles in the collection of information designed to detect threats, the interdiction of activity and individuals known to represent a danger and support for recovery efforts that follow any incident. National resources need to link to regional and local counterparts as well as other uniformed personnel, such as transit and housing authority police, fire investigators, private resources, including security guards and even the general public. Three key strategies include (1) improve the effectiveness of information collection to support threat identification, (2) improve and speed up collection and dissemination of information across a variety of law-enforcement-related organizations, and (3) data management and analysis, particularly data federation technology. This set of techniques allows rapid, flexible interconnection of data from various sources to allow investigators with proper authorization to view the total picture. In this way, disparate information from national intelligence and local law enforcement can be combined with minimal effort to identify suspicious activity and reach appropriate conclusions. This analysis can be distributed securely to those with a need to know. The end result allows existing public safety resources to be shaped into a net with a finer mesh, without the need to reorganize reporting structures or to reengineer information systems.

Table 25.1 (Continued)

Defense and Intelligence

Defense and intelligence frequently lead effort in detection and interdiction of safety and security threats. The application of IT to these disciplines is already widespread and increasing dramatically. Particularly important to the intelligence community are data management techniques that safeguard sensitive intelligence data and allow its appropriate use, including complex analysis without compromising sources to those without a need to know. The application of data federation technology offers significant promise in this area. When properly linked with the communications and collaboration technologies that support public safety and public health initiatives, the intelligence community can control the release of its insights and enable action by government agents across a wide variety of jurisdictions. Both defense and intelligence initiatives benefit from the creation of new linkages among government layers and between government and private sector organizations. These linkages support the collection of intelligence data, securing the data, and the careful release of screened and declassified insights to law enforcement.

challenge is to create brand new processes or transform existing processes supported by appropriate technologies and enabled by the people who can make them work.

Staffing the project teams is another critical steering committee responsibility. Pick the best and brightest and choose your partners wisely. At a minimum, populate teams with experts from each stakeholder group in each of three key disciplines – human resources, information technology, and process change. Deploy project team(s) by establishing a program office for each.

Information technology (IT) expertise is absolutely critical to both the governing steering committee and the individual project teams. IT itself may be the focus of one of the security projects – protecting critical IT infrastructure. Non-IT steering committee and team members need to understand technology capabilities and emerging technologies. Reach out to research and peers worldwide to learn how others are managing similar issues. Examples are everywhere. Faced with 7 million fans at the 2006 World Cup of Soccer, Munich, prepared for traffic control, crowd control and potential mass casualty incidents with satellite connectivity for voice, data, and video among multiple government entities, hospitals, mobile units, and command centers. New York City implemented its real-time crisis center using data warehouse capabilities to search widely diverse and fragmented systems. Now, within minutes, the two-dozen officers and detectives in the crisis center can mine 5 million state criminal records, 20 million NYC criminal files, 31 million national crime records, and 33 billion public records. Coupled with other technologies such as satellite imaging and mapping, capability extends to pinpoint criminal data against geographical data. This same Crime Information Warehouse technology is used by customs and immigration. The National Geospatial Intelligence Agency now provides unclassified imagery in disaster and humanitarian relief efforts. Again, satellite imagery intelligence is available – this time through on demand web-based access – to the military, state and local governments, disaster relief agencies, and rescue and recovery workers for any number of purposes in catastrophic events.

And, finally, the steering committee will grapple with numerous challenges and has a responsibility to proactively resolve each of them. Potential challenges include, but are not limited to, the following: Are privacy issues adequately addressed? What policies need to be adopted by stakeholder groups to share people and resources across departments and jurisdictions? How will the project(s) be funded? Are roles and responsibilities among stakeholders clear? Are data and processes transparent? Will the enterprise architecture support the strategy? Is there a strong focus on measuring performance and outcome, not just statistics? How can we collect public comment and engage citizens?

Understanding the Strategic Interplay of People, Process, and Technology

Effective management models are at the disposal of steering committees to launch and drive security enhancements to completion. The "Three Dimensions of Change" in Fig. 25.1 is one high-level illustration of an effective strategy to manage the complexity of people, processes, and technologies in tandem over time, across multiple projects and organizations. On the vertical axis, processes evolve from stand-alone processes to cross-boundary integration of multiple processes. On the horizontal axis, information technology

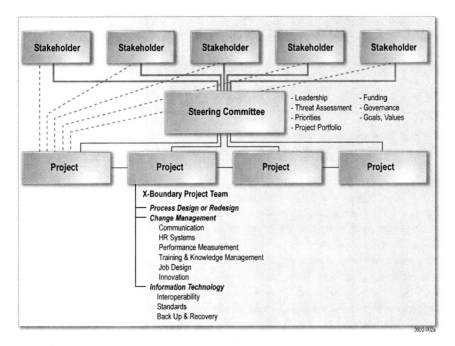

Fig. 25.1 Cross-boundary governance model

infrastructure progresses from individual support of a specific process to support of many processes. Individual projects progress in a stair-step fashion from the starting point toward the upper-right quadrant. The key variable that determines how quickly an organization can progress toward its goal is the management of people and culture, which is depicted on the diagonal (Fig. 25.2).

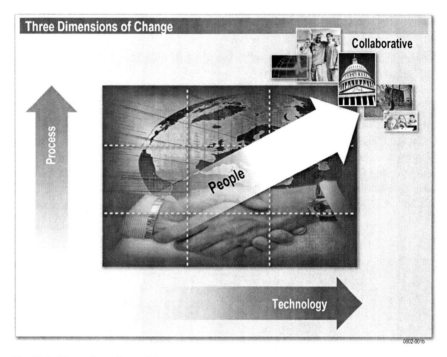

Fig. 25.2 Three dimensions of change

As projects are selected for implementation, the new security goals drive new processes. New processes drive the selection of new technologies. Together, new processes and new technologies create an environment of change that affects people. This is the critical junction where the project team needs members with expertise in process, expertise in information technology, and expertise in change management in order to design the security solution together.

In the following sections – people, process, and technology – proven techniques are presented to help understand and effectively manage the dynamics among the three during implementation. These approaches are also scaleable from an individual intra-governmental initiative to major cross-boundary initiatives involving multiple stakeholders.

People

An organization's culture is self-sustaining. It reinforces itself every day through every employee. With no conscious intent, each new employee is indoctrinated into the existing culture – good or bad. The "culture" or, more precisely, every individual who works in the organization, mirrors a collective, embedded orientation. If the overall cultural predisposition is to maintain the status quo, the rigorous demands of change create bewildered, frustrated, and anxious employees. Any effort that involves multiple organizations creates a challenge to adopt a common cultural orientation for the project(s). In a worst-case scenario, organizational paralysis can occur in the face of change. According to IBM's 2004 Global Business Consulting study, 75% of all transformations fail to fully deliver; and, nine out of ten reasons are related to people!

Team members bring their own respective cultural orientations to the project team from their "home" organization (stakeholder group). So, not only will project teams with members from various stakeholder organizations need to develop a common cultural orientation for the project team, but also each stakeholder's organization will be affected by new processes inherent to new security initiatives and *those* cultures also need to adapt to the inevitable changes. It is a tall order. Fortunately, the change management strategy in Fig. 25.3 has a track record that shapes cultures to support a desired future state.

The outer circle depicts the change cycle beginning with a trigger for change – in this case a portfolio of homeland security enhancements. Project team members with human resource responsibilities will need to communicate the steering committee's vision, strategy, and plans.

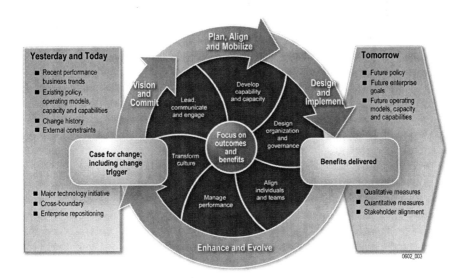

Fig. 25.3 Management of change

The support strategies depicted in the inner circle are critical to project implementation. Human resource policies that govern incentives, promotions, pay, employee development, recruiting, and performance measurement enable change. Modify approaches to training, promotions, reward systems, and management development to align with project goals. Changing the HR system, particularly the learning system, is the most visible way to do this. Recognition is a key tool that senior leaders can manage personally. There are few techniques, which are as powerful or as infectious as public recognition delivered personally by a senior leader to people who demonstrate desired behavior.

Mobilize leaders at every level, placing emphasis on consistent communication and on the need to lead and manage to a new set of operating values. Build consensus about the change. An essential step managing across multiple projects is breaking down silos. Employ a vigorous communications program inclusive of internal and cross-boundary stakeholders throughout the change cycle. The use of a web portal to facilitate communications, collaboration, and e-learning is a proven, effective technique. Deployment of a web portal may be the most productive first step in when the leadership anticipates significant culture change. Effective collaboration tools, reinforced by recognition and reward, helps people become less protective of jobs, organizations, and the status quo and open up to collaboration with other agencies, customers, and partners.

Understand both organization and individual capabilities. Identify any shortfalls in capacity against what's needed and address these as a priority. This may include capability assessments, readiness assessments, skills assessments, and delivery alternatives considering in-sourcing and out-sourcing. Employ knowledge management and transfer knowledge using "train the trainers" and "black belts." Traditional training programs generally emphasize "how-to" activities. Lift training out of an automation focus and shape it into viable education, skills transfer, and knowledge management.

Identify appropriate performance measures for the transition and new organization. Measure effectiveness regularly at all levels – individual, team, overall project, and across projects – using balanced scorecards, employee appraisals, and/or dashboards. Monitor progress toward achieving the desired benefits. Define standards/descriptions for jobs, roles, and functions. Define competency levels and associated values for job/role and function. Ensure continuous learning and development is in place. Do not lose sight of continual improvement so that when a new change trigger arises, subsequent waves of change can be accommodated.

Project teams need to remain focused on addressing the cultural issues associated with the people affected by the change. Design the new organization to realize the target vision. Adjust and streamline governance arrangements (developing new, if necessary) to improve timeliness/effectiveness of decisions and to support both the new organization and the change program. Create focus and accountability. Clarify accountability for, and improve timeliness/effectiveness of, decision making. Address job design from top to bottom for the employees involved in the new processes. Define roles, authorities, and reporting mechanisms. Descriptions of new behaviors and expectations should specify plans to develop new tools and train the workforce to perform more fulfilling jobs in the future.

The cumulative results of addressing "people" efforts in the execution of projects can and do change cultures.

Technology

The complexities of homeland security – from natural disasters to border protection to chemical terrorism – make it impossible to turn to a single technology solution. To avoid deployment of a series of disjointed capabilities, the project team needs to establish strategies around broad, functional areas of concentration and then procure and deploy compatible information technology (IT) components within those areas.

IT expertise on project teams is critical to educate other members about available and emerging technologies that may be applicable to the security goal. More importantly, the role of IT members is to guide the project team through the adoption of basic principles to ensure that effective technologies deliver business value. Some basic guiding principles include

- Focus on capabilities that are used every day – not just in times of emergency.
- Use IT as a complement to human judgment, not as a substitute for it.
- Help people to locate one another, communicate, collaborate, and do their jobs better.
- Deliver timely and accurate information to front-line people who can make decisions and take action.
- Integrate existing systems and technologies around redesigned business processes.
- Select and integrate technologies in support of evolving processes in ways that leverage the people who deliver the results.
- Advance security in ways that do not create expensive, highly secured zones that can be bypassed in favor of adjacent, unsecured targets.
- Incorporate sound practices for protection of critical IT assets including information access, secure networks, backup, recovery, flexibility, and open standards.
- Consider near-term technologies that can be integrated with others over the long term, thus minimizing scrap and replacement before anticipated end of life.
- Reduce the risks of technology adoption.

Technology itself may be the main focus of one or more of the security projects – either the protection of critical IT infrastructure or project-specific IT. For example, the capture and management of video surveillance data is at the center of many public safety and homeland security strategies. The City of Detroit Police Department became dissatisfied with their videotape capabilities. The sheer volume of 1,000 physical tapes per day made efficient management virtually impossible. When tapes were misplaced, evidence was lost. The department transformed its outdated system to an advanced digital and wireless communications infrastructure, including video surveillance and security services. The system includes automatic digital video recording and automatic upload of information to the central precinct computer when officer cars reach precinct stations. In the event of a problem, the precinct can remotely view, manage, and control a police car's camera and video system, helping to provide timely assistance that may be needed.

The following graphic depicts a world-class approach to selecting technology solutions that is driven by homeland security goals, functional modeling across stakeholder groups, shared IT services across stakeholder groups, and open standards (Fig. 25.4).

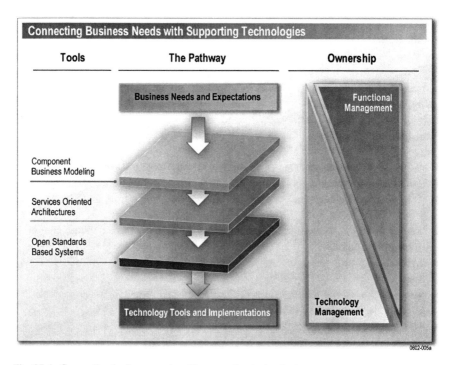

Fig. 25.4 Connecting business needs with supporting technologies

Once the security goal is communicated to the project team, the first step is to develop a high-level model of the organization's functional (or business) components. For example, the goal of the project may be to create a seamless, integrated wireless communications capability across multiple organizations. In this project example, the IT sub-team would identify and model all the functional components related to emergency communications across groups involved. This method, called Component Business Modeling, builds on traditional tools used to describe business processes and functions, but does so in a way that brings clarity to the value offered by today's technology choices. To begin, the team needs to understand the discrete functional components within each organization involved and how they might interact with one another. Invariably the team will discover functional components that are used by multiple organizations in multiple processes. Component Business Modeling (or CBM) provides a view of an *entire* system, outside of the constraints of organizational silos. The result is particularly valuable to resolve redundant and/or conflicting processes, technology implementations, and breakdowns in dependencies across organizational boundaries.

The next step is to map existing information technology assets across the identified functional components. Technologies that support each component are evaluated to highlight gaps, incompatibilities, and identify opportunities to share services among agencies or departments. This emerging technology strategy is called Services Oriented Architectures (SOA). The emphasis in SOA is on the word "services." Information technology provides services that support business requirements. Together, the analyses of functional components and existing technologies across those components can be reassembled to deliver maximum value with minimum cost and risk. In plain terms, the senior leadership on the steering committee can say: "this is how we want to operate collectively to accomplish our security goal." With that direction, the information technology experts on project teams can move forward to turn that vision into a workable plan for information systems across functional components. Finally, sharing IT services may improve service delivery levels at reduced costs and improved reliability. Just as re-engineering back-office functions reduces costs and provides savings that can be reinvested, so can sharing IT assets. Not only can shared services reduce cost, but they can also accelerate implementation of integrated infrastructures critical to today's security needs by introducing reusable assets. The team can also consider alternative sourcing arrangements and prioritize the implementation of emerging technologies

In order to implement shared services, the IT team members focus next on cross-boundary adoption of open standards. The world has learned the value of standards to connect people and technology. Any world traveler is familiar with the awkward process of using an electric plug adapter to address the lack of global standards for electricity. Information technology that supports safety and security requirements has its own set of challenges brought on by lack of standards. We see this in many forms – from communications radios that do not operate across jurisdictions to differences in terminology to conflicting doctrine. Unfortunately, these incompatibilities have both the greatest negative impact and the greatest public visibility in times of emergency or disaster. Both technology and functional managers have awakened to the need for improved standards, particularly as it relates to homeland security. Significant examples of meaningful progress include the work being done by eight mid-Atlantic governments under the All Hazards Consortium and the discussion facilitated by the Emergency Interoperation Consortium with strong support from the US Department of Homeland Security.

Process

The shifting sands of security threats dictate continual process adaptation and the continual infusion of technologies. The expensive alternative is to create a frozen process that becomes intractable as soon as modification is required to respond to a new threat or to introduce an enhanced technology. Therefore, from the beginning, accept process change as a constant. Then plan accordingly. Fortunately, pursuing continuous process improvement has become a science over the past decade. Proven approaches – with documented results in time, money, and effectiveness – are available for leaders.

Once functional components have been identified (CBM) and opportunities are identified to share IT resources (SOA), the nitty–gritty work begins – designing each discrete step in a new process or re-engineer steps in an existing process. Premier among process re-engineering approaches is Lean Sigma. Lean Sigma is a combination of Lean Manufacturing and Six Sigma approaches. Lean Sigma is built upon a business philosophy, a quality measurement, and a continuous improvement process with the aim to redesign processes to achieve high-performance. The approach has steadily evolved from its early days – from reducing manufacturing defects and improving reliability of products at Motorola – to a robust process redesign strategy applied across all industries from banking to telecom, to insurance, and to government. As a result, IBM's Global Business Consulting adopted Lean Sigma as its reengineering approach worldwide, across industries (Fig. 25.5).

Lean Sigma techniques can be used at both the steering committee and the project team level. Goals are developed by the committee for each security project through a series of leadership workshops. This helps to prioritize goals against a performance scorecard, and second, prioritize potential projects against how well they support the overall stakeholder goals. Typically, ranked and prioritized projects are then subjected to a series of filters to determine if they meet minimum thresholds for expected results, size, duration, and what methods are likely to best be utilized to produce the desired result. Appropriate projects are then assigned.

At the project team level, process experts conduct analyses that generally include detailed mapping of current processes and design of new processes. *This is the critical junction where process, information technology, and human resource team*

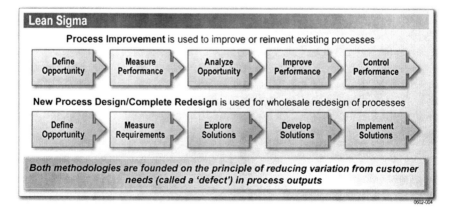

Fig. 25.5 Lean Sigma

members design the security solution together. What are relevant technologies? How will they interoperate? What are the implications for employee job design and training? Process redesign experts are often referred to as "black belts," a term Motorola coined to recognize the special skill sets needed to untangle deep-seated process problems. The approach also institutionalizes learning and organization knowledge and memory. Black belts teach others and capabilities mature over time into a high-performance capability to continuously adapt processes as needed.

Develop a business case for each security project in the portfolio that clearly states how it will help achieve its strategic priority or goal. Scope projects for 6-month completions. This short-time period for completion of projects brings focus and enhances the discovery of root causes, which leads to permanent solutions to process problems.

The absence or failure to meet a requirement is considered a "defect" in Lean Sigma terms. For example, one requirement may be "seamless emergency communications among neighboring jurisdictions." The next step is to understand what is causing the defect through root cause, data, and process analysis methods.

One example of a Lean Sigma implementation is the US Office of the Principal Legal Advisor (OPLA). OPLA provides legal services for the Immigration and Customs Enforcement Agency within the US Department of Homeland Security. Each year, the agency was spending US $1.2 million of its budget on some 60,000 cases that had to be rescheduled or dismissed due to missing documentation. With its budget tightening and its image flagging, the agency decided to revamp its entire operation. Using Lean Sigma, it surveyed its 19 client agencies to understand their needs and implemented ongoing processes to capture and act on agency feedback. As part of its operational overhaul, OPLA installed a computer system to centrally maintain all documents and reinvented mailroom processes to prevent lost documentation. Attorneys can now search and view documents online from their offices – and will eventually be able to access the system from all courtrooms.

Once the project is up and running, a formal process management system is recommended to monitor process performance and to assign responsibility that the improvements are sustained. A process owner and team continue to monitor and recommend additional cycles of improvement. Process management is characterized by process owners monitoring (1) the critical parameters of each process through process dashboards and (2) the critical customer requirements through customer scorecards that feed back actual business process performance from the customer's perspective to the process team.

In Conclusion

The challenges inherent in cross-boundary security initiatives are many. Planning preparedness and response raises the bar for collaboration, for compatible technologies, and for people who embrace change to accomplish a greater good. Leading-edge technologies are available, reliable, and affordable. But the soft stuff is indeed still the hard part – governance of cross-boundary initiatives, strategy, staffing vibrant project teams, instilling leadership, changing old habits through new human resource systems, and selecting technology and process methods that are up to the task. The good news is that leaders around the world are already demonstrating effective approaches highlighted in this chapter. The great news is that their experiences and emerging disciplines, like modeling functional components and sharing technology resources, are making it easier for others to follow in their footsteps and deliver similar results.

Appendix: Primer in Security Technologies

The following technology capabilities show particular promise in security applications. Technology tools are most effective when used in combination with each other. For example, the use of identification technologies and physical security greatly improves the security of access to government facilities.

- Messaging and collaboration: Some of the easiest improvements to achieve in safety and security are attainable through basic technologies that allow government people to locate one another and exchange information. These tools are especially well suited to assist people in doing their jobs rather than do the jobs for them. Capabilities deployed in this space include basic e-mail and instant messaging, directories that identify government and private sector experts whose assistance may be needed in times of emergency, and collaboration tools to support teams of people. The defining characteristic is flexibility. Many government disciplines rely on pre-defined teams of people whose communication needs are predictable. However, the cadre of talent required to identify, interdict, and respond to emergency situations is highly unpredictable, and the tools that support them need to enable rapid team formation and deployment. Business processes that support these approaches may need to be aligned across many organizations to allow people who never have met before to work effectively once they are connected as a team.
- Communications within and between organizations: Communications channels allow people to get in contact and stay in contact. Most government employees already have basic Internet and data connectivity at the office desktop using local area and wide-area networks. The greatest attention in this space today is focused on providing the same reliable connections to employees deployed in the field, improving the reliability and security of data communications that are already in place, and enabling tighter connections between government and non-government entities such as transportation companies, utilities, and financial institutions. Deployments include wireless communications, encrypted data links for highly sensitive information, and network redundancy.
- Data management and analysis: These tools, for many years the mainstay of the intelligence community, have become more common in all aspects of safety and security. The advantages of effective data gathering and analysis are found in lower cost and shorter cycle time to deliver information to decision makers. This includes cross-referencing large data files to identify criminal activity, assessing

epidemiological information that could be the first indicator of a bioterrorism incident, or reviewing cargo manifests to validate the trustworthiness of the shippers of hundreds of containers on an inbound ship. The most interesting new technologies include data federation tools that allow interconnection of databases without actually moving them and tools that gather and analyze data from public sources such as the Internet.

- Emergency preparedness and response: The most essential and easiest to implement are steps to protect government infrastructure such as data centers and networks in the event they are disabled. This is frequently referred to as continuity of operations. The same approach can be applied to all types of infrastructure including transportation and utilities. Some interesting emerging capabilities involve the use of computer simulations to model the impact of emergency conditions on such areas as traffic flow and the use of massive, multiple-player gaming technologies to enable teams of first responders to train and drill on how to work together.
- Identification and authentication: Many aspects of security require the government to establish and validate a person's identity. This is most visible in border crossing, for which the combination of a travel document (passport or visa) and a visual inspection has been the standard. Traditional approaches are easy to foil and do not achieve the level of security desired by most countries today. The use of biometrics, such as fingerprint recognition and smart documents such as passports or visas with identification chips installed, is effective for fast and reliable authentication of individuals. These tools enable employee access to buildings, authorization for logging on to systems, and even access of first responders to emergency scenes. Emerging areas of face recognition, radio-frequency identification tags, and integration of physical security systems with computer security systems extend these capabilities. Although concerns about privacy may slow deployment of the full range of capabilities, technology either exists today or will soon be available to enable fast, inexpensive, reliable authentication of individuals in a wide range of environments. These identification processes, in turn, support validation of authority and determination of trustworthiness. The end result is the ability to secure assets, facilities, and borders and to concentrate scarce inspection resources on those people whose identities cannot be validated or whose trustworthiness is in question.
- Surveillance, site security, and physical assets: The expansion of IT in support of security is not limited to traditional data. Increasingly, critical data include multimedia such as digital images, digital video, and voice. In public places such as airports, output from surveillance cameras is digitized to improve the efficiency of transmission, storage, and analysis. New software tools allow computers to "watch" these video streams and to alert security personnel if certain pre-defined conditions are met. These pre-defined conditions may include abandoned parcels, tailgaters at security doors, and traffic in restricted areas. The net result of these advances is the ability to address genuine threats and incidents, rather than conduct routine, repetitive tasks. The extension of these capabilities includes facilities such as military bases, public places, government buildings, and other critical infrastructure.

Index

A

Activity-Based Accounting (ABC), 5
All Hazards Consortium, 281
Alliance or The Federation, 50 n1
Amber Alerts, 124, 146, 166
Ambulance services, 5, 6, 10
Amtrak, 170, 192
Anaheim Convention Center, 159, 164
Analog Radios, 199–200
Analog Spectrum, 39
Angel Stadium of Anaheim, 159, 170
Anti-Terrorism Advisory Councils (ATACs), 121, 129 n6
Area Maritime Security Committee (AMSC), 103, 114
Ashcroft, J., 120
Atlantic Hurricane Season, 53–60
Auerbach, J., 25
Austin Independent, 218, 219, 227
Automated traffic law enforcement, 178, 179, 181, 182, 183, 184
Automatic Vehicle Locator (AVL), 165, 223, 224
Axelrod, B., 16, 185–189

B

Baarsma, B., 207–216
Barton Creek Greenbelt, 219
Bay Area Rapid Transit (BART), 111
Bay Area Regional Interoperable Communication System (BayRICS), 111
BayEx 2008, 106
Black belts, 278, 283
Blackstone, E. A., 1–20
Blagojevich, R. R., 181
BLM (Custer Grasslands), 205
Border Enforcement Security Task Forces (BESTs), 44, 49
Border security, 41–52, 271, 272

Boston Public Health Commission (BPHC), 24, 29
Building Owners and Managers Association (BOMA), 254
Bureau of Alcohol Tobacco and Firearms, 257
Bureau of Information and Telecommunications' (BIT), 203
Burrell, Y., 99–116

C

California's Electronic Data Information System (EDIS), 166
Cameras, 4, 15, 16, 18, 112, 115, 126, 162, 163, 164, 166, 171, 174, 176, 178, 179, 180, 181, 182, 183, 184, 193, 230, 244, 247, 249, 255, 256, 257, 280, 285
Capital Metropolitan Transportation Authority (CapMetro), 218, 219, 225, 230
Carafano, J. J., 8, 41–52
Cardozo High School, 244
Carnegis, J., 163
Cecil Commerce Center, 58
CEOs for Cities, 191
Chertoff, M., 51 n6, 249, 255
Chicago Bears, 258
ChicagoFIRST, 254
Chicago's Central Business District, 256
Chief Technology Officer (OCTO), 242, 243, 245, 250, 251
Cicilline, D. N., 191–196
Cities Readiness Initiative (CRI), 24, 26, 27
Citizen Information Center (CIC), 55
Code of Virginia (2005), Section 44–146, 18, 262
Collins, P., 220
Combined Transportation, Emergency & Communications Center (CTECC), 225–226, 227, 229

Community Emergency Response Teams (CERT), 59
Community Oriented Policing Services (COPS), 44, 196, 220
ComNet-Ericcson, 219
Component Business Modeling (CBM), 281, 282
Comprehensive Emergency Management Plan, 36, 54
Computer Aided Dispatch (CAD), 162, 221–223, 227, 229, 230, 236, 249
ComStat (COMputer analysis of STATistics), 111, 112
Continuity of government (COG), 140, 141, 145–146, 264, 266, 285
Continuity of operations (COOP), 18, 36, 100, 261–268
Coplink, 236
Costa, D., 196
Crime Information Warehouse technology, 274
Criminal Alien Program (CAP), 50
Current Technologies Corporation, 178
Customs cross designation, 50

D

Daley, R. M., 18, 253–259
Data Exchange Hub (DEH), 245
Data network, 16, 186, 188–189, 246
DC Armory, 244
DC-NET, 246, 247, 248, 249, 251
Delaware Information & Analysis Center (DIAC), 149–157
Dellums, R. V., 11, 99–116
DelValle Institute for Emergency Preparedness, 29
Department of Corrections (DOC), 198, 244
Department of Health, 244
Department of Homeland Security (DHS), 1, 38, 44, 45, 49, 51 n5, n6, 68, 118, 128 n1, 145, 150, 151, 154, 156, 163, 196, 205, 221, 230, 233–239, 244, 254, 257, 281, 283
Department of Justice (DOJ), 128 n3, 152, 196, 199, 220, 234
Department of Streets and Sanitation, 255
Department of Transportation, 51 n9, 108, 171, 182, 193, 197, 218, 222, 225, 227, 230, 244, 257
Department of Water Management, 255
Department of Youth Rehabilitation Services, 244
Digital city, 177–184
Digital Loop Cabinets (DLC's), 188
Digital radio, 199–200, 202, 204

Disaster declaration, 3, 185
Document and Benefit Fraud Task Forces (DBFTFs), 49
Doll, O., 197–205
Drake, R., 8, 31–40
Drug trafficking organizations (DTOs), 50 n1
Duval County Debris Management Plan, 54, 58–59

E

E911, 208, 248, 249
Eckels, R., 74
EDS, 160, 162, 163, 167, 175, 176
Ehrlich, R. L, Jr., 15, 117–129
Emergency Alert System (EAS), 35
Emergency Interoperation Consortium, 281
Emergency Management Accreditation Program (EMAP), 60, 262
Emergency Operations Center (EOC), 11, 17, 18, 34, 36, 54, 55, 60, 82, 83, 103, 104, 107, 108, 115, 161, 171, 175, 192, 196, 225, 226, 229, 248, 266
Emergency Preparedness Division (EPD), 24, 28, 55, 56, 60
Emergency Support Function (ESF), 56
Enterprise Linux Operating System, 235
Enterprise Virtual Operations Center (EVOC), 160, 161, 162, 163–168, 171, 172–175, 176 n1, n2
Esserman, D., 196
E Team Emergency Management Software, 60
Everglades, 185, 186
Executive Order 44 (EO 44), 264
Extendable Markup Language (XML), 176 n2

F

Federal Bureau of Investigation (FBI), 103, 156, 170, 171, 254, 259
Federal Communications Commission (FCC), 217, 219, 243, 245
Federal Disaster Assistance Programs, 57
Federal Emergency Management Agency (FEMA), 3, 94, 107, 262
Federally Declared Disaster events, 57
Federal Preparedness Circular (FPC), 262
FF&W (Sandhill), 205
Field Intelligence Group (FIG), 122, 123
Fire department, 3, 5, 27, 83, 85, 86, 90, 104, 108, 115, 165, 166, 167, 173, 174, 199, 223, 225, 229, 230, 237, 244, 254, 255, 257, 258, 259
Fire/Emergency Medical Services (FEMS), 243
Fort Lewis and McChord AFB, 208

Fusion center, 15, 44, 49, 118–120, 121, 123, 128, 142, 143, 144, 145, 149, 150, 151, 153, 154, 155, 156, 157

G

Garrett, H., 9, 81–86
Gasparilla festival, 238
Gaspar, J., 238
Global positioning system (GPS), 163, 236
Golden Guardian, 106, 170–172
Governor's Office of Homeland Security (GOHS), 103, 118
Green Bay Packers, 258

H

Hakim, S., 1–20
Hammer, M., 269
Hams, 189
Hazards US (HAZUS), 107
Home Front Command (HFC), 64, 65, 68, 69, 70 n1, n4
Homeland Defense Journal's Continuity of Government, 264
Homeland security (HLS), 1–20, 36, 38, 39, 44, 45, 49, 50 n1, 51 n5, 68, 83, 86, 88, 89, 103, 106, 118, 122, 123, 124, 128, 131–147, 150, 151, 154, 155, 156, 163, 170, 186, 191, 192, 193, 194, 196, 205, 221, 230, 233–239, 241, 244, 246, 247, 248, 249, 252, 253, 254, 255, 257, 269, 270, 277, 279, 280, 281, 283
Homeland Security Task Force (HSTF), 87, 92
House Bill 1292, 198
Housing authority, 254, 273
Houston-Galveston Area Council (H-GAC), 88, 89, 90, 91, 92, 95
Hurricane Charlie, 16
Hurricane Ike, 3
Hurricane Katrina, 2, 3, 7, 9, 10, 11, 23, 24, 31, 55, 73–79, 81–86, 93, 94, 95, 96, 97, 98, 106, 139, 140, 141, 145, 165, 244
Hurricane Rita, 2, 7, 10, 11, 23, 24, 73–79, 81–86, 93, 95, 96, 97, 98, 229
Hurricanes Charley, 54, 185, 186, 187
Hurricane Wilma, 16, 93, 185, 187

I

IBM's 2004 Global Business Consulting study, 277
Iden, R., 163
Illinois Emergency Management Agency, 254
Immigration and Nationality Act (INA), 48
Incident-Based Reporting (IBR), 214
Incident Command System (ICS), 26, 34

Information technology (IT), 63, 115, 125, 139, 140, 141, 160, 161, 178, 208, 209, 261–268, 274, 275, 276, 279, 281, 282
Integrated Border Enforcement Team (IBET), 46
Integrated justice, 131, 133–139, 141, 142, 143, 147
Integrated wireless surveillance, 16, 178, 179, 181, 184
Intel Cell, 256, 257
Intelligence Reform and Terrorism Prevention Act of 2004, 245
Intelligent Access Points (IAPs), 194
Interagency Operations Centers (IOC), 114
International Monetary Fund (IMF), 150, 244
Internet protocol (IP), 194, 196
Interoperable communications, 6, 16–17, 37, 38, 39, 45, 94, 110–111, 246, 263
Interoperable Communications Technology Assistance Program (ICTAP), 234, 235, 237
Interstate Identification Index (III), 50
Iorio, P., 17, 233–239
Israel National Research Center for Disasters, 69

J

John A. Wilson Building, 242
Joint Application Development (JAD), 235
Joint Interagency Task Force, 49
Joint Operations Center (JOC), 17, 18, 238, 254–255, 256, 257, 258–259
Joint Terrorism Task Force (JTTF), 44, 122, 126, 154
Justice Silos, 131, 132–133, 147

K

Kaine, T., 249, 261–268
Kirschenbaum, A., 10, 61–71

L

Lake Austin, 219
Lake Michigan, 257
Lake Travis, 219
Law Enforcement Activity and Data System (LEADS), 208, 209, 210–213, 214, 215
Law Enforcement Assistance Administration (LEAA), 208
Law Enforcement Support Agency (LESA), 208, 210, 212
Law Enforcement Support Center (LESC), 50
Leadership in Energy and Environmental Design (LEED), 226
Lean Sigma, 282, 283

LION Apparel, 90
Loop Cabinets (DLC's), 188

M

Making Officer Redeployment Effective
    (MORE), 209
Maryland Coordination and Analysis Center
    (MCAC), 118, 120–125, 126–127, 128
Mayors Emergency Alert Notification System
    (MEANS), 29
Mayors' Urban Design Institute, 191
Medical Reserve Corps (MRC), 23–30, 107
Memorial Coliseum, 82, 83
Menino, T. M., 8, 23–30
MESH network, 192, 193–194, 195, 196
Messier, L., 196
Metropolitan Police Department (MPD), 243
Metropolitan Statistical Areas (MSA), 111, 234
Microsoft Office SharePoint Server
    (MOSS), 236
Microsoft Sequel Server, 238
Mid-Atlantic All Hazards Forum, 270
Minner, R. A., 16, 149–157
Minuteman, 45
Mission Support Platform, 162
Mississippi river, 186
Mitchell SRC, 205
Mobile Data and Transportation Management
    (RDMT), 218, 219, 222, 223
Mobile data computer (MDC), 152, 223–225
Mobile data terminal (MDT), 179, 183, 203
Model city initiative, 110
Morales, A., 18, 269–285
Motorola, 192, 193, 195, 199, 219, 228,
    282, 283
Mudd, J. V., 16, 185–189
Municipal Information Services (MIS), 83

N

Narragansett Bay, 193
National Capital Region (NCR), 243, 245
National Crime Information Center (NCIC),
    50, 150
National Drug Intelligence Center, 41, 50 n1
National Geospatial Intelligence Agency, 274
National Governors Association, 20, 51 n4
National Guard, 2, 16, 45, 103, 120, 154,
    155, 156
National Hurricane Center, 53
National Incident Management System
    (NIMS), 34, 54, 56, 141, 234, 236
National Information Exchange Model
    (NIEM), 137, 138

National Infrastructure Protection Program
    (NIPP), 145, 234
National Leagues of Cities (NLC), 32, 36, 39
National Response Plan (NRP), 141, 145, 239
NCR Interoperability Project (NCRIP), 245
ND National Grasslands, 205
Neptune Coalition, 104
NGO organizations, 63
Norton, E. H., 249
NPS (Mount Rushmore fire crews), 205

O

Oakland Board of Port Commissioners, 101
O'Brien, M., 99–116
Office of the Chief Medical Examiner, 244
Office for Domestic Preparedness (ODP),
    163, 234
Office of Emergency Management and
    Communications (OEMC), 254, 255, 258
O'Hare Airport, 13, 14, 177, 181
O'Hare International, 256
Olson, T., 75
Operation Rio Grande, 44

P

Pandemic Influenza, 24, 27, 115, 264, 266
Pasquale, F. A, Dr., 177–184
Peck, S., 242
Pennsylvania Justice Network (JNET),
    133–139, 143
Perry, R., 220
Peyton, J., 8, 53–60
Points of Dispensing (PODs), 24, 26, 27
Police Department, 27, 33, 103, 105, 111, 112,
    114, 115, 125, 163, 165, 168, 169, 173,
    178, 179, 183, 184, 199, 208, 212, 223,
    225, 229, 230, 235, 243, 255, 258, 279
Port Charlotte, 185
Port of Oakland, 11, 99–116
Port of Tacoma, 208
Pringle, C., 16, 159–176
Private sector, 1–20, 35, 48, 52 n14, 65, 66, 67,
    69, 90, 91, 105, 118, 121, 141, 150, 151,
    153, 155, 156, 160, 161, 162, 175, 210,
    262, 270, 271, 274, 284
Privatization, 61–71
Project Seahawk, 49
Providence Emergency Management Agency,
    192, 194
Providence Hurricane Barrier, 193
Public–private partnership (PPP), 7, 10, 11, 19,
    20, 43, 47, 48, 50, 90, 91, 92, 160, 270
Public Safety Broadband Trust (PSBT), 39

Public Safety Communications Center, 248, 249
Public Safety Interoperable Communications (PSIC), 45
Public Safety Radio System (PSRS), 186, 188
Public sector, 2, 4, 9, 10, 19, 37, 61, 62, 63, 64, 65, 69, 70, 77, 78, 160, 161, 210

R
Ramsey, T. S., 18, 269–285
Raytheon Corporation, 238
Real ID, 43, 46, 145
Red Cross, 35, 36, 63, 74, 75, 77, 78, 85, 97, 107, 244, 254
Red Hat Linux, 238
Red light technology, 181–183
Regional Logistics Center (RLC), 11, 87, 88–92
Regional Radio System (RRS), 219–220, 225, 228, 229, 230
Regional Wireless Broadband Network (RWBN), 245
Reliant complex (the Astrodome and a convention center), 75, 78
Remote Central Office (RCO), 188
Rendell, E., 15, 131–147
Reverse 9-1-1, 95
Ridge, T., 133
Rounds, M. M., 197–205
Rudman Report, 1, 7

S
SAFECOM, 38, 221, 230
St. Louis Area Regional Response System (STARRS), 270
2002 Sarbanes-Oxley Act, 3
School District (AISD), 84, 218, 219, 227
September 11, 2001, (9/11), 139, 149, 159, 241, 245, 246, 248
Services Oriented Architectures (SOA), 281
Sheriff's Office, 53, 222, 235, 236, 238
Singel, M., 133
Sioux Falls, 198
Smith, R., 165
Smithsonian, 244
South Dakota Codified Law 34-45-33, 198
Space and Naval Warfare (SPAWAR), 235
Speaker, A., 42
Special needs, 11, 54, 56–57, 76, 83, 84, 86
Spectrum Coalition, 245
Stafford Act, 57
State Defense Force (SDF), 45–46
State police, 2, 10, 125, 129 n9, 131, 132, 134, 142

State Radio in South Dakota, 197
Statewide Communications Interoperability Plan (SCIP), 221
Steering committee, 139, 173, 222, 263, 266, 270, 271, 274, 275, 277, 281, 282
Strategic National Stockpile, 24, 27
Synchronous optical network (SONET), 189, 246

T
Tampa Bay Safety Net, 237, 238, 239
Tampa Bay Urban Area Security Initiative (TBUASI), 233, 238
Tampa Gasparilla festival, 238
Technical Assistance (TA), 234
Technion – Israel Institute of Technology, ix
Terrorism, 9, 13, 14, 42, 43, 83, 107, 118, 119, 120, 121, 122, 127, 154, 157, 159, 175, 191, 234, 269, 272, 279
Terrorism Risk Insurance Act, 14
Terrorism Risk Insurance Extension Act (TRIEA), 14
Texas Association of Regional Councils (TARC), 221
Texas Radio Coalition (TxRC), 220, 221
Three Dimensions of Change, 275, 276
Tip line, 15, 154
TotalCare$^{®}$, 90
Tracking, Review, Approval and assignment, Case control, Electronic Distribution (TRACED), 213, 214
Transit Authority, 84, 243, 254, 258
Transportation Safety Administration, 254
Trunked technology, 200, 219

U
UHF, 192, 198, 199, 204, 219
Unified Communications Center (UCC), 247, 248
United States Park Police (USPP), 244
United Way, 76
Urban Area Homeland Security Strategy (UAHSS), 234
Urban Area Security Initiative (UASI), 105, 106, 163, 233, 234, 246
Urban Area Working Group (UAWG), 233, 234, 236
Urban Shield, 106
US-Canadian border, 42, 43, 46
US Coast Guard, 156, 254
US Conference of Mayors (USCM), 87, 92, 191
US-Mexican border, 42

US Office of the Principal Legal Advisor
    (OPLA), 283

V

Very high frequency (VHF), 104, 192, 197,
    198, 199, 201, 202, 204, 205, 219
Virginia Department of Emergency
    Management (VDEM), 262
Virginia Emergency Operations Center
    (VEOC), 266, 267, 268
Virginia Emergency Response Team (VERT),
    262, 263, 267
Virginia Municipal League, 265
Virtual operations, 16, 160
VisiCad Mobile software, 223
Voice Over IP (VoIP), 189, 268

W

Wallace, D. G., 10, 87–98
WAPA, 205
Warner, M., 262
Washington Metropolitan Area Transit
    Authority (WMATA), 243, 244

Washington's WRC-TV, 244
Watch Section, 122–123, 124, 125, 126, 127,
    129 n7
WebEOC, 83, 86, 168, 171, 172, 267, 268
Web portal, 160, 278
Welter, J., 173
Western Hemisphere Travel Initiative (WHTI),
    43, 46, 51 n6
White, B., 73–79
Wi-Fi, 82, 83, 86, 113, 162, 170, 183, 258
Williams, A. A., 18, 241–252
Wireless Accelerated Responder Network
    (WARN), 243
Wireless communication, 16, 18, 111, 220,
    245, 270, 279, 280, 284
Wireless interoperable network, 241
Wood, T., 169
2006 World Cup, 274
World Health Organization, 42
World Trade Center, 117, 191
Wynn, W., 17, 217–231

Breinigsville, PA USA
05 October 2009

225195BV00001B/1/P